Ancient Households on
the North Coast of Peru

Ancient Households on the North Coast of Peru

EDITED BY

Ilana Johnson,
David Pacifico, and
Robyn E. Cutright

UNIVERSITY PRESS OF COLORADO
Louisville

© 2021 by University Press of Colorado

Published by University Press of Colorado
245 Century Circle, Suite 202
Louisville, Colorado 80027

 The University Press of Colorado is a proud member of
the Association of University Presses.

The University Press of Colorado is a cooperative publishing enterprise supported, in part, by Adams State University, Colorado State University, Fort Lewis College, Metropolitan State University of Denver, Regis University, University of Colorado, University of Northern Colorado, University of Wyoming, Utah State University, and Western State Colorado University.

∞ This paper meets the requirements of the ANSI/NISO Z39.48–1992 (Permanence of Paper).

ISBN: 978-1-64642-090-2 (hardcover)
ISBN: 978-1-64642-091-9 (ebook)
https://doi.org/10.5876/9781646420919

Library of Congress Cataloging-in-Publication Data

Names: Johnson, Ilana, editor. | Pacifico, David, editor. | Cutright, Robyn E., editor.
Title: Ancient households on the north coast of Peru / Ilana Johnson, David Pacifico, Robyn E. Cutright.
Description: Louisville : University Press of Colorado, [2021] | Includes bibliographical references and index.
Identifiers: LCCN 2020033053 (print) | LCCN 2020033054 (ebook) | ISBN 9781646420902 (hardcover) | ISBN 9781646420919 (ebook)
Subjects: LCSH: Indians of South America—Peru—Pacific Coast—Social life and customs—Case studies. | Household archaeology—Peru—Pacific Coast—Case studies. | Material culture—Peru—Pacific Coast. | Indians of South America—Dwellings—Peru—Pacific Coast. | Indians of South America—Peru—Pacific Coast—Antiquities. | Dwellings, Prehistoric—Peru—Pacific Coast. | Social archaeology—Peru—Pacific Coast.
Classification: LCC F2230.1.S7 A63 2021 (print) | LCC F2230.1.S7 (ebook) | DDC 985/.01—dc23
LC record available at https://lccn.loc.gov/2020033053
LC ebook record available at https://lccn.loc.gov/2020033054

Cover photograph of Pampa Grande by Ilana Johnson; figurine photographs courtesy of Museo Larco, Lima.

Contents

Ancient Households on
the North Coast of Peru

1

Diverse, Dynamic, and Enduring

Ancient Households on the North Coast of Peru

DAVID PACIFICO AND ILANA JOHNSON

The enduring presence of domestic contexts in the archaeological record means that the household perspective is as valuable as ever for deciphering the cultural beliefs and practices of Peru's ancient inhabitants. Building on a long tradition of household archaeology, this book contributes new case studies focusing on ancient households on the north coast of Peru. All of the studies in this volume build upon previous efforts in household archaeology in the Andes. Many also invoke related perspectives, including community archaeology (e.g., Canuto and Yaeger 2000) and neighborhood archaeology (e.g., Pacifico and Truex 2019b). Accordingly, the cases that follow should be considered complementary to earlier studies and parallel approaches.

Nevertheless, the findings here suggest that revision is needed to our understanding of households. Specifically, this volume emphasizes hitherto unrealized dynamism, mutability, and diversity of Precolumbian houses and households. Following a century of archaeological research focusing on the monumental and mortuary contexts of North Coast archaeological sites, this volume presents the first transtemporal synthesis of household research in the North Coast and, in so doing, covers more than 1,000 years of coastal prehistory. The material diversity presented in this volume suggests that households take different forms within a single culture or even settlement. Households serve a variety of purposes that change over time, causing the same household to leave different archaeological indices depending on the spatial and temporal context within which the household functioned. In

DOI: 10.5876/9781646420919.c001

addition, households combine, fragment, and recombine in new configurations, which suggests that they have fluid relationships with larger-scale settlements like neighborhoods, communities, cities, and states. Fluidity does not necessarily imply weak relationships. Instead, it indicates the dynamic nature of social and political alliances on the North Coast in prehistory. The underlying factors that affect household diversity and dynamism are faced by families around the world. Population movement can be coordinated with agricultural cycles, kinship organization can be reorganized by economic changes, or local identities can be resilient or disappear in the face of culture change. We can therefore use the newly discovered household contexts presented in this book to compare ancient Andean case studies with those from other times and places. These complex nuances and their comparative promise attest to the vitality and relevance of household archaeology for exploring human culture and society in the past.

CATEGORIES OF THOUGHT

Household archaeology is the study of daily life, domestic practices, and household social organization. This archaeological approach has existed for many decades, if not centuries if we count early excavations at Pompeii (Ceram 1979). Yet there is only tacit agreement about the terms used to investigate and analyze archaeological households. In place of explicit agreement, many archaeologists hover around a set of concepts that are "good to think with." Here we highlight four interrelated categories of thought that have provided traction in household archaeology: materiality, practice, scale, and symbolism. We highlight these categories in particular, because the cases detailed in this volume both build on the momentum of these terms but also suggest new intellectual trajectories described by these terms within household archaeology. We would also highlight that these intellectual categories implicate one another as essential dimensions for analysis, and they are likely to be difficult to disentangle. This complexity is an optimistic one, for it highlights the promise of new and rich understandings of the past from the perspective of residential life.

MATERIALITY: HOUSE AND HOUSEHOLD

Household archaeology requires simultaneous attention to the physical remains of residential structures (viz. houses) and the material remains of the people who lived, worked, and visited with and around the structure (Ames 1996; Blanton 1994; Haviland 1985; Hirth 1993; Netting 1982; Netting et al. 1984; Wilk and Rathje 1982). An early, useful definition endures in Andean archaeology. This definition is entirely focused on materiality; it defines the household as "the smallest architectural and artifactual assemblage repeated across a settlement" subject to site formation processes during habitation, abandonment, and afterward (LaMotta and Schiffer 1999; Stanish 1989, 11). This archaeological definition focuses on the materiality both of houses themselves as well as the physical remains of people and activities that took place within them. Moreover, this definition emphasizes the fundamental nature of households to their wider social contexts. Attention to both container and contained is an essential and enduring characteristic of household archaeology (Hendon 2010).

A focus on the materiality of houses can help drive clear, local material indicators. For example, an elemental pattern based strictly on materiality is found among urban Moche houses—defined by multipurpose rooms with benches as well as access to essential areas, including storage (Bawden1977, 1978, 1982; Brennan 1982; Chapdelaine 2009; Lockard 2005, 2009; Shimada 1994). Additional architectural indices of social meaning can also be defined by focusing on the materiality of houses and households, including architecture intended to shape movement, provide privacy, impose restriction, and elaborate on design standards (Moore 1992, 1996, 2003). Floors, ramps, and wall finishes can be used to indicate household status (Attarian 2003a, 2003b; Bawden 1982; Campbell 1998; Johnson 2010; Klymyshyn 1982; Topic 1977, 1982; Van Gijseghem 2001). Residence morphology and artifact decoration can indicate household ethnicity and immigration episodes (Aldenderfer and Stanish 1993; Dillehay 2001; Johnson 2008; Kent et al. 2009; Rosas Rintel 2010; Swenson 2004; Vaughn 2005). The materiality of assemblages within houses is also meaningful. Finewares and high-value items can be considered markers for household status or ethnic identity (Bawden 1983, 1986, 1994; Gumerman and Briceño 2003; Johnson 2010; Mehaffey 1998; Rosas Rintel 2010; Stanish 1989). Plant and animal remains can signal distribution patterns, economic organization, and wealth and status of household inhabitants (Gumerman 1991; Hastorf 1991; Pozorski 1976; Pozorski and Pozorski 2003; Rosello et al. 2001; Ryser 1998; Shimada and Shimada 1981; Tate 1998; Vasquez and Rosales 2004).

At the end of the twentieth century, archaeologists began to expand and revise this earliest definition of Andean archaeological households (e.g., Janusek 2004, 2009; Nash 2009). A more recent revision of the traditional definition would direct our attention away from a single fundamental pattern and toward the potential diversity of households within a single settlement (Bawden 1982; Pacifico 2014; Shimada 1994; Uceda Castillo and Morales 2002, 2003, 2005, 2006; Uceda Castillo et al. 1997, 1998, 2004; Vogel 2003, 2012). Certainly, this approach complicates archaeological research, but it also promises to reveal richer pictures of life in the past.

The cases detailed in this volume challenge many assumptions about the materiality of households and our interpretations of households' material remains.

Overwhelmingly, the materiality of households is variable. For example, at Caylán (chapter 3) and Wasi Huachuma (chapter 4), residential structures were modified to meet the changing needs of variable household membership, while at Huaca Colorada (chapter 6), ritual modification of an archetypal house was central to social solidarity.

PRACTICE: HOUSEHOLDS AS CORPORATE GROUPS

In complement to the material definition of archaeological households, a practice-centered definition endures as well: households are corporate task groups. As task groups, households are taken to be the fundamental social units of production, distribution, transmission, and reproduction (Wilk and Rathje 1982). These abstract tasks take specific forms such as dwelling and decision-making (Blanton 1994, 5); attached, independent, or embedded specialization (Costin 1991a; Janusek 1999); making pots and brewing beer (Jennings and Chatfield 2009; Pacifico 2014); scheduling (Salomon 2004, 46); selective consumption (Burger 1988, 133); ritual practice (chapter 8; Vogel 2003, 2012), and managing the domestic economy of household members (Hirth 2009). Focusing on households as corporate groups has honed attention on bottom-up reconstructions of life in the past, often invoking the domain of everyday life. Much of today's household research focuses on the individuals who make up the household and the interactions between them and the rest of the community.

Practice-based strategies in household archaeology reveal intrahousehold complexities. At the most basic level, households are made up of people going about their daily lives. People are rational actors making active choices about their subsistence, social, and political strategies (Cowgill 2000). Household members are inherently interdependent but do not always act with regard to the greater good of the group because "the domestic group consists of social actors differentiated by age, gender, role, and power whose agendas and interests do not always coincide" (Hendon 1996, 48). Households provide an arena in which to explore the physical remains of past individuals' actions, because people have the most control over their daily activities, the majority of which likely take place within and near residential spaces. Therefore, this arena of investigation provides insight into the domain in which people make the most personal decisions pertaining to their well-being and that of fellow household members. For example, the use and deposition of gendered personal artifacts in and around the house suggests strong intrahousehold reproduction of gender identities and gendered practices (chapter 5). Other household practices were variable in response to external and internal forces. While the materiality of houses at Caylán (chapter 3) likely shifted in response to household need, at Pedregal (chapter 8) some household economic practices shifted under the demands of new Chimú overlords, while other household practices remained the same. Household practices also served as corporate strategies used to signal affiliation (at Ventanillas in chapter 8) and autonomy (at Talambo in chapter 9).

SCALE: HOUSEHOLD, COMMUNITY, AND NEIGHBORHOOD

Households rarely exist in isolation, and so it is essential to consider the scalar relationships households shared with wider communities. Methodologically, household archaeology shares interests (and often overlaps) with community archaeology and the archaeology of neighborhoods. Both communities and neighborhoods incorporate households. Communities may not necessarily entail clear material correlates or physical spaces, as communities are often defined in large part by ideational components, such as a sense of belonging, conception of identity, and subcultural habitus. Neighborhoods are clearer cases because of their necessarily spatial and material components.

Households have a scalar relationship with communities because households and their members in part comprise communities (Vaughn 1997). Early anthropologists and archaeologists often envisioned the community as a "relatively static, conservative, closed, and homogeneous social unit" made up of individuals living near each other, sharing cultural values, and carrying out similar daily activities within the larger community area (Yaeger and Canuto 2000, 3; e.g., Murdock 1949). However, this perspective often erroneously equates an archaeological site with a social community (Marcus 2000, 231). Instead, we propose that communities are social groups composed of individuals and subgroups sharing spatial, practical, temporal, and conceptual commonalities (Pacifico 2014; Yaeger and Canuto 2000, 5). In this volume, we are particularly sympathetic to the notion of the political community—an entity that draws individuals, groups, and households into a community based on shared interests under a regime of power that marshals spatial, practical, and temporal similarities to create a shared conception of identity (sensu Bawden 2001; Marcus 2000).

Neighborhoods share clearer scalar relationships with households because neighborhoods are emplaced communities that come into being through construction of and interaction with the physical landscape, often during periods of mass migration (Innis-Jiménez 2013, 61–65; Pacifico and Truex 2019a). Neighborhoods constitute a *social* community but can be studied as a *physical* space in which people share a common locality and orientation (Gottdiener 1985; Hallman 1984). Archaeologically, a neighborhood is a small area within a larger social landscape that contains dwellings and often community facilities (Hutson 2016; Smith and Novic 2012; Stone 1987).

Socially, neighborhoods provide a context in which social, economic, and political networks are created and where norms are reinforced and modified (Hallman 1984; Pacifico and Truex 2019a; Redfield 1960). Houses, neighborhoods, and wider settlement scales may be interdependent precisely because they are nested (Jacobs 1961). This interdependence amplifies the political nature of communities, for neighborhoods often function as political communities with local leaders or representatives that report to higher authorities (Hallman 1984; Lazar 2008; Pacifico 2019; Stone 1987). As elements within a political landscape, households "in urban neighborhoods represent resources in knowledge, information, creativity, commitment, and energy . . . and can channel these resources into constructive pursuits" (Henig 1982, 38).

Because of the politics they imply, scalar relationships between households and communities are important to investigate. Cases in this volume suggest diverse kinds of household-community relationships that may have both social and archaeological consequences. As detailed in several chapters (chapter 5 regarding portable items; chapters 7, 8, and 9 regarding architecture), domestic material culture can signal positive and negative relationships between wider political communities. While household-neighborhood linkages seem clearer due to neighborhoods' necessarily material characteristics, the peripatetic nature of household conglomerates (chapter 4) highlights the need to lend a critical eye toward even this more friendly category of scale.

Symbolism: Household as Cosmogram, Household as Charged Space

The symbolic valence of residential life operates recursively in two scalar directions: households symbolizing community form and community form shaping household morphology. While traditional Western attitudes toward households might posit a sharp distinction between private and public space, archaeological research increasingly highlights the political and ritual nature of houses and household activities (Manzanilla 1996; Widmer and Storey 1993). Indeed, the household itself is sometimes interpreted as a conceptual map for wider social relationships. For example, at Galindo, Garth L. Bawden (1982) interprets residential configuration as an index of community configuration. Similarly, Alan Kolata (1997) argues that both Inka and Egyptian royal houses provided the conceptual model on which the polity operated: the *hyper-oikos*. The reverse case should also be considered, wherein the social community provides the conceptual map by which the house is laid out. Indeed, it is probable that these two symbolic modes inform one another. Archaeologically, we might be able to track the shifts in conceptual configurations by tracking changes in house form through time within a single settlement.

The symbolic nature of houses within a wider social and conceptual scale is most evident in this volume in the case of Huaca Colorada (chapter 6), where the seasonal renovation of a ritual structure-*cum*-archetypal house played a central role in reproducing social solidarity. Nevertheless, more quotidian examples in this volume (figurines, chapter 5; architectural reference, chapters 7, 8, and 9) reinforce the importance of residences as symbolic spaces. However, we are again cautioned from becoming too comfortable in our middle-range theory by chapters 3 and 4, which highlight the mutability of households and residential morphology.

ETHNOGRAPHIC, ARCHAEOLOGICAL, AND ANDEAN HOUSES AND HOUSEHOLDS

Overwhelmingly, the chapters in this volume suggest that Precolumbian Andean households defied the use of a singular model because houses were internally diverse within single societies, sometimes peripatetic, and capable of combining, splitting, and recombining while maintaining integrity all along. Still, many aspects of earlier approaches to households are either confirmed by the studies in this volume or provide the foundation for the new conclusions drawn in the chapters that follow. Three broad categories of study have provided the groundwork for finding and interpreting the remains of Precolumbian North Coast households: previous archaeological research on households, ethnographic research on households, and the application of these antecedents' theory and method into specifically Andean contexts. Household archaeology has been particularly influential to this volume in exploring social reproduction and economic production in domestic contexts. This volume picks up on those themes and extends them with new foci on scale and symbol. Ethnographic research has been particularly influential to this volume by providing analogies for interpreting the material remains of social affinity (e.g., kinship, family), economic production, and household responses to social change. Specifically, Andean studies have been particularly influential on this volume in exploring models of Andean households (e.g., nuclear families or extended family patiogroups) and providing suggestions of how households interrelated.

ARCHAEOLOGICAL ANTECEDENTS IN FINDING AND INTERPRETING HOUSES AND HOUSEHOLDS

In comparison to monumental structures, residential structures are relatively small, materially impoverished, and poorly preserved. Worse yet, they are often the first remains to be destroyed by "modernizing" developments because they are considered to be expendable. For these reasons, a primary concern in household archaeology has been to identify the archaeological indicators of households and to determine what social phenomena they might index before they are erased. Most of the early household studies focused on defining the household as an archaeological entity, ideally in terms of a single material pattern that could be isolated for analysis and compared across cultures (Blanton 1994; Wilk and Rathje 1982). However, since the household is a social unit made up of people cooperating economically, it is not always circumscribed to a single dwelling, making it a challenge for archaeologists to identify the social unit in the archaeological record (Ashmore and Wilk 1988). Because there is not always a one-to-one correlation between dwelling and family or dwelling and household, early archaeological research that focused on the household as an essentialized unit of analysis merits revisiting (Hendon 1996).

The challenge of household archaeology is that archaeologists recover static remains of people who lived in a dynamic world. Archaeologists are faced with the additional challenge, then, of discerning, defining, and analyzing households through their material correlates in hopes of reconstructing past social organization. From dwellings and artifacts, archaeologists attempt to reconstruct the activities, beliefs, and behaviors of past people. From a palimpsest of static material remnants, archaeologists strive to reconstruct the dynamic social, economic, and political systems within which people lived.

Household archaeology has used residential remains for inferring social structure in the past. The analysis of household organization yields more valuable information when investigating general categories of basic domestic functions, which can then be compared among households or across communities and cultures. While it has often been asserted that households are the primary context within which reproduction and socialization takes place (e.g., Wilk and Netting 1984; Wilk and Rathje 1982), we might reconfigure this as a question: *Are* households the primary contexts for this? Or do other social groups provide equally or more important contexts for socialization in some societies?

In any case, social structure and social reproduction are key topics in household archaeology. Households are considered a culturally rich context for the socialization of children because "they embody in microcosm many of the dimensions of [social and cultural] context" (Deetz 1982, 724). Since children absorb and learn the basic structure of society within the context of the household, remnants of these ideas and norms permeate the physical remains of the house. The layout and organization of space tells us about the importance of certain activities, the division of labor, and the size and organization of the family. The decoration of utilitarian and valuable items provides us with clues to the wealth, social status, religious ideology, and ethnicity of members in a given household. Such material elements formed important parts of the socialization process as instantiated in everyday life. In this regard, households are one of the most important units of analysis for archaeologists because they provide small contexts rich in cultural information for intensively studying past human behavior and social structure (Wilk and Netting 1984, 2).

Household archaeology has also explored both the nature and meaning of economic activities in the past. Households are typically the smallest context in which collaborative economic production occurs and are the means for organizing production activities and the level of output (Hendon 1996). The organization of production is clearly "affected by cultural rules, codes, and the division of labor within a society," and these rules are flexible so that people can adapt their social units of production to the specific labor requirements of particular tasks (Wilk and Netting 1984, 7). The products of production fulfill both subsistence needs, such as food and utilitarian items, and social needs, such as prestige and ritual goods and services. Food preparation and craft production have received the most attention by archaeologists because they leave a distinct and interpretable pattern in the archaeological record (Brumfiel and Earle 1987; Costin 1991a, 1991b). Investigating food preparation allows us to reconstruct the diet, use of the natural environment, and gender relations in the past (Costin 1996, 1998). Craft production often occurs in the household or adjacent to it and also requires a specialized tool assemblage. These tools provide us with information on the nature of production, including scale, intensity, standardization, and specialization (Costin 1991b; Uceda Castillo and Armas 1997, 1998). Non-utilitarian craft production is an important indicator of social organization, especially when compared across households (Chapdelaine et al. 1995, 2001; Helms 1993; Rengifo and Rojas 2005). Households that produce valuable goods have control over the distribution of desirable and status-building items, thus resulting in a social and sometimes political advantage (Brumfiel and Earle 1987; Russell et al. 1998; Swenson and Warner 2012).

Distribution is also an important activity of households and involves the movement of materials and products from the producers to the consumers (Wilk and Netting 1984). Distribution begets consumption but adds the element of contact between households that would otherwise be ignored. The economic, social, and political contexts of production are evidenced in the patterns of distribution and consumption (Costin 1991a). Distribution and consumption leave traces in the archaeological record that can inform us about demand, distribution, and "stimulating force(s)" behind the production of different goods (Costin 1991a, 3). Variable access to valuable goods reflects differences in economic power and legitimizes existing social hierarchies in stratified societies. Patterns of consumption reveal both economic and ideological bases of elite hegemony. They also reflect how elites control a subjugated population, finance their activities, reinforce status distinction, and justify social differentiation (Costin and Earle 1989).

ETHNOGRAPHIC EXPLORATIONS OF AFFINITY, CHANGE, AND PRODUCTION
Ethnographic research has helped shape the way archaeologists interpret the material remains of domestic units, because ethnographic models help shape middle-
range theories for probing the meaning of domestic archaeological assemblages.
Ethnographic analogy can help us better understand kinship and affinity, responses
to social changes, and cooperation and production as manifested in household
archaeological assemblages. Domestic groups are dynamic and fluid entities that
follow a developmental cycle similar to that of a living organism (Fortes 1971, 2).
Social reproduction occurs first and foremost in the domestic group through a
cyclical process of cultural reinforcement of norms and practices, culminating in
the dissolution of the original domestic unit and the succession of its descendant
groups (Fortes 1971). Kinship organization, domestic economies, and gender relations are shaped by—and materialized in—houses, because households are where
children become socialized to the cultural norms of society. Houses and households
are therefore laden with intentional and subliminal social messages about family
organization, social values, and gender ideologies. Ethnographic and ethnohistoric
accounts are essential for decoding those messages and provide important insider
viewpoints that would otherwise be elusive to the outside investigator. For example,
in chapter 5, ethnohistoric accounts of shamanistic practices help interpret ritual
objects found in the archaeological record.

One way ethnographic research contributes to analogical insight is by providing living illustrations of the social dimensions of kinship, family, and household
units—dimensions that may be archaeologically invisible but interpretable using
ethnographic case studies. Understanding marriage patterns (monogamy, polyg-
yny) or residence patterns (matrilocal, patrilocal) is almost impossible without
written records or oral accounts. Ethnographic examples are especially important
here, given the subtle complexities of parsing family, household, and kinship. While
the family is a kinship group, the household is a social unit that shares in production and consumption activities (Bender 1967). Families can be explored alongside
households, but the researcher must be aware that the two are not always correlated. Ethnographic accounts show us that some families live in the same structure,
some in several structures linked together by a communal courtyard, and others in
separate areas or villages altogether (Coupland 1996; Haviland 1988). In addition,
some households can be made up of several families, an entire lineage, or kin and
unrelated individuals (Coupland and Banning 1996; Manzanilla 1996).

A specific example of the nuanced connection among kinship, household, and
domestic property is the *société à maison*, or "house society," as invoked in chapter
6. The "house society" was originally outlined by Claude Lévi-Strauss (1982) as a
corporate-based dwelling unit that was not formed strictly around family, lineage,

or clan membership, but rather on cultural determinants of identity and member-ship that could include affinal, political, or negotiated relationships (e.g., Hayden and Cannon 1982; Manzanilla 1996; Touretellot 1988). The concept of the house society illustrates the complexities of defining the household through merely physi-cal remains due to the fluidity of household occupation throughout the year and cultural ideals dictating household membership and inheritance (Gillespie 2000). However, the concept is essential for understanding the complexities of household membership, interpreting residential goods, and discerning the symbolic role of households as a link to the imagined origins of corporate groups. It is also a model of membership that helps illuminate the dynamic nature of households' spatial and temporal configuration. Giles Spence Morrow (chapter 6) marshals *sociétés à maison*—a concept originally applied to European contexts—to the Jequetepeque Valley, Peru, to tie together space, people, and practices.

Ethnographic studies have also helped us better understand how households are affected by social change. Such studies can have important implications for under-standing the dynamic nature of households (e.g., mutability, flexibility, adaptability) as well as for interpreting the diversity observed in household remains across time and space. For example, when the Matsigenka Indians of the Peruvian Amazon moved from small, dispersed hamlets to the large village settlement at Camaná, hinterland social organization was replicated within the new socially organized space (Baksh 1984). People moved into clustered groups within the village but remained close to related kin: "Like stones in a mosaic, hamlets retain their shape even when combined into a larger village" (Johnson 2003, 169). Similarly, Susan Lobo (1992) found that when twentieth-century villagers relocated to Lima, they partially reproduced the sociospatial landscape of their previous settlement in their new urban context.

Ethnographic cases also provide meaningful models for understanding interac-tion, cooperation, and production among households in the archaeological record. The comfort of familiar social organization combined with the economic benefits of sharing labor and resources with kin predicts that people are more likely to coop-erate with relatives when confronted with a new and daunting social environment. This was the case with Michael Baksh's (1984) account of the Matsigenka. This pattern has been observed archaeologically at many incipient urban settlements around the world (e.g., Johnson 2010; Postgate 1990; Widmer and Storey 1993). This generalized pattern helps archaeologists understand household organization at the kin, lineage, and neighborhood levels in different domestic contexts. In chap-ter 3, David Chicoine, Hugo Ikehara, and Jessica Ortiz draw upon ethnohistoric and historic models of *parcialidades* and *señorios* as benchmarks for interpreting the material components of Precolumbian households, especially with respect to production. In chapter 7, David Pacifico explores the extent to which household diversity is related to household labor resources and level of participation in a multiscalar urban ritual economy.

Scholars tend to view Precolumbian Andean households as if they took one of two forms: the nuclear family or an extended family in some configuration often related to the *ayllu* model. As Donna Nash (2009, 210) observes, these two household forms are typically thought to articulate with other such groups in one of two ways: as vertical archipelagos in the highlands (especially in the south) following John Murra's (1985) famous model and as horizontally interconnected specialist communities (especially on the north coast of Peru) as described by María Rostworoski de Diez Conseco (1977). These models are necessarily applied through the backward-facing lens of colonial intervention. So this pair of binary categories is only a broad-brush characterization of myriad households in the past. Moreover, these categories are often challenged in the dispersed literature focusing on Andean households.

While ethnographic accounts of Andean families in the Colonial Period suggest that nuclear families were common, there is a strong likelihood that this interpretation was influenced by colonialism itself as colonial forces aimed to reconfigure indigenous society around "rational" models fitting Catholic Spanish values (Stanish 1989, 1992). Alternatively, many archaeologists explore archaeological households through the lens of the *ayllu*. The *ayllu* is a kinship model based on duality that can encompass several or hundreds of families, though the term can carry connotations of location, resource allocation, and political affiliation (D'Altroy 2002; Janusek 2004; Wernke 2013). Both of these models draw most heavily on highland cases (Nash 2009, 208), though detailed historical and ethnographic accounts suggest that even highland households are more complicated than implied by the nuclear/extended binary. For example, Enrique Mayer's (2002) transhistorical study of households suggests pulsating combination and dispersion, because nuclear families and extended communities meet their respective basic needs through periodic communion and individualization. Moreover, this dynamism accounts even for inanimate (through Western eyes) objects. Catherine Allen's (1998) account of Andean households suggests that domestic items can become members of households, and so household dynamism includes nonhuman members because both human and nonhuman beings share a fundamental essence of being as well as reciprocal responsibilities to one another.

In the expansive literature on North Coast archaeology, some of these underemphasized details are present in the largely dispersed studies on households. In them we see quite a diversity of houses and households within and between societies. The seminal volume *Chan Chan: Andean Desert City* (Moseley and Day 1982) presents a number of distinct patterns in houses and households. This diversity gives us pause to reconsider traditional binary models. Kenneth Day (1982, 63) explains that Chan Chan's most iconic architecture, the *ciudadela*, served as royal residences that contrasted with at least two other contemporaneous residential forms: elite compounds and small irregular agglutinated rooms (SIAR). Alexandra Klymyshyn (1982, 124) explains that among the thirty-five elite compounds, there are six different variations in these residences, which housed intermediate elites. John R. Topic (1982, 148–57) explores commoner residences in depth at Chan Chan. He famously describes these dense compounds of innumerable internal divisions and notes that they follow three patterns: neighborhood-like clusters, platform-top clusters, and anomalous patterns (Topic 1982, 150). Indeed, Topic (1982, 153–7) even notes a variety of kitchen configurations, including formal, informal, and communal kitchens. At Chan Chan alone, then, there are more than a dozen residential forms practiced within the capital of the Chimú Empire.

A more expansive review shows diverse approaches to North Coast households and more diverse findings than we might anticipate in terms of house morphology, household form, and the contours of domestic authority. For example, Bawden's (1982) study of Galindo suggests a connection between residence form and community organization. The variety of residence forms found by archaeologists, then, problematizes simple models in understanding Andean households on the North Coast. Christopher J. Attarian's (2003b) study suggests that during the Early Intermediate Period in the Chicama Valley, ceramic manufacture and distribution reflect the intentional choices of households in asserting household and community identity. Furthermore, Hendrik Van Gijseghem's (2001) study of houses at Moche revealed three types of residences relating to differences in status and family configuration. The volume *Domestic Life in Prehispanic Capitals: A Study of Specialization, Hierarchy, and Ethnicity* (Manzanilla and Chapdelaine 2009) expands on Van Gijseghem's (2001) findings, with half the essays dedicated to a variety of Andean cases. Claude Chapdelaine's (2009) examination of residents at Huacas de Moche argues that, despite some differences, Moche residences were typified by central, multipurpose rooms with benches. Their domestic assemblages indicate that these urban dwellers were deeply reliant on—and therefore tied to—hinterland populations (Chapdelaine 2009). Despite a certain dependency on people outside the city, Hélène Bernier's (2010) study of craft production at Moche also suggests a certain level of household autonomy in production.

In subsequent North Coastal societies, we see that house forms, household composition, and household autonomy also seem variable. Topic's (2009) revisiting of Chimú commoners demonstrates that the overarching Chimú control of production still left much space in domestic economies for certain forms of autonomy. This finding resonates with the conclusions Jerry Moore (1989) draws about the domestic economy and state involvement at the later Chimú-Casma site of Manchán. In addition, Melissa Vogel's (2012) study of Cerro la Cruz, in the Chao Valley, points to microscale symbolism evidenced in the small sacrifices (e.g., twists of hair) residents made in their houses. These are evidence of autonomy at least in the domain of domestic ritual. David Pacifico's findings at the Casma state capital El Purgatorio (chapter 7) indicate multiple different contemporaneous household configurations.

In complement to dispersed studies, we find only two volumes to date dedicated to Andean household archaeology that explore the *ayllu* model of Andean households in one or more of the connotations it carries. Mark Aldenderfer and Charles Stanish's (1993) *Domestic Architecture, Ethnicity, and Complementarity in the South-Central Andes* set the stage for future household archaeology in the Andes. Acknowledging the potential diversity of household forms, essays in that volume aim to probe for ethnic identity and juxtaposition, to explore complementarity models in the Andes, and to "seek the smallest architectural and artifactual assemblage repeated over a settlement" (Stanish 1989, 11). Similarly, Terence D'Altroy and Christine Hastorf's (2001) volume *Empire and Domestic Economy* explores the productive pursuits and political integration of households from a political-economic standpoint.

In the following section, we summarize the findings of the subsequent chapters in this book, some of which challenge the very integrity of the term *household*. We find residences that are both monumental and symbolic entities for orienting larger settlements. We find households that shapeshift as they move across the landscape in a seasonal cycle; we find household items that give insight into the intricate social relations in the most intimate settings; and, of course, we find that households rarely exist in a vacuum, and we are prompted to explore the different kinds of relationships different households may have with their neighbors, neighboring settlements, and neighboring societies.

NEW FINDINGS ON NORTH COAST HOUSEHOLDS

This volume adds several new case studies to a growing number of investigations into the daily lives of past Andean people. In the second chapter of this volume, Brian R. Billman provides a historical perspective on the changing nature of household studies on the north coast of Peru, from early studies on the forms and functions of households to the modern focus on intersectionality, social change, resilience, and sociopolitical dynamics. Billman outlines the value of a household perspective in contributing to a historical investigation of social change. As a person's worldview is shaped by the social dynamics and cultural messages embedded in household structures, fragments of that worldview are left for us in the archaeological remains of dwellings and household objects. Billman outlines important perspectives for constructing archaeological histories of households, including determining household duration, reconstructing development cycles, and discerning the impacts of political domination. To reveal the social history of a North Coast river valley, researchers must compare rural-urban, commoner-elite, and food-craft-producing households to provide a holistic picture of ancient life on the north coast of Peru.

In the third chapter, David Chicoine, Hugo Ikehara, and Jessica Ortiz provide an in-depth architectural analysis of the house compounds of Caylán located in the Nepeña Valley (figure 1.1). The Early Horizon on the southern North Coast (table 1.1) was marked by major social reorganization, as seen in the abandonment of Initial Period centers, the rejection of Cupisnique imagery, and the development of urban settlements, defensive sites, and conflict. One of these urban settlements was Caylán, where Chicoine and colleagues documented forty house compounds with domestic refuse coordinated around a central plaza. Each compound had two to three subunits that combined to represent a single integrated household and social unit. Baffled entries show an emphasis on privacy, while formally planned compounds with little modification show shared cultural views on household construction and organization. Chicoine and colleagues also found a lack of permanent internal architecture, such as storerooms and benches, in the compounds, suggesting that rooms could easily be modified to accommodate changing activities and demographics.

In chapter 4, Guy S. Duke questions the permanence of Late Moche domestic settlements in the Jequetepeque hinterland and, instead, proposes that households comprised a mobile social unit with seasonal rounds of habitation related to production and ritual cycles. The presence of temporary residential architecture lacking food production tools at the site of Wasi Huachuma suggests seasonal occupation at the site and fluid changes to the composition of the household and community throughout the year (figure 1.1). Ceremonial architecture at the site also suggests that formal structures were used as part of a religious round as community members came together for seasonal rituals and rites of passage. Instead of being tied to a specific village or city, farmers and fishermen needed flexibility and fluidity to meet the seasonal demands of food production, economic exchange, social life, and religious observations.

Next, Ilana Johnson analyzes the iconography and distribution of figurative household artifacts within Moche domestic contexts at the sites of Pampa Grande

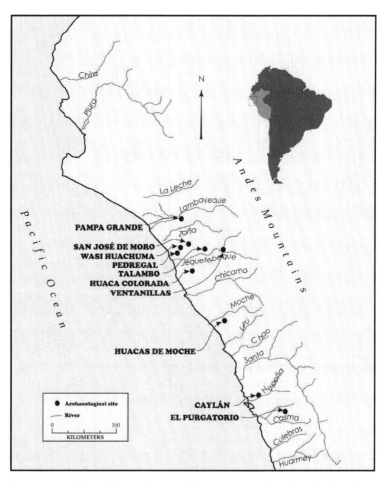

FIGURE I.I. Map of the north coast of Peru showing the archaeological sites discussed in this volume

and Huacas de Moche (figure 1.1). Figurines and whistles from household and production contexts provide important insight into gender ideologies and engendered ritual practices. Female figurines are common in household contexts and are associated with spaces and artifacts typically used by women, whereas male or supernatural whistles were used as part of public rituals and processions outside the dwelling. The ubiquity of female figurines in domestic contexts through all time periods and across sites indicates their consumption as gender-infused objects reflecting the daily concerns of the lower-class majority. Modern ethnographic and ethnohistoric accounts describe the practitioners of shamanic rituals related to the female life cycle and provide many parallels with the ritual objects and religious specialists represented in Moche art.

In the sixth chapter, Giles Spence Morrow explores the ceremonial architecture at Huaca Colorada as a representation of a symbolic household (figure 1.1). Architectural renovation and sacrifice were essential rituals for constructing community and group identity. Artistic representations of elite individuals under gabled roof structures served as a powerful cultural symbol of the archetypal Moche household, and ritualized domestic structures atop ceremonial huacas constructed and reflected fundamental domestic ideologies. Whether these structures were actual elite houses or merely ritualized domestic symbols, they served as an idealized representation of a central house or communal identity. Ritualized renovation of the structures on top of huacas served to forge community bonds and metaphorically re-create the archetypal household as well as the activities carried out inside it. The (re)construction of the idealized home in these contexts creates a communal or ancestral home for the inhabitants of the village or city, thus solidifying community membership and cooperation.

David Pacifico, in chapter 7, employs a neighborhood archaeology approach to studying social diversity, hierarchy, and inequality among nonelite households at the site of El Purgatorio, which served as the former capital of the Casma Polity (figure 1.1). Individual inhabitants, families, and household units contribute to the social construction of urban settlements as much as community organizers and rulers. At El Purgatorio, low- and high-status commoners lived in small, single-family residences, while middle-status households consisted of large multiroom complexes with internal differentiation, suggesting several nuclear families sharing space and economic tasks. Wealth at El Purgatorio was measured through access to space and participation in neighborhood or city-wide feasts and rituals. Wealth in these terms did not affect each household's ability to secure reliable access to food and protein, as these were distributed rather evenly across domestic contexts. Instead, wealth was accumulated in the form of social status, amount of residential space, and embeddedness in the competitive feasting cycle.

In chapter 8, Robyn E. Cutright explores the similarities and differences in household form and organization among the Moche, Lambayeque, and Chimú Periods (table 1.1). Changes in ceramic forms and function between the Moche and Lambayeque Periods signal significant shifts in cuisine and cultural practices related to consumption. This supports the prevailing notion that the Moche collapse caused dramatic cultural upheaval with far-reaching effects even down to the household level. Cutright compares two case studies from domestic sites on the North Coast that illustrate the plurality of strategies employed by households to meet their social, political, and economic needs in the face of political change. At the site of Ventanillas, local elites incorporated Lambayeque domestic and ceremonial architecture styles as a way of signaling cultural affiliation and elite status (figure 1.1). At the site of Pedregal, households increased production of cotton and maize to meet the new demands of the Chimú State, but domestic organization and activities changed little from the preceding time period. Rather than being passive entities easily affected by sociocultural changes, individual households made conscious decisions about whether to incorporate imperial changes into their everyday lives.

Next, Kari A. Zobler employs an endurance perspective in looking at household responses to sociopolitical change. The location of Talambo at the neck of the Jequetepeque Valley allowed for water control and socioeconomic independence, which buffered households from the effects of the Moche collapse that affected other parts of the valley (figure 1.1). Specialized production at the household level continued uninterrupted through the Transitional Period, which also saw an increase in building construction and dietary variability. In addition, the lack of fineware ceramics from either the Cajamarca or San José de Moro polities suggests local autonomy and endurance by the residents of Talambo during a time of significant change elsewhere in the region.

In the final chapter, Edward Swenson provides a theoretical analysis of the case studies presented in this volume and explores the prevailing themes, missing elements, and directions for future research. The daily activities and routines carried out by household members are actively political in nature as individuals engage or reject social norms and traditions; therefore, diversity in the domestic realm of the North Coast should be seen as reflecting contradictory political formations with cultural effects at the level of the household and beyond. Ultimately, residences, household objects, and domestic activities are not only reflections of identity, status, and practice but are also integral to constructing and realizing the larger sociopolitical institutions in which they are embedded.

DYNAMIC HOUSEHOLDS: A NEW PERSPECTIVE ON NORTH COASTAL RESIDENTIAL LIFE

Since ethnographic, archaeological, and Andean models of household life influence the framework by which we interpret subsequent archaeological remains, the research reported in this volume directs us to contemplate revising those models within the discourse of anthropological archaeology. The case studies here first and foremost emphasize the variability of households on the precolonial North Coast.

Variability, in some cases, means dynamically adaptive. Houses seemed able to change their production strategies depending on the political and ecological contexts

TABLE 1.1. Comparison of Andean time periods on the North Coast, South Coast, and Highlands

	General Andean Periods	North Coast	South Coast	Highlands
AD 1476–1534	Late Horizon	Chimú-Inka	Inka	Inka
AD 1400 AD 1200 AD 1000	Late Intermediate Period	Lambayeque/Chimú/Casma	Chincha/Chancay/Ica	Colla/Aymara
AD 800 AD 600	Middle Horizon		Coastal Wari	Wari/Tiwanaku/Cajamarca
		Transitional		
AD 400 AD 200	Early Intermediate Period	Moche	Nasca	Recuay
200 BC 400 BC 600 BC 900 BC	Early Horizon	Cupisnique	Paracas	Chavin/Pukara
1200 BC 1400 BC 1800 BC	Formative	Formative	Formative	Formative

they faced. The corporate group model of households still holds, but the dynamism of household strategies (sensu Mayer 2002) needs to be recognized, as does the potential for diverse archaeological remains related to those strategies (e.g., Sheets 2000).

Variability means mutability in other cases. Houses and households were physically mutable at Caylán (chapter 3), as they remodeled their interiors to meet changing activities and membership. The enactment of mutability took on overt social significance during ritual modification at Huaca Colorada (chapter 6). Households were mutable in their morphology as they moved across the landscape around WasiHuachuma (chapter 4), taking on new configurations depending on place and time in their peripatetic cycle.

Variability means diversity in still other cases, where multiple kinds of houses, households, and suites of domestic practice were found within single settlements and societies. Houses and households took on different morphologies depending on social status *within* the broad "commoner" class at El Purgatorio (chapter 7). They housed individuals who experienced the home in different ways with respect to gender enculturation and domestic rituals at Pampa Grande and Huacas de Moche (chapter 5). Houses and households could also defy binary categorizations such as "ritual" or "residential." At Huaca Colorada, a ritual-residential structure both played symbolic roles and highlighted the importance of domestic reproduction (chapter 6).

Variability also applies to household strategies of articulation, interaction, and affiliation with extramural groups. They took on a variety of economic activities depending on the context in which they found themselves, as evidenced by household activities through time at Ventanillas and Pedregal (chapter 8). They also made agentive decisions at those settlements as to how they might incorporate broader political economic institutions into their own daily and household activities. At Talambo (chapter 9), settlement location and water strategies show a clear effort to manage household and community articulation with wider social institutions, both in terms of resisting outside changes and providing for household and settlement continuity and stability.

CONCLUSION: A NEW IMAGE OF THE NORTH COAST?

The cases presented here confirm the importance of household archaeology to Andean anthropological archaeology. The themes raised by household archaeology are central to deeper concerns within anthropology: the topics of materiality, scale, practice, and social symbolism. Moreover, the social models drawn upon in our cases—those of the *ayllu*, nuclear families, and patio groups—are all known from other studies. However, the cases here draw these trusted intellectual tools into new configurations. More important, the cases in this volume highlight the mutability of our objects of analysis and direct us to find ways of capturing, examining, and characterizing households as moving targets.

New directions in household archaeology on the North Coast and elsewhere should account for the variability of households *within* a society and ask what that variability tells us about the social structure of that society. Future investigations should take the cases here as evidence that the ritual and residential, the private and public, the symbolic and the instrumental, the familiar and the extra familiar worlds may often be well mixed. If that's the case, then perhaps the biggest question raised by the cases in this volume is about the ways households articulated with other groups. What models of social solidarity might be implied, then, by households that join, split, and recombine and by settlements that selectively engage or buffer themselves from expansive polities? We might then think of the North Coast not only as characterized by Rostworowski's (1977) "horizontalism," by *ayllu*-like moieties, by patio groups and huacas, but also as a dynamic patchwork of people, residents, and relationships that left behind an archaeological record that seems more complex than ever before.

REFERENCES

Aldenderfer, Mark, and Charles Stanish. 1993. "Domestic Architecture, Household Archaeology, and the Past in the South-Central Andes." In *Domestic Architecture, Ethnicity, and Complementarity in the South-Central Andes*, edited by Mark Aldenderfer, 1–12. Iowa City: University of Iowa Press.

Allen, Catherine. 1998. "When Utensils Revolt: Mind, Matter, and Modes of Being in the Pre-Columbian Andes." *RES* 33: 19–27.

Ames, Kenneth M. 1996. "Life in the Big House: Household Labor and Dwelling Size on the Northwest Coast." In *People Who Live in Big Houses*, edited by Gary Coupland and E. B. Banning, 131–150. Monographs in World Archaeology 27. Madison, WI: Prehistory Press.

Ashmore, Wendy, and Richard R. Wilk. 1988. "Household and Community in the Mesoamerican Past." In *Household and Community in the Mesoamerican Past*, edited by Richard R. Wilk and Wendy Ashmore, 1–27. Albuquerque: University of New Mexico Press.

Attarian, Christopher J. 2003a. "Pre-Hispanic Urbanism and Community Expression in the Chicama Valley, Peru." PhD dissertation, University of California, Los Angeles.

Attarian, Christopher J. 2003b. "Cities as a Place of Ethnogenesis: Urban Growth and Centralization in the Chicama Valley, Peru." In *The Social Construction of Ancient Cities*, edited by Monica Smith, 184–211. Washington, DC: Smithsonian Institution Press.

Baksh, Michael. 1984. "Cultural Ecology and Change of the Machiguenga Indians of the Peruvian Amazon." PhD dissertation, University of California, Los Angeles.

Bawden, Garth L. 1977. "Galindo and the Nature of the Middle Horizon in Northern Coastal Peru." PhD dissertation, Harvard University, Cambridge, MA.

Bawden, Garth L. 1978. "Life in the Pre-Colombian Town of Galindo." *Field Museum of Natural History Bulletin* 3: 16–23.

Bawden, Garth L. 1982. "Community Organization Reflected by the Household: A Study of Pre-Columbian Social Dynamics." *Journal of Field Archaeology* 9: 165–183.

Bawden, Garth L. 1983. "Cultural Reconstitution in the Late Moche Period: A Case Study in Multidimensional Stylistic Analysis." In *Civilization in the Ancient Americas: Essays in Honor of Gordon R. Willey*, edited by Richard Leventhal and Alan L. Kolata, 211–235. Albuquerque: University of New Mexico Press.

Bawden, Garth L. 1986. *Early Middle Horizon Ceramic Innovations from the Moche Valley of the Peruvian North Coast*. Museum of Anthropology Miscellaneous Series 64. Albuquerque: Maxwell Museum, University of New Mexico.

Bawden, Garth L. 1994. "Nuevasformas de cerámica Moche V procedentes Galindo." In *Moche: Propuestas y perspectivas [Actas del primer coloquiosobre la cultura Moche, Trujillo*

12 al 16 de abril de 1993], edited by Santiago Uceda Castillo and Elías Mujica, 207–222. Lima: Travaux de l'Institue Francais d'Etudes Andines 79.

Bawden, Garth L. 2001. "The Symbols of Late Moche Social Transformation." In *Moche Art and Archaeology in Ancient Peru*, edited by Joanne Pillsbury, 285–307. New Haven, CT: Yale University Press.

Bender, Donald R. 1967. "A Refinement of the Concept of Household: Families, Co-residence, and Domestic Functions." *American Anthropologist* 69: 493–504.

Bernier, Hélène. 2010. "Craft Specialists at Moche: Organization, Affiliations, and Identities."*Latin American Antiquity* 21(1):22–43.

Blanton, Richard. 1994. *Houses and Households: A Comparative Study*. New York: Plenum.

Brennan, Curtiss T. 1982. "The Origin of the Urban Tradition on the Peruvian North Coast." *Current Anthropology* 23: 247–254.

Brumfiel, Elizabeth M., and Timothy K. Earle. 1987. "Specialization, Exchange, and Complex Societies: An Introduction." In *Specialization, Exchange, and Complex Societies*, edited by Elizabeth M. Brumfiel and Timothy K. Earle, 1–9. Cambridge: Cambridge University Press.

Burger, Richard. 1988. "Unity and Heterogeneity within the Chavín Horizon." In *Peruvian Prehistory*, edited by Richard W. Keatinge, 99–144. Cambridge: Cambridge University Press.

Campbell, Catherine. 1998. "Residential Architecture and Social Stratification: A Comparison of Two Sites in the Moche Valley, Peru." Master's thesis, Northern Arizona University, Flagstaff.

Canuto, Marcello A., and Jason Yaeger, eds. 2000. *The Archaeology of Communities: A New World Perspective*. New York: Routledge.

Ceram, C. W. 1979. *Gods, Graves, and Scholars: The Story of Archaeology*, 2nd revised ed. New York: Vintage.

Chapdelaine, Claude. 2009. "Domestic Life in and around the Urban Sector of the Huacas of Moche Site, Northern Peru." In *Domestic Life in Prehispanic Capitals: A Study of Specialization, Hierarchy, and Ethnicity*, edited by Linda Manzanilla and Claude Chapdelaine, 181–196. Memoirs of the Museum of Anthropology 46. Ann Arbor: University of Michigan Press.

Chapdelaine, Claude, Greg Kennedy, and Santiago Uceda Castillo. 1995. "Activación Neutrónica en el estudio de la producción local de la cerámica ritual en el sitio Moche, Perú." *Bulletin del'Institut Francais d'Études Andines* 24(2): 183–212.

Chapdelaine, Claude, Greg Kennedy, and Santiago Uceda Castillo. 2001. "Neutron Activation Analysis of Metal Artefacts from the Moche Site, North Coast of Peru." *Archaeometry* 43(3): 373–391.

Costin, Cathy L. 1991a. "Craft Specialization: Issues in Defining, Documenting, and Explaining the Organization of Production." *Archaeological Method and Theory* 3: 1–56.

Costin, Cathy L. 1991b. "Craft Production Systems." In *Archaeology at the Millennium: A Sourcebook*, edited by Gary M. Feinman and T. Douglas Price, 273–328. New York: Kluwer.

Costin, Cathy L. 1996. "Exploring the Relationship between Gender and Craft in Complex Societies: Methodological and Theoretical Issues of Gender Attribution." In *Gender and Archaeology*, edited by Rita P. Wright, 111–132. Philadelphia: University of Pennsylvania Press.

Costin, Cathy L. 1998. "Introduction: Craft and Social Identity." In *Craft and Social Identity: Archaeological Papers of the American Anthropological Association*, edited by Cathy L. Costin and Rita P. Wright, 3–16. Malden, MA: Wiley-Blackwell.

Costin, Cathy L., and Timothy Earle. 1989. "Status Distinction and Legitimization of Power as Reflected in Changing Patterns of Consumption in Late Pre-Hispanic Peru." *American Antiquity* 54(4): 691–714.

Coupland, Gary. 1996. "The Evolution of Multi-Family Households on the Northwest Coast of North America." In *People Who Lived in Big Houses: Archaeological Perspectives on Large Domestic Structures*, edited by Gary Coupland and E. B. Banning, 121–130. Madison, WI: Prehistory Press.

Coupland, Gary, and E. B. Banning. 1996. "Introduction: The Archaeology of Big Houses." In *People Who Lived in Big Houses: Archaeological Perspectives on Large Domestic Structures*, edited by Gary Coupland and E. B. Banning, 1–9. Madison, WI: Prehistory Press.

Cowgill, George L. 2000. " 'Rationality' and Contexts in Agency Theory." In *Agency in Archaeology*, edited by Marcia-Anne Dobres and John Robb, 51–60. New York: Routledge.

D'Altroy, Terence. 2002. *The Incas*. Malden, MA: Blackwell.

D'Altroy, Terence, and Christine Hastorf. 2001. *Empire and Domestic Economy*. New York: Springer.

Day, Kenneth. 1982. "Ciudadelas: Their Form and Function." In *Chan Chan: Andean Desert City*, edited by Michael Moseley and Kenneth Day, 55–66. Albuquerque: University of New Mexico Press.

Deetz, James. 1982. "Households: A Structural Key to Archaeological Explanation." *American Behavioral Scientist* 25(6): 717–724.

Dillehay, Tom D. 2001. "Town and Country in Late Moche Times: A View from Two Northern Valleys." In *Moche Art and Archaeology in Ancient Peru*, edited by Joanne Pillsbury, 259–284. New Haven, CT: Yale University Press.

Fortes, Meyer. 1971. "Introduction." In *The Developmental Cycle in Domestic Groups*, edited by Jack Goody, 1–14. Cambridge: Cambridge University Press.

Gillespie, Susan D. 2000. "Lévi-Strauss: Maison and Sociétés à Maisons." In *Beyond Kinship: Social and Material Reproduction in House Societies*, edited by Rosemary A. Joyce and Susan D. Gillespie, 22–52. Philadelphia: University of Pennsylvania Press.

Gottdiener, Mark. 1985. *The Social Production of Urban Space*. Austin: University of Texas Press.

Gumerman, George. 1991. "Subsistence and Complex Societies: Diet between Diverse Socio-Economic Groups at Pacatnamú, Peru." PhD dissertation, University of California, Los Angeles.

Gumerman, George, and Jesus Briceño. 2003. "Santa Rosa—Quirihuac y Ciudad de Dios: Asentamientos rurales en la parte media del valle de Moche." In *Moche: Hacia el Final del milenio*, Volume 1, edited by Santiago Uceda Castillo and Elías Mujica, 217–244. Trujillo, Peru: Universidad Nacional de Trujillo.

Hallman, Howard W. 1984. *Neighborhoods: Their Place in Urban Life*. Beverly Hills: Sage.

Hastorf, Christine. 1991. "Gender, Space, and Food in Prehistory." In *Engendering Archaeology*, edited by Joan M. Gero and Margaret W. Conkey, 135–188. Malden, MA: Wiley-Blackwell.

Haviland, William A. 1985. *Excavations in Small Residential Groups of Tikal: Groups 4F-1 and 4F-2*. Tikal Report 19. Philadelphia: University of Pennsylvania Museum.

Haviland, William A. 1988. "Musical Hammocks at Tikal: Problems with Reconstructing Household Composition." In *Household and Community in the Mesoamerican Past*, edited by Richard R. Wilk and Wendy Ashmore, 121–134. Albuquerque: University of New Mexico Press.

Hayden, Brian, and Arnold Cannon. 1982. "The Corporate Group as an Archaeological Unit." *Journal of Anthropological Archaeology* 1: 132–158.

Helms, Mary. 1993. *Craft and the Kingly Ideal: Art, Trade, and Power*. Austin: University of Texas Press.

Hendon, Julia A. 1996. "Archaeological Approaches to the Organization of Domestic Labor: Household Practice and Domestic Relations." *Annual Review of Anthropology* 25: 45–61.

Hendon, Julia A. 2010. *Houses in a Landscape: Memory and Everyday Life in Mesoamerica*. Durham, NC: Duke University Press.

Henig, Jeffrey R. 1982. *Neighborhood Mobilization: Redevelopment and Response*. New Brunswick, NJ: Rutgers University Press.

Hirth, Kenneth. 1993. "The Household as an Analytical Unit: Problems in Method and Theory." In *Prehispanic Domestic Units in Western Mesoamerica: Studies of the Household,*

Compound, and Residence, edited by Richard S. Santley and Kenneth G. Hirth, 21–36. Boca Raton: CRC Press.

Hirth, Kenneth. 2009. "Craft Production, Household Diversification, and Domestic Economy in Prehispanic Mesoamerica." In *Housework: Craft Production and Domestic Economy in Ancient Mesoamerica*, edited by Kenneth Hirth, 13–32. Archaeological Papers of the American Anthropological Association 19. Malden, MA: Wiley.

Hutson, Scott. 2016. *The Ancient Urban Maya: Neighborhoods, Inequality, and Built Form*. Gainesville: University of Florida.

Innis-Jiménez, Michael. 2013. *Steel Barrio: The Great Mexican Migration to South Chicago, 1915–1940*. New York: New York University Press.

Jacobs, Jane. 1961. *The Death and Life of Great American Cities*. New York: Random House.

Janusek, John W. 1999. "Craft and Local Power: Embedded Specialization in Tiwanaku Cities." *Latin American Antiquity* 10(2): 107–131.

Janusek, John W. 2004. *Identity and Power in the Ancient Andes: Tiwanaku Cities through Time*. New York: Routledge.

Janusek, John W. 2009. "Residence and Ritual in Tiwanaku: Hierarchy, Specialization, Ethnicity, and Ceremony." In *Domestic Life in Prehispanic Capitals: A Study of Specialization, Hierarchy, and Ethnicity*, edited by Linda Manzanilla and Claude Chapdelaine, 159–180. Memoirs of the Museum of Anthropology 46. Ann Arbor: University of Michigan Press.

Jennings, Justin, and Melissa Chatfield. 2009. "Pots, Brewers, and Hosts: Women's Power and the Limits of Central Andean Feasting." In *Drink, Power, and Society in the Andes*, edited by Justin Jennings and Brenda J. Bowser, 200–232. Tallahassee: University Press of Florida.

Johnson, Allen W. 2003. *Families of the Forest: The Matsigenka Indians of the Peruvian Amazon*. Berkeley: University of California Press.

Johnson, Ilana. 2008. "Portachuelo de Charcape: Daily Life and Political Power in the Hinterland during the Late Moche Period." In *Arqueología Mochica nuevas enfoques: actas del primero congreso internacional de jóvenes investigadores de la cultura Moche*, edited by Luis Jaime Castillo Butters, Hélène Bernier, Gregory Lockard, and Julio Rucabado, 261–274. Lima: Pontificia Universidad Católica del Perú.

Johnson, Ilana. 2010. "Households and Social Organization at the Late Moche Period Site of Pampa Grande, Peru." PhD dissertation, University of California, Los Angeles.

Kent, Jonathan D., Teresa Rosales Tham, Victor Vásquez Sánchez, Richard A. Busch, and Catherine M. Gaither. 2009. "Gallinazo and Moche at the Santa Rita 'B' Archaeological Complex, Middle Chao Valley." In *Gallinazo: An Early Cultural Tradition on the Peruvian North Coast*, edited by Jean-Francois Millaire and Magali Morlion, 167–179. Los Angeles: Cotsen Institute of Archaeology Press.

Klymyshyn, Alexandra M. U. 1982. "Elite Compounds in Chan Chan." In *Chan Chan: Andean Desert City*, edited by Michael E. Moseley and Kent C. Day, 119–143. Albuquerque: University of New Mexico Press.

Kolata, Alan. 1997. "Of Kings and Capitals: Principles of Authority and the Nature of Cities in the Native Andean State." In *The Archaeology of City States: Cross-Cultural Approaches*, edited by Deborah L. Nichols and Thomas H. Charlton, 245–254. Washington, DC: Smithsonian Institution Press.

LaMotta, Vincent M., and Michael B. Schiffer. 1999. "Formation Processes of House Floor Assemblages." In *The Archaeology of Household Activities*, edited by Penelope Allison, 19–29. New York: Routledge.

Lazar, Sian. 2008. *El Alto, Rebel City: Self and Citizenship in Andean Bolivia*. Durham, NC: Duke University Press.

Lévi-Strauss, Claude. 1982. *The Way of the Masks*. Translated by Sylvia Modelski. Seattle: University of Washington Press.

Lobo, Susan. 1992. *A House of My Own: Social Organization in the Squatter Settlements of Lima, Peru*. Tucson: University of Arizona Press.

Lockard, Gregory D. 2005. "Political Power and Economy at the Archaeological Site of Galindo, Moche Valley, Peru." PhD dissertation, University of New Mexico, Albuquerque.

Lockard, Gregory D. 2009. "The Occupational History of Galino, Moche Valley, Peru." *Latin American Antiquity* 20(2): 279–302.

Manzanilla, Linda. 1996. "Corporate Groups and Domestic Activities at Teotihuacan." *Latin American Antiquity* 7(3): 228–246.

Manzanilla, Linda, and Claude Chapdelaine, eds. 2009. *Domestic Life in Prehispanic Capitals: A Study of Specialization, Hierarchy, and Ethnicity*. Memoirs of the Museum of Anthropology 46. Ann Arbor: University of Michigan Press.

Marcus, Joyce. 2000. "Toward an Archaeology of Communities." In *The Archaeology of Communities: A New World Perspective*, edited by Marcello A. Canuto and Jason Yaeger, 231–242. New York: Routledge.

Mayer, Enrique. 2002. *The Articulated Peasant: Household Economies in the Andes*. Boulder: Westview.

Mehaffey, Douglas T. 1998. "Broken Pots and Life in Two Rural Moche Villages: Pottery Analysis, Interpretations, and Comparisons." Master's thesis, Northern Arizona University, Flagstaff.

Moore, Jerry D. 1989. "Pre-Hispanic Beer in Coastal Peru: Technology and Social Context of Prehistoric Production."*American Anthropologist* 91(3):682–695.

Moore, Jerry D. 1992. "Pattern and Meaning in Prehistoric Peruvian Architecture: The Architecture of Social Control in the Chimú State." *Latin American Antiquity* 3(2): 95–113.

Moore, Jerry D. 1996. *Architecture and Power in the Ancient Andes: Architecture of Public Buildings*. Cambridge: Cambridge University Press.

Moore, Jerry D. 2003. "Life behind Walls: Patterns in the Urban Landscape on the Prehistoric North Coast of Peru." In *The Social Construction of Ancient Cities*, edited by Monica Smith, 81–103. Washington, DC: Smithsonian Institution Press.

Moseley, Michael, and Kenneth Day, eds. 1982. *Chan Chan: Andean Desert City*. Albuquerque: University of New Mexico Press.

Murdock, George P. 1949. *Social Structure*. Macmillan, New York.

Murra, John. 1985. "El 'Archipelago Vertical' Revisited." In *Andean Ecology and Civilization: An Interdisciplinary Perspective on Andean Ecological Complementarity, Papers from the Wenner-Gren Foundation for Anthropological Research Symposium no. 91*, edited by Yoshio Masuda, Izumi Shimada, and Craig Morris, 3–13. Tokyo: University of Tokyo.

Nash, Donna. 2009. "Household Archaeology in the Andes." *Journal of Archaeological Research* 17:205–261.

Netting, Robert McC. 1982. "Some Truths on Household Size and Wealth." *American Behavioral Scientist* 25(6): 641–662.

Netting, Robert McC., Richard R. Wilk, and Eric J. Arnould. 1984. "Introduction." In *Households: Comparative and Historical Studies of the Domestic Group*, edited by Robert McC. Netting, Richard R. Wilk, and Eric J. Arnould, xiii–xxxviii. Berkeley: University of California Press.

Pacifico, David. 2014. "Neighborhood Politics: Diversity, Community, and Authority at El Purgatorio, Peru." PhD dissertation, University of Chicago.

Pacifico, David. 2019. "Neighborhood as Nexus: A Trans-Historical Approach to Emplaced Communities." In *Excavating Neighborhoods: A Cross-Cultural Perspective*, edited by David Pacifico and Lise Truex, 114–132. Washington, DC: Archaeological Papers of the American Anthropological Association.

Pacifico, David, and Lise Truex, eds. 2019a. *Excavating Neighborhoods: A Cross-Cultural Perspective*. Washington, DC: Archaeological Papers of the American Anthropological Association.

Pacifico, David, and Lise Truex. 2019b. "Why Neighborhoods? The Neighborhood in Archaeological Theory and Practice." In *Excavating Neighborhoods: A Cross-Cultural Perspective*, edited by David Pacifico and Lise Truex, 5–19. Washington, DC: Archaeological Papers of the American Anthropological Association.

Postgate, J. Nicholas. 1990. "Excavations at Abu Salabikh, 1988–89." *Iraq* 52:95–106.

Pozorski, Sheila. 1976. "Prehistoric Subsistence Patterns and Site Economics in the Moche Valley, Peru." PhD dissertation, University of Texas, Austin.

Pozorski, Sheila, and Thomas Pozorski. 2003. "La arquitectura residencial y la subsistencia de los habitantes del sitio de Moche: evidencia recuperada por el Proyecto Chan Chan—Valle de Moche." In *Moche: Hacia el final del milenio*, vol. 1, edited by Santiago Uceda Castillo and Elías Mujica, 119–150. Trujillo, Peru: Universidad Nacional de Trujillo.

Redfield, Robert. 1960. *The Little Community*. Chicago: University of Chicago Press.

Rengifo, Carlos, and Carol Rojas. 2005. "Especialistas y centros de producciónen el complejoarqueológicoHuacas de Moche: evidencias de un taller orfebre." In *Proyecto arqueológico Huaca de la Luna: Informe técnico 2004*, edited by Santiago Uceda Castillo and Ricardo Morales, 377–390. Trujillo, Peru: Final report submitted to the Instituto Nacional de Cultura, La Libertad.

Rosas Rintel, Marco. 2010. "Cerro Chepen and the Late Moche Collapse in the Jequetepeque Valley, North Coast of Peru." PhD dissertation, University of New Mexico, Albuquerque.

Rosello, Eufrasia, Victor Vasquez, Arturo Morales, and Teresa Rosales. 2001. "Marine Resources from an Urban Moche (470–600 AD) Area in the Huacas del Sol y de la Luna Archaeological Complex (Trujillo, Peru)." *International Journal of Osteoarchaeology* 11: 72–87.

Rostworowski de Diez Canseco, María. 1977. *Costa Peruana Prehispanica*. Lima: Institutio de EstudiosPeruanos.

Russell, Glenn S., L. Leonard Banks, and Jesus Briceño. 1998. "The Cerro Mayal Workshop: Addressing Issues of Craft Specialization in Moche Society." In *Andean Ceramics: Technology, Organization, and Approaches*, edited by Izumi Shimada, 63–89. Philadelphia: University of Pennsylvania, Museum of Archaeology and Anthropology.

Ryser, Gail. 1998. "Beans: Prehistoric Indicators of Social Relations and Organization in the Moche Valley, Peru." Master's thesis, Northern Arizona University, Flagstaff.

Salomon, Frank L. 2004. *The Cord Keepers: Khipus and Cultural Life in a Peruvian Village*. Durham, NC: Duke University Press.

Sheets, Payson. 2000. "Provisioning the Ceren Household: The Vertical Economy, Village Economy, and Household Economy in the Southeastern Maya Periphery." *Ancient Mesoamerica* 11: 217–230.

Shimada, Melody, and Izumi Shimada. 1981. "Explotación y manejo de los recursos naturales en Pampa Grande, sitio Moche V: significado del análisis orgánico." *Revista del Museo Nacional* 45:19–73. Lima.

Shimada, Izumi, 1994. *Pampa Grande and the Mochica Culture*. Austin: University of Texas Press.

Smith, Michael E., and Juliana Novic. 2012. "Introduction." In *The Neighborhood as a Social and Spatial Unit in Mesoamerican Cities*, edited by M. Charlotte Arnauld, Linda R. Manzanilla, and Michael E. Smith, 1–26. Tucson: University of Arizona Press.

Stanish, Charles. 1989. "Household Archaeology: Testing Models of Zonal Complementarity in the South Central Andes." *American Anthropologist* 91(1): 7–24.

Stanish, Charles. 1992. *Ancient Andean Political Economy*. Austin: University of Texas.

Stone, Elizabeth. 1987. *Nippur Neighborhoods*. Studies in Ancient Oriental Civilization 44. Chicago: Oriental Institute of the University of Chicago.

Swenson, Edward R. 2004. "Ritual and Power in the Urban Hinterland: Religious Pluralism and Political Decentralization in Late Moche Jequetepeque, Peru." PhD dissertation, University of Chicago.

Swenson, Edward R., and John Warner. 2012. "Crucibles of Power: Forging Copper and Forging Subjects at the Moche Ceremonial Center of Huaca Colorada, Peru." *Journal of Anthropological Archaeology* 31(3): 314–333.

Tate, James. 1998. "Maize Variability in the Moche Valley, Peru." Master's thesis, Northern Arizona University, Flagstaff.

Topic, John R. 1982. "Lower Class Social and Economic Organization at Chan Chan." In *Chan Chan: Andean Desert City*, edited by Michael E. Moseley and Kent C. Day, 145–175. Albuquerque: University of New Mexico Press.

Topic, John R. 2009. "Domestic Economy as Political Economy." In *Domestic Life in Prehispanic Capitals: A Study of Specialization, Hierarchy, and Ethnicity*, edited by Linda Manzanilla and Claude Chapdelaine. Memoirs of the Museum of Anthropology 46. Ann Arbor: University of Michigan Press.

Topic, Teresa. 1977. "Excavations at Moche." PhD dissertation, Harvard University, Cambridge, MA.

Tourtellot, Gair. 1988. "Developmental Cycles of Households and Houses at Seibal." In *Household and Community in the Mesoamerican Past*, edited by Richard R. Wilk and Wendy Ashmore, 97–120. Albuquerque: University of New Mexico Press.

Uceda Castillo, Santiago, and José Armas. 1997. "Los talleres alfareros en el centro urbano Moche." In *Investigaciones en la Huaca de la Luna 1995*, edited by Santiago Uceda Castillo, Elías Mujica, and Ricardo Morales, 93–104. Trujillo, Peru: Universidad Nacional de Trujillo.

Uceda Castillo, Santiago, and José Armas. 1998. "An Urban Pottery Workshop at the Site of Moche, North Coast of Peru." In *Andean Ceramics: Technology, Organization, and Approaches*, edited by Izumi Shimada, 91–110. MASCA Research Papers in Science and Archaeology, supplement to vol. 15. Philadelphia: University of Pennsylvania, Museum of Archaeology and Anthropology.

Uceda Castillo, Santiago, and Ricardo Morales, eds. 2002. *Proyecto arqueológico Huaca de la Luna: Informe técnico 2001*. Trujillo, Peru: Final report submitted to the Instituto Nacional de Cultura, La Libertad.

Uceda Castillo, Santiago, and Ricardo Morales, eds. 2003. *Proyecto arqueológico Huaca de la Luna: Informe técnico 2002.* Trujillo, Peru: Final report submitted to the Instituto Nacional de Cultura, La Libertad.

Uceda Castillo, Santiago, and Ricardo Morales, eds. 2005. *Proyecto arqueológico Huaca de la Luna: Informe técnico 2004.* Trujillo, Peru: Final report submitted to the Instituto Nacional de Cultura, La Libertad.

Uceda Castillo, Santiago, and Ricardo Morales, eds. 2006. *Proyecto arqueológico Huaca de la Luna: Informe técnico 2005.* Trujillo, Peru: Final report submitted to the Instituto Nacional de Cultura, La Libertad.

Uceda Castillo, Santiago, Elías Mujica, and Ricardo Morales, eds. 1997. *Investigaciones en la Huaca de la Luna 1995.* Trujillo, Peru: Universidad Nacional de Trujillo.

Uceda Castillo, Santiago, Elías Mujica, and Ricardo Morales, eds. 1998. *Investigaciones en la Huaca de la Luna 1996.* Trujillo, Peru: Universidad Nacional de Trujillo.

Uceda Castillo, Santiago, Elías Mujica, and Ricardo Morales, eds. 2004. *Investigaciones en la Huaca de la Luna 1998–1999.* Trujillo, Peru: Universidad Nacional de Trujillo.

Van Gijseghem, Hendrik. 2001. "Household and Family at Moche, Peru: An Analysis of Building and Residence Patterns in a Prehispanic Urban Center." *Latin American Antiquity* 12(3): 257–273.

Vasquez, Victor, and Teresa Rosales. 2004. "Arqueozoología y arqueobotánica de Huaca de la Luna 1998–1999." In *Investigaciones en la Huaca de la Luna 1998–1999*, edited by Santiago Uceda Castillo, Elías Mujica, and Ricardo Morales, 315–336. Trujillo, Peru: Universidad Nacional de Trujillo.

Vaughn, Kevin. 1997. "Archaeological Investigations at Marcaya: A Village Approach to Nasca Sociopolitical and Economic Organization." PhD dissertation, University of California, Santa Barbara.

Vaughn, Kevin. 2005. "Household Approaches to Ethnicity on the South Coast of Peru: The Domestic Architecture of Early Nasca Society." In *Us and Them: Archaeology and Ethnicity in the Andes*, edited by Richard M. Reycraft, 86–103. Los Angeles: Cotsen Institute of Archaeology Press.

Vogel, Melissa. 2003. "Life on the Frontier: Identity and Sociopolitical Change at the Site of Cerro la Cruz, Peru." PhD dissertation, University of Pennsylvania, Philadelphia.

Vogel, Melissa. 2012. *Frontier Life in Ancient Peru: The Archaeology of Cerro la Cruz.* Gainesville: University Press of Florida.

Wernke, Steve. 2013. *Negotiated Settlements: Andean Communities and Landscapes under Inka and Spanish Colonialism.* Gainesville: University Press of Florida.

Widmer, Randolph J., and Rebecca Storey. 1993. "Social Organization and Household Structure of a Teotihuacán Apartment Compound: S3W1:33 of the Tlajinga Barrio." In

Prehispanic Domestic Units in Western Mesoamerica, edited by Robert S. Santley and Kenneth G. Hirth, 87–104. Boca Raton: CRC Press.

Wilk, Richard R., and Wendy Ashmore, eds. 1988. *Household and Community in the Mesoamerican Past*. Albuquerque: University of New Mexico Press.

Wilk, Richard R., and Robert McC. Netting. 1984. "Households: Changing Forms and Functions." In *Households: Comparative and Historical Studies of the Domestic Group*, edited by Robert McC. Netting, Richard R. Wilk, and Eric J. Arnould, 1–28. Berkeley: University of California Press.

Wilk, Richard R., and William L. Rathje. 1982. "Household Archaeology." *American Behavioral Scientist* 25(6): 617–639.

Yaeger, Jason, and Marcello A. Canuto. 2000. "Introducing an Archaeology of Community." In *The Archaeology of Communities: A New World Perspective*, edited by Marcello A. Canuto and Jason Yaeger, 1–15. New York: Routledge.

2

New Directions in Household Archaeology

Case Studies from the North Coast of Peru

BRIAN R. BILLMAN

The social world is accumulated history . . .

PIERRE BOURDIEU (1986, 241)

PROLOGUE

Imagine for a moment that we studied the Mediterranean world, not the north coast of Peru, and that this volume was about the period from AD 200 to 1460 *in the Mediterranean world.* In this strange parallel universe, archaeologists in the Mediterranean focused almost exclusively on the rise of Christianity. Nearly all of their research was about just one ritual of Christianity, a strange and mysterious ritual involving the transformation of wine and bread into the flesh and blood of the son of God. This ritual was performed only at monumental temples by powerful priests, who were dressed in elaborate regalia. In the ritual, a central figure was presented with the blood and flesh of the son of God, which he consumed. The main research questions were about identifying the archaeological remains of the Presentation Ritual, which was depicted in religious artwork of the period. The quest for proof that this ritual actually occurred led to excavations at the largest temple complexes, where large polychrome friezes and extraordinary royal tombs were discovered. These excavations revealed that, indeed, the Presentation Ritual did take place and that Christian institutions were remarkably stable from AD 200 to 1460. There was extraordinary continuity in iconography, religious art, and architecture throughout that long period. Rome emerged

DOI: 10.5876/9781646420919.c002

as the first pan-Mediterranean center of the Presentation Cult, but soon after, Constantinople became a rival religious center. Archaeologists believed that in terms of iconography, art, and architecture, there was a Christian Culture West and a distinct Christian Culture East. Because of their focus on temples, royal tombs, and the Presentation Ritual in this strange and distant parallel universe, archaeologists failed to identify some of the most important historical processes in Western history. They failed to identify the fall of the Western Roman Empire, the rise and fall of the Byzantine Empire, and the rise of Western European kingdoms. Fortunately, that parallel universe really doesn't exist. It's mere fantasy. It doesn't bear any resemblance to the north coast of Peru.

A ROAD NOT TAKEN

On the north coast of Peru in the 1970s and early 1980s, a cohort of young archaeologists embarked on a new direction in north coast archaeology: household archaeology as defined by Robert McC. Netting, Richard R. Wilk, and others (see Netting et al. 1984b; Wilk and Rathje 1982). Although long a staple of research in other areas of the world, most notably the American Southwest and Mesoamerica, systematic, multidisciplinary investigation of household dwellings and domestic middens was new to the north coast. These researchers sought to understand social life and social change on the north coast through the excavation of diverse samples of households, both at urban centers and in rural sustaining areas. Much was happening. John Topic had completed his magnum opus on crafting households in the urban barrios of Chan Chan (J. Topic 1977, 1982). Richard Keatinge (1974, 1975) and Shelia G. Pozorski (1979, 1982) completed a multidisciplinary study of households at Cerro la Virgen, the main settlement in the hinterland of Chan Chan (see also Griffis 1971). Pozorski (1976, 1978, 1982) had finished her dissertation, which presented the results of her rigorous quantitative analysis of a large sample of household middens in the Moche Valley, ranging in date from the start of the Late Preceramic through the Late Horizon. At the site of Moche, Theresa L. Topic (1977, 1982) conducted the first ever excavation of Moche households, giving us our first view of the layout of household architecture there. Her excavation in the nuclear core of the site revealed 5 m of stratified deposits of domestic architecture and middens. Moche wasn't a vacant ceremonial center as others had imagined (Schaedel 1972, 1985). At Galindo, the Late Moche Phase political capital of the Moche Valley, Garth Bawden systematically excavated a large sample of household structures, ranging from the lowest status to the highest status at the site. His dissertation was one of the first quantitative analyses of variation in household wealth in the Andes (Bawden 1977, 1982).[1] In the Lambayeque Valley, Izumi Shimada (1994) conducted large-scale excavation of households at the sprawling Late Moche urban center of Pampa Grande.

We were on the verge of a revolution in north coast archaeology. Sure, *ciudadelas*, chamber tombs, and huacas were great, but households—households were the key. The driving notion was that household archaeology was crucial to understanding the development of urban centers and the rise and fall of states and empires on the north coast. In this period, households mattered.

And then the revolution was over. Household archaeology largely ended on the north coast by the mid-1980s. Jerry D. Moore's (1981, 1985, 1991) research in the barrios of Manchán and at Quebrada Santa Cristina and Thomas and Shelia Pozorski's (1986) excavations at Pampa de las Llamas were some of the last household excavations conducted on the north coast for a decade.

Maybe it was the discovery of the polychrome friezes at Huaca de la Luna and El Brujo in 1990 and 1991 (Franco Jordán et al. 1994, 1996; Uceda Castillo 2001; Uceda Castillo et al. 1994). Maybe it was the royal chamber tombs at Sipán, San José de Moro, and Batán Grande, each one loaded with fineware pottery (rich in iconography) and ceremonial regalia made of gold, silver, copper, turquoise, lapis lazuli, and *Spondylus* (Alva Alva and Donnan 1993; Castillo Butters 2001; Castillo Butters and Donnan 1994; Donnan and Castillo Butters 1994; Shimada et al. 2004). Then there were the finds of sacrificial victims at Huaca de la Luna and El Brujo (Bourget 2001a, 2001b; Verano 1998, 2001a, 2001b).

By 1990, the archaeology of the North Coast had shifted dramatically to the almost exclusive study of the elite culture of Moche and Sicán. The focus was on the excavation of elite tombs, temples, and human sacrificial victims in conjunction with the interpretation of iconographic narratives depicted on murals, metal objects, and pottery. The household archaeology of the 1970s and 1980s proved to be a road not taken and opportunities missed.

This volume picks up where the revolution in household archaeology ended around thirty years ago. Here we see some of the results of a small group who have been quietly doing detailed, multidisciplinary household archaeology on the north coast of Peru. This renaissance in household archaeology is a hybrid of many influences. For instance, my main influence is the long tradition of household archaeology in the southwest United States (for example, Lightfoot 1994; Varien 1999), while others may find their inspiration in Mesoamerica (for example, Flannery 1976; Flannery and Marcus 2005; Smith 1987, 1993; Smith et al. 1999) or the southeast United States (Pluckhahn 2010; Wilson 2008). Nonetheless, we are unified in the belief that society and social change is best viewed from the bottom up. We are also unified by a group of methods that includes 100 percent screening of excavated fill, systematic collection of samples for fine-screening and special analysis, and rigorous reconstruction of formation processes and context. This approach is fundamentally multidisciplinary, integrating ethnobotany, palynology, zooarchaeology, bioarchaeology, archaeochemistry (residual and bone chemistry analysis), metallurgy, geoarchaeology, and ceramic and lithic analysis. It is also fundamentally context-driven in that it involves the systematic analysis and recording of the processes that formed each context (Schiffer 1985, 1987), what Kent Lightfoot (Lightfoot et al. 1998) calls the contextual approach.

In this chapter, I begin by examining the question: Why households? Drawing on the chapters in this volume, I outline a series of crucial research questions for the north coast that can be best addressed through the investigation of households. I advocate a social historical approach to understanding social change (aka bottom up), drawing inspiration from the Social History and Annals schools of thought (see, for example, Braudel 1992a, 1992b, 1992c; Hobsbawm 1996a, 1996b, 1996c). Further, I argue that Pierre Bourdieu's (1986) concept of three forms of capital (economic, social, and cultural capital) may hold a key to addressing questions concerning the integration of households into communities and overarching political organizations. New theories and new questions require new methods, new manners of work. Household archaeology is, at its foundation, a practiced-based discipline. Based on the experience of the contributors to the volume (and my own experience in the Andes and the Southwest), I discuss four best practices in household archaeology for the north coast of Peru and perhaps beyond.

WHY HOUSEHOLDS?

The articles in this volume and elsewhere (see Costin and Earle 1989; D'Altroy and Hastorf 2001a, 2001b; Deetz 1976; Nash 2009; Robin 2003, 2013a, 2013b; Smith 1993; Smith et al. 1999) demonstrate the importance of the household perspective in understanding historical processes of social, political, and economic change. If we have learned anything over the last thirty years of theoretical debate, we have learned that people matter; people are agents of social change. However, people are not free agents; they act within historically specific structures, such as the physical environment, ecological relationships, demographic processes, gender roles, social organizations, political institutions, and, most important, the distribution of various forms of capital (social, cultural, and economic) (Bourdieu 1977, 1986). These structures shape history and are shaped by history (Bourdieu 1977).

Households are one of the most important structuring agents in human societies. Households are groups of people who (1) are bonded by marriage, blood (fictive or biological), or other means, (2) pool labor to advance the common purposes of the household, and (3) live together at least some of the time or have the right of co-residence (see Netting et al. 1982; Wilk and Rathje 1982).[2] One of the primary purposes of households through time has been to maintain the well-being of their members, especially the raising of children, who come into the household by birth, adoption, fostering, or captivity.[3] Even in our modern era of mass media, schools, and government, the household remains the key locus of enculturation of children, where social norms are learned and gender roles are defined (see Brumfiel 1991; Gagnon et al. 2013; Gero and Conkey 1991; Hastorf 1991; Hendon 1997; Johnson, this volume; Lambert et al. 2012; Lightfoot et al. 1998; Roth 2010; Tringham 1991, 1994; Voss 2008; Weismantel 1988, 1989). Further, we use households to protect our families[4] from natural disasters (floods, earthquakes, or droughts) and adapt to changing times.[5] People use households to pool labor and risk and to acquire and hold various forms of capital.

At the household level, social statuses are negotiated, goods and services are produced, and labor is accumulated or extracted by overarching institutions or social movements. Since the beginning of full-time farming and herding, nearly all of the food consumed by people was produced by household-based farms. This has changed only recently with the creation of corporate farms and multinational food corporations. Nonetheless, even today, a significant percentage of global food production is from family farms. Based on agricultural censuses, Benjamin E. Graeub and his colleagues (2016) estimate that globally today, family farms constitute over 98 percent of all farms and that family farms work on 53 percent of agricultural land. Smallholding households are an enduring rural institution around the world (Netting 1993).[6] Households are not passive agents but actively structure and reproduce ecological, economic, social, and political relationships.

The clear implication is that households matter because households are the fundamental social grouping in human society, infinitely varied in possible forms but universal in core. This is not to say that all households are the same throughout history and prehistory (see discussion in chapter 1, this volume). The hallmark of the human household is its diversity of forms. Variation is limited only by human imagination and history.

In the Andes, households were the foundation of political organizations in prehistory. During the Late Intermediate Period (LIP) and Late Horizon (AD 900–1533), households paid the taxes and tributes that supported the political economies of chiefly societies, states, and empires of the Andean world, a practice that continued during the reign of the Spanish Empire.[7] Furthermore, most of the craft goods circulating in ancient Andean societies were produced within households. For instance, painted Moche pottery, ceramic figurines, and instruments were likely produced in home workshops at political centers (Uceda Castillo and Armas Asmad 1997, 1998). However, there were exceptions to household crafting, most notably the chosen women who weaved for the Inka royalty and the craft workshops of Húanaco Pampa, which apparently were worked by *mit'a* laborers who traveled there to work.

Households have been overlooked for so long in the Andes and other regions for many reasons. The great monuments and works of art of the ancient Andes capture the eye and take hold of the imagination. However, they cannot be fully understood without studying the households that produced the labor, materials, and skills that built those monuments and crafted the works of art. In this volume, Johnson's study of Moche figurines reveals that the rituals performed at the grand monuments did not encompass all Moche rituals and beliefs. A different set of rituals was performed within households, which focused on woman's knowledge, fertility, and female activities. Figurines may have played a key role in the definition of gender roles within the household (see also Ringberg 2007).

To understand the historical development and structure of prehistoric societies on the north coast and elsewhere in the Andes, we must understand the relationships between political institutions and households, royal and noble households, royal and commoner households, crafting and farming households, and urban and rural households. From historical and ethnographic sources, we know that households are often the locus of intense political activity, such as coalition building (see Blanton 1994 for a review of this issue). The chapters in this volume provide examples of political activities within households on the north coast. Chapters by Chicoine and colleagues and Pacifico reveal that collective political action often takes place within residences. Their case studies reveal that groups of extended families formed corporate units that resided together within large, walled compounds at urban centers. Households were actively negotiating their political position in a larger urban setting by conducting elaborate feasts and performances within residential compounds.

Households can also be a source of social change. Although individuals have agency, social change happens through group action. As the fundamental human social group, households often formed the foundations of social change. When ancient tyrants imposed taxes, the impact was felt at the household level (see, for instance, Brumfiel 1991; Costin and Earle 1989; Cutright, this volume, 2009, 2010, 2011, 2015; D'Altroy and Hastorf 2001a, 2001b; Smith 1993; Smith et al. 1999). In the Andes, we have countless cases of peasant households unifying in revolt against the Spanish Empire and later against postcolonial Andean nation-states. The chronicles describe many rebellions against the Inka Empire by local ethnic groups. In the Andes, the peasants were not a "sack of potatoes," to use Karl Marx's infamous insult of the role of peasant households in social change. Unfortunately, very few Andean archaeologists have investigated household resistance in the prehistoric era. Resistance is an important direction in Andean archaeology, especially for the north coast, because of the long history of the rise and fall of centralized polities.

Studying the full range of households on the North Coast allows us to investigate fundamental questions of broad anthropological interest. The chapters in this volume directly or indirectly engage with such fundamental issues, including:

- What strategies were used by royal and noble families to extract labor and resources from rural and urban households? How did those strategies change through time?
- How did households resist states and empires?
- Were rural households transformed by the formation of urban centers, ceremonial centers, and centralized polities? If so, to what degree and in what ways?
- What were the size range and the structure of urban households? How did urban households form, and how were they similar to or different from rural households?
- What were the relationships between urban and rural households?
- Did rural and urban households adopt the beliefs and religious practices associated with states and empires? Is there evidence of resistance to state religions?
- What were the economic impacts of states and empires on households?
- How did social stratification develop over the *longue durée* of prehistory? What forms of capital did royal and noble households control? How was capital distributed across households?
- How did gender roles and relationships change over the *longue durée* of prehistory? How did the formation of centralized polities impact gender roles?

TOWARD NEW DIRECTIONS IN HOUSEHOLD THEORY

To investigate these questions, we need to do more theory building. General theories of political power are crucial to our understanding of north coast polities. In this conceptual territory, we need to continue to build on the theoretical work of Bray (2003), Costin and Earle (1989), D'Altroy (1992), D'Altroy and Earle (1985), DeMarris et al. 1996, Earle (1997), Earle and Spriggs (2016), Haas (1982, 1987), Hastorf (1993), and Schreiber (1992).

A promising addition to this long tradition of the study of political power in anthropology is the notion of capital. Pierre Bourdieu (1986, 241) defines capital as "accumulated labor (in its materialized form or its 'incorporated,' embodied form) which, when appropriated on a private, i.e., exclusive, basis by agents or groups of agents, enables them to appropriate social energy in the form of reified or living labor."[8] In other words, capital is accumulated labor that has the potential to yield gains for the holders. This resonates with the conception of political power (aka social power) as the ability of leaders to get people to do things through the application of positive or negative sanctions (Adams 1975; Earle 1997; Haas 1982; Mann 1986). In essence, political power is based on the control of capital because political power is based on the control of accumulated labor that yields gains.

Human capital can take many forms or guises (Bourdieu 1986). In our contemporary world, capital is monetized in a myriad of financial instruments, such as paper and electronic money, stocks, bonds, futures, loans, insurance, reinsurance, derivatives, and credit default swaps, to name a few. Bourdieu (1986) proposes broadening this conception of capital by defining three forms of capital: economic, social, and cultural. All three forms are accumulated labor, but by different means and in different forms. Politics and daily life are structured by types and quantities of capital held by households, political organizations, and other institutions (Bourdieu 1986).

The logic of this theoretical approach implies that to understand the rise and fall of ancient states and empires, we must understand changes in the distribution of various forms of capital across a wide range of households. Our challenge is to examine how households were linked together into durable networks of human capital.

For instance, the primary source of economic capital in prehistoric agrarian societies on the coast of Peru was irrigation systems. These systems were the result of modest to truly massive investments of labor and expertise (Billman 2002, 2010; Hayashida 2006; Huckleberry et al. 2012; Moseley and Deeds 1982; Ortloff et al. 1985; Pozorski 1987). They were durable capital investments that yielded substantial, sustainable annual returns in the form of rents, foodstuffs, and industrial crops (cotton, for instance). Sustaining these systems of economic capital—this vast human-made landscape—required continuous investment of labor and expertise. The distribution of forms of economic capital across households, and the networks of households through which economic capital flowed, structured ancient political and social life on the coast. Other potential forms of ancient Andean economic capital may have included rights to fisheries, herds, pasture, bosque seco, and mines and control of craft workshops. For instance, control of potters, metalsmiths, and other crafting households was an important source of capital for Moche and Chimú leaders (Billman 2010; J. Topic 1977, 1982; Uceda Castillo and Armas Asmad 1997, 1998).

Bourdieu (1986, 249) defines social capital as "the aggregate of the actual or potential resources which are linked to possession of a durable network of more or less institutionalized relationships of mutual acquaintance and recognition—or in other words, to membership in a group—which provides each of its members with the backing of the collectivity-owned capital, a 'credential' which entitles them to credit, in the various senses of the word." In other words, social capital is labor that is accumulated through social networks, such as kinship networks (e.g., moieties, clans, or lineages), systems of reciprocity, feasts, clubs, churches, secret societies, and political patronage networks. In the Prehispanic era on the north coast, social capital no doubt took many forms. In the LIP, groups of commoners formed *parcialidades*, which were probably corporate, resource-owning lineages (Cock 1986; Netherly 1977, 1984, 1990; Ramirez 1996). Each *parcialidad* specialized in an occupation, such as farming, fishing, or crafting; and each paid "rent" to a *curaca*, who "owned" the land or fishery. These *curacas* were organized into noble or royal lineages, which were arranged in a hierarchy with the reigning royal lineage at its paramount. For households in the LIP, membership in a *parcialidad* may have been the primary means of accessing social capital.

Cultural capital is labor accumulated in the acquisition of knowledge, such as time spent in formal education, apprenticeship, religious training, pilgrimages, rites of passage, and other forms of the quest for knowledge (Bourdieu 1986). Cultural capital also includes labor expended in the acquisition of the manners and tastes of a particular class, occupation, caste, or other group identities. Cultural capital is the basis of social distinction (Bourdieu 1984). The origins and structure of social stratification cannot be understood without an understanding of the production and distribution of cultural capital and cultural goods (often called "prestige goods" in the archaeological literature) (see, for instance, Bray 2003; Hastorf 2003). Sacred knowledge, iconography, rituals, sacred objects, and ancestral mummies were perhaps some of the dominant forms of objectified cultural capital on the coast perhaps as far back as the Late Preceramic Period.

Economic, social, and cultural capital can be embodied, objectified, or institutionalized. For instance, cultural capital can be objectified in iconographic texts, ritual objects, monuments, temples, sacred places, and landscapes; embodied by dress, speech, and manners, including tattooing and cranial modification; or institutionalized by the creation of formal positions of authority, religious or bureaucratic offices, schools, laws, and formal ritual practices (Bourdieu 1986).

Economic, social, and cultural capital are also fungible. One form of capital may be converted to other forms of capital. How households, groups, and leaders converted capital is key to understanding social processes (Bourdieu 1986). On the north coast, cultural capital may have played a key role in accumulating economic and social capital. In the Initial Period and Early Horizon in the Moche Valley, leaders invested far more labor in the construction of monuments for the public performance of ritual than was invested in irrigation (Billman 2002). Irrigation systems were small and were likely built and maintained by small rural communities (Billman 2002). Ritual performance (aka cultural capital) may have been the primary means by which supralocal leaders tapped into the economic capital of small autonomous irrigation systems.

HOUSEHOLD HISTORIES AND THE SOCIAL
HISTORY OF ANCIENT HOUSEHOLDS

Households are fundamentally labor accumulated in various forms. Historically, people have used households to acquire, defend, and transmit capital to subsequent generations. Likewise, political organizations, such as factions, states, empires, and institutionalized religions, have relied on households as sources of economic, social, and cultural capital. Consequently, the investigation of household histories (individually and in groups such as communities and neighborhoods) is crucial to understanding how households and polities were linked by the flow of various forms of capital.

One might call this approach to investigating households biographical or historical. However, I think of it as *social history* in the tradition of the French Annals School (see, for example, Braudel 1992a, 1992b, 1992c) and the British Social History movement (see, for example, Hobsbawm 1996a, 1996b, 1996c). By social history, I mean the view of history from the bottom up. Rather than focusing exclusively on rulers and their customs and practices (the capital of "*haute*" culture), a social history approach contextualizes the elite realm of rulers within the wider world of farming, crafting, and fishing households (see discussion of *fields* in Bourdieu 1977). Social history is the integrated history of political, social, economic, and ecological change from the perspective of the masses. Regardless of whether one embraces Bourdieu's conception of forms of capital, the chapters in this volume demonstrate the utility of a social historical approach to households.

This emerging emphasis on the social history of households has brought fundamental changes in the way archaeology is done on the north coast. The great diversity of household forms and their flexibility in the face of change present archaeologists with many challenges. Excavating a household is different from excavating cemeteries and mounds (no surprise there). Household archaeology is, in essence, a group of flexible *best practices* in fieldwork and analysis rather than a rigid rulebook of recipes. Best practices are derived from lessons we have learned through the critical examination of collective experience. The term *tried and true* comes to mind.

Our collective experience over the last twenty years of household archaeology on the north coast of Peru has demonstrated that four best practices are key to doing good household archaeology:

- Documentation of the occupational history of dwellings, especially the history of remodeling and the duration of occupation
- Comprehensive data recovery through 100 percent screening of all fill types (with a few exceptions) in combination with the systematic collection of floor and bulk fill samples from all contexts for fine-screening and special analysis[9]

- Systematic identification and coding of fill and context types through the rigorous analysis of formation processes
- Quantitative multidisciplinary analysis of household remains.

DOCUMENTATION OF HOUSEHOLD HISTORIES

To build a social history of any valley on the north coast, the history of a large sample of households from a cross-section of society must be documented: rural and urban commoner households, rural and urban elite households, and fishing and crafting. One of the keys to social history is understanding the political and social landscape in which households were situated through the integration of settlement pattern data and household histories (e.g., see Varien 1999). Although time-consuming, the systematic documentation of a comprehensive sample of households is essential for understanding the social history of regions and social processes.

The main physical manifestation of ancient households is the residential structure or structures and their associated activity areas, extramural features, and trash deposits—aka the home (Moore 2012; see also chapter 1, this volume). Understanding household histories requires complete or near-complete surface collection and excavation of dwellings, as well as sampling of middens and extramural activity areas. Although a time-consuming process, comprehensive documentation of floors, features, walls, and associated middens is central to the process. For instance, one must systematically record the number of layers of plaster on floors and walls, bonding/abutting walls, sealed doors, sealed floor features, remodeling of hearths, and similar items. When complete stripping of plaster and floors cannot be implemented, strategically placed test pits (aka *windows*) can provide this information. Micromorphology, geochemical analysis, and analysis of microartifacts from floors hold much promise for taking the analysis of households to a new level (see Parker and Sharratt 2017; Parker et al. 2018).

In addition to new methods, doing household archaeology requires the development of special kinds of middle-range theory. To do household archaeology well means developing usable middle-range theories of spatial grammar, gendered use of space, duration of occupation, room function, household demography, household development cycles, seasonality of occupation, and modes of abandonment.[10] These are key dimensions of household life, which must be analyzed before we can get to broad questions of social change. We cannot skip ahead. We must build upward toward grand conclusions by constructing chains of inference concerning the quotidian aspects of household theory. To develop middle-range theory, we need more ethnoarchaeological studies of fishing, herding households, vernacular architecture, and other traditional practices on the north coast (for example, see Hudson's 2011 study of contemporary Huanchaco fishing households).

Estimating the duration of occupation of dwellings is key to understanding social organization (chapters by Duke and Zobler, this volume; Pauketat 1989; Schlanger 1991; Varien 1999; Warrick 1988). Long multigenerational occupations of great houses may signal the development of hereditary distinctions and of accumulated, heritable capital (see chapters in this volume by Chicoine et al., Pacifico, and Morrow). Among rural farmers on the north coast, the construction of durable multigenerational household compounds from stone and adobe may indicate the development of hereditary rights to arable land and the formation of smallholder households (Netting 1993). Within urban centers, long-term occupations of residential compounds may signal the development of hereditary occupations. For instance, the superposition of four potting households at the site of Moche indicates the long-term presence of households of potters in one particular neighborhood at the sites, perhaps for several centuries (Uceda Castillo and Armas Asmad 1997, 1998). This suggests the emergence of hereditary occupational specialization in pottery production. These types of durable household compounds contrast with the short-term residences of new immigrants or transitory, seasonal workers.

Estimating the duration of occupation of households, therefore, is essential for understanding households and social change (see chapters by Duke and Zobler, this volume).[11] Although there is a large, diverse literature on duration of occupation, few of these techniques have been applied on the north coast (for exceptions, see Moore and Gasco 1990; Ringberg 2012). Duration of occupation can be estimated from discard rates of cooking vessels (see, for instance, de Barros 1982; Deboer 1974; Pauketat 1989; Varien and Mills 1997; Varien and Potter 1997; Wilson 2008) and from studies of the use-life and durability of vernacular architecture (Lightfoot 1994; McIntosh 1974; Moore and Gasco 1990; Wilson 2008). More ethnoarchaeology and experimental archaeology needs to be done on the various forms of traditional, vernacular architecture on the north coast (for examples from other regions, see Deal 1985; Deetz 1982; Graham 1993, 1994; Hayden and Cannon 1982a, 1982b; Joyce and Johannessen 1993; Kamp 2000; Kent 1992; Kramer 1982; Lawrence 1999; LeBlanc 1971; LeeDecker 1994; Murray 1980; Narroll 1962; Oswald 1987; Rathje and McGuire 1982; Rocek 1988; Stevenson 1982).

Household development cycle is another crucial dimension of social life (Goody 1971; Netting et al. 1984b; Prossor et al. 2012; Weismantel 1989; Wilk and Netting 1984; Wilson 2008). Households have cycles of growth and decline. Within an urban neighborhood or rural village, there may be the remains of households that appear poorer than others because they are smaller and have fewer of certain types of artifacts, such as fineware pottery. However, these differences might not reflect hereditary social stratification but rather differences in household cycle. Such dwellings might be small and have limited artifact assemblages because they were abandoned in the early stage of development, not because they occupied a lower class status. Newly established households, formed by young married couples, may appear poor compared to their parental homes (Weismantel 1989). To find evidence of poverty in prehistory, we must compare household structures of similar duration of occupation. We must look for long-term evidence of enduring poverty. For instance, Zobler's excavations at Talambo (this volume) revealed an initial occupation consisting of the remains of a modest *quincha* domestic compound, which was transformed into a more durable stone and adobe compound in the second phase of occupation. Might this superposition be the result of the household development cycle rather than social status?

Duration of occupations and household cycle studies are also essential for examining household resilience. Chapters by Cutright and Zobler in this volume underscore the importance of duration of occupation as a measure of household resilience in the face of climatic perturbations, such as El Niño events, and the rise and fall of regional polities. This research indicates that some households in the Jequetepeque Valley were more resilient because of their location in relation to the valley's irrigation system and their position in the regional social landscape.

In addition to issues of resilience, social stratification, and status, house histories can reveal the impacts of political domination. At important junctures of social change, such as empire conquest, households may shift in size, composition, and residence in response to new imperial taxes (see, for instance, Brumfiel 1991; Costin and Earle 1989; Cutright, this volume, 2009, 2010, 2011, 2015; D'Altroy and Hastorf 2001a, 2001b; Smith 1993; Smith et al. 1999). Consequently, understanding the construction history and remodeling of residential structures is also a key to understanding regional political change.

COMPREHENSIVE DATA RECOVERY

In combination with comprehensive surface collection and excavations of dwellings, a social historical approach to households and social change requires a focus on "small things forgotten," to use James Deetz's (1976) famous phrase. This means screening 100 percent of the fill from dwellings and middens, combined with systematic sampling for pollen, phytolith, macrobotantical, microartifact, and geochemical analysis. We should collect a 5- or 10-liter sample from every context investigated as well as systematically collect samples of floor material.

The issue of screening is one that divides Peruvian and North American archaeologists. In the United States and Canada, where monumental architecture and royal tombs are largely absent, archaeologists primary deal with small residential sites and hunting-and-gathering camps. Consequently, North Americans automatically screen all deposits unless there is a clear and compelling reason to skip screening certain fill types. Our default setting is screening. In contrast, Peruvian archaeologists, especially those on the north coast, come from a different tradition, one that focuses on temple and tomb excavations. Typically, massive volumes of looted back dirt and wallfall must be removed to reveal the architecture, murals, and burial chambers. However, when this monumental approach is applied to household excavations, the result is the excavation of large areas without screening or only limited screening of certain features, such as burials. This approach has been useful in that it has revealed internal layout of households and the spatial organization of residential sectors at urban centers (Chapdelaine 2001, 2002, 2003; Uceda Castillo et al. 1997, 1998, 2000, 2004, 2006, 2008). However, much information is lost, ultimately limiting the kinds of questions we can ask.

Comprehensive screening of household architecture and domestic middens is essential for understanding the socioeconomic status of households, household activities, use of space, household histories, and formation processes, to name a few. There is no substitute, no viable alternative. For instance, when digging floors, point-plotting of artifacts in contact with the floor is not sufficient for understanding the activities that happened on the floor. Many of the larger items on the floor may have been deposited after abandonment of the room, either as trash or by natural agents, while large items associated with room activity were removed prior to abandonment or scavenged after abandonment (Cameron 1991; LaMotta and Schiffer 1999; Lightfoot 1993; Schiffer 1985; Tani 1995).

Experience demonstrates that the small items, such as bone or shell fragments, carbonized seeds, and small artifacts, are the best indicators of room activity. These small remains cannot be quantified without the screening of floor fill and the collection of samples for fine-screening and special analysis. In the American Southwest, archaeologists excavate the fill in contact with the floor as a separate level, known as "floor fill." This is usually an arbitrary level of fill within 5 cm to 10 cm of the floor. Screening and bulk sampling of this floor fill layer can reveal a wealth of information on the use of floor surfaces and abandonment processes.

Comprehensive screening, however, should not be limited to floor fill. Even seemingly sterile room fill, or at least a significant sample, should be screened. Too often, room fill is seen as an inconvenience that must be removed as quickly as possible to get to the "*in context*" goodies. However, room fill can reveal the history of the abandonment of the room and its transition into the archaeological record. We really cannot understand floor assemblages without understanding fill-associated fill assemblages. Screening allows the archaeologist to systematically identify the processes that formed episodes of fill through the recovery and analysis of ecofacts and artifacts from the fill.

Perhaps equally important, the process of screening forces us to slow down and look at the structure of the fill as well as its cultural and natural constituents. Screening gives us a lot to think about as well as the time to think, observe, and mull over ideas as we work our way down to floors.

SYSTEMATIC IDENTIFICATION OF FILL AND CONTEXT TYPES

Screening is not just about artifact and ecofact recovery. It is also about systematically and rigorously defining formation processes, fill types, and contexts. Identifying how deposits are formed is the single most important inference in household archaeology (no doubt this is true for archaeology in general). Human actions result in assemblages of artifacts and ecofacts, but not all assemblages are the direct result of human actions. Distinguishing between sediments formed from natural processes and those formed by human actions is crucial, requiring multiple lines of evidence for accurate interpretations. Every subsequent inference we make will probably be wrong if we don't get this right.

While it is possible to identify fill types and formation processes without screening, it is easier to do this effectively and accurately when all or most of the fill is screened. Too many important details are lost when screening is not done. Screening forces us to look at the cultural *and* noncultural constituents of the fill (known as clasts in the parlance of geomorphology).

Most of my time digging is spent taking notes, talking about the fill and architecture with the excavators, and regularly scraping, poking, and picking at fill with my blunt-nosed trowel. I also spend a good deal of time at the sorting table to get a handle on the type, size, and shape of rocks in the fill (e.g., rounded, subangular, or angular); the quantity, type, and sizes of artifacts and ecofacts; and the state of preservation and modification of cultural constituents.

For instance, a valuable piece of information is sherd size. Average sherd size is a good proxy of formation processes. Primary trash deposits are often characterized by the presence of many large sherds (especially large conjoining pieces). With movement from primary to secondary to tertiary contexts, sherds are broken into smaller and smaller pieces. Also, modern and prehistoric foot traffic and salt crystal formation from ocean breezes can chew up sherds.

Sherd wear, such as eroded surfaces or rounded edges, is another indicator of the processes that reworked deposits after their initial deposition by human agents. In the lab, sherd size and wear (both use-wear and postdepositional wear) can be systemically analyzed, and field observations can be tested. In addition to sherd size and wear, analysis of formation processes must involve analysis of other clasts as well as the structure of fill. Multiple lines of evidence must be used to infer formation processes. None of this, of course, is possible without screening and bulk sample collection.

Exceptions to screening can be made only after we have determined with certainty how a specific stratum of fill was formed *and* that little meaningful information will be lost by not screening. Also, sometimes constraints on time, such as the imminent destruction of the site or part of the site, require us to cut corners on screening.

In addition to examining the clasts in each layer of fill, we must examine the structure of the fill as it is being excavated as well as the relationship of fill layers to architecture and features. Alas, we are all too likely to cut corners by rapidly shoveling out fill, believing "it's okay; all will be revealed in the profile." However, a profile is a two-dimensional slice of three-dimensional layers of fill. I first became aware of the limits of profiling when I worked with complex superpositions of floors and trash deposits at Cerro la Virgen in the Moche Valley. We found that excavation usually revealed far more stratigraphic complexity than was observable in the profile. Typically, many more floors were found during the excavation than were visible in the profile.

While working with Gary Huckleberry on the north coast as well as with other geoarchaeologists in coastal California and in the American Southwest, I noticed that geoarchaeologists treat a profile differently than do archaeologists. Many times I've cut a nice, straight profile, outlined the fill layers, and blown off every speck of dust, only to see—to my horror—the geoarchaeologist attack the pristine profile with a geologic hammer or small pick. The reason for this is that geoarchaeologists want to see the structure of the fill, the range and density of clasts, and the orientation of sediments and clasts, among other things.

My point is simple: fill types and contexts need to be defined through critical examination of fill during excavation. If carefully excavated and screened, the formation processes of each layer of fill can be identified, described, and then systematically coded. Likewise, the context of fill can be systematically and consistently coded. By coding fill and context, analysts can sort their data by the same categories, such as primary trash, secondary redeposited trash, wallfall, general architectural fill, floor fill, floor contact, subfeature fill, or construction fill. Systematic coding of provenience data and the construction of a relational database are the twin foundations for quantitative, multidisciplinary analysis.

QUANTITATIVE MULTIDISCIPLINARY ANALYSIS

Household archaeology requires a multidisciplinary team of researchers. Household excavations often yield an extraordinary quantity and diversity of ecofacts and artifacts. This is especially true for the north coast, where preservation is often ideal because of hyperarid conditions. This means collaboration among ceramicists, paleoethnobotanists, zooarchaeologists, and archaeochemists (for residue and isotope studies). Additional collaboration may be necessary with metallurgists, textile specialists, lithic analysts, geoarchaeologists, palynologists, and bioarchaeologists. The project leader as director of excavations should be tasked with description, analysis, and interpretation of architecture and stratigraphy. To be effective, analysts need to work off a descriptive manuscript on the excavations and architecture in draft form, ideally with accompanying photographs, maps, profiles, and cross-sections.

To integrate all these various lines of investigation by specialists, a project needs a well-designed relational database (usually in Access). On our projects in the Moche Valley, we use a provenience designation system and a specially designed Access database. The mother file, or Provenience Data file (PD file), contains all of the data on each provenience investigated (whether that be a level in a unit, a surface collection unit, a test trench, looter hole, profile, grab sample, or any other unit of space). The type of unit, feature information, context, fill type, methods employed, dates, recorder, elevations, disturbance, and other descriptive provenience data are coded and entered into the PD file. All of the information in this file is linked to specialist data files through the use of provenience designation numbers, known as PD numbers. There is a PD log for every site, with proveniences investigated designated as PD 1 through PD n. A unique number is created for each item in the catalog by combining PD numbers with their associate Field Specimen numbers (e.g., PD 1 and its associated FS 1, 2, 3, and so on, equals 1.01, 1.02, 1.03, and so on).

A PD system and relational database ensures that all of the analysts are using the same provenience data when they build tables or do statistical tests. It also enables analysts to sort their data by fill types, context, feature types, room types, and so on, which are coded in the Provenience Data file. A combined PD system and relational database also allows researchers to do multivariate spatial analysis of patios, rooms, and structures by integrating all specialist data (see, for instance, Allison 1999; Flannery and Marcus 2005).

One final point on multidisciplinary analysis is the importance of standardized measures and tests. Many different statistical tests and quantitative measures are used in this volume. We need to cooperate more in this area so we can compare households across our projects. Three specific measures are ideal for cross-project analysis: ubiquity, abundance, and richness. These measures have become standard in paleoethnobotanical analysis (Gumerman 1991, 2002; Hastorf 2003; Hastorf and Popper 1988; Popper 1988; VanDerwarker and Peres 2010; VanDerwarker et al.

2013). They also can be used in artifact analysis (Earle et al. 1987). Another important standard measure is the ratio of corn kernels to cobs, which can be used to track tribute payment and use (Cutright 2009, 2010, 2015; Scary 2003; Welch and Scary 1995).

Likewise, we need to standardize the analysis and reporting of faunal remains (see Reitz and Shackley 2012; Reitz and Wing 2008). Surprisingly, no one has studied the frequency and distribution of bone elements on the north coast of Peru. By looking at the distribution of body parts of deer and camelids between households or between sites, we can examine status difference, and differential access to prime cuts as well as regional systems of exchange (Jackson and Scott 2003; Miller and Burger 1995; Pohl 1994). Also important are data on the age distribution of camelids and deer in assemblages, which can be used to reconstruct herd management and cropping patterns.

CONCLUSION

In sum, archaeological research on the north coast of Peru since 1990 has focused almost exclusively on the cultural capital of the Moche and Chimú nobles and royalty: art and iconography, public architecture, wealthy tombs, and elaborate rituals. Although these were important forms of cultural capital, we cannot understand ancient societies on the north coast without understanding the distribution of economic, social, *and* cultural capital across households. By doing household archaeology, we are essentially recasting the study of north coast prehistory as a study of long-term social history. Only time will tell if household studies will flourish on the north coast or if this will be another revolution lost.

ACKNOWLEDGMENTS

Many thanks to Robyn, Ilana, and David for putting together this volume and for their years of work on north coast households. I'm especially appreciative of comments by them, Alicia Boswell, and two anonymous reviewers. Their commentary greatly improved the chapter. Many archaeologists over the years have directly contributed to my education in household archaeology. These include Tony Boudreaux, Jesus Breceño, Cory Breternitz, Barker Farris, Celeste Gagnon, Jonathan Haas, Jean Hudson, Gary Huckleberry, John Marcoux, Patrick Mullins, Jennifer Ringberg, Chris Rodning, Julio Rucabado, Kathy Schreiber, Evan Surridge, Amber Vanderwarker, Mark Varien, and Greg Wilson. Any errors or outlandish assertions found in the chapter are not their fault but mine alone.

NOTES

1. Bawden's work was truly pioneering. Since his excavations at Galindo, the analysis of household wealth has become a mainstay of household archaeology (see, for example, Abrams 1994; Carmean et al. 2011; Costin and Earle 1989; Cutright 2009, 2010; Cuéllar 2013; D'Altroy and Hastorf 2001a; Earle et al. 1987; Flannery and Marcus 2005; Gumerman 1991, 2002; Jackson and Scott 2003; LeCount 1999; Lightfoot et al. 1998; Netting 1982; Pohl 1994; Rathje and McGuire 1982; Robin 2013a, 2013b; Smith 1987, 1993; Smith et al. 1999; Vaughn 2004; Webster and Gonlin 1988; Webster et al. 1998; Welch and Scary 1995; Wilk 1983; Wright 2014).

2. This volume provides a glorious diversity of definitions of the term *household*. While some researchers focus on social structure (such as Lévi-Strauss; see Zobler, this volume), others define households by the activities they share, that is, by the functions households perform (Chicione et al., this volume; Lightfoot 1994; Netting 1993; Wilk and Netting 1984; Wilk and Rathje 1982). As Pacifico and Johnson discuss in chapter 1, there are many layers to the concept of households. Rather than striving for a consensus on a single definition, we need to embrace conceptual diversity.

3. There are, of course, exceptions to this, especially in utopian movements. Shaker communities, which began in the United States in the 1800s, prohibited procreation; not surprisingly, those communities didn't last long.

4. By families I am broadly referring to groups of people closely related by blood, marriage, adoption, or other means. I'm not referring to some imagined, modern American nuclear family from the 1950s.

5. I use the term *adapt* in a broad sense, meaning to adjust to changing circumstances. I'm not using "adaptation" in the biological or ecological sense or in the sense of old-school, processual ecofunctionalism (for instance, Binford 1962, 1968; Isbell 1978; Plog 1974). Rather, I use the term to acknowledge that people, individually and in groups, are capable of developing solutions to problems presented by historical circumstances. People are also capable of disastrous failures, by which I mean environmental degradation, political and social chaos, genocide, world wars, and other historical horrors of human society.

6. Netting's research on smallholder economies has much to offer north coast archaeologists. Netting (1993, 2) defines smallholders as "rural cultivators practicing intensive, permanent diversified agriculture on relatively small farms in areas of dense population. The family household is the major corporate social unit for mobilizing agricultural labor, managing productive resources, and organizing consumption." Further, he states: "Smallholders practice *intensive agriculture*, producing relatively high annual yields or multicrop yields from permanent fields that are seldom or never rested, with fertility restored and sustained by practices such as thorough tillage, crop diversification and rotation, animal husbandry, fertilization, irrigation, drainage, and terracing. I'm not talking about amber waves of grain

but about gardens and orchards, about rice paddies, dairy farms, and *chinampas*" (Netting 1993, 3). This is likely a good model for examining changes in agricultural production since the introduction of irrigation agriculture on the coast circa 3,000 BC.

7. I'm not using the terms *states* and *empires* to mean evolutionary types (such as Service 1972); nor do I mean European notions of the nation-state (as conceived by Locke, Hume, Ricardo, Marx, Engels, and others). Rather, I am referencing the long indigenous tradition of centralized polities in the Andes, such as the Wari, Chimú, and Inka, as well as smaller formations such as the *señorios* of the Peruvian coast and the chiefdoms of the Ecuadorian highlands. Much of our understanding of Andean statecraft comes from ethnohistoric accounts in Spanish and indigenous chronicles and court documents.

8. Bourdieu's definition is based on conventional definitions of capital found in the classic works of political economy by Marx, Smith, and Ricardo.

9. My inclusion of 100 percent screening of fill and systematic collection of samples for special analysis may seem out of place in a chapter on "Future Directions" in household archaeology. However, the limited use of these practices on the north coast and in many other regions in the Andes still remains a fundamental impediment to advancing our knowledge of prehistoric social change. Most of the publications on household archaeology on the North Coast are still based on excavations of large areas without screening. Consequently, there is little contextual information on the distributions of artifacts and ecofacts and formation processes. Quantitative analysis and comparisons of artifacts and ecofacts within and between households are difficult, if not impossible.

10. Mode of abandonment is largely overlooked in Andean archaeology. One of the most important results of mode of abandonment studies is that floor assemblages cannot be assumed to represent the activities that took place within rooms. Associated middens adjacent to domestic structures are often the best places to investigate household activities and differences in status or wealth.

11. "Thus, without accurate estimates of the length of occupation, we cannot adequately evaluate any anthropological theory—for example, theory concerning the development of political complexity—that involves the interpretation of assemblage diversity, settlement patterns, or population size" (Varien and Potter 1997, 196).

REFERENCES

Abrams, Elliot M. 1994. *How the Maya Built Their World: Energetics and Ancient Architecture.* Austin: University of Texas Press.

Adams, Robert M. 1975. *Energy and Structure: A Theory of Social Power.* Austin: University of Texas Press.

Allison, Penelope, ed. 1999. *The Archaeology of Household Activities.* London: Routledge.

Alva Alva, Walter, and Christopher B. Donnan. 1993. *Royal Tombs of Sipán*. Los Angeles: Fowler Museum of Culture History, University of California.

Bawden, Garth. 1977. "Galindo and the Nature of the Middle Horizon of the North Coast of Peru." PhD dissertation, Harvard University, Cambridge, MA.

Bawden, Garth. 1982. "Community Organization Reflected by the Household: A Study of Pre-Columbian Social Dynamics." *Journal of Field Archaeology* 9: 165–181.

Billman, Brian R. 2002. "Irrigation and the Origins of the Southern Moche State on the North Coast of Peru." *Latin American Antiquity* 13 (4): 371–400.

Billman, Brian R. 2010. "How Moche Rulers Came to Power: Investigating the Emergence of the Moche Political Economy." In *New Perspectives on Moche Political Organization*, edited by Jeffrey Quilter and Luis Jaime Castillo Butters, 179–198. Washington, DC: Dumbarton Oaks Press.

Binford, Lewis R. 1962. "Archaeology as Anthropology." *American Antiquity* 28 (2): 217–225.

Binford, Lewis R. 1968. "Post-Pleistocene Adaptations." In *New Perspectives in Archeology*, edited by Sally R. Binford and Lewis R. Binford, 313–341. Chicago: Aldine Publishing Company.

Blanton, Richard E. 1994. *Houses and Households: A Comparative Study*. New York: Plenum.

Bourdieu, Pierre. 1977. *Outline of a Theory of Practice*. Cambridge: Cambridge University Press.

Bourdieu, Pierre. 1984. *Distinction: A Social Critique of the Judgment of Taste*. Cambridge, MA: Harvard University Press.

Bourdieu, Pierre. 1986. "The Forms of Capital." In *Handbook of Theory and Research for the Sociology of Education*, edited by John Richardson, 241–258. New York: Greenwood.

Bourget, Steve. 2001a. "Children and Ancestors: Ritual Practices at the Moche Site of Huaca de la Luna, North Coast of Peru." In *Ritual Sacrifice in Ancient Peru*, edited by Elizabeth P. Benson and Anita G. Cook, 93–119. Austin: University of Texas Press.

Bourget, Steve. 2001b. "Rituals of Sacrifice: Its Practice at Huaca de la Luna and Its Representation in Moche Iconography." In *Moche Art and Archaeology in Ancient Peru*, edited by Joanne Pillsbury, 89–109. New Haven, CT: Yale University Press.

Braudel, Fernand. 1992a. *Civilization and Capitalism, 15th–18th Centuries*, vol. 1: *The Structures of Everyday Life*. Berkeley: University of California Press.

Braudel, Fernand. 1992b. *Civilization and Capitalism, 15th–18th Centuries*, vol. 2: *The Wheels of Commerce*. Berkeley: University of California Press.

Braudel, Fernand. 1992c. *Civilization and Capitalism, 15th–18th Centuries*, vol. 3: *The Perspective of the World*. Berkeley: University of California Press.

Bray, Tamara L. 2003. "Inca Pottery as Culinary Equipment: Food, Feasting, and Gender in Imperial State Design." *Latin American Antiquity* 14: 3–28.

Brumfiel, Elizabeth M. 1991. "Weaving and Cooking: Women's Production in Aztec Mexico." In *Engendering Archaeology: Women and Prehistory*, edited by Joan Gero and Margret Conkey, 224–251. Oxford: Basil Blackwell.

Cameron, Catherine M. 1991. "Structure Abandonment in Villages." In *Archaeological Method and Theory*, vol. 3, edited by Michael B. Schiffer, 155–194. Tucson: University of Arizona Press.

Carmean, Kelli, Patricia McAnany, and Jeremy A. Sabloff. 2011. "People Who Live in Stone Houses: Local Knowledge and Social Difference in the Classic Maya Puuc Region of Yucatan, Mexico." *Latin American Antiquity* 22: 143–158.

Castillo Butters, Luis Jaime. 2001. "The Last of the Mochicas: A View from the Jequetepeque Valley." In *Moche Art and Archaeology in Ancient Peru*, edited by Joanne Pillsbury, 307–332. New Haven, CT: Yale University Press.

Castillo Butters, Luis Jaime, and Christopher B. Donnan. 1994. "La ocupación moche de San José de Moro, Jequetepeque." In *Moche: Propuestas y Prospectivas. Actas del Primer Coloquio sobre la Cultura Moche (Trujillo, 12 a 16 de abril de 1993)*, edited by Santiago Uceda Castillo and Elias Mujica Barrada, 93–146. Lima, Peru: Institute Francais d'Etudes Andines.

Chapdelaine, Claude. 2001. "The Growing Power of a Moche Urban Class." In *Moche Art and Archaeology in Ancient Peru*, edited by Joanne Pillsbury, 69–87. New Haven, CT: Yale University Press.

Chapdelaine, Claude. 2002. "Out in the Streets of Moche: Urbanism and Socio-political Organization at a Moche IV Urban Center." In *Advances in Andean Archaeology and Ethnohistory*, edited by William H. Isbell and Helaine Silverman, 53–88. New York: Plenum.

Chapdelaine, Claude. 2003. "La ciudad de Moche: urbanismo y estado." In *Moche: Hacia el Final del Milenio. Actas del Segundo Coloquio sobre la cultura Moche*, edited by Santiago Uceda Castillo and Elias Mujica Barrada, 247–285. Trujillo, Peru: Universidad Nacional de Trujillo and Pontificia Universidad Católica del Perú.

Cock, Guillermo A. 1986. "Power and Wealth in the Jequetepeque Valley in the Sixteenth Century." In *The Pacatnamu Papers*, vol. 1, edited by Christopher B. Donnan and Guillermo A. Cock, 171–182. Los Angeles: Fowler Museum of Culture History, University of California.

Costin, Cathy Lynne, and Timothy K. Earle. 1989. "Status Distinctions and the Legitimation of Power as Reflected in Changing Patterns of Consumption in Late Prehispanic Peru." *American Antiquity* 54 (4): 691–714.

Cuéllar, Andrea M. 2013. "The Archaeology of Food and Social Inequality in the Andes." *Journal of Archaeological Research* 21: 123–174.

Cutright, Robyn E. 2009. "Between the Kitchen and the State: Domestic Practice and Chimú Expansion in the Jequetepeque Valley, Peru." PhD dissertation, University of Pittsburgh, PA.

Cutright, Robyn E. 2010. "Food, Family, and Empire: Relating Political and Domestic Change in the Jequetepeque Hinterland / Comida, familia, e imperio: Relacionando cambios políticos y domésticos en la periferia del Jequetepeque." In *Comparative Perspectives on the Archaeology of Coastal South America*, edited by Robyn E. Cutright, Enrique López-Hurtado, and Alexander Martin, 27–44. Pittsburgh: Center for Comparative Archaeology, University of Pittsburgh.

Cutright, Robyn E. 2011. "Food for the Dead, Cuisine of the Living: Mortuary Food Offerings from the Jequetepeque Valley, Perú." In *From State to Empire in the Prehistoric Jequetepeque Valley, Peru*, edited by Colleen Zori and Ilana Johnson, 83–92. British Archaeological Reports International Series #2310. Oxford: Archaeopress.

Cutright, Robyn E. 2015. "Eating Empire in the Jequetepeque: A Local View of Chimu Expansion on the North Coast of Peru." *Latin American Antiquity* 26: 64–86.

D'Altroy, Terence N. 1992. *Provincial Power in the Inca Empire*. Washington, DC: Smithsonian Institution Press.

D'Altroy, Terence N., and Timothy K. Earle. 1985. "Staple Finance, Wealth Finance, and Storage in the Inca Political Economy." *Current Anthropology* 26 (2): 187–206.

D'Altroy, Terence N., and Christine A. Hastorf. 2001a. "The Domestic Economy, Households, and Imperial Transformation." In *Empire and Domestic Economy*, edited by Terence N. D'Altroy and Christine A. Hastorf, 3–26. New York: Kluwer Academic/ Plenum.

D'Altroy, Terence N., and Christine A. Hastorf, eds. 2001b. *Empire and Domestic Economy*. New York: Kluwer Academic/Plenum.

Deal, Michael. 1985. "Household Pottery Disposal in the Maya Highlands: An Ethnoarchaeological Interpretation." *Journal of Anthropological Archaeology* 4: 243–291.

de Barros, Philip L.F. 1982. "The Effects of Variable Site Occupation Span on the Results of Frequency Seriation." *American Antiquity* 47: 291–315.

Deboer, Warren R. 1974. "Ceramic Longevity and Archaeological Interpretation: An Example from the Upper Ucayali, Peru." *American Antiquity* 39: 335–343.

Deetz, James. 1976. *In Small Things Forgotten*. New York: Anchor Books.

Deetz, James. 1982. "Households: Ethnographic Households and Archaeological Interpretation." *American Behavioral Scientist* 25: 717–724.

DeMarris, Elizabeth, Luis Jaime Castillo Butters, and Timothy Earle. 1996. "Ideology, Materialization, and Power Strategies." *Current Anthropology* 37: 15–31.

Donnan, Christopher, and Luis Jaime Castillo Butters. 1994. "Excavaciones de tumbas de sacerdotistas moche en San José de Moro, Jequetepeque." In *Moche: Propuestas y Prospectivas: Actas del Primer Coloquio sobre la Cultura Moche (Trujillo, 12 a 16 de abril de 1993)*, edited by Santiago Uceda Castillo and Elias Mujica Barrada, 415–424. Lima: Travaux de l'Institute Francais d'Etudes Andines.

Earle, Timothy K. 1997. *How Chiefs Come to Power: The Political Economy in Prehistory*. Stanford, CA: Stanford University Press.

Earle, Timothy K., Terence D'Altroy, Christine Hastorf, Catherine Scott, Cathy Costin, Glenn Russell, and Elsie Sandefur. 1987. *Archaeological Field Research in the Upper Mantaro, Peru, 1982–1983: Investigations of Inca Expansion and Exchange*. Monograph 28. Los Angeles: Institute of Archaeology, University of California.

Earle, Timothy K., and Matthew Spriggs. 2016. "Political Economy in Prehistory: A Marist Approach to Pacific Sequences." *Current Anthropologist* 56: 515–544.

Flannery, Kent V., ed. 1976. *The Early Mesoamerican Village*. New York: Academic Press.

Flannery, Kent V., and Joyce Marcus. 2005. *Excavations at San José Mogote 1*. Memoirs Museum of Anthropology 40. Ann Arbor: University of Michigan.

Franco Jordán, Régulo, César Gálvez Mora, and Segundo Vásquez Sánchez. 1994. "Arquitectura y decoración Mochica en la Huaca Cao Viejo, Complejo El Brujo: Resultados Preliminares." In *Moche: Propuestas y Prospectivas: Actas del Primer Coloquio sobre la Cultura Moche (Trujillo, 12 a 16 de abril de 1993)*, edited by Santiago Uceda Castillo and Elias Mujica Barrada, 147–180. Lima: Travaux de l'Institute Francais d'Etudes Andines.

Franco Jordán, Régulo, César Gálvez Mora, and Segundo Vásquez Sánchez. 1996. "Los descubrimientos arqueológicos en la Huaca Cao Viejo, Complejo 'El Brujo.'" *Ark Inca* 1 (5): 82–94.

Gagnon, Celeste Marie, Brian R. Billman, Jose Carcelén Silva, and Karl J. Reinhard. 2013. "Tracking Shifts in Coca Use in the Moche Valley: Analysis of Oral Health Indicators and Dental Calculus Microfossils." *Ñawpa Pacha* 33 (2): 193–214.

Gero, Joan M., and Margaret W. Conkey, eds. 1991. *Engendering Archaeology: Women and Prehistory*. Oxford: Basil Blackwell.

Goody, Jack. 1971. *The Household Developmental Cycle*. Cambridge: Cambridge University Press.

Graeub, Benjamin E., M. Jahi Chappell, Hannah Wittman, Samuel Ledermann, Rachel Bezner Kerr, and Barbara Gemmill-Herren. 2016. "The State of Family Farms in the World." *World Development* 87: 1–15.

Graham, Martha. 1993. "Settlement Organization and Residential Variability among the Rarámuri." In *Abandonment of Settlements and Regions: Ethnoarchaeological and*

Archaeological Approaches, edited by Catherine M. Cameron and Steve A. Tomka, 25–42. Cambridge: Cambridge University Press.

Graham, Martha. 1994. *Mobile Farmers: An Ethnoarchaeological Approach to Settlement Organization among the Raramuri of Northwestern Mexico*. International Monographs in Prehistory, Ethnoarchaeological Series 3. Ann Arbor: University of Michigan.

Griffis, Shelia. 1971. "Excavation and Analysis of Midden Material from Cerro la Virgen, Moche Valley, Peru." Undergraduate honor's thesis, Harvard University, Cambridge, MA.

Gumerman, George J., IV. 1991. "Subsistence and Complex Society: Diet between Diverse Socio-economic Groups at Pacatnamu, Peru." PhD dissertation, University of California, Los Angeles.

Gumerman, George J., IV. 2002. "Llama Power and Empowered Fishermen: Food and Power at Pacatnamu, Peru." In *The Dynamics of Power*, edited by Maria O'Donovan, 238–256. Center for Archaeological Investigations Occasional Paper 30. Carbondale: Southern Illinois University.

Haas, Jonathan. 1982. *The Evolution of the Prehistoric State*. New York: Columbia University Press.

Haas, Jonathan. 1987. "The Exercise of Power in Early Andean State Development." In *The Development and Origins of the Andean State*, edited by Jonathan Haas, Shelia Pozorski, and Thomas Pozorski, 31–35. Cambridge: Cambridge University Press.

Hastorf, Christine A. 1991. "Gender, Space, and Food in Prehistory." In *Engendering Archaeology*, edited by Joan Gero and Margaret Conkey, 132–159. Oxford: Basil Blackwell.

Hastorf, Christine A. 1993. *Agriculture and the Onset of Political Inequality before the Inca*. Cambridge: Cambridge University Press.

Hastorf, Christine A. 2003. "Andean Luxury Foods: Special Foods for the Ancestors, Deities, and the Elite." *Antiquity* 77: 545–555.

Hastorf, Christine, and Virginia Popper. 1988. *Current Paleoethnobotany: Analytic Methods and Cultural Interpretations of Archaeological Plant Remains*. Chicago: University of Chicago Press.

Hayashida, Frances. 2006. "The Pampa de Chaparrí: Water, Land, and Politics on the North Coast of Peru." *Latin American Antiquity* 17 (3): 243–264.

Hayden, Brian, and Aubrey Cannon. 1982a. "The Corporate Group as an Archaeological Unit." *Journal of Anthropological Archaeology* 1: 132–158.

Hayden, Brian, and Aubrey Cannon. 1982b. "Where the Garbage Goes: Refuse Disposal in the Maya Highlands." *Journal of Anthropological Archaeology* 2: 117–163.

Hendon, Julia A. 1997. "Women's Work, Women's Space, and Women's Status among the Classic-Period Maya Elite at Copan, Honduras." In *Women in Prehistory: North America and Mesoamerica*, edited by Cheryl Claassen and Rosemary Joyce, 33–46. Philadelphia: University of Pennsylvania Press.

Hobsbawm, Eric John Ernest. 1996a. *The Age of Revolution: Europe 1789–1848*. New York: Vintage Books.

Hobsbawm, Eric John Ernest. 1996b. *The Age of Capital: 1848–1875*. New York: Vintage Books.

Hobsbawm, Eric John Ernest. 1996c. *The Age of Empire: 1875–1914*. New York: Vintage Books.

Huckleberry, Gary F., Frances M. Hayashida, and Jack Johnson. 2012. "New Insights into the Evolution of an Intervalley Prehistoric Irrigation Canal System, North Coastal Peru." *Geoarchaeology* 27 (6): 492–520.

Hudson, Jean. 2011. "Pacific Ocean Fishing Traditions: Subsistence, Beliefs, Ecology, and Households." In *Ethnozooarchaeology: The Present and Past of Human-Animal Relationships*, edited by Umberto Albarella and Angela Trentacoste, 49–57. Oxford: Oxbow Books.

Isbell, William H. 1978. "Environmental Perturbations and the Origins of the Andean State." In *Social Archaeology: Beyond Subsistence and Dating*, edited by Charles L. Redman, 303–313. New York: Academic Press.

Jackson, H. Edwin, and Susan L. Scott. 2003. "Patterns of Elite Faunal Utilization at Moundville, Alabama." *American Antiquity* 68: 552–572.

Joyce, Arthur, and Sissel Johannessen. 1993. "Abandonment and the Production of Archaeological Variability at Domestic Sites." In *Abandonment of Settlements and Regions: Ethnoarchaeological and Archaeological Approaches*, edited by Catherine M. Cameron and Steve A. Tomka, 138–156. Cambridge: Cambridge University Press.

Kamp, Kathryn. 2000. "From Village to Tell: Household Ethnoarchaeology in Syria." *Near Eastern Archaeology* 63: 84–93.

Keatinge, Richard W. 1974. "Chimú Rural Administrative Centers in the Moche Valley, Peru." *World Archaeology* 6: 66–82.

Keatinge, Richard W. 1975. "Urban Settlement Systems and Rural Sustaining Communities: An Example from Chan Chan's Hinterland." *Journal of Field Archaeology* 2 (3): 215–227.

Kent, Susan. 1992. "Studying Variability in the Archaeological Record: An Ethnoarchaeological Model of Distinguishing Mobility Patterns." *American Antiquity* 57: 635–660.

Kramer, Carol. 1982. "Ethnographic Household and Archaeological Interpretations: A Case Study from Iranian Kurdistan." *American Behavioral Scientist* 6: 663–675.

Lambert, Patricia, Celeste Marie Gagnon, Brian R. Billman, M. Anne Katzenberg, José Carcelén, and Robert H. Tykot. 2012. "Bone Chemistry at Cerro Oreja: A Stable

Isotope Perspective on the Development of a Regional Economy in the Moche Valley, Perú." *Latin American Antiquity* 23 (2): 144–166.

LaMotta, Vincent M., and Michael B. Schiffer. 1999. "Formation Processes of House Floor Assemblages." In *The Archaeology of Household Activities,* edited by Penelope Allison, 19–29. London: Routledge.

Lawrence, Susan. 1999. "Towards a Feminist Archaeology of Households: Gender and Household Structure in the Australian Goldfields." In *The Archaeology of Household Activities,* edited by Penelope Allison, 121–141. London: Routledge.

LeBlanc, Stephen. 1971. "An Addition to Naroll's Suggested Floor Area and Settlement Population Relationship." *American Antiquity* 36: 210–211.

LeCount, Lisa J. 1999. "Polychrome Pottery and Political Strategies in Late and Terminal Classic Lowland Maya Society." *Latin American Antiquity* 10: 239–258.

LeeDecker, Charles H. 1994. "Discard Behavior on Domestic Historic Sites: Evaluation of Contexts for the Interpretation of Household Consumptions Patterns." *Journal of Archaeological Method and Theory* 1: 345–375.

Lightfoot, Kent G., Antoinette Martinez, and Ann M. Schiff. 1998. "Daily Practice and Material Culture in Pluralistic Social Settings: An Archaeological Study of Culture Change and Persistence from Fort Ross, California." *American Antiquity* 63: 199–222.

Lightfoot, Ricky R. 1993. "Abandonment Processes in Prehistoric Pueblos." In *Abandonment of Settlements and Regions: Ethnoarchaeological and Archaeological Approaches,* edited by Catherine M. Cameron and Steve A. Tomka, 165–177. Cambridge: Cambridge University Press.

Lightfoot, Ricky R. 1994. *The Duckfoot Site,* vol. 2: *Archaeology of the House and Household.* Occasional Paper 4. Cortez, CO: Crow Canyon Archaeological Center.

Mann, Michael. 1986. *The Sources of Social Power.* Cambridge: Cambridge University Press.

McIntosh, Roderick J. 1974. "Archaeology and Mud Wall Decay in a West African Village." *World Archaeology* 6: 154–171.

Miller, George, and Richard L. Burger. 1995. "Our Father the Cayman, Our Dinner the Llama: Animal Utilization at Chavin de Huantar, Peru." *American Antiquity* 60: 421–458.

Moore, Jerry D. 1981. "Chimu Sociocultural Organization: Preliminary Data from Manchan, Casma Valley, Peru." *Ñawpa Pacha* 19: 115–126.

Moore, Jerry D. 1985. "Household Economics and Political Integration: The Lower Class of the Chimu Empire." PhD dissertation, University of California, Santa Barbara.

Moore, Jerry D. 1991. "Cultural Responses to Environmental Catastrophes: Post-El Niño Subsistence on the Prehistoric North Coast of Peru." *Latin American Antiquity* 2: 27–43.

Moore, Jerry D. 2012. *The Prehistory of Home.* Berkeley: University of California Press.

Moore, Jerry D., and Janine Gasco. 1990. "Perishable Structures and Serial Dwellings from Coastal Chiapas." *Ancient Mesoamerica* 1: 205–212.

Moseley, Michael E., and Eric E. Deeds. 1982. "The Land in Front of Chan Chan: Agrarian Expansion, Reform, and Collapse in the Moche Valley." In *Chan Chan: Andean Desert City*, edited by Michael E. Moseley and Kent C. Day, 25–54. Albuquerque: University of New Mexico Press.

Murra, John V. 1980. *Economic Organization of the Inca State.* New Haven, CT: JAI Press.

Murray, Pricilla. 1980. "Discard Location: The Ethnographic Data." *American Antiquity* 45: 490–502.

Narroll, Raoul. 1962. "Floor Area and Settlement Population." *American Antiquity* 27: 587–589.

Nash, Donna. 2009. "Household Archaeology in the Andes." *Journal of Archaeological Research* 17: 205–226.

Netherly, Patricia. 1977. "Local Level Lords on the North Coast of Peru." PhD dissertation, Cornell University, Ithaca, NY.

Netherly, Patricia. 1984. "Management of Late Andean Irrigation Systems on the North Coast of Peru." *American Antiquity* 49 (2): 227–254.

Netherly, Patricia. 1990. "Out of Many, One: The Organization of Rule in the North Coast Polities." In *The Northern Dynasties: Kingship and Statecraft in Chimor*, edited by Michael E. Moseley and Alana Cordy-Collins, 461–487. Washington, DC: Dumbarton Oaks Research Library and Collection.

Netting, Robert McC. 1982. "Some Home Truths on Household Size and Wealth." *American Behavioral Scientist* 6: 641–662.

Netting, Robert McC. 1993. *Smallholders, Householders: Farm Families and the Ecology of Intensive, Sustainable Agriculture.* Stanford, CA: Stanford University Press.

Netting, Robert McC., Richard R. Wilk, and Eric J. Arnould, eds. 1984a. *Households: Comparative and Historical Studies of the Domestic Group.* Berkeley: University of California Press.

Netting, Robert McC., Richard R. Wilk, and Eric J. Arnould. 1984b. "Introduction." In *Households: Comparative and Historical Studies of the Domestic Group*, edited by Robert McC. Netting, Richard R. Wilk, and Eric J. Arnould, xiii–xxxviii. Berkeley: University of California Press.

Ortloff, Charles R., Robert A. Feldman, and Michael E. Moseley. 1985. "Hydraulic Engineering and Historical Aspects of the Pre-Columbian Intravalley Canal Systems of the Moche Valley, Peru." *Journal of Field Archaeology* 12: 77–98.

Oswald, Dana. 1987. "The Organization of Space in Residential Buildings: A Cross-Cultural Perspective." In *Method and Theory for Activity Area Research: An*

Ethnoarchaeological Approach, edited by Susan Kent, 295–344. New York: Columbia University Press.

Parker, Bradley J., Gabriel Prieto Burmester, and Carlos Osores Mendives. 2018. "Methodological Advances in Household Archaeology: An Application of Microartifact Analysis at Pampa La Cruz, Huanchaco, Peru." *Ñawpa Pacha* 38 (1): 57–75.

Parker, Bradley J., and Nicola Sharratt. 2017. "Fragments of the Past: Microartifact Analysis of Use Surfaces at Tumilaca la Chimba, Moquegua, Peru." Advances in Archaeological Practice 5 (1): 71–92.

Pauketat, Timothy R. 1989. "Monitoring Mississippian Homestead Occupation Span and Economy Using Ceramic Refuse." *American Antiquity* 54: 288–310.

Plog, Fred, ed. 1974. *The Study of Prehistoric Change*. New York: Academic Press.

Pluckhahn, Thomas J. 2010. "Household Archaeology in the Southeastern United States: History, Trends, and Challenges." *Journal of Archaeological Research* 18: 331–385.

Pohl, Mary Deland. 1994. "The Economics and Politics of Maya Meat Eating." In *The Economic Anthropology of the State*, edited by Elizabeth M. Brumfiel, 119–148. Lanham, MD: University of America Press.

Popper, Virginia S. 1988. "Selecting Quantitative Measurements in Paleoethnobotany." In *Current Paleoethnobotany*, edited by Christine A. Hastorf and Virginia S. Popper, 53–71. Chicago: University of Chicago Press.

Pozorski, Shelia G. 1976. "Prehistoric Subsistence Patterns and Site Economics in the Moche Valley, Peru." PhD dissertation, University of Texas, Austin.

Pozorski, Shelia G. 1979. "Prehistoric Diet and Subsistence of the Moche Valley, Peru." *World Archaeology* 11 (2): 163–184.

Pozorski, Shelia G. 1982. "Subsistence Systems in the Chimu State." In *Chan Chan: Andean Desert City*, edited by Michael E. Moseley and Kent C. Day, 177–196. Albuquerque: University of New Mexico Press.

Pozorski, Shelia G., and Thomas Pozorski. 1986. "Recent Excavations at Pampa de las Llamas-Moxeke, a Complex Initial Period Site in Peru." *Journal of Field Archaeology* 13 (4): 381–401.

Pozorski, Thomas. 1987. "Changing Priorities in the Chimu State: The Role of Irrigation Agriculture." In *The Origins and Development of the Andean State*, edited by Jonathan Haas, Shelia G. Pozorski, and Thomas Pozorski, 111–120. Cambridge: Cambridge University Press.

Prossor, Lauren, Susan Lawrence, Alasdair Brooks, and Jane Lennon. 2012. "Household Archaeology, Lifecycles, and Status in a Nineteenth-Century Australian Coastal Community." *International Journal of Historical Archaeology* 16 (4): 809–827.

Ramirez, Susan E. 1996. *The World Upside Down: Cross-Cultural Contact and Conflict in Sixteenth-Century Peru*. Stanford, CA: Stanford University Press.

Rathje, William L., and Randall McGuire. 1982. "Rich Men . . . Poor Men: Ethnographic Households and Archaeological Interpretation." *American Behavioral Scientist* 25: 705–715.

Reitz, Elizabeth, and Myra Shackley. 2012. *Environmental Archaeology*. New York: Springer.

Reitz, Elizabeth, and Elizabeth Wing. 2008. *Zooarchaeology*. Cambridge: Cambridge University Press.

Ringberg, Jennifer E. 2007. "Figurines, Household Ritual, and the Use of Domestic Space in a Middle Moche Rural Community." In *Arqueología Mochica: Nuevos Enfoques*, edited by Luis Jaime Castillo Butters, Hèléne Bernier, Gregory Lockard, and Julio Rucabado Yong, 341–358. Lima: Pontificia Universidad Católica del Perú.

Ringberg, Jennifer E. 2012. "Daily Life at Cerro Leon, an Early Intermediate Period Highland Settlement in the Moche Valley, Peru." PhD dissertation, University of North Carolina, Chapel Hill.

Robin, Cynthia. 2003. "New Directions in Classic Maya Household Archaeology." *Journal of Archaeological Research* 11: 307–356.

Robin, Cynthia, ed. 2013a. *Chan: An Ancient Maya Farming Community*. Gainesville: University of Florida Press.

Robin, Cynthia. 2013b. *Everyday Life Matters: Maya Farmers at Chan*. Gainesville: University of Florida Press.

Rocek, Thomas R. 1988. "The Behavioral and Material Correlates of Site Seasonality: Lesson from Navajo Ethnoarchaeology." *American Antiquity* 53: 523–536.

Roth, Barbara J., ed. 2010. *Engendering Households in the Prehistoric Southwest*. Tucson: University of Arizona Press.

Scary, C. Margaret. 2003. "The Use of Plants and Mound-Related Activities at Bottle Creek and Moundville." In *Bottle Creek: A Pensacola Culture Site in South Alabama*, edited by Ian W. Brown, 114–129. Tuscaloosa: University of Alabama Press.

Schaedel, Richard P. 1972. "The City and the Origin of the State in America." *Actas y Memorias del 39 Congreso Internacional de Americanistas* 2: 15–33.

Schaedel, Richard P. 1985. "The Transition from Chiefdom to State in Northern Peru." In *Development and Decline: The Evolution of Sociopolitical Organization*, edited by J. M. Claessen, Peter van der Velde, and M. Estelle Smith, 156–169. South Hadley, MA: Bergin and Garvey.

Schiffer, Michael B. 1985. "Is There a 'Pompeii Premise' in Archaeology?" *Journal of Anthropological Research* 41: 18–41.

Schiffer, Michael B. 1987. *Formation Processes of the Archaeological Record*. Albuquerque: University of New Mexico Press.

Schlanger, Sarah H. 1991. "On Manos, Metates, and the History of Site Occupation." *American Antiquity* 56: 460–474.

Schreiber, Katharina. 1992. *Wari Imperialism in the Middle Horizon Peru*. Museum of Anthropology Anthropological Papers 87. Ann Arbor: University of Michigan.

Service, Elman. 1972. *Origins of the State and Civilization: The Process of Cultural Evolution*. New York: Norton.

Shimada, Izumi. 1994. *Pampa Grande and the Mochica Culture*. Austin: University of Texas Press.

Shimada, Izumi, Ken-ichi Shinoda, Julie Farnum, Robert Corruccini, and Hirokatsu Watanabe. 2004. "An Integrated Analysis of Pre-Hispanic Mortuary Practices." *Current Anthropology* 45 (3): 369–402.

Smith, Michael E. 1987. "Household Possessions and Wealth in Agrarian States: Implications for Archaeology." *Journal of Anthropological Archaeology* 6: 297–335.

Smith, Michael E. 1993. "Social Complexity in the Aztec Countryside." In *Archaeological Views from the Countryside*, edited by Glen Schwartz and Steven Falconer, 143–159. Washington, DC: Smithsonian Institution Press.

Smith, Michael E., Cynthia Heath-Smith, and Lisa Montiel. 1999. "Excavations of Aztec Urban Houses at Yautepec, Mexico." *Latin American Antiquity* 10: 133–150.

Stevenson, Marc G. 1982. "Toward an Understanding of Site Abandonment Behavior: Evidence from Historic Mining Camps in the Southwest Yukon." *Journal of Anthropological Archaeology* 1: 237–265.

Tani, Masakazu. 1995. "Beyond the Identification of Formation Processes: Behavioral Inferences Based on Traces Left by Cultural Formation Processes." *Journal of Archaeological Method and Theory* 2: 231–252.

Topic, John. 1977. "Lower Class at Chan Chan: A Quantitative Approach." PhD dissertation, Harvard University, Cambridge, MA.

Topic, John. 1982. "Lower Class Social and Economic Organization at Chan Chan." In *Chan Chan: Ancient Desert City*, edited by Michael E. Moseley and Kent C. Day, 25–53. Albuquerque: University of New Mexico Press.

Topic, Theresa L. 1977. "Excavations at Moche." PhD dissertation, Harvard University, Cambridge, MA.

Topic, Theresa L. 1982. "The Early Intermediate Period and Its Legacy." In *Chan Chan: Ancient Desert City*, edited by Michael E. Moseley and Kent C. Day, 25–53. Albuquerque: University of New Mexico Press.

Tringham, Ruth E. 1991. "Households with Faces: The Challenge of Gender in Prehistoric Household Architectural Remains." In *Engendering Archaeology: Women and Prehistory*, edited by Joan M. Gero and Margaret W. Conkey, 93–131. Oxford: Basil Blackwell.

Tringham, Ruth E. 1994. "Engendered Places in Prehistory." *Gender, Place, and Culture* 1: 169–203.

Uceda Castillo, Santiago. 2001. "Investigations at Huaca de la Luna, Moche Valley: An Example of Moche Religious Architecture." In *Moche Art and Archaeology in Ancient Peru*, edited by Joanne Pillsbury, 47–67. New Haven, CT: Yale University Press.

Uceda Castillo, Santiago, and José Armas Asmad. 1997. "Los talleres alfareros en el centro urbano Moche." In *Investigaciones en la Huaca de la Luna 1995*, edited by Santiago Uceda Castillo, Elías Mujica Barrada, and Ricardo Morales Gamarra, 93–104. Trujillo, Peru: Facultad de Ciencias Sociales, Universidad Nacional de la Libertad.

Uceda Castillo, Santiago, and José Armas Asmad. 1998. "An Urban Pottery Workshop at the Site of Moche." In *Andean Ceramics: Technology, Organization, and Approaches*, edited by Izumi Shimada, 91–110. MASCA Research Papers in Science and Archaeology, Supplement to vol. 15. Philadelphia: University of Pennsylvania, Museum of Anthropology and Archaeology.

Uceda Castillo, Santiago, Ricardo Morales Gamarra, José Canziani Amico, and María Montoya Vera. 1994. "Investigaciones sobre la arquitectura y relieves policromos en Huaca de la Luna, valle de Moche." In *Moche: Propuestas y Prospectivas. Actas del Primer Coloquio sobre la Cultura Moche (Trujillo, 12 a 16 de abril de 1993)*, edited by Santiago Uceda Castillo and Elias Mujica Barrada. Lima, Peru: Institute Francais d'Etudes Andines.

Uceda Castillo, Santiago, Elías Mujica Barrada, and Ricardo Morales Gamarra, eds. 1997. *Investigaciones en la Huaca de la Luna 1995*. Trujillo, Peru: Facultad de Ciencias Sociales, Universidad Nacional de la Libertad.

Uceda Castillo, Santiago, Elías Mujica Barrada, and Ricardo Morales Gamarra, eds. 1998. *Investigaciones en la Huaca de la Luna 1996*. Trujillo, Peru: Facultad de Ciencias Sociales, Universidad Nacional de la Libertad.

Uceda Castillo, Santiago, Elías Mujica Barrada, and Ricardo Morales Gamarra, eds. 2000. *Investigaciones en la Huaca de la Luna 1997*. Trujillo, Peru: Facultad de Ciencias Sociales, Universidad Nacional de la Libertad.

Uceda Castillo, Santiago, Elías Mujica Barrada, and Ricardo Morales Gamarra, eds. 2004. *Investigaciones en la Huaca de la Luna 1998–1999*. Trujillo, Peru: Facultad de Ciencias Sociales, Universidad Nacional de la Libertad.

Uceda Castillo, Santiago, Elías Mujica Barrada, and Ricardo Morales Gamarra, eds. 2006. *Investigaciones en la Huaca de la Luna 2000*. Trujillo, Peru: Facultad de Ciencias Sociales, Universidad Nacional de la Libertad.

Uceda Castillo, Santiago, Elías Mujica Barrada, and Ricardo Morales Gamarra, eds. 2008. *Investigaciones en la Huaca de la Luna 2001*. Trujillo, Peru: Facultad de Ciencias Sociales, Universidad Nacional de la Libertad.

VanDerwarker, Amber M., Jon B. Marcoux, and Kandace D. Hollenbach. 2013. "Farming and Foraging at the Crossroads: The Consequences of Cherokee and European Interaction through the Late Eighteenth Century." *American Antiquity* 78 (1): 68–88.

VanDerwarker, Amber M., and Tanya Peres, eds. 2010. *Integrating Zooarchaeology and Paleoethnobotany: A Consideration of Issues, Methods, and Cases.* New York: Springer.

Varien, Mark D. 1999. *Sedentism and Mobility in a Social Landscape: Mesa Verde and Beyond.* Tucson: University of Arizona Press.

Varien, Mark D., and Barbara J. Mills. 1997. "Accumulation Research: Problems and Prospects." *Journal of Archaeological Method and Theory* 4: 141–191.

Varien, Mark D., and James M. Potter. 1997. "Unpacking the Discard Equation: Simulating the Accumulation of Artifacts in the Archaeological Record." *American Antiquity* 62: 194–213.

Vaughn, Kevin. 2004. "Households, Craft, and Feasting in the Ancient Andes: The Village Context of Early Nazca Craft Consumption." *Latin American Antiquity* 15: 61–88.

Verano, John W. 1998. "Sacrificios Humanos, Desmembramientos y Modificaciones Culturales en Restos Osteológicos: Evidencias de las Temporadas de Investigación 1995–96 en Huaca de la Luna." In *Investigaciones en la Huaca de la Luna 1996*, edited by Santiago Uceda Castillo, Elías Mujica Barrada, and Ricardo Morales Gamarra, 159–171. Trujillo, Peru: Facultad de Ciencias Sociales, Universidad Nacional de la Libertad.

Verano, John W. 2001a. "The Physical Evidence of Human Sacrifice in Ancient Peru." In *Ritual Sacrifice in Ancient Peru*, edited by Elizabeth P. Benson and Anita G. Cook, 165–184. Austin: University of Texas Press.

Verano, John W. 2001b. "War and Death in the Moche World: Osteological Evidence and Visual Discourse." In *Moche Art and Archaeology in Ancient Peru*, edited by Joanne Pillsbury, 111–125. New Haven, CT: Yale University Press.

Voss, Barbara L. 2008. "Gender, Race, and Labor in the Archaeology of the Spanish Colonial Americas." *Current Anthropology* 49 (5): 861–893.

Warrick, Gary A. 1988. "Estimating Ontario Iroquoian Village Duration." *Man in the Northeast* 36: 21–60.

Webster, David, Barbara Fash, Randolph Widmer, and Scott Zeleznik. 1998. "The Skyband Group: Investigation of a Classic Maya Elite Residential Complex at Copán, Honduras." *Journal of Field Archaeology* 25: 319–343.

Webster, David, and Nancy Gonlin. 1988. "Household Remains of the Humblest Maya." *Journal of Field Archaeology* 15: 169–190.

Weismantel, Mary J. 1988. *Food, Gender, and Poverty in the Ecuadorian Andes.* Prospect Heights, IL: Waveland.

Weismantel, Mary J. 1989. "Making Breakfast and Raising Babies: The Zumbaga Household as Constituted Process." In *The Household Economy: Reconsidering the Domestic Mode of Production*, edited by Richard R. Wilk, 55–72. Boulder: Westview.

Welch, Paul D., and C. Margaret Scary. 1995. "Status-Related Variation in Foodways in the Moundville Chiefdom." *American Antiquity* 60: 397–419.

Wilk, Richard R. 1983. "Little House in the Jungle: The Causes of Variation in House Size among Modern Kekchi Maya." *Journal of Anthropological Archaeology* 2: 99–116.

Wilk, Richard R., and Robert McC. Netting. 1984. "Households Changing Form and Function." In *Households: Comparative and Historical Studies of the Domestic Group*, edited by Robert McC. Netting, Richard R. Wilk, and Eric J. Arnould, 1–28. Berkeley: University of California Press.

Wilk, Richard R., and William L. Rathje. 1982. "Household Archaeology." *American Behavioral Scientist* 6: 617–639.

Wilson, Gregory. 2008. *The Archaeology of Everyday Life at Early Moundville*. Tuscaloosa: University of Alabama Press.

Wright, Kathrine I. 2014. "Domestication and Inequality? Households, Corporate Groups, and Food Processing Tools at Neolithic Catalhoyuk." *Journal of Anthropological Archaeology* 33: 1–33.

3

Cercaduras and Domestic Urban Life in Early Horizon Nepeña, Coastal Ancash

DAVID CHICOINE, HUGO IKEHARA, AND JESSICA ORTIZ

Since the early discovery of dwellings at Huaca Prieta (Bird 1948), Nasca (Kroeber and Collier 1998), Pukara (Kidder 1943), and Pachacamac (Uhle 1991 [1903]), Andeanists have invested systematically more efforts in the study of households and their constituents (Aldenderfer 1993; Nash 2009; Taboada and Angiorama 2003). Scholars have looked at various forms of dwelling arrangements (Brennan 1982; Lau 2010; Topic 1980) and studied the engagement of household members with multiple phenomena, from small-scale economic production, consumption, and differentiation (Bawden 1982; Bermann 1994; Topic 1982; Van Gijseghem 2001; Vaughn 2004) to ethnic identity and group membership (Aldenderfer 1993; Goldstein 2005; Janusek 2004; Morris and Thompson 1985; Stanish 1992; Vaughn 2005), and the interaction of domestic households with larger hegemonic political systems (Bermann 1997; D'Altroy 1992; Hastorf 1993; Jennings and Yépez Álvarez 2001; Lau 2005; Schreiber 1992; Van Gijseghem and Vaughn 2008).

On the north coast of Peru, one particularly salient form of dwelling and social institution is materialized in walled house compounds known as *cercaduras*. While *cercadura* architecture and lifestyles are best documented from late Moche through Chimú times at sites such as Pampa Grande (Shimada 1994), Galindo (Bawden 1982), and Chan Chan (Klymyshyn 1982; Moore 2003), comparatively little is known about earlier forms of enclosed lifeways (Swenson 2004; Warner 2010). This is particularly the case in coastal Ancash, on the southern portion of the north coast of Peru, where Early Horizon studies have traditionally focused on the Chavín and

DOI: 10.5876/9781646420919.c003

Cupisnique religious phenomena and their monumental and artistic expressions (Daggett 1987a; MAAUNMSM 2005; Pozorski and Pozorski 1987; Proulx 1985; Shibata 2010; Tello 1960; Vega-Centeno 2000). In this chapter, we focus on the emergence of urban house compounds and their associated domestic lifestyles during the Early Horizon in the Nepeña Valley, coastal Ancash. Here, settlement pattern data suggest the emergence of a multitiered regional polity centered at the complex of Caylán and the associated development of *cercadura* households.

In 2009, the first scientific excavations at Caylán, the largest Early Horizon settlement in Nepeña, were undertaken (Chicoine and Ikehara 2010). Sixteen weeks of excavations have so far brought evidence on spatial organization, architecture, and material remains (Chicoine and Ikehara 2014). Caylán's urban nucleus consists of dense walled compounds organized into attached colonnaded patios, roofed areas, storerooms, kitchens, middens, fill lots, low platforms, and plazas articulated through baffled entries, corridors, and streets. Caylán stone masonry is very well preserved and visible at the surface. This allowed the delimitation and mapping of more than forty residential enclosures, yielding information on the spatial and social organization of co-residents at Caylán.

In the remainder of the chapter, we briefly review relevant literature on Andean household archaeology and focus on the development of complex urban societies in coastal Ancash during the Early Horizon. Literature on Andean households suggests high degrees of variability through space and time. The reconfiguration of forms of domestic arrangements can be used to explore shifts in macrosocial organization, including the emergence of urbanized settlements. Preliminary spatial data on *cercaduras* at Caylán can be integrated into a working hypothesis on forms of domestic life and put into perspective based on limited excavations at Compound-E, a middle-size residential compound partially excavated in 2010. The implications of the Caylán research are manifold and help to understand broader trajectories of residential architecture and compound lifeways on the north coast of Peru.

BACKGROUND: THE ARCHAEOLOGY OF ANDEAN HOUSEHOLDS

Household archaeology has undergone major renovations since its foundation in processual concerns with class structure, population patterns, and specialized production in the 1960s (e.g., Flannery and Winter 1976; see Carballo 2011; Nash 2009; Pluckhahn 2010; Vaquer 2007). Archaeologists have gradually emphasized the fundamental multifaceted roles of household units in the constitution of societies (Ashmore and Wilk 1988, 1). Focus has shifted away from static views of the social and symbolic meanings of households (e.g., Blier 1987; Deetz 1982) to focus on their active structuring agency and inherent historical contexts (e.g., Bloch 1995; James 1997; see Dean and Kojan 2001, 111–112). One of the enduring problems with households has been defining their economic, social, and political ramifications, as well as their materialization (Nash 2009, 225; Wilk and Netting 1984). In particular, researchers have demonstrated that one cannot simply equate households with the material remains of houses (Rogers 1995, 9; Wilk and Rathje 1982, 620). In the case of Caylán, for instance, it is likely that some of the largest urban compounds were built, maintained, and occupied by multiple households and groups organized at a suprahousehold level (e.g., neighborhood).

Households can be defined along several different axes including kinship, shared identity, economic production, as well as social and biological reproduction (Wilk and Rathje 1982). They are social units that play a key role in structuring human behaviors. At the same time, they are adaptable and serve the goals and strategies of their constituents (Rapoport 1969). Domestic units represent groups of people who co-reside and share domestic activities and decision-making processes (Blanton 1994, 5; see also Patterson 1999). Politically, households are the loci for power dialectics and the negotiation of hierarchies (Bowser and Patton 2004; Lyons 2007). Thomas Pluckhahn (2010, 334) puts forth a flexible and inclusive definition of households as activity groups taking part in one or more of the following practices: production, consumption or distribution, reproduction, co-residence, and enculturation/transmission (see also Ashmore and Wilk 1988, 4; Wilk and Netting 1984, 5).

At the most fundamental level, households represent basic units of economic production and cooperation (Allison 1999, 1; Ashmore and Wilk 1988, 1; Franklin 2004, xiii; Hirth 1993, 21; Robin 2003, 308; Stanley and Hirth 1993, 3). Scholars emphasize the need to clarify the scale of these actions, along with their loci, and the diversity and degrees of specialization of household activities. For instance, members of a household often engage in multiple interrelated production activities and thus can simultaneously enact multiscalar interaction networks (Carballo 2011, 144; Hirth 2006, 275–300). It is indeed significant to nuance the traditional view that households typically engage in self-sufficient, low-intensity production. From that standpoint, high-intensity production is believed to involve full-time specialists working from largely nonresidential places (e.g., Brumfiel and Earle 1987, 4–5; Costin 1991, 3–18). Most scholars now agree that specialized and domestic tasks should not be treated separately (Allison 1999, 8; Cobb 2000, 186–189; Hagstrum 2001, 50–51). Field results from Caylán suggest that urban domestic activities during the Early Horizon were varied, yet focused on the secondary processing of subsistence and clothing goods, as well as tools, vessels, and body adornments. In contrast, the primary processing of agrarian and marine produce is underrepresented and appears to have been carried out at smaller satellites, including the seaside town of Samanco (Chicoine et al. 2016; Helmer 2015; Helmer and Chicoine 2015b).

Socially, individual agency has become emphasized within the more corporate nature of larger domestic groups (Carballo 2011, 150). Here, the basic variable lies in the degree of agency granted to households in relation to the constraints imposed by large-scale, even hegemonic economic and political forces. In the Andes, household dynamics have been alternatively articulated around the concepts of verticality and horizontality (Nash 2009, 210). Models of verticality are grounded in John Murra's (1980) account of Inka ecological complementarity or archipelago in which households are only partially self-sufficient. Tasks are assigned to households, often referred to as *ayllus*, which in turn are granted access to land. Domestic units contribute to communal economies. In contrast, horizontality models steer away from zonal complementarity to emphasize interactions between communities living in similar types of ecosystems (Shimada 1982). Ideas mainly stem out of María Rostworowski's ethnohistorical accounts of north coastal communities described as *parcialidades*. In *parcialidades*, communities of specialists are under the authority of lords. Each lord rules a chiefdom, or *señorío*. Rostworowski (1970, 1975, 1977) describes different levels of interdependencies among occupational specialists whose leaders engaged in exchange networks through which flowed various types of resources, including fish, crops, and manufactured goods. House compounds documented at Prehispanic sites including Huacas de Moche, Pampa Grande, and Chan Chan have been favorably compared to ethnohistorical *señorios* (Nash 2009, 215). In Nepeña, architectural and spatial data from Caylán, Huambacho (Chicoine 2006), Samanco (Helmer 2015), and Sute Bajo (Cotrina et al. 2003) suggest the existence of large, urban households organized as suprakin groups perhaps composed of multiple extended families into neighborhoods (Helmer and Chicoine 2015a; see Pacifico 2014; Smith and Novic 2012). The settlement hierarchy in the lower valley combined with the close stylistic and apparent economic complementarity between communities points to existence of a complex polity potentially analogous to the ethnohistorical accounts aforementioned.

EARLY HORIZON URBANISM AND THE CAYLÁN POLITY

The valley of Nepeña is located in the modern Department of Ancash, on the southern portion of the north coast of Peru, 400 km north of Lima. The small drainage is famous for the spectacular discovery of polychrome friezes and painted murals at the sites of Punkurí, Cerro Blanco de Nepeña, Huaca Partida, and Pañamarca (figure 3.1) (Bonavia 1974; MAAUNMSM 2005; Schaedel 1951; Shibata 2011; Tello 1943; Trever 2017; Trever et al. 2013; Vega-Centeno 2000).

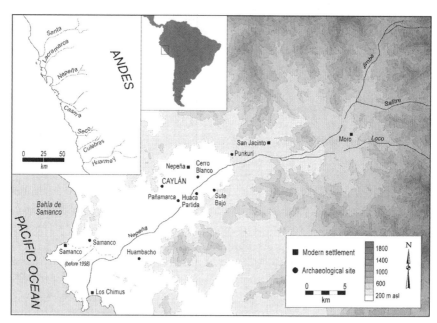

FIGURE 3.1. Map of the Nepeña Valley, Department of Ancash, showing the location of the sites mentioned in the text

This may explain why so little scientific attention has been given to dwelling forms and household units and their implications for understanding ancient cultural developments in coastal Ancash. During the Early Horizon, profound socioeconomic transformations in the region contributed to the development of urban forms of community organization. Changes were perhaps most visible in the abandonment of late Initial Period ceremonial centers and the rejection or avoidance of Cupisnique and Chavín precepts (Chicoine 2010b; Shibata 2010, 2011). Various lines of faunal and floral proxies point to the increased reliance on maize as both a staple crop and to produce fermented alcoholic beverages commonly consumed in festive contexts (Chicoine 2011; Chicoine et al. 2016; Ikehara et al. 2013), as well the introduction of camelids as pack animals (Helmer and Chicoine 2015b; Szpak et al. 2016). Finally, intercommunity tensions rose dramatically as groups relocated to defensible locations and invested unprecedented amounts of time and resources in armed conflicts (Daggett 1987b; Ghezzi 2006; Ikehara 2016). The complex dynamics of these processes need further analysis but synergistically contributed to the nucleation of population at several settlements, including the primary center of Caylán.

While traditional models for the valley have centered on the relationships between local populations and the Cupisnique and Chavín phenomena (Daggett 1987a; Larco 1941; Proulx 1985; Tello 1943, 1960), recent fieldwork has allowed for a reappraisal of Nepeña's chronology and cultural manifestations during the first millennium BC (Chicoine 2010a; Shibata 2004, 2010). Excavations of superimposed architectural contexts at the ceremonial center of Cerro Blanco de Nepeña have been particularly helpful in generating an updated chronological sequence for the Initial Period and Early Horizon. Based on changing patterns of monumental architecture, ceramic styles, and religious imageries, Nepeña archaeologists now operate a four-phases sequence: (1) Huambocayán (1500–1100 BC), (2) Cerro Blanco (1110–800 BC), (3) Nepeña (800–450 BC), and (4) Samanco (450–150 BC) (Shibata 2011).

Habitation sites and dwelling forms have yet to be documented for the Huambocayán and Cerro Blanco Phases. Cerro Blanco developments correspond to the construction of a U-shaped temple with conical adobes and polychrome murals at the center of Cerro Blanco de Nepeña. After a phase of megalithic renovations, the temple appears to gradually lose influence and is ultimately abandoned by the end of the Nepeña Phase by 500 BC. The following Samanco Phase saw the reuse of the Cerro Blanco de Nepeña structures by Early Horizon squatters. In the meantime, some groups, perhaps dissidents from Cerro Blanco de Nepeña and other Nepeña Phase centers, merged at the base of Cerro Caylán, as well as at other valley margin locations including Huambacho, Sute Bajo, and Samanco. Fieldwork at the small elite center of Huambacho identified two walled compounds consisting of rectangular plazas attached to colonnaded patio rooms of different sizes, as well as smaller roofed areas and storerooms. In contrast, more than forty compounds have been identified and mapped at the much larger and complex settlement of Caylán, bringing insights into the organization of Early Horizon *cercaduras* and associated domestic urban lifeways.

CAYLÁN URBAN CENTER (PV31-30)

Caylán is located in the coastal portion of the Nepeña drainage, 15 km from the Pacific coast. The site was first mentioned by Wendell C. Bennett (1939), who spent two days in Nepeña in 1935 (Proulx 1968, 9). Caylán's architecture and dense urban layout were described by Paul Kosok (1965, 208) after a study of aerial photographs and a brief visit in 1949 (see also Horkheimer 1965, 30). The site was then revisited by Donald A. Proulx (1968) as part of the first systematic surface survey of the valley. Proulx (1973, 70, 115–116) identified a Middle Horizon mortuary component based on the presence of Red-White-Black and press-molded pottery sherds exposed

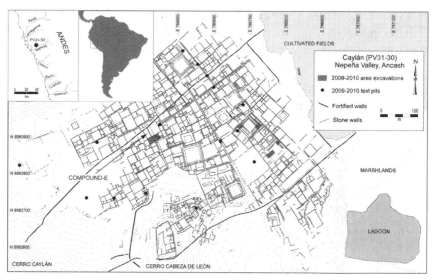

FIGURE 3.2. Plan reconstruction of the standing stone architecture at Caylán showing the location of the excavation units and test pits

through illegal excavation activities. More recently, such artistic expressions have been assigned to Casma cultural developments and the center of El Purgatorio in the neighboring eponymous valley to the south (Pacifico 2014; Vogel 2016; Vogel and Pacifico 2011). Proulx (1985, 46–47), along with his student Richard E. Daggett (1984), revisited the site in the late 1970s and early 1980s, producing sketch maps and further documenting surface materials. Based on the presence of ceramic pan-pipes, polished lithic projectiles, and Early Horizon styles of pottery sherds, including carinated bowls ornamented with stamped circle-and-dot designs, Daggett (1987b, 1999) suggested a major occupation during the first millennium BC.

In 2009, excavations were undertaken at Caylán and confirmed that most structures and material remains belong to an intensive human occupation during the Early Horizon. Fieldwork has allowed the complete mapping of the urban core (figure 3.2). Pedestrian mapping was realized with a Topcon total station theodolite, and the spatial data were compiled into both CAD and GIS databases. Results of surface mapping indicate a complex and diverse Early Horizon settlement composed of an urban core organized as high-quality stone-and-mud compounds articulated through at least a dozen streets. Several low platform mounds and enclosed plazas dot the urban compounds. A ridge-top compound, perhaps a fortress or refuge, is located in the southwest portion of the urban area (figure 3.3). The surrounding

FIGURE 3.3. Photograph of the urban sector at Caylán showing the architectural structures discussed in the text (view to the east)

peripheries are dotted with the remnants of stone-and-mud structures. Modern agrarian activities have destroyed large portions of the Early Horizon settlement, especially in the east sector. The extensive presence of surface ceramic scatters suggests the presence of lower-quality, wattle-and-daub architecture surrounding the urban core.

Pedestrian surface survey revealed extensive evidence for domestic activities, including dense ceramic scatters, heaps of plant remains, mixed midden areas, and 237 grindstones. The distribution of the surface grindstones confirms the importance of plant processing within the urban sector but suggests that domestic activities also extended to peripheral areas where standing stone architecture is absent or destroyed (figure 3.4). Grindstones include large anvils (*batanes*) (n = 36), two-hand portable grinders (*chungos*) (n = 166), and smaller one-hand pestles, hammers, or both (*manos*) (n = 35). The grinding tools are made of different varieties of local granite and are identifiable based on use-wear patterns. Although caution must be exercised when dealing with surface grindstones, as they tend to be recycled over time, the imbalance between the numbers of surface *batanes* and *chungos*—tools that are typically used in conjunction (figure 3.5)—suggests that the former might have been shared between community members, most likely at the *cercadura* level.

FIGURE 3.4. Aerial photograph of Caylán with combined distribution of surface grindstones

In addition to surface evidence, the excavation of 564 m² (~830 m³) yielded further evidence of the intensive domestic activities carried out at Caylán. Excavation methods included vertical and horizontal area excavations, as well as test pits and the clearing of looter pits. We excavated a total of six excavation units (*Unidad de Excavación*, or UE1 through 6), sixteen test pits (*Hoyo de Prueba*, or HP1 through 16), and one looter pit (*Pozo de Huaquero*, or PH1). All materials were screened through a 3 mm mesh, and recovery efforts targeted 100 percent of the archaeological remains. Preservation conditions are excellent, and a vast amount of material remains were recovered. More than 48,000 pottery sherds, 220 kg of

FIGURE 3.5. Photograph of in situ *batán* and *chungos* at Caylán

shells, 10 kg of animal bones, 15 kg of plants, and 90 kg of soil and other samples were collected.

URBAN *CERCADURAS* AT CAYLÁN

Based on careful pedestrian survey and the visual analysis of stone architecture, more than forty house compounds have so far been delimited and recorded at Caylán. Based on access patterns, overall spatial organization, and preliminary excavation data, the compounds are hypothesized to represent discrete residential and social units. The scale of some of the compounds aligns well with the concept of neighborhood (see Arnauld et al. 2012), while it is still unclear if the compounds are organized into broader urban districts (Pacifico 2014; Smith and Novic 2012).

The identified compounds range between 800 and 8,400 m² in total surface area, with an average of 4,500 m² (n = 42, σ = 1,713). Surface observations also suggest the existence of empty lots scattered across the urban sector, as well as monumental constructions that do not conform to the house compound forms. At the moment, three such structures are identified, including a ridge-top structure, a monumental platform complex, and a possible camelid corral or complex of storerooms. These contrast with residential *cercaduras* by one or more of the following features: the scale of their architecture, the width of wall structures and entrances, and unique internal spatial organization. The functions of these anomalous structures remain unclear but could well be linked to the public administration of the city, including defense, economy, and politics. Empty lots, meanwhile, are located in between compounds. They are typically devoid of formal access and appear to have served as opportunistic discard areas.

All compounds interpreted as *cercaduras* or neighborhood compounds share a similar internal spatial logic. They have a single, independent entrance connected to one of the dozen or so streets that cross-cut and divide the urban sector. The streets themselves appear coordinated around a Main Plaza (also known as Plaza Mayor or Plaza-C), the only truly open space at Caylán, currently interpreted as the center of movement and communal city life. Based on test excavations, the ground surface of the Main Plaza appears to have been paved with a layer of small cobbles and gravel, suggesting heavy foot traffic. The open space fronts the largest mound structure at Caylán. Indeed, the 10 m high structure is part of one of the complexes interpreted as a nonresidential building. The façade of the mound is decorated with clay sculptures visible from all across the site. This contrasts markedly with mural art within the house compounds, which is typically invisible to outsiders.

Cercaduras at Caylán were accessed by way of a plaza—typically surrounded on one or more of its sides by outer raised platforms. Clearing operations at Plaza-A have revealed that some platforms were decorated with sculpted geometric designs. The murals were visible to plaza visitors only. The plaza platforms are typically topped by colonnades of rectangular columns that originally supported stone, wood, reeds, and clay roof superstructures. These semipublic spaces subsequently gave access to more private colonnaded patios and roofed areas interpreted as production and living spaces. In sum, each compound had its plaza to mediate the public realm accessed through streets and the domestic, private areas of the patios, production areas, and living quarters. While excavations at the large, particularly monumental Compound-A (~5,200 m^2) brought insights into the architecture and acoustic properties of the plazas (Chicoine and Ikehara 2010, 2014; Helmer and Chicoine 2013; Helmer et al. 2012), fieldwork at the smaller Compound-E (~2,500 m^2) yielded evidence on the spatial organization and subdivision of the more private, domestic space (Ortiz 2012). Some of the *cercaduras* were subdivided into a number of subcompounds. Most compounds appear to have been divided into two or three subunits. Work at Compound-E indicates it was organized into two subcompounds.

Compound-E is located in the southwest quadrant of the urban core, at an average elevation of 134 m asl. The compound can be accessed through a 3 m wide SW-NE street, which cross-cuts a NW-SE street (figures 3.2, 3.3). The latter is interpreted as the main axis of movement at Caylán and leads to the Main Plaza. The entrance of Plaza-E is located ~125 m from the intersection of that street with the main crossroad. The Main Plaza, meanwhile, is located 200 m south of the main intersection. Compound-E is thus located more than 300 m from the main public area. The remoteness of Compound-E from the central public arena is perhaps informative of the status of its residents.

Compound-E measures roughly 58 m by 43 m in a NW-SE axis (58° east of the magnetic north) for a total surface area of ~2,500 m². It contains at least fifteen rooms in addition to the plaza area. Surface evidence allows the clear delimitation of twelve rooms, including Plaza-E (figure 3.6). Meanwhile, horizontal excavations (*Unidad de Excavación* 6, or UE6) sampled 164 m² and yielded significant evidence for domestic activities, including food processing (i.e., grinding, butchering, cooking), storing, spinning, weaving, and resting (figure 3.7). With the exception of one room (Rec-5), which was raised using burned domestic trash, dirt, and sand as fill materials (i.e., secondary deposition), most remains recovered from Compound-E were associated with the last moments of residential activities and left in situ on the plastered floors.

A total of 14,896 pottery fragments were collected during UE6, which represents more than 30 percent of the pottery sherds recovered at Caylán (n = 48,837). This is a rather high frequency considering that UE6 (~165 m³) recovered only 20 percent of the total volume excavated at Caylán (~830 m³). This suggests a higher density of artifact remains in the area. More than 99 percent (n = 14,779) of the sherds from UE6 are associated with the Early Horizon occupation, and 568 sherds yielded information about vessel forms and decorations. Comprising almost 70 percent of the total rim sherds (n = 455), neckless jars, or ollas (n = 309), dominate the assemblage. These open vessels can serve for storage or cooking, although they are more typically associated with the latter. In contrast, finer serving vessels appear in lesser frequencies, with bowls (n = 61, 13.41%), bottles (n = 10, 2.20%), and cups (n = 5, 1.10%) counting for a little more than 15 percent of the rim sherds. Considering the extensive use of gourds as containers and the perishable nature of these artifacts, serving implements are likely underrepresented at Compound-E. Finally, storage vessels take the form of large jars, or *tinajas* (n = 3, 0.66%), and smaller-neck jars, or cántaros (n = 67, 14.73%). Overall, cooking activities at Compound-E, and to some extent small-scale storage, appear to have produced the bulk of the broken pots.

Other fired clay artifacts include sherd discs (n = 142), panpipes (n = 108), and spindle whorls (n = 10). Sherd discs are small round objects made by recycling pottery sherds through abrasive techniques. Their function is unclear, but they could have been used as tokens for various activities, including games. Together with the presence of panpipes, they could be linked to moments of entertainment and

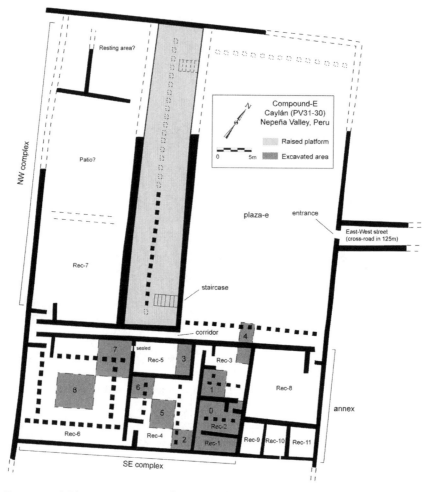

FIGURE 3.6. Plan reconstruction of Compound-E showing the overall architectural organization, the NW and SE Complexes, as well as the rooms delimited during the excavation of UE6 (Rec-1–Rec-6), and the limits of Excavations Unit 6 (0) and its subsequent extensions (1–8)

relaxing. Spindle whorls indicate that spinning activities likely took place within the domestic precinct. Twenty-one fragments (~27 grams) of textiles, mainly plain woven cloth made of cotton, were recovered. Of the stone artifacts recovered, the presence of an in situ *batán* fragment and complete *chungo* on the floor of Rec-6 (UE6–Ext7) is particularly indicative of the food-processing activities realized at

FIGURE 3.7. Photograph of horizontal excavations at Compound-E showing the different extensions that sampled the SE Complex

Compound-E (figure 3.8). The location of the grindstones gallery space created by the patio colonnades confirms the use of shaded areas for production activities.

Excavations documented 125 features associated with the Early Horizon floor contexts and their immediate use and abandonment. They were found either directly on or in the floor matrix, as well as in the layer of windblown sand on top of the floors. The features include holes and depressions (n = 47) likely used as supports for pots (figure 3.9), dried feces (n = 45), hearths (n = 11), mixed trash (n = 12), concentrations of ash (n = 8), complete broken ceramics (n = 1), as well as one complete juvenile dog (n = 1).

ARCHITECTURE AND SPATIAL LOGIC AT COMPOUND-E

In the remainder of the chapter, we focus on the organization of domestic space and the spatial logic of Compound-E, arguing that the *cercadura* represents a single integrated house compound. Architectural data indicate that Caylán builders prioritized a dual emphasis on (1) colonnaded patios as multifunctional activity and production areas and (2) smaller, more remote, and private roofed quarters. Each residential compound also featured a semipublic plaza that had to be traversed

FIGURE 3.8. Photograph of in situ grindstones in Room 6 at Compound-E (UE6-Ext7, Floor Context): broken *batán* and *chungo* (measuring stick = 1 m)

before gaining access to the production and living areas. In sum, architectural priorities included engineering privacy; mitigating sound, smell, and dust; separating production activities from resting, and creating complementary wide/open and small/covered spaces.

We number rooms as *Recinto-x*, or Rec-x. Surface evidence indicates the existence of four distinct spatial components including (1) Plaza-E, (2) an attached annex area of four rooms (Rec-8 through Rec-11), and two residential subdivisions: (3) SE Complex (Rec-1 through Rec-6) and (4) NW Complex (Rec-7 and other rooms). The complexes are interpreted as activity, production, and living areas located behind the nested plaza. Based on their integration and graded access, all the rooms—including Plaza-E—are considered part of a single, integrated house compound. The 2010 excavations focused on the SE Complex, but surface evidence allows for a preliminary consideration of Compound-E's spatial organization as a whole (see Hillier and Hanson 1984).

Plaza-E is the largest room of the compound, covering an area of more than 1,200 m^2. The room is weighed toward the ground area (~867 m^2), while the raised area (~356 m^2) is relatively limited. Upon entering the plaza from the east, visitors were confronted with a 2.5 m tall wall platform, complemented by an additional 2 m high

FIGURE 3.9. Photograph of depressions in the floor of Room 4 at Compound-E (UE6-Ext5, Floor Context) (measuring stick = 1 m)

roof superstructure supported by rectangular columns. The top of the wall platform would have been visible to people standing in the ground area of the plaza. Thirteen columns were visible on top of the raised platform, but many more are hypothesized based on the length of the structure. The columns' layout and dimensions are consistent with colonnaded architecture elsewhere at Caylán and other Early Horizon sites in Nepeña (Chicoine 2006; Chicoine and Ikehara 2010; Cotrina et al. 2003; Helmer 2015). Columns average 46 cm by 52 cm in dimensions and are placed at 80 cm intervals, 2 m from the exterior walls. The bases of the columns were preserved and plastered with plain clay. It is hypothesized that residents of Compound-E could have sat or stood on top of the platform, welcoming guests and visitors who entered the ground area from the street to the east.

From the ground area, the platform was accessible through a pair of inset staircases. The top of the platform stands out as the visual focus of the plaza where the residents of the complex, and perhaps their guests, could have sought shade and sat. Both sides of the plaza ground were colonnaded. In addition to the ~769 m² of open ground area, the lateral gallery spaces provided ~98 m² of shaded areas for dwellers and visitors. Here, social encounters would have been structured through the use of a semipublic space. Attached to Plaza-E, in the SE corner, a doorway led directly to a contiguous series of four smaller rooms (Rec-8 through Rec-11). This annex consists of a 10.2 m by 9.7 m room (~100 m²) (Rec-8)—possibly a patio area—attached to a series of three small rectangular rooms with low walls (Rec-9 through Rec-11).

The smaller rooms collectively cover 45 m². They were most likely roofed and could have served as storage spaces associated with the patio Rec-8. Together, these rooms would have constituted a plaza annex. It has yet to be excavated, but based on its location and overall layout, the rooms could have been used to store goods and prepare food for plaza guests. The hypothesized storerooms (Rec-9 through Rec-11) conform to patterns of expected storage features, including restricted access, relatively small replicated size, agglutinated placement, and lack of a doorway (Warner 2010, 446; see Chapdelaine 2001, figure 5; Day 1982).

To the SE of Plaza-E's platform, a 1 m wide and 22 m long corridor led to a dual doorway and the SE and NW Complexes, respectively. Their location behind the raised platform made the complexes invisible to plaza guests. Excavations focused on the SE Complex, an area measuring 33 m by 15.7 m (~487 m²). A series of six rooms (Rec-1 through Rec-6) were documented, including colonnaded patios and smaller roofed areas. Excavations completely cleared two of the six rooms (Rec-1, Rec-2) and sampled portions of the remaining four (Rec-3 through Rec-6), as well as a limited portion of the southern gallery space of Plaza-E. To the north, the NW Complex covers an analogous surface, with measurements of 40 m by 12.5 m (~495 m²).

The SE Complex consists of three distinct divisions (Units 1 to 3) organized through a graded system of baffled entryways (figure 3.10). The emphasis on graded access in Early Horizon *cercaduras* confirms the concern of urban dwellers and builders with creating hierarchical residential spaces where privacy could be architecturally engineered. The deepest and most remote subdivision, Unit 3, is composed of the rooms Rec-1, Rec-2, and Rec-3. The rooms are interpreted as areas for private domestic interactions, including sleeping. Rec-1, the most remote room of the complex, is a small roofed area measuring 6 m by 2.3 m (~13.5 m²). Rec-2 and Rec-3 are also fairly remote from compound traffic and the affluent activity areas of the Rec-4 and Rec-6 colonnaded patios. The presence of a corridor leading from Rec-4 to Unit 3 materializes the intention to separate the latter from the activity areas of patios Rec-4 and Rec-6. The desire to isolate the dormitories from the noise and smell of the activity areas likely played a key role in the design of the residential space.

Rec-2 is a small colonnaded patio room covering 26 m². The location of the columns and limited size of the room suggest that at least 70 percent of the room was roofed (18 m²). Rec-3, a larger patio covering ~46 m², displays a roofed-to–open area ratio of nearly one. The contiguous colonnaded patios Rec-4 and Rec-6 offered additional open and roofed areas for multiple types of domestic activities, including food preparation, storage, maintenance, and tool manufacture.

Rec-4 (Unit 2) is roughly quadrangular and covers an area of ~95 m². More than half of the ground area was roofed through two colonnades for an estimated eleven columns. The patio was linked to Rec-6 through a baffled entryway located in the

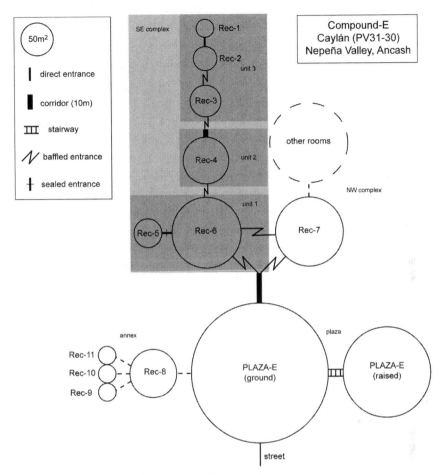

FIGURE 3.10. Gamma analysis and spatial syntax of Compound-E

SW corner. Rec-6 is the largest patio of the complex and the first room accessible from the carrier space of Plaza-E. It measures roughly 15 m by 15 m for a total of ~225 m² and is colonnaded on all four sides. Rec-6 is connected to a small rectangular roofed area (Rec-5) through a direct doorway. Together, these rooms form Unit 1.

Rec-5 is a small roofed area measuring 8.2 m by 4.4 m (~36 m²). The function of Rec-5 is unclear but is related to the use of Rec-6. Its entrance was sealed at some point during the Early Horizon occupation following its reuse as a refuse area and latrine. Cooking, meanwhile, would have been best performed in the open area of the patios.

In sum, only Rec-1 and Rec-5 are column-free rooms and likely to have been completely roofed. The other four rooms all have one or more of their sides colonnaded, thus creating complementary zones of light/open air and shaded/gallery space. Accesswise, it is significant that smaller rooms in Unit 3 are located at the back of the larger patios Rec-4 and Rec-6, a pattern typical of house compounds focusing on the dual design of courtyards as activity areas and smaller covered rooms as living spaces (see Frankel and Webb 2006, 299, for an example from the Bronze Age to Middle Cypriot site of Marki). From that standpoint, the colonnaded patios interpreted as production areas would have provided a buffer zone between the semipublic Plaza-E and the more private sleeping quarters.

Our excavations distinguished two distinct patterns of entryways: (1) baffled entryways for colonnaded patios and (2) direct doorways for noncolonnaded rooms. This suggests that baffled entryways were strategically designed to control foot traffic, visibility, and perhaps air, smell, dust, and sound transference between activity and dwelling areas. Direct doorways, in contrast, appear to articulate private spaces already secluded from higher-traffic activity areas and areas with little need for privacy (e.g., storerooms).

The builders of Compound-E—and other residences at Caylán (see Helmer and Chicoine 2013)—went to great lengths to maximize privacy in the context of urban nucleation and high demographic densities. For instance, Rec-1—located just 15 m as the crow flies from Plaza-E—can only be reached by foot through five doorways, four of them baffled, for a total of more than 80 m. In addition, the corridor connecting Plaza-E with Rec-6 allows the transit of only one person at a time, considerably restricting the flow of people.

It is unclear how many people lived at Compound-E. The total area for Compound-E is estimated at 2,500 m^2, with ~1,000 m^2 dedicated to domestic tasks and living areas. Meanwhile, ~1,450 m^2 are associated with the use of Plaza-E and its annex. Keeping that in mind, we nevertheless venture in speculating about demographic and capacity estimates at Compound-E. Scholars have considered demography and household population estimates (see Hassan 1981). The general consensus is that a strong correlation exists between the surface of roofed areas—interpreted as dwelling spaces—and the number of inhabitants. In the case of the SE Complex, roofed areas cover an area of 275 m^2, with 85 m^2 dedicated to dormitories. Based on the cross-culturally accepted ratio between 4 and 6 m^2/person (Peterson 2006, 72; see Brown 1987; Casselberry 1974; Kolb 1985; LeBlanc 1971; Naroll 1962; Wiessner 1974), between 46 and 68 people could have dwelled in the SE portion of Compound-E, with the dormitories permanently designed for perhaps 14 to 21 people. Considering that a nuclear family is typically composed of fewer than 10 individuals, these estimations suggest that the SE Complex was designed as a permanent residence for an extended family and perhaps more. Indeed, the roofed areas of the patios Rec-4 and Rec-6, as well as the room Rec-5, could have served as dwelling spaces for visitors and other constituents of the extended family. Combined with the presence of another residential complex in the NW portion of Compound-E, the spatial data suggest that residential compounds at Caylán were designed and maintained by a number of extended family groups—in the case of Compound-E, at least two. This further suggests that at least some *cercaduras* were organized into neighborhoods.

Residents of the SE Complex could have shared the activity areas (Unit 1 [Rec-5, Rec-6] and Unit 2 [Rec-4]) with their constituents and even perhaps servants or other attached members of the household unit. The more private living areas (Unit 3 [Rec-1–Rec-3]), located at the back of the patio areas, meanwhile, could have been reserved to family members and close relatives. Here, one has to keep in mind that co-resident groups may be composed of multiple households or form parts of larger households (e.g., Hally 2008, 273; Swanton 1928, 170–171; see Pluckhahn 2010, 334).

DISCUSSION

On the north coast of Peru, the transition into the Early Horizon marked a series of significant changes in architectural forms and settlement organizations (see Warner 2010, 87–96). Large open centers with axial layouts and central mounds were abandoned as coastal populations nucleated at dense settlements strategically associated with irrigation systems and cultivation fields (Billman 1996; Brennan 1982). The development of enclosed lifeways brought about major changes in the structuring properties of the built environment. Here, the changes in the domestic built environment can be interpreted as related to the insufficiencies of residences to fulfill people's expectations (Rapoport 1969; see Van Gijseghem and Vaughn 2008 for an example from the Southern Nasca region). The basic premise here is that built settings accommodate human behaviors (Rapoport 1982). If buildings cease to meet people's perceived needs, builders are likely to modify them or abandon them and relocate. Important changes in socioeconomic networks, ritual life, feelings of security, and patterns of status acquisition and maintenance can all impact house forms (Van Gijseghem and Vaughn 2008, 112). As demonstrated in this chapter, Early Horizon compound life in coastal Ancash was linked to a major realignment of domestic space and activities. Sociopolitically, the emergence of dense, architecturally differentiated habitation centers likely materialized the complexity of social arrangements and increased regional tensions, armed conflicts, and perhaps political centralization in some coastal areas.

Fieldwork at Caylán provides insights into urban-like forms of community organization and domestic lifeways associated with the development of walled house compounds, or *cercaduras*. Recent excavations and abundant material remains allow for the generation of working hypotheses on domestic life and household formations in the context of incipient urbanism in Early Horizon Ancash.

The residents of Compound-E were one of many groups who merged at Caylán. The motivations behind the emergence of the settlement are unclear, but the economic pull of the primary center; its heavy demographic weight, trading potential, and political capital; as well as the need for large-scale communal defensive strategies probably all played significant roles (Chicoine and Ikehara 2014). Preliminary data from fieldwork in 2009 and 2010 suggest that urban groups built, inhabited, and maintained house compounds where significant domestic and other productive activities were carried out. Of those, food processing and craft production are currently the most visible. The social status of each group was likely linked to its size and respective economic success. These materialized in the location, scale, and elaboration of the groups' respective compounds, material wealth, and patterns of consumption. The competition and negotiation of residential space within the crowded urban area must have played a major role in structuring communal interactions and social arrangements.

Compound-E is located within the city center but not in immediate proximity to the central public space (Main Plaza). In addition, its dimensions and degree of elaboration are relatively limited in comparison to other larger and finely ornamented compounds (e.g., Compound-A). Plaza-E, for instance, appears to lack murals and clay friezes, which contrasts with more elaborate monumental structures at the site (e.g., Plaza-A). Yet the fine stone-and-mud masonry and repetitive colonnaded layout stand in stark contrast to the irregularly shaped wattle-and-daub residences hypothesized for the outskirt of the city.

Compound-E, like other *cercaduras* at Caylán, did not grow organically in a fashion typical of vernacular architecture in urban residential contexts. It is a formally designed compound that saw little de facto modification after its initial construction. Yet it was used for domestic tasks associated with two or more extended families of urban residents. Based on the spatial layouts and material assemblages, the most visible production activities include food processing, pottery work, and perhaps textile work.

The redundancy and consistency in the replicated compounds argue for rigid and shared spatial precepts. Yet the lack of specific features inside the patio rooms (e.g., storerooms, benches) argues against distinct predetermined functions. Rather, the use of the space could be altered in an expedient manner, by rearranging the semifixed elements of the built environment (e.g., pots, hearths, grindstones). The need for cool shaded areas, in addition to the well-ventilated open air and sunny zones, was a key architectural concern. Shaded arcades produced by the colonnaded architecture, as well as the possible presence of trees inside the plazas, provided ideal spaces for residents.

More information is needed regarding storage facilities, but the sample excavated does not lend weight to production activities at a large-scale, suprahousehold level. This is different from patterns of Moche urban production documented at Huacas de Moche and Pampa Grande (Johnson 2010; Uceda Castillo and Armas 1998). Rather, the evidence from Caylán conforms well to patterns of generalized production associated with the immediate and medium-term need of multiple household members and their extended group. It is likely that production activities, at least as visible through the presence and relative frequencies of grindstones, were organized at the neighborhood level.

The presence of activity areas and associated remains within the house compounds at Caylán contrasts with data from other sites where walled enclosures were the dominant mode of spatial organization. At the Chimú site of Manchán in Casma, production activities and other domestic tasks were performed outside elite house compounds, inside perishable cane structures surrounding the formal compound architecture (Mackey and Klymyshyn 1990). Chimú *cercaduras* at other sites, including Chan Chan and Farfán, are also interpreted as residences for elite administrators detached from production activities (Mackey 2006). Along the same lines, John Warner (2010) interprets house compounds at the site of Jatanca (400 BC–AD 100) in the Jequetepeque Valley as mostly nondomestic in function.

Warner suggests that the absence of clear hearths, sleeping benches, and storerooms at Jatanca's Compound 1 does not align well with expected domestic contexts. For him, the rigid and repetitive aspects of Jatanca's compounds contrast with the more organic, agglutinated, and informal residences at other urban-like centers, most notably Grupo Gallinazo in the Virú Valley (Bennett 1950; see also Millaire and Eastaugh 2011). It is perhaps significant that, chronologically, the occupation of Compound-E at Caylán overlaps the development of analogous replicated compounds at Jatanca (Warner 2010, 9). The discovery of trash piles, broken tools, floor scatters, hearths, and potholes at Compound-E, however, contrasts with the evidence from Jatanca and suggests a more intensive domestic occupation and production activities. Along those lines, the Caylán data align better with the residential districts documented at El Purgatorio in Casma, where small-scale domestic processing coupled with episodic intensive surplus production for localized communal rituals are inferred (Pacifico, this volume).

The integration of Compound-E members within larger regional human networks remains unclear. Research at other Early Horizon sites, including the small elite center of Huambacho and the seaside town of Samanco, suggests the existence of interdependent, perhaps specialized communities in the lower Nepeña Valley during the Nepeña Phase and in particular the Samanco Phase (Chicoine and Rojas 2012, 2013; Helmer 2015; Helmer and Chicoine 2015b). It is unclear whether urban residents at Caylán *only* had access to semiprocessed materials or if they could also acquire primary goods and raw materials.

More data are needed on the activities carried out within plazas, in particular, feasts. Nevertheless, research at the coeval elite center of Huambacho indicates that communal feasts were key mechanisms to negotiate authority (Chicoine 2011). Here, rooms adjacent to a large monumental plaza (Plaza-A) were used for feasting events and other gatherings, albeit of smaller scale and more fragmented composition than the events carried on inside the plaza. At Compound-E at Caylán, it is still unclear whether visitors and guests were granted access to residential areas at the back of the raised platform of the plaza. Evidence of feasting at contemporary sites suggests that this activity might be revealed during future excavations at Caylán.

The Caylán data indicate the development of well-planned house compounds with clear domestic and productive functions organized within a dynamic urban landscape with multiple organizational levels, from the centralized planning of streets and public spaces to the group-based endeavors linked to the construction, maintenance, and use of monumental house compounds or neighborhoods. As pointed out by Warner (2010) for Jatanca, the presence of multiple compounds within urban centers suggests the existence of several different social groups articulated through complex networks of political alliance, negotiation, and competition. Within emerging urban landscapes, households have the potential to become loci of power affirmation and negotiation, especially when monumental *cercaduras*—some lavishly decorated with sculpted friezes—likely played a major role in status acquisition and maintenance. At Caylán, intergroup hierarchies were materialized in the location, scale, and elaboration of house compounds. It is also likely that the scales of both production and consumption (e.g., feasting) acted as indices of economic prosperity and social capital.

The scale and complexity of Caylán's compounds, in particular as viewed through excavations at Compound-E, contrast with examples of urban residences from Huacas de Moche. For instance, Claude Chapdelaine's (2001) excavations at Compound 9 revealed more than forty rooms of different sizes and shapes—built, occupied, and remodeled over a period of more than 200 years. At least nine rectilinear rooms were enclosed and used for storage, suggesting productive capabilities beyond the household level. More than thirty elite residences had a single attached room that could have been used for feasts and maize beer production. Pending future excavations, results from Compound-E suggest a similar annex linked to the use of a plaza space enclosed within the house compound.

At a broader scale, the emergence of enclosed lifestyles on the north coast of Peru was significant. While most research has focused on the development of Middle Horizon and Late Intermediate Period *cercaduras* (Bawden 1982; Moore 2003), recent findings confirm the appearance of enclosed lifestyles during the Early Horizon (Chicoine 2006; Warner 2010). It is significant to note that Early Horizon walled compounds in Nepeña contrast with Chimú *cercaduras* and other walled compounds documented on the north coast. As noted by Jerry D. Moore (2003), Chimú *cercaduras* materialized a shift in social hierarchies and a desire to exclude nonelite people from royal residences. Here, rulers and their entourage clearly tried to physically isolate themselves from the populace. The Caylán case, rather, suggests the co-residence of groups of various ranks and social roles within a dense urban setting.

At Caylán, co-resident groups could have been organized along multiple and complex networks of interactions, both vertical and horizontal (Helmer and Chicoine 2015b; Szpak et al. 2016). So far, no clear dominant group or ruling family can be recognized from surface architectural evidence. Rather, nucleation appears motivated by a desire to jointly organize defensive strategies and perhaps negotiate land tenure and water management. Yet the urban landscape was packed with groups who likely competed for influence and economic prosperity.

CONCLUSION

Ongoing research at Caylán challenges our traditional understanding of the Early Horizon and brings insights into ancient household institutions on the north coast of Peru. While scholars agree that households stand as basic units of socioeconomic (re)production, urban *cercaduras* at Caylán suggest that large, perhaps multifamily neighborhoods developed during the second half of the first millennium BC in the Nepeña Valley. Our research cautions Andeanists to remain critical and open to exactly what forms households took on the north coast of Peru in the past. At Caylán, each residential compound had an independent entrance, while internal spatial organization indicates subdivisions consistent with co-resident kin (or at least economically cooperative) groups. Preliminary excavation results and demographic estimates from the mid-size Compound-E are consistent with this working hypothesis. Yet we have to keep in mind that tensions might have arisen among the processes of urban integration, the potential for political centralization, and the apparent spatial independence of co-resident groups. Future excavations should yield data on patterns of abandonment, the curation of deserted *cercaduras*, land negotiations, and development of the urban landscape.

At Caylán, the hypothesized generalized patterns of domestic production suggest that urban neighborhoods—composed of several extended families—were relatively self-sufficient within the urban setting. People relied on communal builders whose work integrated different groups at the site level through shared architectural canons and spatial layouts. At the broader regional level, the Caylán community interacted with neighboring groups through subsistence exchange networks that linked inland and coastal settlements.

Finally, it is imperative to explore the relationships between the urban residents and the groups living in the periphery of the monumental core at Caylán. The mapping and preliminary observation of architectural remains indicate the presence of irregular-shaped structures with stone-and-mud foundations and possibly reed-and-mud walls and superstructures. More data are needed from other house compounds at Caylán and elsewhere in Nepeña and beyond to better understand trajectories of house compounds on the southern portion of the north coast at the onset of urbanism in the Andes.

ACKNOWLEDGMENTS

We wish to thank Robyn Cutright, Ilana Johnson, and David Pacifico for the warm invitation to join the list of contributors to this volume. Excavations at Caylán were realized in accordance with Peruvian regulations, and we extend special thanks to the Lima and Chimbote offices of the Ministerio de Cultura. The data analyzed in this chapter were generated with the financial support of the Louisiana Board of Regents, Office of Research and Economic Development at Louisiana State University. Kyle Stich and Jacob Warner helped with the mapping of the grindstones, and Kimberly Munro elaborated figure 3.4. We acknowledge the help of Ashley Whitten in the pedestrian and visual reconnaissance of surface architecture at Caylán. Finally, Ilana Johnson and David Pacifico, as well as two anonymous reviewers, provided valuable comments that significantly strenghtened the final version of this text.

REFERENCES

Aldenderfer, Mark, ed. 1993. *Domestic Architecture, Ethnicity, and Complementarity in the South-Central Andes.* Iowa City: Iowa University Press.

Allison, Penelope M. 1999. "Introduction." In *The Archaeology of Household Activities,* edited by Penelope M. Allison, 1–18. London: Routledge.

Arnauld, M. Charlotte, Linda R. Manzanilla, and Michael E. Smith. 2012. *The Neighborhood as Social and Spatial Unit in Mesoamerican Cities.* Tucson: University of Arizona Press.

Ashmore, Wendy, and Richard R. Wilk. 1988. "Household and Community in the Mesoamerican Past." In *Household and Community in the Mesoamerican Past*, edited by Richard R. Wilk and Wendy Ashmore, 1–28. Albuquerque: University of New Mexico Press.

Bawden, Garth. 1982. "Community Organization Reflected by the Household: A Study in Pre-Columbian Social Dynamics." *Journal of Field Archaeology* 19 (2): 165–181.

Bennett, Wendell C. 1939. *Archaeology of the North Coast of Peru: An Account of Exploration in Viru and Lambayeque*. New York: American Museum of Natural History.

Bennett, Wendell C. 1950. *The Gallinazo Group, Viru Valley, Peru*. Publications in Anthropology 43. New Haven, CT: Yale University Press.

Bermann, Marc. 1994. *Lukurmata: Household Archaeology in Prehispanic Bolivia*. Princeton, NJ: Princeton University Press.

Bermann, Marc. 1997. "Domestic Life and Vertical Integration in the Tiwanaku Heartland." *Latin American Antiquity* 8 (2): 93–112.

Billman, Brian R. 1996. "The Evolution of Prehistoric Political Organizations in the Moche Valley." PhD dissertation, University of California, Santa Barbara.

Bird, Junius B. 1948. "Preceramic Cultures in Chicama and Virú." In *A Reappraisal of Peruvian Archaeology*, edited by Wendell C. Bennett, 21–28. New York: Smithsonian Institution Press.

Blanton, Richard E. 1994. *Houses and Households: A Comparative Study*. New York: Plenum.

Blier, Suzanne Preston. 1987. *The Anatomy of Architecture: Ontology and Metaphor in Batammaliba Architectural Expression*. Cambridge: Cambridge University Press.

Bloch, Maurice. 1995. "The Resurrection of the House amongst the Zafimaniry of Madagascar." In *About the House*, edited by Janet Carsten and Steven Hugh-Jones, 69–83." Cambridge: Cambridge University Press.

Bonavia, Duccio. 1974. *Ricchata Quellccani: Pinturas Murales Prehispánicas*. Lima: Editorial Ausonia.

Bowser, Brenda J., and John Q. Patton. 2004. "Domestic Spaces as Public Spaces: An Ethnoarchaeological Case Study of Houses, Gender, and Politics in the Ecuadorian Amazon." *Journal of Archaeological Method and Theory* 11 (2): 157–181.

Brennan, Curtiss T. 1982. "Cerro Arena: Origins of the Urban Tradition on the Peruvian North Coast." *Current Anthropology* 23 (3): 247–254.

Brown, Barton McCall. 1987. "Population Estimation from Floor Area: A Restudy of 'Naroll's Constant.'" *Behavior Science Research* 22 (1–4): 1–49.

Brumfiel, Elizabeth M., and Timothy K. Earle. 1987. "Specialization, Exchange, and Complex Societies: An Introduction." In *Specialization, Exchange, and Complex*

Societies, edited by Elizabeth M. Brumfiel and Timothy K. Earle, 1–9. Cambridge: Cambridge University Press.

Carballo, David. 2011. "Advances in the Household Archaeology of Highland Mesoamerica." *Journal of Archaeological Research* 19 (2): 133–189.

Casselberry, Samuel E. 1974. "Further Refinement of Formulae for Determining Population from Floor Area." *World Archaeology* 6 (1): 117–122.

Chapdelaine, Claude. 2001. "The Growing Power of a Moche Urban Class." In *Moche Art and Archaeology in Ancient Peru*, edited by Joanne Pillsbury, 69–87. New Haven, CT: Yale University Press.

Chicoine, David. 2006. "Early Horizon Architecture at Huambacho, Nepeña Valley, Peru." *Journal of Field Archaeology* 31 (2): 1–22.

Chicoine, David. 2010a. "Cronología y secuencias en Huambacho, valle de Nepeña, costa de Ancash." *Boletín de Arqueología PUCP* 12: 317–348.

Chicoine, David. 2010b. "Elite Strategies and Ritual Settings in Coastal Peru during the 1st Millennium BC." In *Comparative Perspectives in the Archaeology of Coastal South America*, edited by Robyn Cutright, Enrique López-Hurtado, and Alexander C. Martin, 191–212. Lima, Pittsburgh, and Quito: Fondo Editorial PUCP, Center for Comparative Archaeology, University of Pittsburgh, and Ministerio de Cultura de Ecuador.

Chicoine, David. 2011. "Feasting Landscapes and Political Economy at the Early Horizon Center of Huambacho, Nepeña Valley, Peru." *Journal of Anthropological Archaeology* 30 (3): 432–453.

Chicoine, David, Beverly Clement, and Kyle Stich. 2016. "Macrobotanical Remains from the 2009 Season at Caylán: Preliminary Insights into Early Horizon Plant Use in the Nepeña Valley, North-Central Coast of Peru." *Andean Past* 12: 155–161.

Chicoine, David, and Hugo Ikehara. 2010. "Nuevas evidencias sobre el Periodo Formativo del valle de Nepeña: Resultados preliminares de la primera temporada de investigaciones en Caylán." *Boletín de Arqueología PUCP* 12: 349–370.

Chicoine, David, and Hugo Ikehara. 2014. "Ancient Urban Life in the Nepeña Valley, North-Central Coast of Peru: Investigations at the Early Horizon Center of Caylán." *Journal of Field Archaeology* 39 (4): 336–352.

Chicoine, David, and Carol Rojas. 2012. "Marine Exploitation and Paleoenvironment as Viewed through Molluscan Resources at the Early Horizon Center of Huambacho, Nepeña Valley, Peru." *Andean Past* 10: 284–290.

Chicoine, David, and Carol Rojas. 2013. "Shellfish Resources and Maritime Economy at Caylán, Coastal Ancash, Peru." *Journal of Island and Coastal Archaeology* 8 (3): 336–360.

Cobb, Charles R. 2000. *From Quarry to Cornfield: The Political Economy of Mississippian Hoe Production*. Tuscaloosa: University of Alabama Press.

Costin, Cathy L. 1991. "Craft Specialization: Issues in Defining, Documenting, and Explaining the Organization of Production." *Journal of Archaeological Method and Theory* 3: 1–56.

Cotrina, Jorge, Victor Peña, Arturo Tandaypan, and Elvia Pretell. 2003. "Evidencias Salinar: sitios VN-35 y VN-36, Sector Sute Bajo, valle de Nepeña." *Revista Arqueológica SIAN* 14: 7–12.

Daggett, Richard E. 1984. "The Early Horizon Occupation of the Nepeña Valley, North Central Coast of Peru." PhD dissertation, University of Massachusetts, Amherst.

Daggett, Richard E. 1987a. "Reconstructing the Evidence for Cerro Blanco and Punkuri." *Andean Past* 1 (1): 111–132.

Daggett, Richard E. 1987b. "Toward the Development of the State on the North Central Coast of Peru." In *The Origins and Development of the Andean State*, edited by Jonathan Haas, Shelia Pozorski, and Thomas Pozorski, 70–82. Cambridge: Cambridge University Press.

Daggett, Richard E. 1999. "The Early Horizon in Nepeña: An Update." Paper included in the symposium The Foundations of Coastal Andean Civilizations: Preceramic through the Early Horizon. 64th Annual Meeting of the Society for American Archaeology, Chicago, March 26.

D'Altroy, Terence N. 1992. *Provincial Power in the Inka Empire*. Washington, DC: Smithsonian Institution Press.

Day, Kent C. 1982. "Storage and Labor Service: A Production and Management Design for the Andean Area." In *Chan Chan: Andean Desert City*, edited by Michael E. Moseley and Kent C. Day, 333–349. Albuqerque: University of New Mexico Press.

Dean, Emily, and David Kojan. 2001. "Ceremonial Households and Domestic Temples: 'Fuzzy' Definitions in the Andean Formative." In *Past Ritual and the Everyday*, edited by Christine A. Hastorf, 109–135. Berkeley: Kroeber Anthropological Society, Department of Anthropology, University of California.

Deetz, James F. 1982. "Households: A Structural Key to Archaeological Explanation." *American Behavioral Scientist* 25 (6): 717–724.

Flannery, Kent V., and Marcus C. Winter. 1976. "Analyzing Household Activities." In *The Early Mesoamerican Village*, edited by Kent V. Flannery, 34–47. New York: Academic Press.

Frankel, David, and Jennifer M. Webb. 2006. "Neighbours: Negotiating Space in a Prehistoric Village." *Antiquity* 80 (308): 287–302.

Franklin, Maria. 2004. "Foreword." In *Household Chores and Household Choices: Theorizing the Domestic Sphere in Historical Archaeology*, edited by Kerri S. Barile and Jamie C. Brandon, xiii–xiv. Tuscaloosa: University of Alabama Press.

Ghezzi, Ivan. 2006. "Religious Warfare at Chankillo." In *Andean Archaeology III: North and South*, edited by William H. Isbell and Helaine Silverman, 67–84. New York: Springer Science.

Goldstein, Paul S. 2005. *Andean Diaspora: The Tiwanaku Colonies and the Origins of South American Empire*. Gainesville: University Press of Florida.

Hagstrum, Melissa B. 2001. "Household Production in Chaco Canyon Society." *American Antiquity* 66: 47–55.

Hally, David J. 2008. *King: The Social Archaeology of a Late Mississippian Town in Northwestern Georgia*. Tuscaloosa: University of Alabama Press.

Hassan, Fekri A. 1981. *Demographic Archaeology*. New York: Academic Press.

Hastorf, Christine A. 1993. *Agriculture and the Onset of Political Inequality before the Inka*. Cambridge: Cambridge University Press.

Helmer, Matthew. 2015. *The Archaeology of an Ancient Seaside Town: Performance and Community at Samanco, Nepeña Valley, Peru (ca. 500–1 BC)*. BAR International Series 2751. Oxford: Archaeopress British Archaeological Reports.

Helmer, Matthew, and David Chicoine. 2013. "Soundscapes and Community Organisation in Ancient Peru: Plaza Architecture at the Early Horizon Centre of Caylán." *Antiquity* 87 (335): 92–107.

Helmer, Matthew, and David Chicoine. 2015a. "Neighbourhoods and Incipient Urbanism in the Nepeña Valley, North-Central Coast of Peru circa 500 BCE." *Contributions in New World Archaeology: Journal of the Institute of Archaeology of the Jagiellonian University* 9: 33–50.

Helmer, Matthew, and David Chicoine. 2015b. "Seaside Life in Early Horizon Peru: Preliminary Insights from Samanco, Nepeña Valley." *Journal of Field Archaeology* 40 (6): 626–642.

Helmer, Matthew, David Chicoine, and Hugo Ikehara. 2012. "Plaza Life and Public Performance at the Early Horizon Center of Caylán, Nepeña Valley, Peru." *Ñawpa Pacha: Journal of Andean Archaeology* 32 (1): 85–114.

Hillier, Bill, and Julienne Hanson. 1984. *The Social Logic of Space*. Cambridge: Cambridge University Press.

Hirth, Kenneth G. 1993. "The Household as an Analytical Unit: Problems in Method and Theory." In *Prehispanic Domestic Units in Western Mesoamerica: Studies of the Household, Compound, and Residence*, edited by Robert S. Stanley and Kenneth G. Hirth, 21–39. Boca Raton, FL: CRC Press.

Hirth, Kenneth G., ed. 2006. *Obsidian Craft Production in Ancient Central Mexico*. Salt Lake City: University of Utah Press.

Horkheimer, Hans. 1965. *Identificación y bibliografía de importantes sitios prehispánicos del Perú*. Volume Arqueológicas 8. Pueblo Libre, Peru: Museo Nacional de Antropología y Arqueología.

Ikehara, Hugo. 2016. "The Final Formative Period in the North Coast of Peru: Cooperation during Violent Times." *World Archaeology* 48 (1): 70–86.

Ikehara, Hugo, Fiorella Paipay, and Koichiro Shibata. 2013. "Feasting with Zea mays in the Middle and Late Formative North Coast of Peru." *Latin American Antiquity* 24 (2): 217–231.

James, Steven R. 1997. "Change and Continuity in Western Pueblo Households during the Historic Period in the American Southwest." *World Archaeology* 28 (3): 429–456.

Janusek, John W. 2004. *Identity and Power in Ancient Andes: Tiwanaku Cities through Time*. London: Routledge.

Jennings, Justin, and Willy Yépez Álvarez. 2001. "Architecture, Local Elites, and Imperial Entanglements: The Wari Empire and the Cotahuasi Valley of Peru." *Journal of Field Archaeology* 28: 143–159.

Johnson, Ilana. 2010. "Households and Social Organization at the Late Moche Period Site of Pampa Grande, Peru." PhD dissertation, University of California, Los Angeles.

Kidder, Alfred, II. 1943. *Some Early Sites in the Northern Lake Titicaca Basin: Expeditions to Southern Peru*. Volume Papers 21 (1). Cambridge, MA: Peabody Museum of Archaeology and Ethnology, Harvard University.

Klymyshyn, Alexandra. 1982. "The Elite Compounds in Chan Chan." In *Chan Chan: Andean Desert City*, edited by Michael E. Moseley and Kent C. Day, 119–143. Albuquerque: University of New Mexico Press.

Kolb, Charles C. 1985. "Demographic Estimates in Archaeology: Contributions from Ethnoarchaeology on Mesoamerican Peasants." *Current Anthropology* 26 (5): 581–599.

Kosok, Paul. 1965. *Life, Land, and Water in Ancient Peru*. New York: Long Island University Press.

Kroeber, Alfred L., and Donald Collier. 1998. *The Archaeology and Pottery of Nazca, Peru: Alfred L. Kroeber's 1926 Expedition*. Walnut Creek, CA: Altamira.

Larco, Rafael. 1941. *Los Cupisniques*. Lima: Casa Editorial La Crónica y Variedades.

Lau, George F. 2005. "Core-Periphery Relations in the Recuay Hinterlands: Economic Interaction at Chinchawas, Peru." *Antiquity* 79 (303): 78–99.

Lau, George F. 2010. "House Forms and Recuay Culture: Residential Compounds at Yayno (Ancash, Peru), a Fortified Hilltop Town, AD 400–800." *Journal of Anthropological Archaeology* 29: 327–351.

LeBlanc, Steven. 1971. "An Addition to Naroll's Suggested Floor Area and Settlement Population Relationship." *American Antiquity* 36: 210–211.

Lyons, Diane E. 2007. "Building Power in Rural Hinterlands: An Ethnoarchaeological Study of Vernacular Architecture in Tigray, Ethiopia." *Journal of Archaeological Method and Theory* 14 (2): 179–207.

Mackey, Carol J. 2006. "Elite Residences at Farfán: A Comparison of the Chimú and Inca Occupations." In *Palaces and Power in the Americas: From Peru to the Northwest Coast*, edited by Jessica J. Christie and Patricia J. Sarro, 313–352. Austin: University of Texas Press.

Mackey, Carol J., and Alexandra Klymyshyn. 1990. "The Southern Frontier of the Chimú Empire." In *The Northern Dynasties: Kingship and Statecraft in Chimor*, edited by Michael E. Moseley and Alana Cordy-Collins, 195–226. Washington, DC: Dumbarton Oaks.

Millaire, Jean-François, and Edward Eastaugh. 2011. "Ancient Urban Morphology in the Virú Valley, Peru: Remote Sensing Work at the Gallinazo Group Site (100 BC–AD 700)." *Journal of Field Archaeology* 36 (4): 289–297.

Moore, Jerry D. 2003. "Life behind Walls: Patterns in the Urban Landscape in the Prehistoric North Coast of Peru." In *The Social Construction of Ancient Cities*, edited by Monica Smith, 81–102. Washington, DC: Smithsonian Institution Press.

Morris, Craig, and Donald E. Thompson. 1985. *Huánuco Pampa: An Inca City and Its Hinterland*. London: Thames and Hudson.

Murra, John V. 1980. *The Economic Organization of the Inca State*. Greenwich, CT: JAI Press.

Museo de Arqueología y Antropología y Antropología de la Universidad Nacional Mayor de San Marcos (MAAUNMSM). 2005. *Arqueología del Valle de Nepeña: Excavaciones en Cerro Blanco y Punkurí*. Lima: Museo de Arqueología y Antropología de la Universidad Nacional Mayor de San Marcos.

Naroll, Raoul. 1962. "Floor Area and Population Settlement." *American Antiquity* 27: 587–588.

Nash, Donna. 2009. "Household Archaeology in the Andes." *Journal of Archaeological Research* 17 (3): 205–261.

Ortiz, Jessica. 2012. "Excavaciones en el Conjunto E de Caylán, valle de Nepeña: espacio residencial de élite del Formativo Tardío y Final." Licenciatura BA thesis, Pontificia Universidad Católica del Perú, Lima.

Pacifico, David. 2014. "Neighborhood Politics: Diversity, Community, and Authority at El Purgatorio, Peru." PhD dissertation, University of Chicago, IL.

Patterson, Thomas C. 1999. "The Development of Agriculture and the Emergence of Formative Civilization in the Central Andes." In *Pacific Latin America in Prehistory: The Evolution of Archaic and Formative Cultures*, edited by Michael Blake, 181–188. Pullman: Washington State University Press.

Peterson, Christian E. 2006. "'Crafting' Hongshan Communities? Household Archaeology in the Chifeng Region of Eastern Inner Mongolia, PRC." PhD dissertation, University of Pittsburgh, PA.

Pluckhahn, Thomas. 2010. "Household Archaeology in the Southeastern United States: History, Trends, and Challenges." *Journal of Archaeological Research* 18 (4): 331–385.

Pozorski, Shelia, and Thomas Pozorski. 1987. "Chavin, the Early Horizon and the Initial Period." In *The Origins and Development of the Andean State*, edited by Jonathan Haas, Shelia Pozorski and Thomas Pozorski, 36–46. Cambridge: Cambridge University Press.

Proulx, Donald A. 1968. *An Archaeological Survey of the Nepeña Valley, Peru.* Amherst: Department of Anthropology, University of Massachusetts.

Proulx, Donald A. 1973. *Archaeological Investigations in the Nepeña Valley, Peru.* Amherst: Department of Anthropology, University of Massachusetts.

Proulx, Donald A. 1985. *An Analysis of the Early Cultural Sequence in the Nepeña Valley, Peru.* Amherst: Department of Anthropology, University of Massachusetts.

Rapoport, Amos. 1969. *House Form and Culture.* Englewood Cliffs, NJ: Prentice-Hall.

Rapoport, Amos. 1982. *The Meaning of the Built Environment.* Beverly Hills, CA: Sage.

Robin, Cynthia. 2003. "New Directions in Classic Maya Household Archaeology." *Journal of Archaeological Research* 11: 307–356.

Rogers, J. Daniel. 1995. "The Archaeological Analysis of Domestic Organization." In *Mississippian Communities and Households*, edited by J. Daniel Rogers and Bruce D. Smith, 1–31. Tuscaloosa: University of Alabama Press.

Rostworowski, María. 1970. "Mercaderes del valle de Chincha en la época prehispánica: un documento y unos comentarios." *Revista Española de Antropologia Americana* 5: 135–178.

Rostworowski, María. 1975. "Pescadores, artesanos, y mercaderes costeños en el Perú prehispánico." *Revista del Museo Nacional* 41: 311–349.

Rostworowski, María. 1977. "Coastal Fishermen, Merchants, and Artisans in Prehispanic Peru." In *The Sea in the Pre-Columbian World*, edited by Elizabeth P. Benson, 167–186. Washington, DC: Dumbarton Oaks Research Library and Collections.

Schaedel, Richard P. 1951. "Moche Murals at Pañamarca." *Archaeology* 4 (3): 145–154.

Schreiber, Katharina. 1992. *Wari Imperialism in Middle Horizon Peru.* Ann Arbor: Museum of Anthropology, University of Michigan.

Shibata, Koichiro. 2004. "Nueva cronología tentativa del Período Formativo-Aproximación a la arquitectura ceremonial." *Desarollo arqueológico costa norte del Perú* 1: 79–98.

Shibata, Koichiro. 2010. "Cerro Blanco de Nepeña dentro de la dinámica interactiva del Periodo Formativo." In *El Periodo Formativo y evidencias recientes: cincuenta años de la misión japonesa y su vigencia*, edited by Peter Kaulicke, 287–315. Lima: Pontificia Universidad Católica del Perú.

Shibata, Koichiro. 2011. "Cronología, relaciones interregionales y organización social en el Formativo: esencia y perspectiva del valle bajo de Nepeña." In *Arqueologia de la Costa de Ancash*, edited by Milosz Giersz and Ivan Ghezzi, 113–134. Warsaw and Lima: Centro de Estudios Precolombinos de la Universidad de Varsovia and Institut Français d'Études Andines.

Shimada, Izumi. 1982. "Horizontal Archipelago and Coast-Highland Interaction in North Peru." In *El hombre y su ambiente en los Andes Centrales*, edited by Luis Millones and Hiroyasu Tomoeda, 137–210. Senri Ethnological Studies 10. Osaka: National Museum of Ethnology.

Shimada, Izumi. 1994. *Pampa Grande and the Mochica Culture*. Austin: University of Texas Press.

Smith, Michael E., and Juliana Novic. 2012. "Neighborhoods and Districts in Ancient Mesoamerica." In *The Neighborhood as a Social and Spatial Unit in Mesoamerican Cities*, edited by M. Charlotte Arnauld, Linda R. Manzanilla, and Michael E. Smith, 1–26. Tucson: University of Arizona Press.

Stanish, Charles. 1992. *Ancient Andean Political Economy*. Austin: University of Texas Press.

Stanley, Robert S., and Kenneth G. Hirth, eds. 1993. *Prehispanic Domestic Units in Western Mesoamerica: Studies of the Household, Compound, and Residence*. Boca Raton, FL: CRC Press.

Swanton, John R. 1928. *Social Organization and Social Usages of the Indians of the Creek Confederacy*. Washington, DC: Smithsonian Institution.

Swenson, Edward R. 2004. "Ritual and Power in the Urban Hinterland: Religious Pluralism and Political Decentralization in Late Moche Jequetepeque, Peru." PhD dissertation, University of Chicago, IL.

Szpak, Paul, David Chicoine, Jean-François Millaire, Christine D. White, Rebecca Parry, and Fred J. Longstaffe. 2016. "Early Horizon Camelid Management Practices in the Nepeña Valley, North-Central Coast of Peru." *Environmental Archaeology: The Journal of Human Palaeoecology* 21 (3): 230–245.

Taboada, Constanza, and Carlos Angiorama. 2003. "Buscando los indicadores arqueológicos de la unidad doméstica." *Cuadernos de la Facultad de Humanidades y Ciencias Sociales* 20: 393–407.

Tello, Julio C. 1943. "Discovery of the Chavín Culture in Peru." *American Antiquity* 9 (1): 135–160.

Tello, Julio C. 1960. *Chavín: Cultura Matriz de la Civilización Andina*. Lima: Universidad Nacional Mayor de San Marcos.

Topic, John R. 1980. "Excavaciones en los barrios populares de Chan Chan." In *Chan Chan: Metropoli Chimú, Lima*, edited by Roger Ravines, 267–282. Lima: Instituto de Estudios Peruanos, Instituto de Investigación Tecnologica Industrial y de Normas Tecnicas.

Topic, John R. 1982. "Lower-Class Social and Economic Organization at Chan Chan." In *Chan Chan: Andean Desert City*, edited by Michael E. Moseley and Kent C. Day, 145–175. Albuquerque: University of New Mexico Press.

Trever, Lisa. 2017. *The Archaeology of Mural Paintings at Pañamarca, Peru*. Washington, DC: Dumbarton Oaks Research Library and Collections.

Trever, Lisa, Jorge Gamboa Velásquez, Ricardo Toribio Rodríguez, and Flannery Surette. 2013. "A Moche Feathered Shield from the Painted Temples of Pañamarca, Peru." *Ñawpa Pacha: Journal of Andean Archaeology* 16: 103–118.

Uceda Castillo, Santiago, and José Armas. 1998. "An Urban Pottery Workshop at the Site of Moche, North Coast of Perú." In *Andean Ceramics: Technology, Organization, and Approaches*, edited by Izumi Shimada, 91–110. MASCA Research Papers in Science and Archaeology. Philadelphia: University of Pennsylvania Press.

Uhle, Max. 1991 [1903]. *Pachacamac* (reprint of the 1903 edition *Pachacamac Archaeology: Retrospect and Prospect*, with an introduction by Izumi Shimada). Philadelphia: University Museum of Archaeology and Anthropology, University of Pennsylvania.

Van Gijseghem, Hendrik. 2001. "Household and Family at Moche, Peru: An Analysis of Building and Residence Patterns in a Prehispanic Urban Center." *Latin American Antiquity* 12 (3): 257–273.

Van Gijseghem, Hendrik, and Kevin J. Vaughn. 2008. "Regional Integration and the Built Environment in Middle-Range Societies: Paracas and Early Nasca Houses and Communities." *Journal of Anthropological Archaeology* 27: 111–130.

Vaquer, José María. 2007. "De vuelta a la casa: algunas consideraciones sobre el espacio doméstico desde la arqueología de la práctica." In *Procesos sociales prehispánicos en el sur andino: la vivienda, la comunidad y el territorio*, edited by Axel E. Nielsen, M. Clara Rivolta, Veronica Seldes, Maria Magdalena Vázquez, and Pablo H. Mercolli, 11–35. Córdoba, Argentina: Editorial Brujas.

Vaughn, Kevin J. 2004. "Households, Crafts, and Feasting in the Ancient Andes: The Village Context of Early Nasca Craft Consumption." *Latin American Antiquity* 15 (1): 61–88.

Vaughn, Kevin J. 2005. "Household Approaches to Ethnicity on the South Coast of Peru: The Domestic Architecture of Early Nasca Society." In *Us and Them: Archaeology and Ethnicity in the Andes*, edited by Richard M. Reycraft, 86–103. Los Angeles: Cotsen Institute of Archaeology, University of California.

Vega-Centeno, Rafael. 2000. "Imagen y simbolismo en la arquitectura de Cerro Blanco, costa norcentral peruana." *Bulletin de l'Institut Français d'Études Andines* 29 (2): 139–159.

Vogel, Melissa A. 2016. *The Casma City of El Purgatorio: Ancient Urbanism in the Andes*. Gainesville: University Press of Florida.

Vogel, Melissa A., and David Pacifico. 2011. "Arquitectura de El Purgatorio: capital de la cultura Casma." In *Arqueología de la Costa de Ancash*, edited by Milosz Giersz and Ivan Ghezzi, 357–397. Warsaw and Lima: Centro de Estudios Precolombinos de la Universidad de Varsovia and Institut Français d'Études Andines.

Warner, John. 2010. "Interpreting the Architectonics of Power and Memory at the Late Formative Center of Jatanca, Jequetepeque Valley, Peru." PhD dissertation, University of Kentucky, Lexington.

Wiessner, Polly. 1974. "A Functional Estimator of Population from Floor Area." *American Antiquity* 39 (2): 343–350.

Wilk, Richard R., and Robert McC. Netting. 1984. "Households: Changing Forms and Functions." In *Households: Comparative and Historical Studies of the Domestic Group*, edited by Robert McC. Netting and Richard R. Wilk, 1–28. Berkeley: University of California Press.

Wilk, Richard R., and William L. Rathje. 1982. "Household Archaeology." *American Behavioral Scientist* 25: 617–639.

4

Communities in Motion

Peripatetic Households in the Late Moche Jequetepeque Valley, Peru

GUY S. DUKE

Community is not an unchanging essence, but from time to time and place to place
it is a different phenomenon.

WILLIAM H. ISBELL (2000, 253)

Often, the term *community* is employed as just another word for *village* or *site*,
rooting it in place as an essentially self-contained, bounded entity (e.g., Arensberg
1955; Hollingshead 1948; Kolb and Snead 1997; Murdock 1949; Redfield 1963
[1955]; Wolf 1957). Through this perspective, "'Community' is [often] assumed
to be real and natural. It is internally homogeneous, externally bounded, and characterized by a collective consciousness shared by all affiliates" (Isbell 2000, 243).
Central to this perspective is George Murdock's (1949) concept of "co-residence,"
in which a household is ostensibly defined as people who live together in the
same structure—and communities are more or less agglomerations of individual
households (Isbell 2000; Yaeger and Canuto 2000). This viewpoint can often be
advantageous to archaeologists who are inextricably tied to material remains, but
it is flawed as a conceptualization of communities that fails to recognize them as
dynamic social units.

Counter to this interpretation of "natural communities" is "'community' as process, an imagined community constructed in competing discourses, dynamic, contingent, and contradictory" (Isbell 2000, 245). William H. Isbell's (2000, 249) idea
of "imagined communities" (sensu Anderson 1991), in its assumed volatility and

DOI: 10.5876/9781646420919.c004

dynamism of group membership, embraces the concept that communities are plural and membership in them is impermanent and flexible, a perspective that allows us to read multiple forms of community participation dependent upon context (see also Hegmon 2002; Mac Sweeney 2011; Owoc 2005; Pauketat 2000; Rowe 2014; Varien 1999; Yaeger and Canuto 2000). This dynamism does not exclude placedness in its conception; rather, it emphasizes the social malleability of communities while acknowledging the interactions in time and space through which communities are constructed. Within this conception of communities, households, too, are untethered from specific structures and places and are seen as more fluid in both their location and their membership. Definitions of both community and household thus become predicated on interaction and "doings," invoking Anthony Giddens's (1984) "copresence" rather than place and architecture (see also Anderson 1991; Canuto and Yaeger 2000; Cohen 1985; Fowles 2013; Ingold 2000; Varien and Potter 2008; Varien and Wilshusen 2002).

There is a growing body of evidence that during the Late Moche Period in the northern coastal valleys of Peru, rural populations were highly mobile and were not necessarily inhabitants of towns and villages as part of an urban periphery. Evidence of peripatetic movement of people for purposes of work parties, ritual observances, agricultural production, and trade blurs the lines between the physical and social spaces these activities occupied (Dillehay 2001; Gumerman 2010; Swenson 2018; Swenson and Chiguala 2018). In fact, the Late Moche Jequetepeque Valley was characterized by multiple interconnected residential patterns. The large urban centers appear to have had populations of elite religious and political specialists as well as craft-producing specialists (Bawden 1982, 2001; Chapdelaine 2001, 2009; Johnson 2010; Pozorski and Pozorski 2003; Shimada 2001; van Gijseghem 2001). These groups were also resident in small and intermediate-size settlements in the countryside, though in smaller populations. These two groups of urban and rural elites and specialists were linked directly to one another through ideological paraphernalia and associated social obligations (Castillo Butters 2001; Dillehay 2001; Gumerman 2010; Johnson 2008, 2011; Swenson 2007, 2008; Swenson and Chiguala 2018).

Entangled within this network of large and small elite centers of religious and political observation were the highly mobile communities of agriculturalists and fishers who were not specifically tied to any one settlement, though possibly to specific fields, canals, or both at specific times during the agricultural cycle (see Castillo Butters 2010). These mobile agriculturalists/fishers were connected to the small and large centers through the exchange of materials and political/religious observations but were not necessarily beholden to any one settlement or group of settlements. Previous research has established the relative autonomy of smaller hinterland centers in the Late Moche Jequetepeque Valley[1] (Dillehay 2001; Johnson 2008, 2011; Swenson 2006).

It is important to avoid the assumption that "rural life" is equal to "lower-class laborers." Those in leadership positions may also have been rural and mobile, with only a very select few living in permanent, urban settings. In essence, the concept of spatially bounded communities is inappropriate when discussing the rural populations in the Late Moche Jequetepeque. Instead, I argue that the Late Moche rural household was a mobile social unit that was not fixed to any particular architectural feature or settlement site, instead following economic, ritual, and eminently social rounds throughout the region in which the households resided.

The use of multiple households is common in the Andes, as documented ethnographically, ethnohistorically, and archaeologically (e.g., Contreras 2010; Hirsch 2018; Jurado 2013; Murra 1956; Saignes 1995; van Buren 1996; Wernke 2007). Most studies have focused on the highlands, however, and on John V. Murra's (1956) concept of the vertical archipelago, in which residents of steep highland valleys make use of the variety in altitudinal ecological zones to produce or collect the different products that can grow in each zone. This would entail repeatedly traversing the steep hillsides, usually with residences in at least two of them for occupation during harvesting or planting periods. This model works well for the most part in these valleys but is less easily applied to the coastal lowlands of the Moche. However, as Izumi Shimada (1982) has noted, the coast also has specific ecological zones where specific resources are located and exploited. This raises the possibility of similar patterns of mobility and temporary residences occurring in coastal areas as well.

With this said, it should be remembered that the movement of people is invariably rooted in social contexts. Gregson Schachner (2012, 5) argues that "population movement does not simply result in the transfer of people from one place to another; rather, it is a social context in which people can transform social organization and networks." Schachner (2012, 9–11) invokes the idea of "population circulation," as it is used in geography (see Chapman and Prothero 1985), and details four propositions on mobility: "(1) circulation varies depending on the particular individuals studied, as well as the destination of their moves . . . (2) circulation is often driven by three factors: ecological variability and hazards; 'customary life,' including marriage, warfare, and exchange; and 'the decisions of the elderly, the prestigious, and the socially and economically important' (i.e., social hierarchy) . . . (3) in every society there is a spatial separation of obligations, activities, and goods; and . . . (4) frequent population circulation promotes fluidity in residence, social group membership, and leadership" (Schachner 2012, 10–11).

These four propositions are part of the lens through which I view mobility in the Late Moche Jequetepeque. Late Moche rural mobility may have been rooted in conceptions of social organization that contrasted with those dwelling in urban centers, a conception manifested in the construction of temporary architecture as well as the presence and absence of artifactual assemblages associated with rural life (i.e., agricultural and maritime labor). I argue that residence was highly fluid and that communities were not bounded spatially. These peripatetic households—that is, groups of co-residing individuals whose places of habitation were multiple in location, requiring cyclical movement between residences—were likely the most common form of social organization among rural inhabitants of the Late Moche Jequetepeque Valley.

The idea of an economic round in archaeology and anthropology has traditionally been tied to mobile, nonsedentary or semisedentary gathering, hunting, and fishing groups, with any ritual significance to such a round ascribed to the elevated symbolic importance of the subsistence system within which it is embedded (*sensu* Steward 1938). While I do not agree that a ritual round is necessarily subservient to and dependent upon an economic round—the two are in fact inextricably intertwined—there is no reason to believe that similar rounds were not part of the daily, monthly, and yearly lives of people living in what are considered to be more sedentary societies.

People are always in motion. Whether it is to or from a place of spiritual observance, in pursuit of wild game, from the field house to the field, or from the fishing nets to the market, movement from place to place is integral to the operation of society (Ingold 2000). In actuality, movement and interaction become the social context itself. Trade, religion, subsistence, and politics are all dependent upon them. Even in so-called sedentary societies marked by permanent residences and monumental architecture, people still embark on religious pilgrimages, long-distance trade expeditions, or diplomatic missions. The majority of residents in the Late Moche Jequetepeque, I argue, were constantly moving as members of mobile household groups, likely on a set round of inextricably linked political, religious, and economic significance.

Households as social constructs, as opposed to simply physical structures (*sensu* Bourdieu 1979, 133–153; Lévi-Strauss 1982), have been extensively explored by archaeologists for decades (e.g., Coupland et al. 2009; Cutting 2003; Hodder 1994; Moore 2012; Pauketat and Alt 2005; Robin 2002, 2003; Stanish 1989; Wilk and Rathje 1982). Moche households have become an increasingly prominent avenue of inquiry into Moche societies ever since Garth Bawden (1982) noted the relative lacunae in such research in the early 1980s. Since then, analyses of the domestic sectors at sites such as Galindo (Bawden 1982, 2001), Huacas de Moche (Chapdelaine 2001, 2009; Pozorski and Pozorski 2003; van Gijseghem 2001), Pampa Grande (Johnson 2010; Shimada 1994, 2001), and Huaca Colorada (Gataveckas 2011; Lynch 2013;

Swenson and Chiguala 2018; Swenson et al. 2011, 2012, 2013), among others, have greatly advanced our understanding of Moche domestic life. However, with a few notable exceptions (e.g., Gataveckas 2011; Gumerman and Briceño 2003; Johnson 2008, 2011; Swenson and Chiguala 2018), Moche households have been understood primarily through studies of urban settings, associating domestic life directly with fixed, relatively permanent architectural structures (Bawden 1982; Chapdelaine 2001; Johnson 2010; Pozorski and Pozorski 2003; van Gijseghem 2001).

However, for most of history, urban dwellers have been only a small portion of the population, and this was likely also true in the case of the Late Moche Jequetepeque Valley. As Tom D. Dillehay (2001, 259) asserts, "The archaeological history needs to be tempered by more information excavated from communities in the countryside . . . not just from urban elite architecture and commodities." Dillehay's assertion emphasizes that rural regions operated somewhat autonomously within complex economically and politically entangled systems rather than simply as sources of economic support for, and under the direct or indirect control of, elite urban leaders (*contra* Keatinge 1975). In fact, urban and rural Moche households have recently been shown to differ in their social organization and corporate group composition (see Gataveckas 2011; Gumerman and Briceño 2003; Johnson 2010, 2011; Shimada 2001). The literature on the daily practices of rural populations in the archaeological past, in the Andes and beyond, has grown significantly (see Dillehay 2001; Johnson 2008, 2011; Schwartz and Falconer 1994; Swenson 2004, 2008; Vining 2011). Following these investigations, rural Moche households appear to have been far more flexible and variable than previously acknowledged. This variation and flexibility necessarily calls into question some of our basic assumptions of so-called sedentary societies (Dillehay 2001; Ingold 2000; Isbell 1995, 1996, 2000; Kent 1992; Kent and Vierich 1989; Schachner 2012; Varien 1999).

During the Late Moche Period in the northern coastal valleys of Peru (particularly the Jequetepeque and Zaña), rural populations may have been highly mobile and were not necessarily inhabitants of permanent towns and villages as part of an urban periphery (Dillehay 2001; Gumerman 2010; Swenson and Chiguala 2018). This mobility may have been rooted in conceptions of social organization that contrasted with those dwelling in urban centers. Instead, rural inhabitants likely moved across the landscape as part of cyclical economic and ritual rounds rooted in timed events such as planting/harvest periods, canal maintenance schedules, and the presentation of tribute to local political and religious elites. This cyclical round would have required a certain amount of social flexibility in regard to household and family. It is possible that the rural Moche household was a mobile social unit not fixed to any particular architectural feature or settlement site, instead consisting of a fluid and flexible group of individuals following an economic, ritual, and eminently social round throughout the region in which they resided.

In essence, a large proportion of the population, regardless of socioeconomic position, was highly mobile as part of a politicoeconomic-ritual round. This dynamic interaction is evidenced through mobility across the landscape, a landscape in which permanent architecture does not necessarily equal permanent residence. This is not to say that previously posited, architecturally embedded household analyses from urban regions are incorrect but that they instead account only for one subset of the Moche population—urban dwellers. However, a significant percentage of the Moche lived in the countryside as farmers and fishers and was only occasionally drawn to urban locales. This model of households highlights the contingent and contextual nature of Moche communities.

RURAL MOBILITY IN THE LATE MOCHE JEQUETEPEQUE VALLEY

Evidence of the rapid rise of multiple ceremonial centers in the Jequetepeque Valley (figure 4.1) suggests that the Late Moche Period was one of instability in which previously unified territories fragmented into autonomous and often competing polities (Castillo Butters 2010; Dillehay 2001; Dillehay et al. 2009; Donnan 2011; Rosas Rintel 2007; Swenson 2004, 2007, 2008). This decentralization and internecine conflict has been posited as the result of internal disputes, external invasions, environmental stress, or a combination of these factors (Castillo Butters 2000; Castillo Butters et al. 2008; Rosas Rintel 2010; Swenson 2006, 2007).

A general shift toward the north side of the Jequetepeque during the Late Moche Period was countered by the rise in prominence of Huaca Colorada on the south side (Donnan 2011; Swenson 2012; Swenson et al. 2008, 2009, 2010, 2011). In addition, contact with highland polities intensified, as demonstrated at Huaca Colorada as well as at San José de Moro and Cerro Chepén on the north side of the valley (Castillo Butters 2000; Castillo Butters et al. 2008; Rosas Rintel 2007, 2010; Swenson and Warner 2012; Swenson et al. 2010, 2011, 2012, 2013, 2015). The interrelationships between shifts in religious practices and political interactions with foreign groups are central to the understanding of local concepts of identity. An examination of the fluidity of rural household and community identities provides an alternative perspective to the focus on ceremonial centers that predominates in studies of the Late Moche Jequetepeque Valley (Castillo Butters 2008; Cutright 2010; Rosas Rintel 2007; Swenson 2011, 2012).

To date, rural Moche populations have not been extensively studied, limiting our understanding of Moche social diversity and political organization. In fact, Moche social distinction and political organization are mostly known through studies of

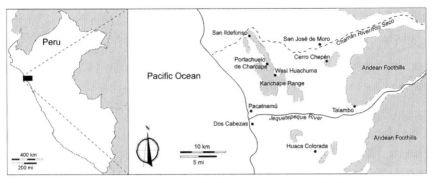

FIGURE 4.1. Map of lower Jequetepeque Valley and sites discussed in this chapter

urbanization, monumental architecture, burials, and feasting economies (Arsenault 1992; Castillo Butters et al. 2008; Gumerman 1997, 2010; Swenson 2006; White et al. 2009). Little attention has been paid to the everyday practices of identity formation and maintenance for the majority of the population—rural farmers/ fishers and rural elites. If people were frequently shifting from location to location as parts of work parties or for ritual observances (which are not mutually exclusive; see Gumerman 2010), then the areas where they performed their domestic tasks were likely to be inextricable from the work and ritual contexts in which they were traveling and their memberships in these groups was likely as fluid as their movements between locations. The separation of domestic and ritual is often problematic (Bourdieu 1979, 133–153; Hendon 2003; Hodder 1994; Hodder and Cessford 2004; Robin 2002). This is particularly true for rural Moche settlements (see Spence Morrow, this volume; Swenson and Warner 2012).

Despite the fact that many, if not most, of the inhabitants of the Late Moche Jequetepeque Valley were likely farmers and fishers, most sites so far investigated had no evidence of farming or fishing tools. Their mobility and regular changes in physical residence likely led them to leave their tools closer to where they used them. One example is the site of Portachuelo de Charcape, located on the west side of a pass across the Santa Catalina Hills. Ilana Johnson (2011, 57) highlights the adobe brick structures located close to the two huacas as likely loci for elite residences, though she notes that the size of the site itself is indicative that it was unlikely that full-time specialists resided at the site. The lack of farming implements recovered during excavations is perplexing, as Moche subsistence was based on agricultural and maritime products, both of which were present in abundance at the site (Johnson 2008, 265–266). Johnson posits three possible scenarios that could explain the lack of agricultural tools at the site: (1) resident agriculturalists removed their tools when they abandoned the site, (2) the tools are located in an as yet unexcavated part of the site, and (3) residents of the site were exclusively maritime fishers, exchanging their products with agriculturalists not resident at the site. As Johnson (2008, 265) explicitly notes, these scenarios are not the only possibilities. With this in mind, I would add a fourth possibility: that agriculturalists and possibly fishers as well had only an ephemeral presence at the site, keeping their tools in locations closer to fields/shore to be retrieved when they were needed.

There is growing consensus that rural Moche communities in the Jequetepeque were semiautonomous, linked in part by ideology and networks of alliances (Castillo Butters 2001; Dillehay 2001; Johnson 2008, 2011; Swenson 2007). This new understanding of Moche social organization resonates with mobility as an integral part of rural life. Johnson (2011, 55) notes that "new emphasis on community participation in burial rituals at the site of San José de Moro . . . may have included groups from other villages in the Jequetepeque Valley." This supports the likelihood of a ritual/economic round that brought farmers, fishers, and villagers to and from a variety of sites, including ritual/administrative centers such as Portachuelo de Charcape and Wasi Huachuma as well as large ceremonial sites like Huaca Colorada and San José de Moro. Broad settlement data support this hypothesis (see Dillehay 2001; Dillehay et al. 2009; Swenson 2004). Dillehay (2001, 267; Dillehay et al. 2009) and his team recorded a significant number of small and intermediate-size Late Moche settlements as well as "many small settlements representing part-time or full-time farmsteads." At the more substantial sites, Dillehay noted the possibility of both permanent residence and seasonal/temporary residence likely associated with farming and fishing. Further, Dillehay (2001, 270) mentions the periodic abandonment and reuse of sites of all sizes but particularly in the countryside, which "presumably had something to do with new kinds of interactions taking place among local social groups."

The small, rural sites of ritual and administrative function that proliferated in the Late Moche Period northern valleys were arguably part of a network of political, economic, and religious nodes of interaction for the residents of the region (Dillehay 2001; Dillehay et al. 2009; Gumerman 2010; Johnson 2008; Swenson 2004, 2008; Swenson and Chiguala 2018). Dillehay (2001, 272–273) theorizes that "there may even have been separate spheres of social and economic interaction in late Moche times, characterized by coexisting elite and nonelite economic networks." While he is clear that these ideas are preliminary and somewhat speculative, he asserts that Moche commoners in the countryside were likely relatively autonomous, perhaps even during times with more centralized political structures (Dillehay 2001, 274). While Dillehay does not explicitly explore mobility, the evidence he presents and the theories he posits are interwoven with this premise as a central element. The assertions of temporary residences, varied networks of interaction, and high levels of autonomy among farmers, fishers, and villagers all hint toward a population in motion, moving from sites of economic, political, and religious importance whenever needed. A network such as this would require a mobile population to be viable, such as that described by George J. Gumerman (2010; see also Dietler and Herbich 2001) in regard to peripatetic laborers and festive participation in the Moche world.

Gumerman (2010) identifies Moche mobility through the lens of feasts, and certainly feasting was important. Attendance at life-cycle feasts (e.g., births, deaths, marriages) and work party feasts, as discussed by Gumerman, plus attendance at other social and political obligations involving feasting (see Swenson 2008), was in all likelihood an integral element for mobility. However, there was more to life than feasting, despite its importance to Moche life. Instead, I argue that Late Moche mobility in the lower Jequetepeque Valley was rooted in complex, intertwining, and inseparable elements connected to social life, economic seasonality, and ritual/political expediency. Because of this, household memberships in communities were necessarily fluid.

THE LOWER JEQUETEPEQUE: TWO LATE MOCHE CASES

Huaca Colorada and Wasi Huachuma (Je-64) are two very different archaeological sites in the lower Jequetepeque Valley (see figure 4.1). Huaca Colorada is a large ceremonial center on the south side of the valley, with two lower, flanking "domestic" sectors (Swenson 2018; Swenson and Chiguala 2018; Swenson and Warner 2012; Swenson et al. 2011, 2012, 2013, 2015). Wasi Huachuma, in contrast, is a small site on the north side of the valley featuring a high lookout, evidence of potential elite residence, and a small ramped platform mound (Dillehay et al. 2009, 86–89; Duke 2017, 100–179; Swenson 2004, 609–617). While it is likely that the two sites were not used by the same people—and may have been part of two entirely different polities on different sides of the valley (Swenson 2007, 2008)—evidence for similar patterns of peripatetic movement appears at both.

At these two sites, structures with thick walls with at least two courses of adobe bricks, showing evidence of maintenance, renovation, or both, are thought to have been permanent and indicative of regular occupation. These structures may have seen occasional re-flooring events but do not show evidence of abandonment and reconstruction. In addition, ceremonial ramped/terraced structures with evidence of consistent upkeep were also classified as permanently occupied/used.

In contrast, temporary structures were generally smaller and, if they had walls, were a single course of adobe or stone. Constructed floors of *tapia* were frequently present but were rougher, less formalized, and not necessarily conscribed by walls on all sides. They show evidence of onetime use followed by abandonment and reconstruction of new, similar structures nearby. This is evidenced by the palimpsest of floors (not necessarily placed directly atop previous floors) with thin layers of sand between them, indicating a lack of upkeep after abandonment (see Swenson et al. 2012, 168–190).

The features and artifacts associated with these structures are also important in showing temporary or long-term use (hearths are an excellent example of this). The types of materials in these contexts can tell us what sorts of activities took place in these structures and potentially for how long. On their own, the artifacts are insufficient, but together with their overall contexts they were certainly useful to help understand what items people were bringing and leaving behind at specific locations.

Huaca Colorada

Huaca Colorada is a ceremonial site situated 13 km from the Pacific Coast, in the sand dune–covered coastal lowlands of the southern Jequetepeque Valley. It is the only known large ritual center on the south side of the Jequetepeque River dating to the Late Moche Period (Dillehay et al. 2009; Swenson 2004, 2012). Three sectors delimit the site: Sector B at the summit of the huaca, Sector A below B to the north, and Sector C below B to the south (figure 4.2). Sector B has been identified as the monumental core based on the architecture and presence of sacrificial burials as well as a large midden thought to be the remains of feasting events (Swenson et al. 2010, 2011, 2012, 2013). Sectors A and C have been theorized as residential or domestic productive zones where people made expedient camps and produced crafts for the events at the summit. Distinct rooms with floors and storage chambers on the south side of Sector B may indicate permanent elite residence, while the expedient camps in the other sectors suggest that nonelites occupied these areas ephemerally but repeatedly. The expedient camps of Sector C are focused on below. Sector C is approximately 100 m^2 and is 10 m below and to the south of Sector B, on the lower prominence of a stationary sand dune on which the site is located. (Swenson et al. 2011, 171–172). Excavations here have revealed a number of expediently made structures featuring low adobe walls and rough floors with inset depressions for large pots (Swenson et al. 2011, 2012, 2013). The structures are generally characterized by two low, perpendicular adobe walls and a floor of mixed clay and sand (*tapia*) that was laid down wet in the corners, expanding out to create a living surface that terminated roughly in a square at the end points of the walls (figure 4.3). These structures were quickly assembled and have been found scattered throughout the central portion of Sector C at Huaca Colorada, occasionally overlapping one another. It is likely that these were temporary structures, constructed by household

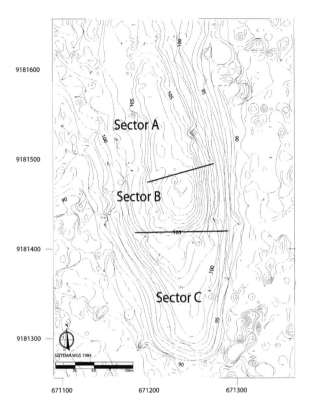

FIGURE 4.2.
Topographic map of
Huaca Colorada with
three primary sectors.
Courtesy, Edward
Swenson

groups during cyclical attendance at the site for political and religious events conducted in the upper ceremonial core in Sector B (Gataveckas 2011; Swenson 2018;
Swenson and Chiguala 2018; Swenson and Warner 2012; Swenson et al. 2011, 2012,
2013). Edward R. Swenson and Jorge Y. Chiguala (2018) have attributed these types
of informal habitations to fluid, daily co-residential practices performed by transitory residential groups.

These structures were venues of primarily quotidian activities as evidenced by
paleobotanical (table 4.1) and zooarchaeological (table 4.2) samples (Vásquez
Sánchez and Rosales Tham 2011, 2012, 2013) and ceramic data (table 4.3) (Swenson
and Warner 2012; Swenson et al. 2011, 2012, 2013). Notably, the contexts excavated
within these structures lack many of the exotic and imported luxury goods, such
as *Spondylus* shell, deer, peanuts, fruit (e.g., guava, pacay, lucuma), and Cajamarca-
style ceramics (Swenson and Warner 2012), found in the Sector B ceremonial core.
Instead, there is a mix of utilitarian and high-status materials but with a definite lean
toward local (e.g., beans, maize, chili peppers, local ceramics) rather than imported

FIGURE 4.3. Expedient *tapia* floor and adobe walls in Sector C at Huaca Colorada. *Courtesy*, Edward Swenson

(e.g., highland ceramics, *Spondylus*) and domestic (e.g., bottle gourds, utilitarian ceramics) rather than ceremonial (e.g., decorated ceramics, peanuts).

Either local elites occupied the expedient structures of Sector C or nonelites gained access to fineware ceramics for use there. Local Moche fineline wares were found in relative abundance (40 sherds, 37.4% of the total ceramics recovered) and this, combined with the lack of highland Cajamarca wares (1 sherd, 0.9% of the total ceramics recovered), emphasizes this local focus and the use of specialized ceramics generally reserved for special events. These structures present other assemblage patterns that are consistent with temporary use. The presence of coca and chili peppers—two plants known for both their ritual significance and importance in daily activities (Cutright 2011, 87; Gumerman 2002)—as well as maize and llama, is consistent with a pattern that makes sense for temporary domestic structures at an important ceremonial site. Rural farmers/fishers either were not part of the attendees/temporary residents at the site or, more likely, they simply did not bring their work tools to the party, as indicated by the lack of agricultural and fishing implements in Sector C at Huaca Colorada.

While there was a substantial amount of permanent architecture, particularly in the ceremonial core at the top of the site in Sector B as well as on the east and south edges of Sector C (Swenson 2012; Swenson and Warner 2012; Swenson

TABLE 4.1. Presence/absence of paleobotanical materials from Sectors C* and B† at Huaca Colorada

Species/Genus (common name)	Sector C Sample*	Sector B†
Acacia sp. (acacia)		Y
Ahnfeltia durvillaei (seaweed)		Y
Arachis hypogaea (peanut)		Y
Bunchosia armeniaca (peanut butter fruit)		Y
Capparis angulata (sapote)		Y
Capparis ovalifolia		Y
Capsicum sp. (pepper)	Y	Y
Citrus aurantium (bitter orange)		Y
Cucurbita moschata (squash/pumpkin)		Y
Erytrhroxilum coca (coca)	Y	Y
Gigartina chamissoi (seaweed)		Y
Gossypium barbadense (cotton)	Y	Y
Gynerium sagittatum (caña brava)		Y
Inga feuillei (pacay)		Y
Ipomoea batatas (sweet potato)		Y
Lagenaria siceraria (bottle gourd)	Y	Y
Paspalum sp. (grass)	Y	Y
Persea americana (avocado)		Y
Phaseolus lunatus (lima bean)		Y
Phaseolus vulgaris (common bean)	Y	Y
Phragmites australis (reed)	Y	Y
Potamogeton sp. (pond weed)		Y
Pouteria lucuma (lúcuma)		Y
Prionitis sp. (seaweed)		Y
Prosopis pallida (algorroba)	Y	Y
Psidium guajava (guava)		Y
Scirpus sp. (aquatic grass)		Y
Solanum sp. (nightshades)		Y
Thevetia peruviana (yellow oleander)		Y
Tillandsia sp. (bromeliad)		Y
Trifolium sp. (clover)		Y
Ulva sp. (sea lettuce)		Y
Zea mays (maize)	Y	Y

* Includes all floors, subfloor fill, floor overburden, hearth, and trash contexts from units 6, 7, 11 (2010) and 4, 5, 7 (2011).
† Includes all units excavated in and around the ceremonial center of the site.

TABLE 4.2. Zooarchaeological remains from Sector C* at Huaca Colorada

Vertebrates

Mammals	NISP	*% of Mammals*	*% of Vertebrates*	*% of Total*
Canis familiaris (dog)	9	5.0	3.6	0.3
Cavia porcellus (Guinea pig)	20	11.0	7.9	0.7
Lama sp. (llama/guanaco)	109	59.9	43.3	3.8
Mammals (unidentified mammal)	17	9.3	6.7	0.6
Muridae (rodent)	24	13.2	9.5	0.9
Otaria sp. (eared seal)	3	1.6	1.2	0.1
Total	182	100.0	72.2	6.4
Fish		*% of Fish*	*% of Vertebrates*	*% of Total*
Anisotremus scapularis (Peruvian grunt)	2	4.2	0.8	0.1
Caulolatilus sp. (percoid fish [e.g., whitefish])	1	2.1	0.4	> 0.1
Cynoscion sp. (sea trout)	4	8.3	1.6	0.1
Fish (unidentified fish)	8	16.7	3.2	0.3
Galeichthys peruvianus (sea catfish)	1	2.1	0.4	> 0.1
Mugil cephalus (flathead mullet)	27	56.3	10.7	1.0
Myliobatis sp. (eagle ray)	1	2.1	0.4	> 0.1
Paralonchurus peruanus (Peruvian banded croaker)	2	4.2	0.8	0.1
Sardinops sagax (South American pilchard)	1	2.1	0.4	> 0.1
Stellifer minor (lined drum)	1	2.1	0.4	> 0.1
Total	48	100.0	19.0	1.7
Birds		*% of Birds*	*% of Vertebrates*	*% of Total*
Bird (unidentified bird)	7	43.8	2.8	0.2
Larus sp. (gull)	2	12.5	0.8	0.1
Phalacrocorax bougainvillii (Guanay cormorant)	5	31.3	2.0	0.2
Zenaida asiatica (white-winged dove)	2	12.5	0.8	0.1
Total	16	100.0	6.4	0.6
Reptiles		*% of Reptiles*	*% of Vertebrates*	*% of Total*
Reptile (unidentified reptile)	1	16.7	0.4	> 0.1
Tropidurus sp. (ground lizard)	5	83.3	2.0	0.2
Total	6	100.0	2.4	0.2
TOTAL VERTEBRATES	252			

Invertebrates

Mollusks	NISP	% of Mollusks	% of Invertebrates	% of Total
Acanthopleura echinata (chiton)	1	> 0.1	> 0.1	> 0.1
Argopecten purpuratus (Peruvian/calico scallop)	1	> 0.1	> 0.1	> 0.1
Cancellaria urceolata (sea snail; nutmeg snail)	1	> 0.1	> 0.1	> 0.1
Cantharus elegans (whelk)	1	> 0.1	> 0.1	> 0.1
Cerithium stercusmuscarum (sea snail)	2	0.1	0.1	0.1
Choromytilus chorus (giant mussel)	2	0.1	0.1	0.1
Donax obesulus (surf clam)	1,044	41.2	40.4	36.8
Enoplochiton niger (chiton)	1	> 0.1	> 0.1	> 0.1
Fissurella crassa (thick keyhole limpet; sea snail)	1	> 0.1	> 0.1	> 0.1
Fissurella maxima (giant keyhole limpet)	1	> 0.1	> 0.1	> 0.1
Helisoma sp. (freshwater snail)	1	> 0.1	> 0.1	> 0.1
Helisoma trivolvis ("ramshorn" land snail)	1	> 0.1	> 0.1	> 0.1
Mesodesma donacium (saltwater clam)	1	> 0.1	> 0.1	> 0.1
Mitra orientalis (miter sea snail)	10	0.4	0.4	0.4
Nassarius dentifer (mud snail; dog whelk; sea snail)	29	1.1	1.1	1.0
Oliva peruviana (Peruvian olive/sea snail)	1	> 0.1	> 0.1	> 0.1
Olivella columellaris (dwarf olives/sea snail)	12	0.5	0.5	0.4
Perumytilus purpuratus (common marine mussel)	30	1.2	1.2	1.1
Polinices uber (moon sea snail)	675	26.7	26.1	23.8
Prisogaster niger (turban sea snail)	185	7.3	7.2	6.5
Pupoides sp. (land snail)	2	0.1	0.1	0.1
Scutalus chiletensis (land snail)	14	0.6	0.5	0.5
Semimytilus algosus (intertidal mussel)	45	1.8	1.7	1.6
Sinum cymba (concave moon ear snail)	47	1.9	1.8	1.7
Solenosteira fusiformis (fusiform goblet)	4	0.2	0.2	0.1
Spisula adamsii (surf clam)	3	0.1	0.1	0.1
Tegula atra (sea snail)	21	0.8	0.8	0.7
Tegula euryomphalus (sea snail)	2	0.1	0.1	0.1
Thais chocolata (locate/rock snail/sea snail)	110	4.3	4.3	3.9
Thais delessertiana (sea snail/rock snail)	1	> 0.1	> 0.1	> 0.1

continued on next page

TABLE 4.2—*continued*

Invertebrates

Mollusks	NISP	% of Mollusks	% of Invertebrates	% of Total
Thais haemastoma (red-mouthed rock shell)	193	7.6	7.5	6.8
Trachycardium procerum (cockle)	1	> 0.1	> 0.1	> 0.1
Trivia radians (false cowry/small sea snail)	1	> 0.1	> 0.1	> 0.1
Turbo fluctuosus (wavy turban/sea snail)	1	> 0.1	> 0.1	> 0.1
Xanthochorus buxea (sea snail/rock snail)	86	3.4	3.3	3.0
Total	2,531	100.0	98.0	89.3
Arthropods		% of Arthropods	% of Invertebrates	% of Total
Platyxanthus orbignyi (crab)	52	100.0	2.0	1.8
Total	52	100.0	2.0	1.8
TOTAL INVERTEBRATES	2,583			
TOTAL ALL	2,835			

* Includes all floors, subfloor fill, floor overburden, hearth, and trash contexts from units 6, 7, 11 (2010) and 4, 5, 7 (2011), excluding burials.

et al. 2011, 2012, 2013), the evidence for permanent residence in relation to this architecture is somewhat uncertain. Sector A was a possible location for longer-term or permanent habitation at Huaca Colorada, which is evidenced by rectilinear structures with rooms and benches as well as series of floors indicating reconstruction and possible reoccupation or potentially permanent occupation and continual maintenance (Swenson et al. 2012, 2013). The ambiguity here arises with the presence of many large face-neck vessels theorized to be used for *chicha* production and grain storage. This could indicate domestic occupation and production or simply that these were storage facilities for occasional feasts. What Swenson and Chiguala (2018) assert is that the variety of household forms found at this one site, ranging from permanent residences to temporary, expedient structures, is clear evidence of a diversity in the domestic realm of the Moche that has not before been properly acknowledged.

WASI HUACHUMA

Wasi Huachuma was a multifunctional site featuring prominent ceremonial architecture, high, flat platforms overlooking the valley, residential architecture, and

TABLE 4.3. Ceramics from Sector C* at Huaca Colorada

	Counts	% of Grade	% of Total
Utilitarian/low grade			
Olla rims	8	13.8	7.5
Cántaro rims	37	63.8	34.6
Ralladores	1	1.7	0.9
Tinaja rims	6	10.3	5.6
Other	6	10.3	5.6
Total	58		54.2
Mid-grade/decorated			
Face-neck cántaros	4	50.0	3.7
Figurines/appliqué pieces	3	37.5	2.8
Other	1	12.5	0.9
Total	8		7.4
High-status serving wares			
Cajamarca (highland)	1	2.4	0.9
Local high-status Moche	40	97.6	37.4
Total	41		38.3
TOTAL ALL	107		

* Includes all floors, subfloor fill, floor overburden, hearth, and trash contexts from units 6, 7, 11 (2010) and 4, 5, 7 (2011), excluding burials.

possible temporary campsites. The site is located on the lower northeast slope of the Santa Catalina Hills, 12 km south of San José de Moro, 10 km northeast of Pacatnamú, and 12 km west of Cerro Chepén—three major centers of political power during the Moche Period in the Jequetepeque Valley (Cusicanqui Marsano 2010; Donnan and Cock 1997; Rosas Rintel 2010) (see figure 4.1).

The site consists of seven distinct sectors delineated by three dry arroyos running northeast from the top of the hills to the irrigated plain below (Dillehay et al. 2009, 86–89; Duke 2017, 100–179; Swenson 2004, 609–617) (figure 4.4). Sector B, the ceremonial core of the site, occupies the central portion of the lower slope of the hill and features a three-tiered, ramped platform mound (Structure B). Sector A is situated to the east of Sector B and encompasses two low hills and an intervening low pass. This zone is located between Arroyo 1 and Arroyo 3 and features a two-tiered terrace structure built within the pass. Sector D is located on the hill 47 m above Sector B and is notable for its two flat platforms at the summit. These flat platforms overlook the site and the farmlands of the valley

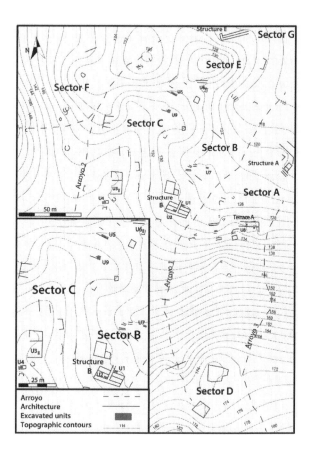

FIGURE 4.4.
Topographic map of
Wasi Huachuma with
inset of sectors discussed
in this chapter.

below. Sector C is located to the west of Sector B and is bordered on the west by
Arroyo 2. It occupies a low ridge and features a number of stone alignments and
disinterred burials and in previous surveys had been identified as the primary
residential sector (Dillehay et al. 2009, 86–89; Swenson 2004, 609–617). Sector
E is situated to the north of Sector C and designates the hill on the north tip of
the ridge. This sector features a series of terraces on the hill slope and an L-shaped
platform at the bottom of the northwest slope. Sector F is located on the west
side of Arroyo 2 and features a number of circular stone alignments. Sector G lies
on the flat area northeast of the base of the Sector E hill and, based on the surface
ceramics collected, was a likely residential/temporary camp area. The evidence
for both permanent and temporary residence at Wasi Huachuma is notable in its
variability. Sections C and E, as well as Sector G, will be focused on below as the
primary residential zones at the site.

SECTORS C AND E

The architecture and excavated materials from Sectors C and E show evidence of permanent habitation and food processing, including burned floors, hearths, food-processing implements—such as grinding stones, cutters and scrapers, and ceramic graters (*ralladores*)[2]—as well as the remains of food items themselves (Duke 2017, 130–161). The preponderance of plain ceramic body sherds (table 4.4), many of which showed signs of burning, in combination with the frequency of hearth contexts associated with floors is highly indicative of food production. The *tapia* floors placed along walls were made up of a single course of construction materials (stone rather than adobe in this case) (figure 4.5). Ultimately, Wasi Huachuma was likely a locale featuring both temporary and permanent residence, as shown by the architectural and artifactual evidence from Sectors C and E.

The structures in Sectors C and E at Wasi Huachuma may have been the locales of repeated reoccupation by the same groups, possibly local elites or food production specialists. The paleobotanical (table 4.5), zooarchaeological (Vásquez Sánchez and Rosales Tham 2014) (table 4.6), and ceramic (table 4.4) assemblages exhibit a mix of utilitarian and high-status materials but with an emphasis on local over imported materials (i.e., no highland ceramics), similar to Sector C at Huaca Colorada. As well, although Wasi Huachuma is close to the ocean as the dove flies, consideration must be given to the large range of hills between the site and the sea. Thus Wasi Huachuma is decidedly oriented to the north and east, toward the wide agricultural plain between the Santa Catalina Hills and the foothills of the Andes. This might, at least in part, explain the low emphasis on marine products in the archaeological assemblage. Excavations did not recover tools specifically associated with agriculture or fishing. The implications appear to be that temporary or semipermanent structures were erected for use during important events located at Wasi Huachuma. The materials recovered were clearly indicative of small-scale food production, making this the possible site for semipermanent or more temporary habitation.

SECTOR G

In addition to Sectors C and E, Wasi Huachuma's Sector G was also a temporary residence area (figure 4.6). While the sample is currently small and comes solely from the surface, the ceramic evidence indicates primary use of utilitarian cooking vessels (table 4.4). The location of Sector G on the north perimeter of the site, nearer to the irrigated fields and furthest from the ceremonial core (Structure B), combined with the predominance of utilitarian cooking and storage vessels from the Sector G surface collection, suggests that this was a likely location for the construction of temporary domestic structures occupied by itinerant farmers/fishers attending events at the site. Unfortunately, time constraints prevented the

FIGURE 4.5. Parallel stone walls with floor in Sector C at Wasi Huachuma

excavation of units in this sector in 2013, but further work here would target this sector to elaborate on this theme.

HUACA COLORADA AND WASI HUACHUMA IN COMPARISON

The evidence from the two sites suggests that they both experienced temporary occupations, though through different modes and prevalence in the styles of occupation, potentially taking place simultaneously at each site. The central portion of Sector C at Huaca Colorada is marked by a series of temporary, expedient structures laid down as needed and abandoned after a brief period of usage, never to be reoccupied, with new structures constructed over the top of or near old ones. A similar pattern at Wasi Huachuma appears in Sectors C and E and may have also taken place in Sector G, though more excavations are needed to establish this. Based on current and admittedly limited evidence from Wasi Huachuma, it is possible that the Sectors C and E were inhabited on a temporary or semipermanent basis by groups with somewhat higher status than those in Sector G. Sector G was also likely more ephemeral than Sectors C and E.

Sector A at Huaca Colorada appears to have been more permanently occupied or at least reoccupied more than once. The closest correlation at Wasi Huachuma is

TABLE 4.4. Ceramics from Sectors C/E* and G† at Wasi Huachuma

	C/E*	% of Grade	% of Total	G†	% of Grade	% of Total
Utilitarian/low grade						
Cántaro rims	3	3.1	3.0	7	50.0	50.0
Olla rims	8	8.3	7.9	3	21.4	21.4
Plain body sherds	84	87.5	83.1	0	0.0	0.0
Tinaja rims	1	1.0	1.0	4	28.6	28.6
Total	96		95.0	14		100.0
Mid-grade/decorated						
Face-neck cántaros	1	50.0	1.0	0	0.0	0.0
Other	1	50.0	1.0	0	0.0	0.0
Total	2		2.0	0		0.0
High-status serving wares						
Local high-status Moche	2	66.7	2.0	0	0.0	0.0
Other	1	33.3	1.0	0	0.0	0.0
Total	3		3.0	0		0.0
TOTAL ALL	101			14		

* Includes all floors, subfloor fill, floor overburden, hearth, and trash contexts from units 6, 7, 11 (2010) and 4, 5, 7 (2011), excluding burials.
† Surface collection.

Sectors C and E, where layers of floors and more permanent stone walls may indicate reoccupation over time, though lacking in the apparent permanence of the architecture noted in Sector A at Huaca Colorada (e.g., full rectilinear structures with benches). The construction of floors and low walls at Wasi Huachuma is reminiscent of the expedient structures in Sector C at Huaca Colorada, yet the presence of floor sequences was more similar to Sector A. Where they differ is in the linear style of construction (i.e., a lack of corners in the walls) and what may be the specific reuse/refurbishing of specific locales, as evidenced by successive floor levels associated with specific walls. The surface collections and appearance here indicate that the residences in Sector G may have been similar in style to Sector C at Huaca Colorada.

The differences in scale and styles between the two sites themselves may also play a role in the level of permanence of architecture and occupation. Huaca Colorada is thought to have been the largest and possibly only major ceremonial site on the south side of the lower valley during its period of use, while Wasi Huachuma was one of a number of small sites of its kind on the north side of the river valley. These

TABLE 4.5. Presence/absence of paleobotanical materials from Sectors C/E* and Structure B[†] at Wasi Huachuma

Taxa	Sector C/E Sample*	Structure B Sample[†]
Acacia sp. (acacia)		Y
Capparis sp.	Y	
Capsicum sp. (pepper)	Y	Y
Cucurbita moschata (squash/pumpkin)	Y	Y
Encelia sp. (desert shrub)		Y
Erytrhroxilum coca (coca)	Y	
Gossypium barbadense (cotton)	Y	
Gynerium sagittatum (caña brava)		Y
Lagenaria siceraria (bottle gourd)		Y
Leguminosae (legumes)	Y	
Phaseolus vulgaris (common bean)	Y	
Phragmites australis (reed)	Y	Y
Pouteria lucuma (lúcuma)	Y	
Prosopis sp. (algorroba)	Y	Y
Solanum tuberosum. (potato)	Y	
Zea mays (maize)	Y	Y

* Includes all floors, subfloor fill, floor overburden, hearth, and trash contexts from units 3, 4, 5, 6, 9 (2013).
[†] Includes all floors, subfloor fill, floor overburden, hearth, and trash contexts from unit 2 (2013).

political and demographic dynamics surely affected the styles of occupation in the area. However, both sites exhibit evidence of construction indicative of use, abandonment, and reconstruction consistent with patterns of mobility among peripatetic farmers/fishers partaking in a ritual/economic/political round.

PERIPATETIC HOUSEHOLDS, PERIPATETIC COMMUNITIES

Huaca Colorada and Wasi Huachuma support a population circulation model, as defined by Schachner (2012) and Gumerman (2010). To return briefly to Schachner's application of "population circulation," the Late Moche Jequetepeque Valley is certainly fertile ground to further explore this archaeologically. The first proposition (varied circulation depending on individuals and destinations) can be understood in the Moche context through the multitude of small and large ceremonial sites with residential components (temporary, semipermanent, or otherwise) alongside the fields and seaside as destinations of equal importance, indicative of

TABLE 4.6. Zooarchaeological remains from Sectors C/E* at Wasi Huachuma

Vertebrates

Mammals	NISP	% of Mammals	% of Vertebrates	% of Total
Artiodactyla (even-toed ungulate)	7	6.4	4.3	3.0
Canis familiaris (dog)	4	3.6	2.5	1.7
Cavia porcellus (Guinea pig)	22	20.0	13.6	9.3
Lama sp. (llama/guanaco)	17	15.5	10.5	7.2
Mammals (unidentified mammal)	4	3.6	2.5	1.7
Muridae (rodent)	56	50.9	34.5	23.7
Total	110	100.0	67.9	46.6

Fish		% of Fish	% of Vertebrates	% of Total
Cynoscion sp. (sea trout)	3	7.5	1.9	1.3
Fish (unidentified fish)	3	7.5	1.9	1.3
Galeichthys peruvianus (sea catfish)	15	37.5	9.3	6.4
Mugil cephalus (flathead mullet)	17	42.5	10.5	7.2
Sardinops sagax (South American pilchard)	1	2.5	0.6	0.4
Stellifer minor (lined drum)	1	2.5	0.6	0.4
Total	40	100.0	24.8	17.0

Birds		% of Birds	% of Vertebrates	% of Total
Bird (unidentified bird)	1	33.3	0.6	0.4
Zenaida asiatica (white-winged dove)	2	66.7	1.2	0.8
Total	3	100.0	1.8	1.2

Reptiles		% of Reptiles	% of Vertebrates	% of Total
Dicrodon sp. (tegu)	8	88.9	4.9	3.4
Reptile (unidentified reptile)	1	11.1	0.6	0.4
Total	9	100.0	5.5	3.8
TOTAL VERTEBRATES	162			

continued on next page

TABLE 4.6—*continued*

Invertebrates

Mollusks	NISP	% of Mollusks	% of Total
Donax obesulus (surf clam)	3	4.1	1.3
Drymaeus tigris (land snail)	1	1.3	0.4
Helisoma sp. (freshwater snail)	5	6.7	2.1
Lymnaea sp. (freshwater snail)	4	5.4	1.7
Polinices uber (moon sea snail)	11	14.9	4.7
Prisogaster niger (turban sea snail)	4	5.4	1.7
Pupoides sp. (land snail)	33	44.6	14.0
Scutalus sp. (land snail)	2	2.7	0.8
Tegula atra (sea snail)	7	9.5	3.0
Thais chocolata (locate/rock snail/sea snail)	3	4.1	1.3
Xanthochorus buxea (sea snail/rock snail)	1	1.3	0.4
Total	74	100.0	31.4
TOTAL INVERTEBRATES	74		
TOTAL ALL	236		

* Includes all floors, subfloor fill, floor overburden, hearth, and trash contexts from units 3, 4, 5, 6, 9 (2013).

a yearly or seasonally prescribed economic, political, and ceremonial round. The second proposition (circulation centered around ecological variability, customary life [e.g., trade, marriage, warfare], and social hierarchy) is also well covered here. The coastal Peruvian ecological zone is highly variable, including desert, irrigated plains, coastal/littoral areas, and access to higher lands on hilltops and up the valleys. Movement between these zones has been well established (see Dillehay 2001; Gumerman 2010; Shimada 1982). In addition, movement for warfare and trade is well established through the archaeological examples (see Dillehay 2001, 266–267; Swenson 2003). The third proposition (the spatial separation of obligations, activities, and goods) has served as one of the primary bases for the arguments presented in this chapter. The idea that fishing ground, agricultural fields, ceremonial centers, trading sites, and locales for political observances were spread out across the landscape and not confined to a single place (e.g., towns or cities) is significant. Lastly, Schachner's fourth proposition (fluidity in residence, group membership, and leadership) is the primary focus of this chapter. Fluidity in residence is demonstrated by the expedient residences at Huaca Colorada and reoccupied structures at Wasi

FIGURE 4.6. Sector G at Wasi Huachuma, facing north from the top of Sector E

Huachuma. The evidence for multiple autonomous rural settlements with shifting alliances highlights the fluidity of leadership, while the presence of differing ceramic assemblages between the various zones of the two sites potentially indicates fluid group membership.

William H. Isbell (2000) noted that many of our ideas of past communities are impositions from later time periods, and others have argued that much of our work as archaeologists has uncritically imposed modernist, Western ontology into non-modern contexts (see Alberti and Bray 2009; Alberti and Marshall 2009; Alberti et al. 2011; Barad 2003; Fowler 2013; Fowles 2013; Marshall and Alberti 2014). In fact, many of our interpretations of the past take a universalist view of humanity, imposing conceptions from our current world onto those of the past. However, the material configurations we see in our archaeological data can and should challenge those conceptions (see Alberti and Marshall 2009; Viveiros de Castro 1998, 2004). If our goal is to attempt to understand the ontologies of past societies in part through analyzing community organization, it is crucial to recognize that a community is not necessarily defined by the social interactions between groups of households in a specific locale. Rather, we should consider the material evidence we recover from such contexts as a means of assessing the potential varieties of alternative community configurations that may have existed in the past.

Households have been argued to be the building blocks of communities (e.g., Arensberg 1955; Hollingshead 1948; Kolb and Snead 1997; Murdock 1949; Redfield 1963 [1955]; Wolf 1957). However, as has been made clear here, the term *community* is problematic (see Yaeger and Canuto 2000). Donna J. Nash (2009) asserts that not only is the household a basic socioeconomic unit wherein activities such as food production, processing, consumption, and disposal occur, but it is also the basic social unit through which social distinctions are materially negotiated. She asserts that to understand the "societal whole" (Nash 2009, 206), archaeologists must look first and foremost at residential data. These data often include paleobotanical and zooarchaeological evidence, tool remains, architectural and spatial information, and ceramic cooking vessels. This interrelated dataset can provide the basis from which to interpret the components and complexities of quotidian practices as including gender constructions and status differentiation (among others). However, this idea of the household as a basic socioeconomic unit is predicated on the idea of a singular household structure in which a bounded group of people reside and conduct their daily lives on a continuous basis. As I have established above, such a structure, not to mention such a group, is not always present, and some structures that have been interpreted as "houses" are not always what they seem.

Change clearly occurred in the Jequetepeque Valley with the onset of the Late Moche Period (Castillo Butters 2001; Dillehay and Kolata 2004; Swenson 2007). I argue that the rural inhabitants of the Late Moche Jequetepeque Valley were the agents of their own destinies during the emerging fluctuations in environmental and political conditions. In short, by executing a mobile pattern of ritual/political observances and economic labor/exchange, rural communities exercised both their local autonomy and their inclusion within larger networks of interaction, also allowing them the flexibility to adjust to the environmental and political fluctuations common during this period. Further studies of rural areas at small ceremonial sites, villages, and farmsteads, in combination with the existing and growing data from urban centers, can only improve upon our knowledge of the diversity and malleability of Moche communities.

ACKNOWLEDGMENTS

I would like to thank Ilana Johnson and Michelle Koons for inviting me to be a part of the 2014 SAA session from which this chapter has sprung. In addition, a sincere thank you to David Pacifico, Ilana Johnson (again), and two anonymous reviewers for their insightful and constructive editorial commentary and suggestions. Edward Swenson, John Warner, and Jorge Chiguala deserve extra appreciation for allowing me to delve into the Huaca Colorada database and for sharing their project photos. My research at Wasi Huachuma would not have been possible without funding from the Wenner-Gren Foundation (Doctoral Dissertation Grant #Gr. 8640). Lastly, thank you to Sarah M. Rowe and Giles Spence Morrow for their commentary and critiques on earlier drafts of this chapter.

NOTES

1. This autonomy was limited in many ways, including obligatory attendance at ritual and administrative events, but was evident in the lack of overarching political structures during this period and in the likelihood that these smaller centers had the ability to shift loyalties or affiliation from other, larger centers or local elites depending on circumstances (see Swenson 2006).

2. Found as part of the Sector C surface collection.

REFERENCES

Alberti, Benjamin, and Tamara L. Bray. 2009. "Animating Archaeology: Of Subjects, Objects, and Alternative Ontologies." *Cambridge Archaeological Journal* 19 (3): 337–343.

Alberti, Benjamin, Severin Fowles, Martin Holbraad, Yvonne Marshall, and Christopher Witmore. 2011. "Worlds Otherwise." *Current Anthropology* 52 (6): 896–912.

Alberti, Benjamin, and Yvonne Marshall. 2009 "Animating Archaeology: Local Theories and Conceptually Open-Ended Methodologies." *Cambridge Archaeological Journal* 19 (3): 344–356.

Anderson, Benedict. 1991. *Imagined Communities: Reflections on the Origin and Spread of Nationalism*. London: Verso.

Arensberg, Conrad M. 1955. "American Communities." *American Anthropologist* 57 (6): 1143–1162.

Arsenault, Daniel. 1992. "Ritual Dietary Practices in Mochica Society: The Context of the Feast." *Recherches amérindiennes au Québec* 22 (1): 45–64.

Barad, Karen. 2003. "Posthumanist Performativity: Toward an Understanding of How Matter Comes to Matter." *Signs* 28 (3): 801–831.

Bawden, Garth. 1982. "Community Organization Reflected by the Household: A Study of Pre-Columbian Social Dynamics." *Journal of Field Archaeology* 9 (2): 165–181.

Bawden, Garth. 2001. "The Symbols of Late Moche Social Transformation." In *Moche Art and Archaeology in Ancient Peru*, edited by Joanne Pillsbury, 285–306. New Haven, CT: Yale University Press.

Bourdieu, Pierre. 1979. *Algeria 1960: The Disenchantment of the World, the Sense of Honour, the Kabyle House or the World Reversed*. Cambridge: Cambridge University Press.

Bourdieu, Pierre. 1984. *Distinction*. Cambridge, MA: Harvard University Press.

Canuto, Marcello A., and Jason Yaeger, eds. 2000. *The Archaeology of Communities*. London: Routledge.

Castillo Butters, Luis Jaime. 2000. "La presencia de Wari en San José de Moro." *Boletín de Arqueología PUCP* 4: 143–179.

Castillo Butters, Luis Jaime. 2001. "The Last of the Mochicas: A View from the Jequetepeque Valley." In *Moche Art and Archaeology in Ancient Peru*, edited by Joanne Pillsbury, 307–332. New Haven, CT: Yale University Press.

Castillo Butters, Luis Jaime. 2010. "Moche Politics in the Jequetepeque Valley: A Case for Political Opportunism." In *New Perspectives in Moche Political Organization*, edited by Luis Jaime Castillo Butters and Jeffrey Quilter, 1–24. Washington, DC: Dumbarton Oaks.

Castillo Butters, Luis Jaime, Julio Rucabado Yong, Martín del Carpio Perla, Katiusha Bernuy Quiroga, Karim Ruíz, Carlos Rengifo, Gabriel Prieto Burmester, and Carole Fraresse. 2008. "Ideología y poder en la consolidacíon, colapso y reconstitucíon del Estado Mochica del Jequetepeque: El Proyecto Arqueoloógico San José de Moro (1991–2006)." *Ñawpa Pacha: Journal of Andean Archaeology* 29: 1–86.

Chapdelaine, Claude. 2001. "The Growing Power of a Moche Urban Class." In *Moche Art and Archaeology in Ancient Peru*, edited by Joanne Pillsbury, 69–88. New Haven, CT: Yale University Press.

Chapdelaine, Claude. 2009. "Domestic Life in and around the Urban Sector of the Huacas of Moche Site, Northern Peru." In *Domestic Life in Prehispanic Capitals: A Study of Specialization, Hierarchy, and Ethnicity*, edited by Linda Manzanilla and Claude Chapdelaine, 181–196. Ann Arbor: Museum of Anthropology, University of Michigan.

Chapman, Murray, and R. Mansell Prothero. 1985. "Circulation between 'Home' and Other Places: Some Propositions." In *Circulation in Population Movement: Substance and Concepts from the Melanesian Case*, edited by Murray Chapman and R. Mansell Prothero, 1–12. London: Routledge.

Cohen, Anthony P. 1985. *The Symbolic Construction of Community*. Chichester: Ellis Horwood.

Contreras, Daniel A. 2010. "Landscape and Environment: Insights from the Prehispanic Central Andes." *Journal of Archaeological Research* 18 (3): 241–288.

Coupland, Gary, Terrence Clark, and Amanda Palmer. 2009. "Hierarchy, Communalism, and the Spatial Order of Northwest Coast Plank Houses: A Comparative Study." *American Antiquity* 74 (1): 77–106.

Cusicanqui Marsano, Solsiré. 2010. *Investigaciones Arqueológicas en Los Asentamientos De San Ildefonso y Cerro Chepén, Valle Bajo De Jequetepeque*. Lima: Pontificia Universidad Católica del Perú (PUCP).

Cutright, Robyn E. 2010. "Food, Family, and Empire: Relating Political and Domestic Change in the Jequetepeque Hinterland." In *Comparative Perspectives on the Archaeology of Coastal South America*, edited by Robyn E. Cutright, Enrique López-Hurtado, and Alexander J. Martin, 27–44. Pittsburgh: Center for Comparative Archaeology, University of Pittsburgh.

Cutright, Robyn E. 2011. "Food for the Dead, Cuisine for the Living: Mortuary Food Offerings from the Jequetepeque Valley, Peru." In *From State to Empire in the Prehistoric Jequetepeque Valley, Peru*, edited by Colleen M. Zori and Ilana Johnson, 83–92. Oxford: Archaeopress.

Cutting, Marion. 2003. "The Use of Spatial Analysis to Study Prehistoric Settlement Architecture." *Oxford Journal of Archaeology* 22 (1): 1–21.

Dietler, Michael, and Ingrid Herbich. 2001. "Feasts and Labor Mobilization: Dissecting a Fundamental Economic Practice." In *Feasts: Theorizing the Feast*, ed. Michael Dietler and Brian Hayden, 240–264. Washington, DC: Smithsonian Institution Press.

Dillehay, Tom D. 2001. "Town and Country in Late Moche Times: A View from Two Northern Valleys." In *Moche Art and Archaeology in Ancient Peru*, edited by Joanne Pillsbury, 259–284. New Haven, CT: Yale University Press.

Dillehay, Tom D., and Alan L. Kolata. 2004. "Long-Term Human Response to Uncertain Environmental Conditions in the Andes." *Proceedings of the National Academy of Sciences (PNAS)* 101 (12): 4325–4330.

Dillehay, Tom D., Alan L. Kolata, and Edward R. Swenson. 2009. *Paisajes Culturales en el Valle del Jequetepeque: Los Yacimientos Arqueológicos*. Trujillo, Peru: Ediciones SIAN.

Donnan, Christopher B. 2011. "Moche Substyles: Keys to Understanding Moche Political Organization." *Boletín del Museo Chileno de Arte Precolombino* 16 (1): 105–118.

Donnan, Christopher B., and Guillermo A. Cock, eds. 1997. *The Pacatnamú Papers*, vol. 2. Los Angeles: Fowler Museum of Cultural History, University of California.

Duke, Guy S. 2017. "Consuming Identities: Communities and Culinary Practice in the Late Moche Jequetepeque Valley, Peru." PhD dissertation, University of Toronto, ON.

Fowler, Chris. 2013. "Dynamic Assemblages, or the Past Is What Endures." In *Archaeology after Interpretation*, edited by Benjamin Alberti, Andrew Meirion Jones, and Joshua Pollard, 235–256. Walnut Creek, CA: Left Coast Press.

Fowles, Severin M. 2013. *An Archaeology of Doings: Secularism and the Study of Pueblo Religion*. Santa Fe, NM: School for Advanced Research Press.

Gataveckas, Katrina. 2011. "Landscape, Household, and Gender in Late Moche Jequetepeque." MA research paper, University of Toronto, ON.

Giddens, Anthony. 1984. *The Constitution of Society: Outline of the Theory of Structuration*. Cambridge: Polity.

Gumerman, George J., IV. 1997. "Botanical Offerings in Moche Burials at Pacatnamú." In *The Pacatnamú Papers: The Moche Occupation*, vol. 2, edited by Christopher B. Donnan and Guillermo A. Cock, 243–249. Los Angeles: Fowler Museum of Cultural History, University of California.

Gumerman, George J., IV. 2002. "Llama Power and Empowered Fishermen: Food and Power at Pacatnamú, Peru." In *The Dynamics of Power*, edited by Maria O'Donovan, 238–256. Occasional Paper 30. Carbondale: Southern Illinois University.

Gumerman, George J., IV. 2010. "Big Hearths and Big Pots: Moche Feasting on the North Coast of Peru." In *Inside Ancient Kitchens: New Directions in the Study of Daily Meals and Feasts*, edited by Elizabeth A. Klarich, 111–131. Boulder: University Press of Colorado.

Gumerman, George J., IV, and Jesus Briceño. 2003. "Santa Rosa—Quirihuac y Ciudad de Dios: Asentamientos Rurales en la Parte Media del Valle de Moche." In *Moche: Hacia el Final del Milenio, Tomo I [Actas del Segundo Coloquio sobre la Cultura Moche: Trujillo, 1 al 7 de agosto de 1999]*, edited by Santiago Uceda Castillo and Elías Mujica, 119–150. Trujillo: Pontificia Universidad Católica del Perú and Universidad Nacional de Trujillo.

Hegmon, Michelle. 2002. "Concepts of Community in Archaeological Research." In *Seeking the Center Place: Archaeology and Ancient Communities in the Mesa Verde Region*, edited by Mark D. Varien and Richard H. Wilshusen, 263–279. Salt Lake City: University of Utah Press.

Hendon, Julia A. 2003. "Archaeological Approaches to the Organization of Domestic Labor: Household Practice and Domestic Relations." *Annual Review of Anthropology* 25 (1): 45–61.

Hirsch, Eric. 2018. "Remapping the Vertical Archipelago: Mobility, Migration, and the Everyday Labor of Andean Development." *Journal of Latin American and Caribbean Anthropology* 23 (1): 189–208.

Hodder, Ian. 1994. "Burials, Houses, Women, and Men in the European Neolithic." In *Architecture and Order: Approaches to Social Space*, edited by Michael P. Pearson and Colin Richards, 51–68. London: Routledge.

Hodder, Ian, and Craig Cessford. 2004. "Daily Practice and Social Memory at Çatalhöyük." *American Antiquity* 69 (1): 17–40.

Hollingshead, August B. 1948. "Community Research: Development and Present Condition." *American Sociological Review* 13 (2): 136–156.

Ingold, Tim. 2000. *The Perception of the Environment: Essays on Livelihood, Dwelling, and Skill*. London: Routledge.

Isbell, William H. 1995. "Constructing the Andean Past or 'As You Like It.'" *Journal of the Steward Anthropological Society* 23 (1–2): 1–12.

Isbell, William H. 1996. "Household and Ayni in the Andean Past." *Journal of the Steward Anthropological Society* 24 (1–2): 249–295.

Isbell, William H. 2000. "What We Should Be Studying: The 'Imagined Community' and the 'Natural Community.'" In *The Archaeology of Communities: A New World Perspective*, edited by Marcello A. Canuto and Jason Yaeger, 243–266. London: Routledge.

Johnson, Ilana. 2008. "Portachuelo de Charcape: Daily Life and Political Power in the Hinterland during the Late Moche Period." In *Arqueología Mochica Nuevos Enfoques: Actas del Primer Congreso Internacional de Jóvenes Investigadores de la Cultura Moche*, edited by Luis Jaime Castillo Butters, Helaine Bernier, Gregory Lockard, and Julio Rucabado Yong, 261–274. Lima: Pontificia Universidad Católica de Perú Fondo Editorial.

Johnson, Ilana. 2010. "Households and Social Organization at the Late Moche Period Site of Pampa Grande, Peru." PhD dissertation, University of California, Los Angeles.

Johnson, Ilana. 2011. "The Development of Semi-Autonomous Communities in the Late Moche Period (AD 600–900)." In *From State to Empire in the Prehistoric Jequetepeque Valley, Peru*, edited by Colleen Zori and Ilana Johnson, 51–64. Oxford: Archaeopress.

Jurado, M. Carolina. 2013. "Doble Domicilio: Relaciones Sociales y Complementariedad Ecológica en El Norte de Potosí (Bolivia) del Temprano Siglo XVII." *Chungara, Revista De Antropología Chilena* 45 (4): 613–630.

Keatinge, Richard W. 1975. "Urban Settlement Systems and Rural Sustaining Communities: An Example from Chan Chan's Hinterland." *Journal of Field Archaeology* 2 (3): 215–227.

Kent, Susan. 1992. "Studying Variability in the Archaeological Record: An Ethnoarchaeological Model for Distinguishing Mobility Patterns." *American Antiquity* 57 (4): 635–660.

Kent, Susan, and Helga Vierich. 1989. "The Myth of Ecological Determinism—Anticipated Mobility and Site Spatial Organization." In *Farmers as Hunters: The Implications of Sedentism*, edited by Susan Kent, 96–130. Cambridge: Cambridge University Press.

Kolb, Michael J., and James E. Snead. 1997. "It's a Small World After All: Comparative Analyses of Community Organization in Archaeology." *American Antiquity* 62 (4): 609–628.

Lévi-Strauss, Claude. 1982. "The Social Organization of the Kwakiutl." In *The Way of the Masks*, 163–187. Seattle: University of Washington Press.

Lynch, Sally. 2013. "A Ceramic-Based Analysis of Feasting and Power at the Moche Site of Huaca Colorada, Jequetepeque Valley, Peru." MA research paper, University of Toronto, ON.

Mac Sweeney, Naoíse. 2011. *Community Identity and Archaeology: Dynamic Communities at Aphrodisias and Beycesultan.* Ann Arbor: University of Michigan Press.

Marshall, Yvonne, and Benjamin Alberti. 2014. "A Matter of Difference: Karen Barad, Ontology and Archaeological Bodies." *Cambridge Archaeological Journal* 24 (1): 19–36.

Moore, Jerry D. 2012. *The Prehistory of Home.* Berkeley: University of California Press.

Murdock, George P. 1949. *Social Structure.* New York: Free Press.

Murra, John V. 1956. "The Economic Organization of the Inca State." PhD dissertation, University of Chicago, IL.

Nash, Donna J. 2009. "Household Archaeology in the Andes." *Journal of Archaeological Research* 17 (3): 205–261.

Owoc, Mary A. 2005. "From the Ground Up: Agency, Practice, and Community in the Southwestern British Bronze Age." *Journal of Archaeological Method and Theory* 12 (4): 257–281.

Pauketat, Timothy R. 2000. "Politicization and Community in the Pre-Columbian Mississippi Valley." In *The Archaeology of Communities,* edited by Marcello A. Canuto and Jason Yaeger, 16–43. London: Routledge.

Pauketat, Timothy R., and Susan M. Alt. 2005. "Agency in a Postmold? Physicality and the Archaeology of Culture-Making." *Journal of Archaeological Method and Theory* 12 (3): 213–237.

Pozorski, Shelia, and Thomas Pozorski. 2003. "La Arquitectura Residencial y la Subsistancia de los Habitants de Sitio de Moche: Evidencia Recuperada por el Proyecto Chan Chan—Valle de Moche." In *Moche: Hacia el final del milenio, Tomo I [Actas del segundo coloquio sobre la cultura Moche: Trujillo, 1 al 7 de agosto de 1999],* edited by Santiago Uceda Castillo and Elias Mujica, 119–150. Trujillo: Pontificia Universidad Católica del Perú and Universidad Nacional de Trujillo.

Redfield, Robert. 1963 [1955]. *The Little Community: Viewpoints for the Study of a Human Whole.* Chicago: University of Chicago Press.

Robin, Cynthia. 2002. "Outside of Houses." *Journal of Social Archaeology* 2 (2): 245–268.

Robin, Cynthia. 2003. "New Directions in Classic Maya Household Archaeology." *Journal of Archaeological Research* 11 (4): 307–356.

Rosas Rintel, Marcos. 2007. "Nuevas Perspectivas Acerca del Colapso Moche en el Bajo Jequetepeque." *Bulletin de l'Institut Français d'Études Andines* 36 (2): 221–240.

Rosas Rintel, Marcos. 2010. "Cerro Chepén and the Late Moche Collapse in the Jequetepeque Valley, North Coast of Peru." PhD dissertation, University of New Mexico, Albuquerque.

Rowe, Sarah M. 2014. "Community and Memory at the Late Valdivia Site of Buen Suceso, Ecuador." PhD dissertation, University of Illinois, Urbana-Champaign.

Saignes, Thierry. 1995. "Andean Tribute, Migration, and Trade: Remapping the Boundaries of Ethnicity and Exchange." In *Ethnicity, Markets, and Migration in the Andes at the Crossroads of History and Anthropology*, edited by Brooke Larson, Olivia Harris, and Enrique Tandeter, 167–195. Durham, NC: Duke University Press.

Schachner, Gregson. 2012. "Population Circulation and the Transformation of Ancient Zuni Communities." PhD dissertation, University of Arizona, Tucson.

Schwartz, Glenn M., and Steven E. Falconer, eds. 1994. *Archaeological Views from the Countryside: Village Communities in Early Complex Societies*. Washington, DC: Smithsonian Institution Press.

Shimada, Izumi. 1982. "Horizontal Archipelago and Coast-Highland Interaction in North Peru: Archaeological Models." *Senri Ethnological Studies Osaka* 10: 137–210.

Shimada, Izumi. 1994. *Pampa Grande and the Mochica Culture*. Austin: University of Texas Press.

Shimada, Izumi. 2001. "Late Moche Urban Craft Production: A First Approximation." In *Moche Art and Archaeology in Ancient Peru*, edited by Joanne Pillsbury, 176–205. New Haven, CT: Yale University Press.

Stanish, Charles. 1989. "Household Archeology: Testing Models of Zonal Complementarity in the South Central Andes." *American Anthropologist* 91 (1): 7–24.

Steward, Julian H. 1938. *Basin-Plateau Aboriginal Sociopolitical Groups*. Bulletin 120. Washington, DC: Bureau of American Ethnology, Smithsonian Institution.

Swenson, Edward R. 2003. "Cities of Violence: Sacrifice, Power, and Urbanization in the Andes." *Journal of Social Archaeology* 3 (2): 256–296.

Swenson, Edward R. 2004. "Ritual and Power in the Urban Hinterland: Religious Pluralism and Political Decentralization in Late Moche Jequetepeque, Peru." PhD dissertation, University of Chicago, IL.

Swenson, Edward R. 2006. "Competitive Feasting, Religious Pluralism, and Decentralized Power in the Late Moche Period." In *Andean Archaeology III: North and South*, edited by William H. Isbell and Helaine Silverman, 112–142. New York: Springer.

Swenson, Edward R. 2007. "Adaptive Strategies or Ideological Innovations? Interpreting Sociopolitical Developments in the Jequetepeque Valley of Peru during the Late Moche Period." *Journal of Anthropological Archaeology* 26 (2): 253–282.

Swenson, Edward R. 2008. "San Ildefonso and the 'Popularization' of Moche Ideology in the Jequetepeque Valley." In *Arqueología Mochica Nuevos Enfoques: Actas del Primer Congreso Internacional de Jóvenes Investigadores de la Cultura Moche*, edited by Luis Jaime Castillo Butters, Helaine Bernier, Gregory Lockard, and Julio Rucabado Yong, 411–431. Lima: Pontificia Universidad Católica de Perú Fondo Editorial.

Swenson, Edward R. 2011. "Stagecraft and the Politics of Spectacle in Ancient Peru." *Cambridge Archaeological Journal* 21 (2): 283–313.

Swenson, Edward R. 2012. "Moche Ceremonial Architecture as Thirdspace: The Politics of Place-making in the Ancient Andes." *Journal of Social Archaeology* 12 (1): 3–28.

Swenson, Edward R. 2018. "Assembling the Moche: The Power of Temporary Gatherings on the North Coast of Peru." *World Archaeology* 29: 1–24.

Swenson, Edward R., and Jorge Y. Chiguala. 2018. "Relaciones entre el espacio ritual y doméstico en el valle Jequetepeque, Perú." *Bulletin De l'Institut Français d'Études Andines* 47 (2): 195–216.

Swenson, Edward R., Jorge Y. Chiguala, and John P. Warner. 2008. *Proyecto de Investigacion Arqueologica Jatanca—Huaca Colorada, Valle de Jequetepeque: Informe Final, Temporada 2007.* Lima: Ministerio de Cultura.

Swenson, Edward R., Jorge Y. Chiguala, and John P. Warner. 2009. *Proyecto de Investigacion Arqueologica Jatanca—Huaca Colorada, Valle de Jequetepeque: Informe Final, Temporada 2008.* Lima: Ministerio de Cultura.

Swenson, Edward R., Jorge Y. Chiguala, and John P. Warner. 2010. *Proyecto de Investigacion Arqueologica Jatanca—Huaca Colorada, Valle de Jequetepeque: Informe Final, Temporada 2009.* Lima: Ministerio de Cultura.

Swenson, Edward R., Jorge Y. Chiguala, and John P. Warner. 2011. *Proyecto de Investigacion Arqueologica Jatanca—Huaca Colorada, Valle de Jequetepeque: Informe Final, Temporada 2010.* Lima: Ministerio de Cultura.

Swenson, Edward R., Jorge Y. Chiguala, and John P. Warner. 2012. *Proyecto de Investigacion Arqueologica Jatanca—Huaca Colorada, Valle de Jequetepeque: Informe Final, Temporada 2011.* Lima: Ministerio de Cultura.

Swenson, Edward R., Jorge Y. Chiguala, and John P. Warner. 2013. *Proyecto de Investigacion Arqueologica Jatanca—Huaca Colorada, Valle de Jequetepeque: Informe Final, Temporada 2012.* Lima: Ministerio de Cultura.

Swenson, Edward R., Francisco Seoane, and John P. Warner. 2015. *Proyecto de Investigacion Arqueologica Jatanca—Huaca Colorada, Valle de Jequetepeque: Informe Final, Temporada 2015.* Lima: Ministerio de Cultura.

Swenson, Edward R., and John P. Warner. 2012. "Crucibles of Power: Forging Copper and Forging Subjects at the Moche Ceremonial Center of Huaca Colorada, Peru." *Journal of Anthropological Archaeology* 31 (3): 314–333.

van Buren, Mary. 1996. "Rethinking the Vertical Archipelago: Ethnicity, Exchange, and History in the South Central Andes." *American Anthropologist* 98 (2): 338–351.

van Gijseghem, Hendrik. 2001. "Household and Family at Moche, Peru: An Analysis of Building and Residence Patterns in a Prehispanic Urban Center." *Latin American Antiquity* 12 (3): 257–273.

Varien, Mark D. 1999. *Sedentism and Mobility in a Social Landscape: Mesa Verde and Beyond.* Tucson: University of Arizona Press.

Varien, Mark D., and James M. Potter, eds. 2008. *The Social Construction of Communities: Agency, Structure, and Identity in the Prehispanic Southwest.* Lanham, MD: Rowman and Littlefield.

Varien, Mark D., and Richard H. Wilshusen, eds. 2002. *Seeking the Center Place: Archaeology and Ancient Communities in the Mesa Verde Region.* Salt Lake City: University of Utah Press.

Vásquez Sánchez, Victor, and Teresa E. Rosales Tham. 2011. "Restos de Fauna y Vegetales de Huaca Colorada, Valle de Jequetepeque—Temporada 2010." In *Informe Final Proyecto Arqueologico Jatanca–Huaca Colorada, Valle Jequetepeque Temporada 2010,* apendice 1, edited by Edward R. Swenson, Jorge Y. Chiguala, and John P. Warner. Lima: Ministerio de Cultura.

Vásquez Sánchez, Victor, and Teresa E. Rosales Tham. 2012. "Restos de Fauna y Vegetales de Huaca Colorada, Valle de Jequetepeque—Temporada 2011." In *Informe Final Proyecto Arqueologico Jatanca–Huaca Colorada, Valle Jequetepeque Temporada 2011,* apendice 1, edited by Edward R. Swenson, Jorge Y. Chiguala, and John P. Warner. Lima: Ministerio de Cultura.

Vásquez Sánchez, Victor, and Teresa E. Rosales Tham. 2013. "Restos de Fauna y Vegetales de Huaca Colorada, Valle de Jequetepeque—Temporada 2012." In *Informe Final Proyecto Arqueologico Jatanca–Huaca Colorada, Valle Jequetepeque Temporada 2012,* apendice 1, edited by Edward R. Swenson, Jorge Y. Chiguala, and John P. Warner. Lima: Ministerio de Cultura.

Vásquez Sánchez, Victor, and Teresa E. Rosales Tham. 2014. "Restos de Fauna y Vegetales del Sitio Je64, Valle de Jequetepeque—Temporada 2013." In *Proyecto de Investigación Arqueologica: la Vida Doméstica y la Dieta en Wasi Huachuma (Je-64), Valle Jequetepeque—Informe Final de Temporada 2013,* edited by Guy S. Duke and Jessica J. Ramirez Goicochea, apendice 1. Lima: Ministerio de Cultura.

Vining, Benjamin R. 2011. "Ruralism, Land Use History, and Holocene Climate in the Suches Highlands, Southern Peru." PhD dissertation, Boston University, MA.

Viveiros de Castro, Eduardo. 1998. "Cosmological Deixis and Amerindian Perspectivism." *Journal of the Royal Anthropological Institute* 4 (3): 469–488.

Viveiros de Castro, Eduardo. 2004. "Exchanging Perspectives: The Transformation of Objects into Subjects in Amerindian Ontologies." *Common Knowledge* 10 (3): 463–484.

Wernke, Steven A. 2007. "Negotiating Community and Landscape in the Peruvian Andes: A Transconquest View." *American Anthropologist* 109 (1): 130–152.

White, Christine, Andrew Nelson, Fred Longstaffe, Gisela Grupe, and Achim Jung. 2009. "Landscape Bioarchaeology at Pacatnamú, Peru: Inferring Mobility from δ13C and δ15N Values of Hair." *Journal of Archaeological Science* 36 (7): 1527–1537.

Wilk, Richard R., and William L. Rathje. 1982. "Household Archaeology." *American Behavioral Scientist* 25 (6): 617–639.

Wolf, Eric R. 1957. "Closed Corporate Peasant Communities in Mesoamerica and Central Java." *Southwestern Journal of Anthropology* 13 (1): 1–18.

Yaeger, Jason, and Marcello A. Canuto. 2000. "Introducing an Archaeology of Communities." In *The Archaeology of Communities*, edited by Marcello A. Canuto and Jason Yaeger, 1–15. London: Routledge.

5

Figures of Moche Past

Examining Identity and Gender in Domestic Artifacts

ILANA JOHNSON

Artistic themes depicted on domestic artifacts are reflective of larger social and cultural ideologies and provide us with a valuable window into everyday social dynamics (Bawden 1982; Gero 2001). Although representations of women are rare in Moche elite-sponsored art, they are abundant in household artifacts throughout all time periods and sites in the Moche region. Feminine identities are sensitive to cultural change and reflect sociopolitical institutions that shape the status of women and the meaning of gender within a particular society (Costin 1996, 1998; Hastorf 1991; Tringham 1991, 1994). Gender is created in the household, both directly by observing social roles, divisions of labor, and familial interactions and indirectly by being exposed to cultural symbols embedded in household items (Ashmore and Wilk 1988; Blanton 1994; Deetz 1982; Hastorf 1991; Hendon 1996, 1997, 2009; Wilk and Netting 1984; Wilk and Rathje 1982). In this way, domestic artifacts provide an important window for understanding household-state relations because they take on ideologies and symbolism disseminated by the state, while at the same time, states must build on the ideas and practices of households to maintain their legitimacy (DeMarrais et al. 1996; Halperin 2014; Shimada 1994). Households can also challenge state ideologies by engaging with alternative representations and practices to satisfy domestic needs not addressed by the state (Halperin 2014). Different activities depicted on male and female figurative artifacts reflect ideologies related to public and private gender roles. The ubiquity and quantity of female figurines in domestic contexts at Moche settlements indicate their consumption as

DOI: 10.5876/9781646420919.c005

gender-infused objects reflecting the concerns of the lower-class majority as they went about their daily lives.

In this chapter, I present my analysis of 645 figurines and 152 figurative whistles, including artifacts excavated from the ancient settlements of Pampa Grande, Huacas de Moche, and San José de Moro, coupled with collections from the Museo Larco and the UCLA Moche Archive. I also incorporate data from Alexandra Morgan's (2009) analysis of Moche figurines from numerous museum and private collections from around the world. I combine a contextual analysis of excavated artifacts with an iconographic comparison of key visual elements and an ethnographic investigation of female shamanism in South America to construct a holistic viewpoint of the role these objects played in the daily lives of ancient Moche people.

Contextual analysis of ritual artifacts such as figurines can shed light on their use as personal or public ritual objects (Flannery 1976). The figurines and whistles excavated from household contexts at Pampa Grande and Huacas de Moche provide especially important insights into gender ideologies and domestic concerns not expressed in state-sponsored media. Moche figurines almost always depict females as indicated by dress, hairstyle, or genitalia, whereas figurative whistles typically depict male warriors, musicians, and supernatural beings (figure 5.1). Female figurines are found with great frequency in lower- and middle-class households and are absent from public and religious buildings, suggesting they were used in personal household rituals (Hubert 2010; Johnson 2010; Limoges 1999; Ringberg 2008). Although whistles are also found in household contexts, the fact that they depict state-sponsored icons and were used to play music suggests that they were stored in houses but used in communal rituals related to calendric ceremonies or rites of solidarity. Female figurines are found in Moche households of all time periods; however, whistles disappear from domestic contexts during the Late Moche Period (AD 600–900). This change corresponds with major iconographic shifts in the region, including the disappearance of many of the icons commonly found on whistles (McClelland 1990). Figurines continue to be common domestic objects in later periods, and the Labretted Lady found on figurines at Pampa Grande (figure 5.2) continues to be an important female religious figure in the subsequent Lambayeque culture (Cordy-Collins 2001; Johnson 2010).

FIGURINES, IDENTITY, AND MATERIALITY

Analysis and comparison of household figurative artifacts illuminate the nature of gender identities within the urban context of Moche cities. Urban environments form and are formed by the individuals who inhabit their space, meaning that households reflect social ideologies while at the same time constructing them (Deetz 1982; Hendon 2009; Janusek 2004; Smith 2003). City inhabitants share

FIGURE 5.1. *Left*: female figurine; *right*: male whistle. Artifacts from the Huacas de Moche; author photos

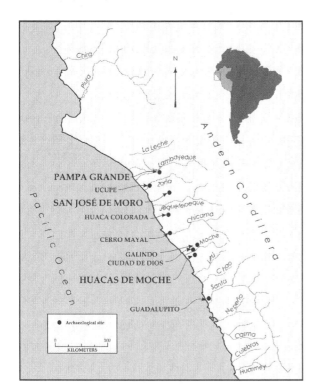

FIGURE 5.2. Map of the Moche region showing archaeological sites discussed in this chapter

a common urban ethos, physical surroundings, sense of culture, general religious knowledge, and participation in city-wide festivals and rites (Smith 2003). At the individual, family, and community levels, however, people have different social and economic statuses, access to state religion, ethnic affiliation, gender roles, specializations or occupations, and household organization. These identities are both actively and unconsciously expressed in material culture. The urban environment and, more specifically, the domestic contexts within them provide a rich opportunity to understand the construction of social identity in relation to others within a shared and circumscribed space (Janusek 2004).

As objects that linked home to society, figurines highlight an important dialectic between subject and object. Their creation, use, and discard all reflect vital aspects of their significance in Moche society and the role they played in constructing human experience. Figurative representations on household objects allow us to contextualize social practices according to the groups that were producing and consuming them (Hendon et al. 2013). Figurines were part of a dynamic system of belief, ritual, and performance integrated into the daily experiences of household inhabitants (Halperin 2014). They represent past agency and reflect socially meaningful practices, actions, and interactions at a very personal level (Hendon 1996).

Figurines have a pervasive presence in Moche domestic assemblages and likely played an important role in the construction of female identities and interactions in relation both to other women and to Moche society more broadly. Figurines have been interpreted as effigies, votives, or amulets used by women for household and fertility-related ceremonies (Marcus 2000). They thus represent powerful symbols of female rituals, ideologies, and social roles within Moche society. Figurines were likely used during individualistic or shamanistic rites carried out within the household related to curing illness, ancestor veneration, and rites of passage, such as menarche, pregnancy, and childbirth (Zeidler 2000). Female shamans involved in these ceremonies were likely regarded as bearers of knowledge and healing powers not available to men (Chavez Hualpa 2000). As physical representations of female animism, figurines shaped private, gender-specific activities oriented toward ritual healing. These symbols would have constructed cultural notions of femininity from an early age and had important implications for Moche society as a whole.

FEMALE SHAMANISM ON THE NORTH COAST OF PERU

Numerous Spanish accounts from the seventeenth century mention the presence of high-status female leaders, known as *Capullanas*, on the north coast of Peru (Cruz Villegas 1982). This practice can be traced back at least to the Late Intermediate Period (AD 1000–1400) when females ruled provinces while men went off to battle

(Fernández Villegas 1989). Thirty-two *Capullanas* have been documented in the Piura region between AD 1500 and 1781, and many more are known to have existed in the Lambayeque region as well. There are a few significant parallels between the powerful females of the Colonial Period and the females depicted on figurines during the Prehispanic periods. Pedro Pizarro (1571) noted that many of the *Capullanas* had pierced lips near their chin (labret piercing), and they filled the holes with gold and silver jewelry. Labret piercings were first depicted in Moche iconography at several northern settlements such as Pampa Grande and San José de Moro and continued to be symbols of high female status in the subsequent Lambayeque culture (Cordy-Collins 2001). In addition, *Capullanas* often wore their hair loose on their shoulders without braids, which distinguished them from lower-status women (Fernández Villegas 1989). Several of the female icons depicted on Moche figurines also wear their hair loose, while simple female figurines are often depicted with head coverings or braids.

The themes present on Moche figurines reference female concerns—such as fertility, childbirth, and childrearing—and include elements from religious ceremonies such as the Presentation Theme and Coca Chewing Ceremony. This suggests that they were used (at least in part) as ritual items associated with shamans and midwives. Numerous modern and Prehispanic ethnographic accounts have documented the role of female shamans and curers on the north coast of Peru and offer us glimpses into cultural practices that can be traced back to Chimú and possibly even Moche time periods. In the modern-day Moche village community located near the ancient ruins of Huacas de Moche, John Gillin (1945) observed the practice of a prominent female shaman who specialized in *curandismo*. Gillin found two classes of *curanderas*: shamans who were more esoteric and focused on illnesses of the body and mind, and midwives who focused more narrowly on the health of pregnant women and children. The female shamans typically handled specialized (culture-bound) illnesses such as *El Susto* (when a person suffers from constant fear because the soul has left the body), *La Admiración* (intense emotion stemming from viewing a deformed person), and *El Ojeo* (the bad energy that results from being envied by someone else; i.e., the evil eye). Midwives assisted with childbirths and tended to women's prepartum and postpartum needs (Chavez 2000; Gillin 1945).

Fabiola Chavez Hualpa (2000) conducted a more recent and in-depth ethnographic study of *curanderas* in the provinces of Ayabaca and Huancabamba in the Department of Piura. She found that midwives do more than help with childbirth; they cover the entire vital reproductive cycle from menarche to menopause. The moon, a powerful feminine symbol and deity among the Moche, continues to play an important role today in the shamanic practices related to menstruation, conception, pregnancy, and childbirth—with different lunar phases relating to beneficial or ominous prognostications for women and their children (Chavez Hualpa 2000, 193, 207). Midwives are charged with helping women with healthy lactation, and they perform rituals to help cure "bad," "cold," or "sleepy" milk (Chavez Hualpa 2000, 212–214). They also attend to infants in the first years of life to help those who "cry in the womb" or those born with "delicate shadows" (Chavez Hualpa 2000, 214). Chavez Hualpa found that the main difference between midwives and shamans was their use of supernatural entities. The midwives cured illnesses and culture-bound syndromes that commonly afflicted women, while shamans were considered to be "master healers" who offered more elaborate therapies and directly called upon the supernatural world for help with their healing (Chavez Hualpa 2000).

This distinction between midwives and shamans helps us understand the differences between simple and elaborate figurines found at ancient Moche sites. The simple figurines depict connections with midwifery such as genitalia and infants and emphasize notions of femininity, procreation, and childrearing. In contrast, the elaborate figurines with identifiable individuals holding prescribed items contain links to supernatural elements and religious ceremonies. These individuals may have called upon supernatural forces during shamanic rituals related to metaphysical concerns affecting women and their particular needs.

Another connection between modern shamanic practices and Moche artifacts is with the use of pendants as ritual talismans. Chavez Hualpa (2000) found that the most widespread syndrome among women was *La Envidia*, when a pregnant woman becomes the victim of envy by a sterile woman. This can result in suffering during childbirth, disease or deformity in the child, or death of the mother. Women employed a variety of talismans to protect themselves and their babies but most commonly used a charmed pendant in the shape of a cross around their neck (Chavez Hualpa 2000, 182). Excavations in the domestic sectors of Pampa Grande and Huacas de Moche revealed significant quantities of miniature figurines with holes at the top so they could be suspended on cords and presumably worn as necklaces. Since Moche figurines show strong connections to notions of fertility and childbirth, they may have served a similar purpose as protective charms for expecting mothers. The continuity of practices between the Prehispanic and modern time periods suggests a long-standing tradition that has been altered by social and religious changes brought about by the introduction of Christianity in the sixteenth century (e.g., the use of crosses instead of figures).

FIGURES IN MOCHE ART

Female figurines and pendants are ubiquitous in Moche households across the North Coast and are typically encountered broken in trash deposits and hearths

FIGURE 5.3. *Left*: female figurines with hands on torso; *middle*: holding a baby; *right*: playing a drum. *Courtesy*, Museo Larco, Lima—Perú ML013849, ML013460, ML013296

(Limoges 1999; Ringberg 2008). The fact that they are so numerous and fragmentary suggests that they were used often and may have been deliberately broken as part of particular domestic rituals or shamanic interventions (Limoges 1999). Simple female figures are depicted without detailed headdresses or clothing and can be found in three poses: with their hands on their torsos, holding a baby, or playing a drum (figure 5.3). Fifty percent of the figurines analyzed indicated sex through visible genitalia, while another 20 percent indicated feminine gender through hairstyle, dress, or activity. In addition to the generic female figurines, three prominent female icons were identified during my analysis. Two have been previously identified and investigated: the Priestess and the Labretted Lady (Castillo Butters 2005; Castillo Butters and Rengifo 2008; Cordy-Collins 2001). The third icon is the Feline Headdress Female, for whom there is no precedent. She is typically depicted with a double-chamber rattle and is associated with coca chewing (table 5.1).

In contrast to female depictions on figurines, males are most commonly depicted on decorative whistles and reflect a distinct masculine identity embedded in warrior-related themes (table 5.2). Whistles are common in households at Huacas de Moche (Limoges 1999; Uceda Castillo and Armas 1998) and hinterland sites, such as Ciudad de Dios (Ringberg 2008). They depict scenes typical of statesponsored art related to public religion and rituals. Many of the whistle figures are musicians playing flutes and trumpets, similar to fineline representations of ceremonial processions (figure 5.4). This similarity suggests that they were used during public events and allowed nonelites to actively take part in ceremonies, thereby fostering a sense of inclusive identity for participants. Several supernatural beings are

TABLE 5.1. Counts of figurine types

Collection	Hands on Torso	Holding Baby	Playing Drum	Labretted Lady	Feline Headdress	Priestess	Pendants	Total
Moche Archive	33	11	0	11	2	6	0	63
Museo Larco	288	18	0	12	15	6	0	339
Huacas de Moche	96	11	3	0	7	0	24	141
Pampa Grande	20	0	7	16	0	0	6	49
San José de Moro	35	2	0	12	0	1	3	53
Total	472	42	10	51	24	13	33	645
Morgan (2009)	178	20	7	23	8	13	9	258

TABLE 5.2. Counts of whistle types

Collection	Supernatural	Warrior	Musician	Figure with Bag and Rope	Total
Moche Archive	12	8	5	3	28
Museo Larco	22	30	22	6	80
Huacas de Moche	9	19	9	5	42
Pampa Grande	0	0	0	0	0
San José de Moro	0	2	0	0	2
Total	43	59	36	14	152

FIGURE 5.4. Whistles depicting musicians. *Left*: pan flute (Museo Larco, Lima—Perú ML014792); *middle*: trumpet; *right*: back of whistle (artifact from the Huacas de Moche; author photo)

FIGURE 5.5. Whistles depicting supernatural beings. *Left*: Ai Aipec/Rayed Deity/ Warrior Priest (Museo Larco Lima—Perú ML014820); *middle*: Strombus Monster (artifact from the Huacas de Moche; author photo); *right*: Owl Deity playing a strombus trumpet (UCLA Moche Archive)

also represented on whistles, including the Strombus Monster, the Bird Priest, the Owl Deity, and Ai Aipec (Warrior/Sun Priest) (figure 5.5). The depiction of these popular and identifiable icons further supports the interpretation of whistles as accoutrements for use in public communitywide rituals and festivals. The Priestess was the only female depicted on whistles, and she is typically shown wearing high-status regalia and bearing symbols of the Presentation Theme. This theme in Moche fineline art depicts the culminating ceremony of the Warrior Narrative, where the blood of sacrificed prisoners is presented to Ai Aipec (Donnan 1976). It is possible that ceremonies such as these were performed in visible spaces, where community members could attend and watch while at the same time participating with whistles, rattles, drums, and other musical instruments.

THE PRIESTESS

The Priestess is the best-known female figure in Moche art (Castillo Butters 2005; Donnan and Castillo Butters 1992, 1994; Hocquenghem and Lyon 1980), and figurines depicting her iconic features have been found in museum collections and limited archaeological contexts. The Priestess is one of the few females with a prominent role in Moche public rituals. She is a key figure in the Presentation Theme, where she presents a disc and a goblet (presumably of blood) to Ai Aipec at the culmination of a series of ritual bloodlettings and sacrifices involving captured prisoners (Bourget 2001a, 2001b; Donnan 1978). She is also closely related to the moon and is often depicted with lunar imagery or riding in a crescent moon-shaped boat (McClelland 1990). The moon has a deep history in the Andes of being associated with menstruation, pregnancy, and childbirth and may indicate that the Priestess also served as an important deity related to the realm of women and reproduction.

In figurine form, she is depicted with or without a plumed headdress but always identified by two long braids, a goblet, and a large disc (figure 5.6). She is often shown with a snarling fanged mouth, suggesting that her role in Moche ritual involved transformation to a supernatural state. Most examples of the Priestess come from museum collections, but figurines have been found archaeologically in the elite residential sector at Galindo (Lockard 2005), in a grave on the north side of Huaca de la Luna (Morgan 2009), and above the chamber tomb of a Priestess burial at San José de Moro (Saldaña 2014).

Although figurines are most common in household contexts, fourteen figurines were included as burial offerings in Late Moche Period graves at San José de Moro. Of the skeletons whose sex and age could be determined, nine were child or infant graves, while four were adult females (figure 5.7). We have long suspected that figurines were important ritual items related to the female life cycle, but the discovery of figurines exclusively in female and child graves shows a strong connection between figurines and religious beliefs related to female-child life cycles and death. The inclusion of figurines in individual graves suggests that they were ritual items imbued with supernatural power specific to a particular person. Perhaps they were

FIGURE 5.6. Priestess figurines. *Left*: with plumes; *right*: without plumes. *Courtesy*, Museo Larco, Lima—Perú, ML013881, ML013933

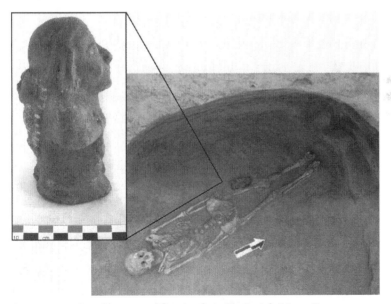

FIGURE 5.7. Female grave and figurine from San José de Moro. *Courtesy*, Archive Programa Arqueológico San José de Moro

FIGURE 5.8. Labretted Lady figurines. *Left*: playing drum; *right*: hands on torso. Artifacts from Pampa Grande; author photos

meant to protect the individual beyond the grave or honor the specific way they died, such as during childbirth or due to postnatal issues or illnesses.

THE LABRETTED LADY

The Labretted Lady was an important icon to the inhabitants of the northern Moche region, as evidenced by the large number of representations found on figurines in households and mortuary contexts. The conspicuous display of key identifiable features, such as the heart-shaped head, beaded jewelry, and labret piercing, points to the emergence of a new feminine cultural icon during the Late Moche Period that may have replaced earlier icons as the predominant figure associated with feminine shamanism (figure 5.8). The Labretted Lady is often depicted playing a large hand-held drum, which is a continuation of an earlier theme portrayed on non-labretted figurines. It is significant that men in Moche art are always shown playing flutes and trumpets, which provides an interesting juxtaposition to our current gender ideologies, where percussion is considered masculine and wind instruments are often associated with femininity (Donna Nash, personal communication, 2014). Female drummers continue to be prominent figures in the Lambayeque and Wari cultures and are often depicted in state-sponsored media such as fineware pottery and textiles (Cordy-Collins 2001; Rowe 1979).

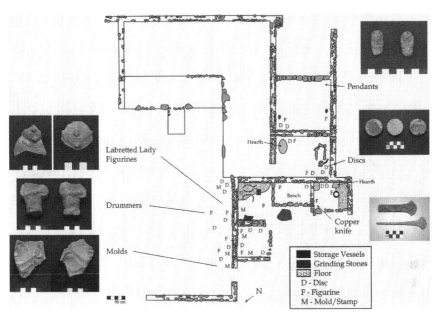

FIGURE 5.9. Ceramic production workshop and artifacts from Pampa Grande; author photos

The Labretted Lady has been found in mortuary contexts at San José de Moro (Cordy-Collins 2001), Cerro Campana (Ubbelohde-Doering 1966), and Úcupe (Bourget 2007), as well as in domestic contexts at Huaca Colorada (Swenson and Warner 2012). The most widespread documented use, however, comes from Pampa Grande, where these figurines were ubiquitously found in household contexts on the Southern Pediment (Johnson 2010). The fact that the Labretted Lady was only depicted on figurines at Pampa Grande and is absent from all state-produced art suggests that she was a cult icon used by nonelite inhabitants of the city, outside the realm of state-created and state-mandated religion. This is reinforced by the recovery of mold fragments for the production of Labretted Lady figurines in the middle-class domestic complexes at Pampa Grande, indicating that they were produced, distributed, and used by inhabitants of the Southern Pediment independent of the governing infrastructure (figure 5.9) (Johnson 2010).

At Pampa Grande, figurines were most often found in general-purpose living rooms, indicating that they were used alongside or in conjunction with other domestic activities (figure 5.10). The figurines were also found in the same contexts as spindle whorls and needles. Since weaving is typically associated with females in Moche iconography (Arsenault 1991) and in burials (Donnan and McClelland

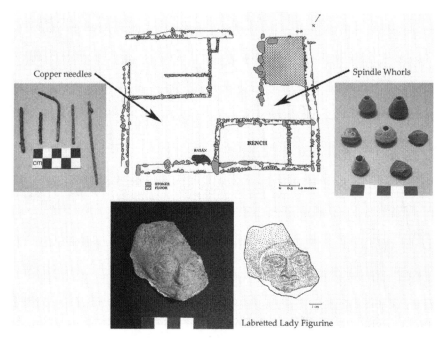

FIGURE 5.10. Living room with figurine fragments and spindle whorls; author photos

1997), this association suggests that they were used by women and were important cultural icons linked to the domestic sphere and specific feminine interests. In later periods, the role of the Labretted Lady shifted to a more prominent position in the iconography of the Lambayeque (Sicán) culture, signifying a further elevation in status for this iconic figure during the Late Intermediate Period (Cordy-Collins 2001). In addition, the labret jewelry and loose hair continued to be a symbol of powerful female identity and were used to signal high status and rulership by *Capullanas* during the late Prehispanic and Colonial time periods (Fernández Villegas 1989; Pizarro 1571).

The pervasiveness of Labretted Lady figurines at Pampa Grande provides evidence for independent specialized production of nonutilitarian items with important cultural messages attached to them (Costin 1996, 1998). Figurines were used and produced in household settings and reflect the desires and concerns of the producers, not the state superstructure. The conspicuous display of key identifiable features, such as the heart-shaped head, beaded jewelry, and labret piercing, points to the emergence of a feminine cultural icon that played an important role in gender identities and domestic ritual (Johnson 2010). These items were produced and distributed at the household level and were likely used for personal rituals related to the female life cycle. They may have been used by midwives attending to women and infants in their homes or as part of individualistic rites performed by the women themselves in response to specific needs, wants, or fears.

THE FELINE HEADDRESS FEMALE

During my analysis, I came across a previously uninvestigated female icon with a set of identifiable features depicted on household figurines. This female is found depicted on both figurines and figurative stirrup-spout bottles and is symbolically linked to rituals related to childbirth and coca chewing. The fact that this icon is found in everyday domestic contexts and is associated with ritual childbirth vessels suggests a possible ritual institution in Moche society related to female concerns. The figure has several key identifiable features, most notably a headdress consisting of a horizontal band with a feline head on the front. Variants of the headdress include multiple feline heads or feline paws on each side of the band (figure 5.11). Felines are one of the most common animals invoked in Amerindian rituals and often communicate with shamans (Alva 2000; Stone 2011). They also often merge with humans during trances or hallucinogenic experiences brought about by the use of medicinal plants such as coca. In addition, modern-day *curanderas* employ jungle animals like the puma to cure and prevent *La Llacama*, or postpartum depression and illness (Chavez Hualpa 2000). Pumas are considered strong animals charged with mythological power, and eating the meat of the puma will infuse the woman with its power. Since the meat is scarce, *curanderas* often keep the bones of pumas for use in cooking or bathing (Chavez Hualpa 2000, 211).

The Feline Headdress Female also typically carries a double-chamber rattle with a rope and less frequently is depicted holding a lime container and stick (figure 5.11). Both the feline headdress and the lime container are also associated with male and female individuals in figurative representations on stirrup-spout bottles found at the Museo Larco. The females are shown with long dresses and loose hair, holding a lime container in one hand and a rattle in the other. Males are shown with short tunics, holding lime containers or gourds and a variety of different types of rattles. In addition, feline heads and paws and lime containers are common symbols in the Coca Chewing Ceremony in Moche fineline art; however, to date, no female figures have been identified in depictions of that particular ceremony. Coca was one of the most sacred plants in ancient South America and was used by curers for healing purposes and by shamans to enter trances and transfigure into felines (Alva 2000). Shamans have the power to converse with or take on the attributes of jaguars

FIGURE 5.11. Feline Headdress Female figurines. *Left*: holding a child; *middle:* holding a lime container, spoon, and double-chamber rattle; *right*: holding a rope and double-chamber rattle. *Courtesy*, Museo Larco, Lima—Perú ML013448, ML013274, ML013308

or pumas, which are considered to be the most powerful animals on the continent and a general symbol of divinity.

At the sites of Huacas de Moche and Cerro Mayal, several figurines depicting the Feline Headdress Female were uncovered archaeologically in the ceramic workshops and general household contexts (Jackson 2008; Uceda Castillo and Armas 1998). A figurine depicting the feline headdress was also discovered in a grave at the western foot of Huaca de la Luna as part of the Uhle excavations (Morgan 2009). In addition, this grave contained two figurines of females holding babies and two figurines of seated individuals holding lime containers and sticks. This association further suggests that the Feline Headdress Female was connected with both childbirth and coca-chewing rituals.

In the Urban Zone at the Huacas de Moche, figurines with feline headdresses have been discovered in several general household contexts. In addition, the Feline Headdress Female was found in significant quantities in the ceramic production workshop associated with Architectural Complex 35 (figure 5.12). This building was a mixed-use structure that served both domestic and production purposes. It was likely inhabited by an extended family that shared production responsibilities for a variety of ceramic objects, including figurines. This workshop is believed to have been part of a much larger "potters' *barrio* complex" that may have included several workshops (Uceda Castillo and Armas 1997; 1998, 107). The workshop was composed of nine main rooms, including one to mix clay with water in large storage vessels, one to form the ceramics using molds, one for drying completed forms,

FIGURE 5.12. Feline Headdress Female figurines from CA-35 ceramic workshop at Huacas de Moche; author photo

and one for elaborating the pottery with applications. Over 1,000 mold fragments were uncovered for making various vessel types, such as figurines, trumpets, stirrup-spout bottles, face-neck jars, and applications. In addition to the ceramic forms just mentioned, the workshop produced whistles, ocarinas, pendants, spindle whorls, jars, and rattles. Two burials discovered in the complex revealed individuals with professional traumas related to pottery production evident on their bones and large amounts of high-quality items in their graves. This suggests that the potters of the Huacas de Moche were part of the middle class who also "had some control over the Moche ideological and cosmological realm through pottery production" (Uceda Castillo and Armas 1998, 107).

FIGURE 5.13. Birthing bowl. *Courtesy*, Museo Larco, Lima—Perú ML004355

FIGURINES, SEX, AND CHILDBIRTH

At the site of Cerro Mayal in the neighboring Chicama Valley, the double-chamber rattle and rope held by the Feline Headdress Female has been found associated with birthing bowls in the ceramic workshop (figure 5.13) (Jackson 2008). Two mold fragments for the production of birthing bowls contained incised drawings of rattles on the exterior. Margaret A. Jackson suggests that the rattle is conceptually linked to giving birth either through the umbilical tail of the rope or through the shamanistic connection to fertility rituals. She goes on to identify the rattle image as a "visual vocabulary unit" used to symbolize an abstract cultural reference to the act of childbirth or rituals related to pregnancy and childbirth (Jackson 2008, 103). This indirect link between the Feline Headdress Female and birth rituals provides yet another link between the use of figurines in rites related to fertility and childbirth. The Feline Headdress Female may have even served as a prominent religious specialist (or may represent a class of religious specialists) attending to female-centric concerns, practices, and medical procedures. Other carvings on the outside of figurine molds provide us with important associations not intrinsically visible

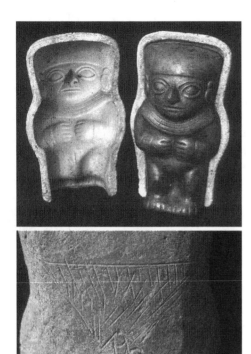

FIGURE 5.14. Incised genitalia on a figurine mold. *Courtesy*, UCLA Moche Archive

in the symbolism of the objects. The most common carving found associated with figurines is female genitalia (sometimes with male genitalia in tandem), indicating that figurines were symbolically associated with sex and procreation (figure 5.14).

The association of the rattle and rope with childbirth and the figurines with procreation paints a dynamic picture of the roles these objects played in Moche daily life. They were simple representations with wide-reaching social implications. They reflect the lack of control Moche women must have felt over the reproductive process and the incorporation of tamable supernatural forces into the realm of feminine concerns and ideals. At the same time, they reflect the strength and power females had as the source of new life and the control female icons like the Feline Headdress Female had over a dangerous and mysterious realm.

CHANGING FEMININE IDENTITIES IN THE LATE MOCHE PERIOD

Moche figurines were one of the main avenues for the artistic expression of feminine identity and reflect female prerogatives, ideologies, and concerns. The Late

Moche Period marks an important transition in gender relations, with high-ranking female religious figures becoming more prominent in Moche art and visual culture. This can be seen in the disappearance of male figures in domestic contexts and the elevated importance of female icons such as the Priestess and the Labretted Lady. This period also marks the elevation of female status on the north coast of Peru as a whole, which can be seen in the increasing frequency of female depictions on ceramics (McClelland et al. 2007), the shift to female sacrificial victims in ritual contexts (Swenson 2012; Swenson and Warner 2012), and the emergence of prominent female dynasties such as the Priestess of San José de Moro (Castillo Butters 2005; Castillo Butters and Rengifo 2008) and the Labretted Lady of Pampa Grande (Cordy-Collins 2001; Johnson 2010).

Figurines were distributed locally in Moche cities and addressed the needs and desires of the popular class. Figurines allowed women to engage in activities and rituals pertinent to their unique concerns that were not addressed in the more prominent ceremonies carried out at the temples (Johnson 2010). Monumental media reflects the cultural ideals of the ruling minority and serves to legitimize the political and social ideologies essential to the maintenance of power. In contrast, household objects reflect gender and domestic ideologies of the lower- and middle-class majority, highlighting choices and concerns experienced as part of everyday life. The ubiquity of figurine fragments in Moche households suggests that these items were used frequently and may have even been deliberately broken as part of the rituals in which they were used (Johnson 2010; Limoges 1999; Ringberg 2008). They were likely used as talismans for protection from supernatural forces believed to be harmful to women who were trying to become pregnant, were currently with child, or had recently given birth. In addition, the identifiable female icons may have represented an institution of female *shamans* with special knowledge and abilities beyond those of traditional midwives. The iconic figurines likely had greater ritual significance and may have been used in limited, perhaps more specialized rituals. These ancient practices may have been similar to the ones carried out by modern-day female *shamans* who specialize in the treatment of culture-bound illnesses resulting from fears of supernatural forces.

CONCLUSION

Females are virtually absent from public art, but their absence does not necessarily indicate a lack of importance in Moche society. Moche women appropriated elements of the state religion into their own ritual realm, ones that were relevant to their personal daily experiences. In addition, the production of Labretted Lady figurines in the middle-class households of Pampa Grande suggests that the residents engaged in the production of artifacts with important ritual significance outside the purview of state-sponsored workshops. Women developed, produced, and disseminated cult religious objects for use in private, personalized rituals related to daily feminine experiences and needs.

Although Moche society valued masculinity and ferocity, females would have been honored as the givers of life and the source of new warriors. It is no surprise, then, that figurines served as important symbols of fertility, conception, and midwifery linked to the very notion of femininity in Moche society. The Feline Headdress Female and the Labretted Lady were powerful women who were revered for their knowledge and shamanic abilities in a realm typically fraught with mystery and fear. The social messages embedded in these household objects emphasize the female power to give and protect life, reinforcing the strength and significance of female religious specialists. In a world where women were mostly excluded from prominent rituals and events, figurines express important messages with a wide distribution and daily social penetrance. These subtle messages would have affected the beliefs and practices of all community members, reaffirming social roles and gender ideologies while also serving as a vehicle for long-term changes in both female identities and social roles.

ACKNOWLEDGMENTS

I would like to thank Luis Jaime Castillo Butters, Christopher Donnan, Santiago Uceda Castillo, Nadia Gamarra, Carol Rojas, and Ulla Holmquist for helping me gather the figurine data for this project. I would also like to thank the National Science Foundation, Cotsen Institute of Archaeology, UCLA Department of Anthropology, and Institute of American Cultures for helping fund my research at Pampa Grande. Finally, I would like to thank all the wonderful people who helped me in the field and beyond. Carol Rojas and Carlos Wester were invaluable co-directors in the field, and my fieldwork would not have been possible without the hard work of my field and lab assistants Ana Sofía Linares, Mayra Frausto, John Dietler, Colleen Zori, David Oshige, Barbara Carbajal, Rebecca Rudolf, Ursula Kruger, Jerome Howard, Jesús Rubio, Nestor Suxe, Luís Rubio, Etmanuel Ramirez, Rolando Flores, Ernesto Santoyo, Salvador Rubio, Agustín Rubio, and Demetrio de la Cruz.

REFERENCES

Alva, Walter. 2000. "Sacerdotes, Shamanes y Curanderos en la Cultura Moche." In *Shamán: La Búsqueda*, edited by Walter Alva, Luis Hurtado, Mario Polia, and Fabiola Chavez, 23–44. Cordoba, Spain: Imprenta San Pablo.

Arsenault, Daniel. 1991. "The Representation of Women in Moche Iconography." In *The Archaeology of Gender: Proceedings of the Twenty-Second Annual Conference of the Archaeological Association of the University of Calgary*, edited by Dale Walde and Noreen D. Willows, 313–326. Calgary, Alberta: University of Calgary Archaeological Association.

Ashmore, Wendy, and Richard R. Wilk. 1988. "Household and Community in the Mesoamerican Past." In *Household and Community in the Mesoamerican Past*, edited by Richard R. Wilk and Wendy Ashmore, 1°27. Albuquerque: University of New Mexico Press.

Bawden, Garth. 1982. "Community Organization Reflected by the Household: A Study of Pre-Columbian Social Dynamics." *Journal of Field Archaeology* 9: 165–181.

Blanton, Richard E. 1994. *Houses and Households: A Comparative Study*. New York: Plenum.

Bourget, Steve. 2001a. "Children and Ancestors: Ritual Practices at the Moche Site of Huaca de la Luna, North Coast of Peru." In *Ritual Sacrifice in Ancient Peru*, edited by Elizabeth P. Benson and Anita G. Cook, 93–119. Austin: University of Texas Press.

Bourget, Steve. 2001b. "Rituals of Sacrifice: Its Practice at Huaca de la Luna and Its Representation in Moche Iconography." In *Moche Art and Archaeology in Ancient Peru*, edited by Joanne Pillsbury, 89–109. New Haven, CT: Yale University Press.

Bourget, Steve. 2007. "Proyecto Huaca El Pueblo Complejo Arqueológico Ucupe Investigaciones Arqueológicas del Periodo Intermedio Temprano del Valle de Zaña, Costa Norte del Perú." La Libertad: Unpublished final report submitted to the Instituto Nacional de Cultura.

Castillo Butters, Luis Jaime. 2005. "Las Señoras de San José de Moro: Rituales funerarios de mujeres de élite en la costa norte del Perú." In *Divina y humana, La mujer en los antiguos Perú y México*, edited by Marta Castañeda Landázuri and Guillermo Astete, 18–29. Lima: Ministerio de Educación.

Castillo Butters, Luis Jaime, and Carlos E. Rengifo. 2008. "Identidades funerarias femeninas y poder ideológico en las sociedades Mochicas." In *Los Señores de los Reinos de la Luna*, edited by Krzysztof Makowski, 2–33. Colección de Arte y Tesoros del Perú. Lima: Banco de Crédito del Perú.

Chavez Hualpa, Fabiola. 2000. "Soñadoras, Terapeutas y Carismáticas de los Andes del Norte: Un Perfil Antropológico." In *Shamán: La Búsqueda*, edited by Walter Alva, Luis Hurtado, Mario Polia, and Fabiola Chavez, 163–224. Cordoba, Spain: Imprenta San Pablo.

Cordy-Collins, Alana. 2001. "Labretted Ladies: Foreign Women in Northern Moche and Lambayeque Art." In *Moche Art and Archaeology in Ancient Peru*, edited by Joanne Pillsbury, 247–257. New Haven, CT: Yale University Press.

Costin, Cathy L. 1996. "Exploring the Relationship between Gender and Craft in Complex Societies: Methodological and Theoretical Issues of Gender Attribution." In *Gender and Archaeology*, edited by Rita P. Wright, 111–132. Philadelphia: University of Pennsylvania Press.

Costin, Cathy L. 1998. "Introduction: Craft and Social Identity." In *Craft and Social Identity: Archaeological Papers of the American Anthropological Association*, edited by Cathy L. Costin and Rita P. Wright, 3–16. Malden, MA: Wiley-Blackwell.

Cruz Villegas, Jacobo. 1982. *Catacaos: Origen y Evolucion Historica de Catacaos*. Piura, Peru: Centro de Investigación y Promoción del Campesinado.

Deetz, James. 1982. "Households: Ethnographic Households and Archaeological Interpretation." *American Behavioral Scientist* 25: 717–724.

DeMarrais, Elizabeth, Luis Jaime Castillo Butters, and Timothy Earle. 1996. "Ideology, Materialization, and Power Strategies." *Current Anthropology* 37: 15–31.

Donnan, Christopher B. 1976. *Moche Art and Iconography*. Los Angeles: UCLA Latin American Center Publications.

Donnan, Christopher B. 1978. *Moche Art of Peru: Pre-Columbian Symbolic Communication*. Los Angeles: UCLA Fowler Museum of Cultural History.

Donnan, Christopher B., and Luis Jaime Castillo Butters. 1992. "Finding the Tomb of the Moche Priestess." *Archaeology* 45 (6): 38–42.

Donnan, Christopher B., and Luis Jaime Castillo Butters. 1994. "Excavaciones de tumbas de sacerdotisas en San José de Moro, Jequetepeque." In *Moche: Propuestas y perspectivas [Actas del primer coloquio sobre la cultura Moche, Trujillo 12 al 16 de abril de 1993]*, edited by Santiago Uceda Castillo and Elías Mujica, 415–424. Lima: Travaux de l'Institut Francais d'Etudes Andines.

Donnan, Christopher B., and Donna McClelland, eds. 1997. *The Pacatnamú Papers, vol. 2: The Moche Period*. Los Angeles: UCLA Fowler Museum of Cultural History.

Fernández Villegas, Oswaldo. 1989. "Las Capullanas: Mujeres curacas de Piura siglos XVI–XVIII." *Buletín de Lima* 66: 11, 43–50, Peru.

Flannery, Kent V. 1976. "Contextual Analysis of Ritual Paraphernalia from Formative Oaxaca." In *The Early Mesoamerican Village*, edited by Kent V. Flannery, 333–344. Walnut Creek, CA: Left Coast Press.

Gero, Joan M. 2001. "Field Knots and Ceramic Beaus: Interpreting Gender in the Peruvian Early Intermediate Period." In *Gender in Pre-Hispanic America*, edited by Cecilia Kline, 15–55. Washington, DC: Dumbarton Oaks.

Gillin, John. 1945. *Moche: A Peruvian Costal Community*. Publication 3. Washington, DC: Smithsonian Institution, Institute of Social Anthropology.

Halperin, Christina T. 2014. *Maya Figurines: Intersections between State and Household*. Austin: University of Texas Press.

Hastorf, Christine. 1991. "Gender, Space, and Food in Prehistory." In *Engendering Archaeology: Women and Prehistory*, edited by Joan M. Gero and Margaret W. Conkey, 135–188. Oxford: Blackwell.

Hendon, Julia A. 1996. "Archaeological Approaches to the Organization of Domestic Labor: Household Practice and Domestic Relations." *Annual Review of Anthropology* 25: 45–61.

Hendon, Julia A. 1997. "Women's Work, Women's Space, and Women's Status among the Classic-Period Maya Elite at Copan, Honduras." In *Women in Prehistory: North America and Mesoamerica*, edited by Cheryl Claassen and Rosemary Joyce, 33–46. Philadelphia: University of Pennsylvania Press.

Hendon, Julia A. 2009. *Houses in a Landscape: Memory and Everyday Life in Mesoamerica*. Durham, NC: Duke University Press.

Hendon, Julia A., Rosemary Joyce, and Jeanne Lopiparo. 2013. *Material Relations: The Marriage Figurines of Prehispanic Honduras*. Boulder: University Press of Colorado.

Hocquenghem, Anne-Marie, and Patricia J. Lyon. 1980. "A Class of Anthropomorphic Supernatural Females in Moche Iconography." *Ñawpa Pacha: Journal of Andean Archaeology* 19: 27–48.

Hubert, Erell. 2010. "Fonctions et significations des figurines mochicas de la vallée de Santa, côte nord du Pérou." In *De l'archéologie analytique à l'archéologie sociale*, edited by Claude Chapdelaine, Adrian L. Burke, and Brad Loewen, 243–264. Quebec: Recherches Amérindiennes.

Jackson, Margaret A. 2008. *Moche Art and Visual Culture in Ancient Peru*. Albuquerque: University of New Mexico Press.

Janusek, John W. 2004. *Identity and Power in the Ancient Andes*. New York: Routledge.

Johnson, Ilana. 2010. "Households and Social Organization at the Late Moche Site of Pampa Grande, Peru." PhD dissertation, University of California, Los Angeles.

Limoges, Sophie. 1999. *Etude Morpho-stylistique et Contextuelle des Figurines du Site Moche, Perou*. Montreal: Université de Montreal.

Lockard, Gregory D. 2005. "Political Power and Economy at the Archaeological Site of Galindo, Moche Valley, Peru." PhD dissertation, University of New Mexico, Albuquerque.

Marcus, Joyce. 2000. "Towards an Archaeology of Communities." In *The Archaeology of Communities: A New World Perspective*, edited by Marcello A. Canuto and Jason Yaeger, 231–242. New York: Routledge.

McClelland, Donna. 1990. "A Maritime Passage from Moche to Chimú." In *Northern Dynasties: Kingship and Statecraft in the Kingdom of Chimor*, edited by Michael E. Moseley and Alana Cordy-Collins, 75–106. Washington, DC: Dumbarton Oaks.

McClelland, Donna, Donald McClelland, and Christopher B. Donnan. 2007. *Moche Fineline Painting from San José de Moro*. Los Angeles: UCLA Fowler Museum of Cultural History.

Morgan, Alexandra. 2009. *The Pottery Figurines of Pre-Columbian Peru, vol. 1: The Figurines of the North Coast*. British Archaeological Reports S1941. Oxford: Archeopress.

Pizarro, Pedro. 1571. *Relación del descubrimiento y conquista de los reinos del Perú*. Translated by Guillerma Lohmann Villena (1986). Colleción Clásicos Peruanos. Lima: Pontificia Universidad Católica Perú.

Ringberg, Jennifer E. 2008. "Figurines, Household Rituals, and the Use of Domestic Space." In *Arqueología Mochica nuevas enfoques: actas del primero congreso internacional de jóvenes investigadores de la cultura Moche*, edited by Luis Jaime Castillo Butters, Hélène Bernier, Gregory Lockard, and Julio Rucabado, 341–357. Lima: Pontificia Universidad Católica del Perú.

Rowe, Anne P. 1979. "Textile Evidence for Huari Music." *Textile Museum Journal* 18: 5–18.

Saldaña, Julio. 2014. "Proyecto Arqueologico San José de Moro Informe Técnico 2014." Edited by Luis Jaime Castillo Butters. La Libertad: Unpublished final report submitted to the Instituto Nacional de Cultura.

Shimada, Izumi. 1994. *Pampa Grande and the Mochica Culture*. Austin: University of Texas Press.

Smith, Monica L. 2003. "Introduction: The Social Construction of Ancient Cities." In *The Social Construction of Ancient Cities*, edited by Monica L. Smith, 1–35. Washington, DC: Smithsonian Institution Press.

Stone, Rebecca R. 2011. *The Jaguar Within: Shamanic Trance in Ancient Central and South American Art*. Austin: University of Texas Press.

Swenson, Edward. 2012. "Warfare, Gender, and Sacrifice in Jequetepeque Peru." *Latin American Antiquity* 23 (2): 167–193.

Swenson, Edward, and John P. Warner. 2012. "Crucibles of Power: Forging Copper and Forging Subjects at the Moche Ceremonial Center of Huaca Colorada, Peru." *Journal of Anthropological Archaeology* 31 (3): 314–333.

Tringham, Ruth E. 1991. "Households with Faces: The Challenge of Gender in Prehistoric Household Architectural Remains." In *Engendering Archaeology: Women and Prehistory*, edited by Joan M. Gero and Margaret W. Conkey, 93–131. Oxford: Basil Blackwell.

Tringham, Ruth E. 1994. "Engendered Places in Prehistory." *Gender, Place, and Culture* 1: 169–203.

Ubbelohde-Doering, Heinrich. 1966. *On the Royal Highways of the Inca: Archaeological Treasures of Ancient Peru*. New York: Praeger.

Uceda Castillo, Santiago, and José Armas. 1997. "Los talleres alfareros en el centro urbano Moche." In *Investigaciones en la Huaca de la Luna 1995*, edited by Santiago

Uceda Castillo, Elías Mujica, and Ricardo Morales, 93–104. Trujillo, Peru: Facultad de Ciencias Sociales, Universidad Nacional de la Libertad.

Uceda Castillo, Santiago, and José Armas. 1998. "An Urban Pottery Workshop at the Site of Moche." In *Andean Ceramics: Technology, Organization, and Approaches*, edited by Izumi Shimada, 91–110. MASCA Research Papers in Science and Archaeology, Supplement to vol. 15. Philadelphia: University of Pennsylvania, Museum of Anthropology and Archaeology.

Wilk, Richard R., and Robert McC. Netting. 1984. "Households' Changing Form and Function." In *Households: Comparative and Historical Studies of the Domestic Group*, edited by Robert McC. Netting, Richard R. Wilk, and Eric J. Arnould, 1–28. Berkeley: University of California Press.

Wilk, Richard R., and William L. Rathje. 1982. "Household Archaeology." *American Behavioral Scientist* 6: 617–639.

Zeidler, James A. 2000. "Gender, Status, and Community in Early Formative Valdivia Society." In *The Archaeology of Communities: A New World Perspective*, edited by Marcello A. Canuto and Jason Yaeger, 161–181. New York: Routledge.

6

Pillars of the Community

*Moche Ceremonial Architecture as Symbolic Household at
Huaca Colorada, Jequetepeque Valley, Peru*

GILES SPENCE MORROW

The sacred might dwell at home. Given the pivotal place dwellings have in the human
experience and the capacity of our houses to shelter both mundane tasks and complicated meanings, it is not surprising that people make their dwellings into sacred
homes. What is surprising are the elaborate and diverse ways in which we do this.

JERRY D. MOORE (2012, 179)

This volume seeks to explore the variation of ancient domestic life on the north
coast of Peru by focusing on the understudied aspects of quotidian routines through
what has been described as "household archaeology" (Douglass and Gonlin 2012;
Gillespie 2007; Nash 2009). In this chapter, an analysis of the ritual practices at
the ceremonial center of Huaca Colorada in the Jequetepeque Valley permits a
critical reassessment of conventional definitions of the house and "domestic" life.
I consider at what scale the concept of "household" can be applied to the study of
ancient lifeways, of which we have little more than temporally distant ethnographic
comparisons to serve as conceptual foundations. Although the monumental architecture of the north coast of Peru is disproportionately overinvestigated, I argue in
this chapter that there is value in approaching what we define as ceremonial structures from a household perspective, to reinterpret those spaces contained within
monumental or "ritualized" architecture as symbolic houses and in direct relationship to more prosaic domestic contexts (Gillespie 2007). Questioning the assumed
opposition of "house" and "temple" in the Moche context also serves to culturally

DOI: 10.5876/9781646420919.c006

contextualize the application of "commoner" and "elite" as heuristics to ancient Moche individuals and their spaces in a way that avoids the imposition of contemporary constructions of status, class, and privilege. Thus the use of these seemingly fundamental categories should not be applied without a critical examination of our definitions of the assumed relationships between elites and commoners within the ancient community under investigation.

In critiquing ahistorical models of elite-commoner interactions, it is still likely that there was some degree of resistance to centralized power among the Moche as based on contemporary analogies. However, it is equally possible that people's relationship to differing institutions of authority defined positions in life and attachment to place that were accepted as such without coercion and aided by participation in ritualized activities. In other words, the self-identifications, dependencies, and obligations of different status groups—often glossed simplistically as elite or commoner—varied from culture to culture and must be contextualized within historically specific conceptual schemes and structures of practice. In her recent study of the conceptual dialogue between vernacular and monumental architecture in the Maya Lowlands during the Terminal Classic Period (800–950 CE), Christina Halperin (2017, 114) describes the mutual influence between each architectural category and the social statuses they reference, suggesting that commoner and elite architectural styles likely informed each other reciprocally. In light of this argument, an analysis of elite residential occupation and the possible "domestic" qualities of their monumental structures must be taken into consideration, paying attention to both the convergences and differences between high-status and commoner residential spaces. Although beyond the scope of the current discussion, such a comparison should include an examination of the types of foods that were served, materials produced, and the assumed roles that were performed by both elite and common participants within the greater community.

For instance, performing and assuming the responsibilities of an elite identity among the Moche may have amounted to accepting a death sentence. This is suggested by the discovery of portrait vessels of individually identifiable authority figures at Huacas de Moche depicted in other ceramics as captives ready for sacrifice later in life, likely after a generation of rule (Donnan 2004; Uceda Castillo 2001b). Assuming that "elite" leaders likely served as conduits of communication with the cosmos through the medium of sacrifice, they thus constituted a vital component of the larger social collective. Unlike, then, Feudal barons in Medieval Europe or members of parliament (but perhaps closer to idealized representations of Roman and Chinese emperors), Moche elites were viscerally committed to the continuity of the community as living stewards rather than simply as expropriating "lords." If members of an elite household were perceived as deified ritual practitioners, then it stands to reason that the lordly residence in question would be freighted with heightened symbolic meaning. This symbolism no doubt influenced conceptions of home, place, identity, and cosmos as part of an ongoing dialogue between vernacular and monumental expressions of these ideals. In other words, conceptions and experience of the quotidian—for different status groups—can only be properly understood in terms of their convergence or contradictions with different ideologies of life and emplacedness, including culturally specific notions of the home. As interlocutors between their community and cosmic, ontological others, the ceremonial arenas of Moche elites were likely perceived as the ultimate place of origins, becoming, and life itself. For many Moche, then, a sense of home, community, and well-being—qualities often ascribed to the private house in the modern context—may have been attributed more to the residences and ceremonial arenas of lordly ritual specialists than to the often transient and makeshift vernacular dwellings documented in certain regions of the Moche world, including the Jequetepeque Valley (see Duke, this volume). If Moche elites appear to have been invested with ensuring the well-being and continuity of the society of which they were a part, then such roles no doubt shaped conceptions and experiences of identity and "rootedness."

In the following analysis I examine rituals of architectural renovation and sacrifice at Huaca Colorada in the Jequetepeque Valley of Peru not as exotic or aberrant rites but as fundamental to local constructions of (imagined) communities and identity (Hobsbawm and Ranger 1983). Seasonal and cyclical rites of architectural construction appear to have reaffirmed bonds of community in relation to a specific sacred locale—in a way that seems to have created a large collective "home" defined here as a place of cooperation and belonging.

SYMBOLIC AUTHORITY AND THE POWER OF THE HOUSE

During the 1987 rescue excavations of the remains of a heavily looted Moche tomb at Huaca Rajada near Sipán in the Reque Valley, a remarkable copper scepter was discovered, unique in its form and manufacture. Decorated with an elaborately detailed architectural model of an open gable-roof structure, the building depicted was fringed on four sides by a portico embellished with sculpted war clubs, or *porras* (Alva and Donnan 1993, 48–49). There is little doubt that this singular artifact served as a rather unambiguous emblem of office. The associated grave goods further indicated that the original occupant held a privileged status in life, perhaps on par with that of the Señores de Sipán (Alva 1999, 26; 2012).

An unusual aspect of this particular architectural depiction is that its roof line was embellished with miniature metal heads bearing horn-like projections, a stylistic representation not known to have a correlate in full-scale architecture elsewhere (Wiersema 2010). Months after the scepter was salvaged, fragmented ceramic war club decorations bearing the same horned human heads were found in closely associated architectural fill (Alva 1999, 30–34). The proximity of the scepter to these full-scale decorative elements suggests a strong correlation between the represented and actual ceremonial architecture once found atop the huaca. As such, this suggests that these adornments had been destroyed at or before the time of the deceased's internment, possibly as a means of entombing symbolic architectural elements with the person most closely associated with the structure; perhaps the unusual *porras* themselves even served as portraits of the interred (Alva 2012).

The gable-roof architectural spaces depicted in the Sipán scepter and on numerous ceramic vessels are widely accepted as representations of architectural complexes that have been uncovered archaeologically on the summits of many huacas across the north coast of Peru (Shimada 1994; Wiersema 2010). With mounting evidence that these structures served both ceremonial and residential functions for elite members of Moche society, I argue that the visual shorthand of a simple open gable-roof structure was a highly charged symbol of the archetypical household and closely associated divine authority often shown seated beneath these iconic structures (Bourget 2003; Chapdelaine 2006; Chapdelaine et al. 2003; Franco et al. 1994, 2003; Wiersema 2010, 2015) (figure. 6.1). In concert with the great wealth of iconographic depictions of what are assumed to represent religious activities found in Moche ceramics, excavation of the ceremonial complexes found atop adobe huacas across the North Coast supports the notion that these monuments served as the loci of elaborate ceremonial activities that may have mirrored domestic ideals or ideologies of home and territory (for an exploration of elite residences as archetypical households in the Andes, see Kolata's [1996] Weberian analysis of the Andean city) (Benson 2012; Bourget 2001, 2006, Donnan 1982; Hocquenghem 1987).

Recent research directed by Edward R. Swenson, Jorge Y. Chiguala, Francisco Seoane, and John P. Warner has investigated precisely such a structure at the summit of Huaca Colorada in the Jequetepeque Valley, excavations that have provided clear evidence of socially regenerative ritual performances centered on communal efforts of reconstruction (Swenson 2012, 2015, 2018a, 2018b). An analysis of the complex architectural biography of Huaca Colorada suggests that the structures at the peaks of huacas symbolized corporate affinity that embodied the connection between the wider community and a deified elite. This symbolic bond was reinforced physically through incorporative acts of construction as well as human and animal sacrifice linked to dedicatory and termination rites of architectonic renewal (Herva 2010; Spence Morrow 2018; Spence Morrow and Swenson 2018; Swenson

FIGURE 6.1. Various depictions of gable-roof structures from Moche ceramic vessels from the Berlin Ethnological Museum: (*a*) VA18282, (*b*) VA 17637, and Museo Larco—Lima, Perú (*c*) ML002875, (*d*) ML031752, (*e*) ML002892

2015, 2018a, 2018b; Swenson et al. 2011, 2012, 2013, 2015, 2017). As a form of symbolic household reproduction, I argue that acts of construction and renovation would have extended kin-based ideologies of home and identity across generations through an embodied process of "cultural construction and contestation" (Pauketat and Alt 2005). These renovation histories clearly suggest that architectural renewal was fundamental to the ideological construction of society and likely tied to intertwined agricultural and cosmological cycles that connected social, religious, political, and environmental aspects of daily life (Prieto Burmester 2008). By housing the ruling elite at the peak of huaca structures, even if on a temporary, rotational, or purely symbolic basis, I suggest that the entire monument symbolized an idealized central house. Identification with a deified authority figure thus served to legitimize and incorporate individuals into their community through regular participation in feasting and ritualized public activities.

Claude Lévi-Strauss's (1982) concept of the *société à maison*, or "house society," refers to communities documented ethnographically that ascribe central importance to material and conceptual aspects of the house in expressing group identity and organizing social relations. A number of archaeologists have recently applied this perspective to their interpretations of past social organization (Beck 2007; Driessen 2010; Gillespie 2000a, 2000b; González-Ruibal 2006; Joyce and Gillespie 2000; Weismantel 2014). In a similar manner, I propose that the Moche conception of the domestic sphere may have incorporated and extended beyond our notion of the quotidian to align more closely to Lévi-Strauss's (1982) conceptualization of the *maison*. Within his problematically reductive categorization, Lévi-Strauss defines the *maison* as "a corporate body holding an estate made up of both material and immaterial wealth, which perpetuates itself through the transmission of its name, its goods, and its titles down a real or imaginary line, considered legitimate as long as this continuity can express itself in the language of kinship or of affinity and, most often, of both" (Lévi-Strauss 1982, 174).

Following Susan D. Gillespie's (2000a, 3) consideration of the material markers of house societies as inextricably linked to their temporal and spatial dimensions, a key function of the house is to "anchor people in space and to link them in time." House societies as defined by Lévi-Strauss are self-defined and reproduced through particular narratives of history that often rely on architectural biographies. The built environment materializes social memory and generational continuity that transcends changes in familial alliances, household membership, or leadership structures It is this sense of temporality that serves to "embody a collective memory about the past, a reference to origins that often forms a salient bond uniting house members" that seems to be expressed through the sequence of renovations that took place at Huaca Colorada, as outlined later in this chapter (Gillespie 2000a, 3). This social arrangement resembles both the exclusive household compounds documented at Huacas de Moche but also the numerous regional huacas that appear to have marked the territorial boundaries of urban and rural Moche communities (Lévi-Strauss 1982, 174; van Gijseghem 2001). By interpreting Moche social organization as comparable but certainly not identical to classic *société à maisons*, I argue that monumental huacas materialized membership within a larger community, extending a common identity across the sphere of Moche influence that negotiated situated notions of place within the landscape vital to each distinct community (Gillespie 2000a, 2000b).

MOCHE POLITICAL AND RELIGIOUS ORGANIZATION

The Moche of the north coast of Peru most accurately refers to a political and religious ideological framework that persisted though much of the Andean Early Intermediate and Middle Horizon Periods (AD 100–800) (Bawden 1996; Quilter and Castillo Butters 2010; Shimada 1994; Uceda Castillo and Mujica 1994, 2003). Often considered to represent one of the earliest state polities in the Americas, Moche societies were defined by a highly stratified social structure (Bawden 1996; Billman 2002; Shimada 1994). The Moche iconographic corpus suggests that ideology and power were theocratic and linked to highly formalized ceremonies, usually focused on interactions between individuals of clearly elevated status who are often shown seated beneath a simple roofed structure (Hocquenghem 1987; Jackson 2008; Wiersema 2010). Elaborate narrative scenes depict distinct activities with a repeated cast of characters who are often participating in elaborate ritual events. With deceivingly self-explanatory titles such as the "Sacrifice Ceremony" ("Presentation Theme") and the "Burial Theme," there are clear indications that the known suite of Moche iconographic scenes was likely re-enacted by elite ritual practitioners who were subsequently buried in their regalia and accompanied by the same material symbols of their status depicted in the iconography (Alva and Donnan 1993; Golte 2009; Quilter 1997) (figure 6.2).

The interconnected and interdependent complex of art, architecture, and action that combined to form Moche religious ideology was "didactic, meant to impress upon their audience who was victorious and who was vanquished, who was the sacrificer and who was the victim, who was the ruler and who was the ruled" (Quilter 2001, 41). Defined by cycles of warfare, prisoner capture, and human sacrifice, the activities depicted likely served to legitimate religious authority; however, the relationship between Moche political theology and their cosmogonic myths is poorly understood and the subject of considerable debate (Alva and Donnan 1993; Bourget 2006; Donnan 1978; Golte 2009; Hill 1998; Swenson 2003). The iconographic and archaeological corpus strongly indicates, however, that the ritual control of human life, death, and regeneration was reciprocally balanced based on the notion that destruction enabled creation, a belief that applied as viscerally to the built environment as it did to human subjects (Bourget 2006; Swenson 2003, 2012).

With death as a liminal and necessary phase in the process of creation and becoming, the transformation of the human body or architectural space through sacrifice constituted a vital generative force of life, cosmos, time, authority, and ultimately the creation of "place" itself. This sacrificial ontology appears to have persisted across the Moche sphere, with repeated dedication and termination rites at Moche centers indicating that Moche conceptions of place clearly considered architectural spaces as vital, living entities in their own right (Swenson 2013, 2018b). Indeed, notions of

FIGURE 6.2. Rollout drawing of Burial Theme. Adapted from drawing by Donna McClelland in the Moche Archive, Dumbarton Oaks, Washington, DC

home, territory, and place specific to the Moche must take into account these central ideologies of life, creation, and death as interdependent modes of being deeply embedded in the landscape (Swenson 2011, 2012, 2018b).

Following this line of thought, the huaca form itself has often been interpreted as a mimetic simulation or miniaturization of the mountains that form the foothills of the Andes along the Pacific Coast, closely in keeping with the pan-Andean veneration of mountain peaks as both deified ancestors and the locus of supernatural and generative power (Bastien 1978; Bawden 1996; Kolata 1993; Swenson and Warner 2016; Uceda Castillo 2001a, 2001b). Exemplifying this multiscalar symbolic tradition, Huaca de la Luna, located at the base of the coastal massif known as Cerro Blanco, served as the primary ceremonial center for the urban settlement in the toponymic Moche Valley (Bawden 1996). The ongoing excavations at the monumental complex of plazas, ramps, and platforms at this site have provided critical information for our interpretations of Moche religious and political ideology (Uceda Castillo 2001a, 2001b).

The walls that frame the large public plaza at the base of Huaca de la Luna are emblazoned with tiers of brightly painted high-relief adobe friezes depicting fanged deities, predatory animals, spiders, warriors, captured prisoners, and cosmic landscapes. The spatial arrangement of these friezes has been argued to present a distinct hierarchical relationship between the actors (Jackson 2008; Uceda Castillo 2001a). The enduring importance of these highly visible murals is clearly evident in the fact that multiple layers of similar decoration have been found below the latest surface, suggesting that the entire monument was renovated and renewed during construction cycles that carefully encased and reiterated the ideological messages presented by earlier phases. As such, Huaca de la Luna and perhaps all Moche huacas existed as living timepieces, chronotopic spaces that underlined the enduring yet dynamic ideals expressed through the monument (Bakhtin 1981; Spence Morrow 2018; Swenson 2012, 2018a, 2018b). Atop this sequence of friezes at Huaca de la Luna sits a series of elevated interior chambers and platforms that served as central stages for the sacrificial rituals performed within view of the substantial open plaza, public acts that no doubt underwrote the theocratic ideologies of Moche polities (Bourget 2001; Swenson 2012). As spaces specifically designed to present ritual acts and powerful symbols to gatherings of people from across a given territory, such ceremonial loci allowed members of a specific situated community to receive, consume, and incorporate the ideas those rituals and symbols represented in order to reify their connection as a group.

The ceremonial complex of Huaca de la Luna is thought to represent the foundational template that was replicated at the numerous satellite centers found in valleys north and south of the Moche Valley, most spectacularly at the Huaca Cao Viejo in the Chicama Valley where a nearly identical scalar version of the monument was constructed (Franco et al. 1994, 2003) (figure 6.3). In essence, the territorial expansion of Moche religious and political ideology can be interpreted as a mimetic process of reiterative reproduction at multiple scales centered on the symbolic replication of territory that no doubt implicated understandings and experiences of domestic space. As such, the connection between the natural and built environment was materialized through a repeated canon of symbolically charged combinations of visual art, architecture, and action. Although the similarities of this ideological complex suggest a degree of continuity across the region, recent investigations have questioned the existence of a territorial Moche State; it seems increasingly apparent that Moche political organization varied considerably from area to area, with each river drainage along the coast exhibiting unique variation on the central religious and political themes (Castillo Butters and Donnan 1994a, 1994b; Quilter 2002; Quilter and Castillo Butters 2010).

Inaugurated by social and environmental upheavals, the Late Moche (Moche V) Period (ca. AD 600–850) has left us with considerable evidence of major transformations in Moche society. During the transition from the Middle to Late Moche Periods (ca. AD 600–650), evidence from ice cores extracted from the Quelccaya glacier in south-central Peru indicates that a severe drought associated with El Niño–Southern Oscillation (ENSO) events occurred between AD 593 and 594 (Shimada et al. 1991). In his work at Huaca de la Luna, Steve Bourget (2001, 91; 2016) has made a convincing argument that relates an apparent surge in sacrificial ceremonies at that site to increased social stress and instability related to drastic environmental changes. Under these pressures, the subsequent Late Moche Period was an era marked by massive demographic and ideological

FIGURE 6.3. Comparison of views from the plazas of Huaca de la Luna (*left*) and Huaca Cao Viejo (*right*)

restructuration that saw a diversification and popularization of Moche religious culture in new territories across the region, including the Jequetepeque and Lambayeque Valleys to the north (Dillehay and Kolata 2004a, 2004b; Swenson 2004). Current radiocarbon dates collected from the foundational phases of construction of Huaca Colorada firmly situate the initial occupation of the site to precisely this same transformative period (Swenson et al. 2011, 2012, 2013, 2015, 2017). Accordingly, the intensity and regularity of the phases of architectonic renovation and renewal at Huaca Colorada over a relatively short period of time (~100–150 years according to the current set of radiocarbon dates) may suggest a population facing considerable stress that sought constant renegotiation and reaffirmation of the bonds of community through material acts of ritualized reconstruction of a symbolic home.

HUACAS AS FOCI OF TERRITORY AND IDENTITY

As the Moche culture lacked a written language, it was through an inextricably linked combination of iconography and architecture that the desired messages—including those of home, territory, and emplacedness—were disseminated to the public. The huaca form, or any highly visible monumental structure for that matter, was intended to be emotionally evocative and physically arresting, and the original builders' desired impact is often felt to this day.

Although his primary research concern focuses on public architecture in the ancient Andes, Jerry Moore (1996b) has discussed the clearly residential functions of many Moche monumental structures, comparing known domestic assemblages from Huaca de la Luna in the Moche Valley to Huaca Fortaleza at Pampa Grande. In marked distinction to the enclosed and restricted elite residences at Pampa

Grande, he points to evidence that those areas interpreted as residential atop the earlier site of Huaca de la Luna were relatively accessible, a difference that is interpreted as an expression of the increased social stresses between commoners and elites on the north coast of Peru during the Late Moche Period. As noted by Donna J. Nash (2009) in her consideration of Izumi Shimada's work at Pampa Grande, if workshops were located in the residences of overseeing elites, the political economy of production would have differed from the family- and kin-managed production documented at Huacas de Moche. As this latter situation does not appear to be the case, Nash (2009) argues that Shimada successfully demonstrated that the administration of a central authority controlled production while not physically imbedded in household space. As will be suggested below, the position of the elite residential structure high atop Moche huacas may have served in a symbolic surveillance capacity, with the production districts as dedicated activity nodes that mimic functional spaces in an idealized household. In this way, the sites surrounding huacas such as those at Pampa Grande and Huaca Colorada would have operated as an extended corporate group, with the central huaca representing a macrocosmic house, a symbol of residence of which every member of the community was part and through which their social identity was forged.

The above discussion of the spatial interrelationship among residential, production, and ceremonial space demonstrates that the interpretation of public events and the architectural creation of public spaces must not be confined strictly to monuments and large plazas but need to take the entire settlement into consideration (see Chicoine et al., this volume; Ossa et al. 2017). In terms of Huaca Fortaleza, the overall orientation of the site as well as the organization of the residential and industrial compounds clearly puts the monumental structure as the focus of attention, visible from every area of the city. Although Huaca Colorada represents the central node of a much more compact settlement in comparison to Pampa Grande, the experience of staged performances of the huaca is worth reiterating. As will be discussed below, a series of public ceremonial platforms along the eastern facade of Huaca Colorada was intended to be seen from the enclosed plaza at the base of the structure.

Accepting that Moche huacas served as the ceremonial loci of ritual activity throughout their sphere of influence and across time, they join the continuum of Precolumbian cultures that focused arguably theocratic social order through the monumental lens of centrally placed ceremonial structures in both rural and urban contexts (Guengerich 2014; Halperin 2017; Millaire 2016; Swenson 2004, 2007, 2008). As the foci for communal actions of identity formation that cite elements of the quotidian, when domestic ideals are referenced in ceremonial structures, symbolic representations that cite these spaces serve as microcosmic depictions of a

particular worldview while macrocosmically reifying the household as encompassing the larger community (Herva 2010). Numerous examples of miniature architectural models have been documented in ancient funerary contexts cross-culturally,
with many of these remarkable miniatures condensing ideals of the physical dwelling as a sacred domestic space. Indeed, these material depictions of vernacular and
monumental households served as the conceptual stages on which life was lived
and identity continually performed, even in death (Bradley 2003, 2005; Castillo
Butters et al. 2011; Kirch 2000; Wiersema 2010, 2012).

Similar to the miniature houses in funerary contexts in other cultures (and comparable to two-dimensional depictions of such structure on Moche fineline ceramics), three-dimensional models of the gable-roof elite residences were also of central
significance to the political theologies of Late Moche communities. Until recently,
the relationship between these very real architectural spaces and their depiction in
the Moche artistic corpus was assumed to have been quite straightforward, with
architectural components of these structures reduced to a simple descriptive shorthand to clearly communicate the specific setting of ritual activity within painted
and modeled scenes. This line of thinking also extended to describe a particular
subset of looted Moche *maquetas*, relatively crudely fashioned and unfired ceramic
models of architectural compounds that were excavated in situ from the elaborate
burials found at the elite Moche funerary site of San José de Moro in the early 1990s
(Castillo Butters 2000a, 2000b, 2001, 2003; Castillo Butters et al. 1997; McClleland
2010). Following twenty-one years of excavation at this site, a collection of forty-
four such *maquetas* have been documented and conserved, with many of the tombs
containing numerous architectural models in a single context (Castillo Butters
2007; Castillo Butters et al. 2011). Made of friable unfired clay, the *maquetas* found
so far are all less than 50 cm square and are constructed and finished in much the
same way buildings of the period would have been: rectangular in plan and slipped
and painted with red, black, and white pigments (Castillo Butters et al. 1997, 127).
Three of the so-called Priestess burials for which San José de Moro is famous contained *maquetas* that were seemingly locally made, perhaps even constructed within
the tomb itself during mortuary rituals of interment (Castillo Butters et al. 1997,
2011; Wiersema 2010).

Due to the overwhelming spatial similarity of one particular excavated *maqueta*
to a detailed map of a small huaca platform structure at the site of Portachuelo
de Charcape in the hinterland of the Jequetepeque Valley, Edward R. Swenson con-
vincingly suggested that the *maquetas* from the tombs at San José de Moro were
representations of real rather than imagined spaces (Castillo Butters et al. 1997;
Johnson 2011; McClelland 2010; Swenson 2004, 2008, 415–421) (figure 6.4).
Charcape is an example of one of many relatively small ramped huaca-like structures

FIGURE 6.4. Comparison of *maqueta* from tomb M-U729 at San José de Moro to the plan of the *tablado* found in the Portachuelo de Charcape. Adapted from Swenson 2006

called *tablados* found throughout the Jequetepeque Valley, thought to represent scaled-down versions of the massive platform mounds found at Late Moche sites of more central importance, such as Huaca Colorada (Swenson 2004; Wiersema 2010). Given this correspondence, it seems that *maquetas* may have served as symbolic tomb substitutes for the full-scale *tablados* found in the hinterlands of the same valley, possibly as markers of community identity.

Suggesting that these models served as a substitute for the ritual architecture associated with the deceased would speak to the personal value and connection individuals likely held *vis-à-vis* ritually charged spaces. If this were the case, having a representation of the specific layout of the gable-roof complex of their home huaca may have served as an emblem of their affiliation. Considering that funerary traditions serve as a sort of theater for and about the living, the inclusion of architectural depictions in Moche burials highlights the importance of these spaces in the reification of community and territory identity. In comparing these models to the gable-roof structures at the summits of huacas, the visual shorthand of a simple roof becomes a charged symbol of a particular elite ritualized household that incorporated members of a specific community through ritual participation. Reinforced by ritual performances of social destruction and regeneration, the huaca stood as a marker of corporate affinity with an elite household, a symbol of identity uniting diverse communities into a single cooperative or ceremonial body. As such, the ritual performances assumed to have occurred within these structures likely underlined the continued legitimacy of both the leadership and the community as a whole. If social identity was in fact forged within these ceremonial spaces, acts of renovation in these profoundly powerful places must have marked particularly charged liminal periods. These ceremonial construction efforts necessitated combined acts of destruction and renewal, involving communal labor efforts in the process of architectural renovation that must have been fundamental to the construction of Moche huacas.

ARCHITECTURAL RENOVATION AS SOCIAL REPRODUCTION

In Andean and Mesoamerican archaeological contexts, rituals of architectural renovation—either additive or reductive—materialized acts of both social and cosmic termination and dedication (Swenson 2015). Largely based on comparisons to the well-documented cosmological-temporal principles of destruction and regeneration linked to calendrical and agricultural cycles and dynastic succession that have been well established in ancient Mesoamerica, architectural renewal in Andean contexts is also considered to have involved highly ritualized acts (Friedel 1998; Hocquenghem 2008; Mock 1998; Prieto Burmester 2008). The sequence of construction phases at Moche huacas is fruitfully compared to Mesoamerican rites of architectural renovation and served in part to impart meaning to daily life for those who were involved in the construction and use of these spaces. Moche huacas were special places where quotidian acts of construction and communal consumption were elevated to community-making rituals that also metaphorically represented production and reproduction more generally (e.g., sexual, agricultural, artisanal). The intense efforts involved in reconstruction made and remade the archetypical house just as other rituals referenced the making and remaking of the cosmos and the agricultural resources so closely tied to the annual cycles on which the rhythms of such ceremonies were based.

The above-mentioned stepped ceremonial platforms, widely depicted in both two and three dimensions in Moche ceramic art, can now be understood in terms of these rituals of architectural termination and rededication (Castillo Butters 2011; Wiersema 2010, 2012, 2015). As discussed, the ubiquity of these representations strongly suggests the central importance of these structures in Moche religious ideology, a hypothesis corroborated by the archaeological investigation of the numerous monumental adobe brick huacas found across the the riverine landscapes of the north coast of Peru. Direct evidence of this architectural tradition is unquestionably present, as the remains of a highly remodeled and carefully curated room complex containing a stepped platform were recently excavated at Huaca Colorada in the southern Jequetepeque Valley. This structure has proved to be one of the closest physical analogs to the ritual platforms depicted in Moche iconographic representations (Swenson et al. 2011, 2012, 2013, 2015, 2017).

HUACA COLORADA AS ANCESTRAL HOUSE

The largest Late Moche settlement on the southern bank of the Jequetepeque Valley, Huaca Colorada is located approximately 100 km north of the Huacas de Moche at the base of Cerro Cañoncillo in an arid region known as the Pampa de Mojucape (figure 6.5). Surrounded by a settlement covering approximately 24 hectares, Huaca Colorada is an elongated adobe brick platform structure built atop a modified sand dune; it measures approximately 390 m by 140 m and rises nearly 20 m at its highest point. Differentiated into three distinct sectors, the principal ceremonial precinct (Sector B) discussed in this chapter is located at the peak of the structure above and between two manufacturing and residential areas on the lower tiers situated to the north and south (figure 6.6). Serving as the ceremonial and political headquarters of a powerful polity, the principal religious constructions of the monumental core of Huaca Colorada consisted of nine daises or altars where both visible and secluded ritual performances would have taken place, all of which were ritually interred under floors or construction fill of each sequential renovation (Swenson et al. 2011, 2012, 2013, 2015, 2017). Of the greatest antiquity among this architectural palimpsest of religious practice is a clearly curated and well-preserved sunken chamber containing a central stepped platform or dais that appears to have served as a stage for acts of ritual performance almost identical in form to those depicted in the iconography of Late Moche fineline ceramics (Swenson et al. 2010, 2011; Wiersema 2010) (figure 6.7).

This last phase of use was extraordinarily well preserved due to a clearly intentional termination episode that saw the entire chamber buried in upward of 120 m³ of clean sand fill. This singular termination event encased and preserved two plaster-coated wooden pillars found rising from the platform that no doubt once supported a simple gable roof. Recent excavations that took place in 2014 and 2016 have further complicated the construction sequence of the platform chamber with the discovery of a considerably larger (~4.4 m × 2.2 m) two-step platform directly west of this secluded chamber but oriented in exactly the same north-facing direction as the private platform (figure 6.8). Unlike the platform chamber found in 2010, this newly discovered dais was located at the very eastern edge of the Huaca and was likely visible from the open plaza below that stretches eastward toward the later ruins of the site of Tecapa (figure 6.9). Excavation of this partially eroded secondary platform revealed that it was enlarged laterally at least once before being intentionally destroyed in an intense conflagration that collapsed the gable roof that covered it and sealed the surface of the entire eastern facade of the huaca. Ample evidence of the original roofing material was found among the burned rubble covering this platform, with the impressions of cane bound with twine preserved in remarkably thick (~15 cm) layers of painted clay that clearly covered the entire roof (figure 6.10).

FIGURE 6.5. Location of Huaca Colorada within the Jequetepeque Valley

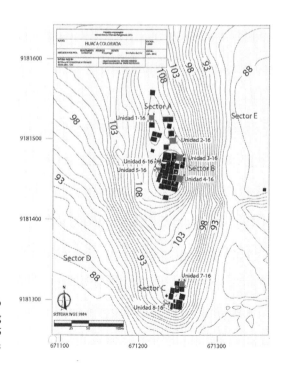

FIGURE 6.6. Contour map of Huaca Colorada showing locations of 2009–2016 excavations

FIGURE 6.7. Western Chamber platform with plaster-coated wooden pillars found during excavation, and depiction of gable-roof platform (*top left*). Adapted from the Christopher B. Donnan and Donna McClelland Moche Archive, Dumbarton Oaks

Considering the size of the platform, the clay-covered roof alone would have been of considerable weight, requiring the support of large wooden posts, the burned bases of which remained imbedded in the platform floor. Excavations immediately north of this burned platform uncovered two additional phases of construction in the form of two overlaid later platforms, both of which were associated with the interment of sacrificial victims (Spence Morrow and Swenson 2019; Swenson et al. 2015, 2017) (figure 6.8).

As this public eastern platform appears to have been built contemporaneous to the earliest phases of the more exclusive platform chamber in the west, it appears that both public and private performances would have been held on these two ritual stages (figure 6.9). The eastern public platform would have been visible to the entire extended community that could have gathered at the base of the huaca in what resembles a large open plaza and is bounded to the west by a high adobe wall, assumed to be associated with the later constructions in Tecapa (figure 6.11). Covering an area measuring approximately 80 m by 100 m, the 8,000 m² space bounded by this plaza could have easily hosted upward of 17,000 ritual participants

FIGURE 6.8. Eastern Terrace platform of Huaca Colorada showing evidence of burning

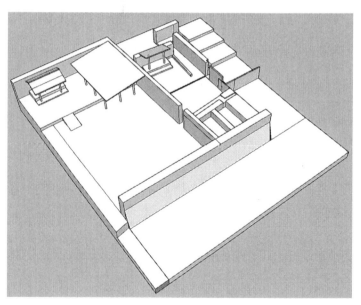

FIGURE 6.9. Three-dimensional model of the relation of Eastern Terrace and Western Chamber platforms at Huaca Colorada

FIGURE 6.10. Cane and twine impressions in burned roofing clay from Eastern Terrace platform

if the upper limit of Jerry D. Moore's plaza occupation density constants are applied (Moore 1996b, 117; Ossa et al. 2017; see Inomata 2006 for similar occupation calculations for the plazas of Tikal, Copán, and Aguateca in Mesoamerica). This walled plaza likely had an earlier and enduring association with Huaca Colorada due to the presence of a considerable retaining wall that runs up across the huaca toward the east and contains and essentially defines the southern limit of Sector B. Although recent excavation and investigation of this wall did not conclusively determine its contemporaneity to the Late Moche construction phases, it appears to have controlled access to the Eastern Plaza, which would have served as the optimal place to observe particular acts that would have taken place on the public platform and later ritual constructions (Swenson et al. 2015) (see figure 6.11).

Later phases of use following the closure of the interior chamber and the sequence of overlaid interments of more visible platforms were clearly designed to maintain visual access to the eastern facade of the huaca. The latest platforms shifted orientation to face Cerro Cañoncillo and the plaza below, construction phases associated with the latest occupations during the post-Moche Transitional Period. There is a clear maintenance of the position of numerous wooden posts as a link to previous

FIGURE 6.11. View from the along the central wall of Tecapa to the Eastern Terrace of Huaca Colorada, with scaled reconstruction of visible platform and gable roof

phases, dynamically preserving fundamental elements of the original structure while allowing for new constructions that conserved certain architectural layouts as the structure was reproduced and renewed. With the construction of a sequence of floors that encapsulated the original north-facing public platform, it appears that there was a concerted effort to maintain the presence of this visible open space to the plaza below while subtly changing the architectural configuration. This constant renewal of the visible public platform is mirrored in the numerous reductions of the private platform in the west as will be discussed below, suggesting that the renovations of both public and private ceremonial spaces were not only reminiscent

FIGURE 6.12. Latest ceremonial platform at Huaca Colorada facing eastward toward Tecapa

of each other but also clearly synchronized. As mentioned, in the last phases of construction, a 90-degree shift in the orientation of the later public ceremonial platforms from north facing to east facing speaks to a fundamental change in the nature of associated activities, possibly related to a new focus on the occupation of Tecapa to the east (figure 6.12).

Following the initial discovery of the latest phase of the private western platform chamber in 2010, two further excavations in 2011 and 2012 defined at least seven distinct phases of renovation of the chamber. Each of these construction phases incrementally reduced the dimensions of the room laterally and vertically, compressing the layout of the original chamber while carefully maintaining and reiterating fundamental components of its spatial organization. These architectural renovations stand as clear evidence of a concerted effort to maintain some vestige of the original spatial orientation of this particular ritual setting while marking the passage of time and the renewal of social order for those involved in its construction and dedication. These reductions clearly define the use of this space as focused on the open gable-roof structure found atop the platform in the southern end of the chamber, with every stage of reduction entombing both the previous space within each of the new floors and walls that marked each phase. Each of these sequential spatial reductions of the private platform chamber at Huaca Colorada was also directly associated with clearly dedicatory acts of human and animal sacrifice (Spence Morrow 2018; Spence Morrow and Swenson 2019; Swenson et al. 2011, 2012, 2013, 2015, 2017) (figure 6.13).

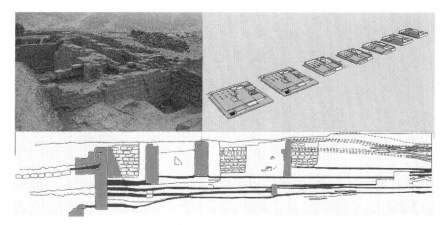

FIGURE 6.13. Profile composite of sequential reductions of Western Chamber platform (*bottom*) and construction phases during excavation (*top left*) and as modeled in three dimensions (*top right*)

Excavation of construction fill that composed the penultimate reduction of the chamber uncovered one of these sacrificial burials, an individual who was rather unceremoniously sprawled across the area, seemingly tossed into the rubble while the space was being reduced (Swenson et al. 2012). Found directly beneath the body were the fragile remains of a large wooden post approximately 30 cm in diameter and nearly 2 m long, laid in the adobe rubble in an almost identical orientation and position as the individual itself. Considering their proximity, relative size, and orientation, this post and the sacrificial victim were clearly interred together in a single event that is suggestive of a symbolic linkage between acts of human and architectural sacrifice (figure 6.14). Atop this construction fill was a circular alignment of adobe bricks surrounding the remnants of a post under which a *Spondylus* shell had been placed—a common dedicatory offering in the construction of Moche architecture (Shimada 1994). This particular architectural element was reminiscent of a series of other adobe post emplacements found at Huaca Colorada in previous seasons. Constructed of levels of mortared adobe bricks arranged in roughly conical forms, these circular shafts tapered downward from approximately 1 m in diameter to 50 cm at their bases, cutting through numerous earlier floors. Often over 2 m deep, these well-like adobe structures were clearly associated with floors on the higher levels of the huaca east of the ceremonial chamber (Rucabado-Yong 2006) (figure 6.15).

The circular adobe bins were aligned and often associated with the remnants of large wooden posts, continually built up over time as new floors were added to the

FIGURE 6.14. Sacrificial victim (*a*) and associated ritualized post burial (*b*) and *Spondylus* shell offering (*d*) in context of post emplacement (*c*)

huaca with each cycle of ceremonial reconstruction (Swenson et al. 2012). Once the western ceremonial chamber had been filled and abandoned in the latest periods of occupation, this higher, more visible eastern area became the focus for ceremonial activity. As mentioned earlier, the uppermost eastern facade of the huaca would have been covered by a veranda made from the alignment of posts, each with its own socket—allowing the huaca to change and grow while maintaining their original positions relative to the huaca, thus renewing space with vertical shifts rather than horizontal reductions (see figure 6.8). This clear desire to maintain the location of posts over time explicitly acknowledged and commemorated previous construction sequences. This ritualized building program created physical conduits through which an association with the past is maintained and where the recycling of the posts provided a continual connection to the earliest iteration of the structure and

FIGURE 6.15. Adobe post emplacement bins (*above*) and suggested construction sequence (*below*)

its ancestral inhabitants. As such, these posts may have held great importance as a kind of vital inherited architectural element that perdured between phases of construction, thereby linking and connecting present, past, and future communities for which this structure served as a powerful instrument of social reproduction. In line with this argument, the choice to bury one of these long-curated posts along with an attendant human sacrifice in the penultimate reduction of the private platform chamber materialized a particularly notable and no doubt powerful act of termination, perhaps even commemorating the fall of a preceding line of rulership and a shift to a new social order.

Parallels of sacrificial rituals that linked acts of architectural change and continuity through the symbolism of post emplacements are also evident in the excavations undertaken by Izumi Shimada at Huaca Loro and Huaca Lercanlech in the Lambayeque Valley during the later Sicán Period (ca. AD 900–1100) (Klaus and Shimada 2016). Investigations at these huacas have uncovered numerous similar columnar adobe post emplacement boxes or sockets that appear to have served the same function as those at Huaca Colorada, suggesting both a symbolic and a functional extension of this particular architectural tradition, although significantly intensified in terms of the relation to sacrificial rites (Klaus and Shimada 2016; Shimada 1990). Within each of these later post sockets, along with small foundation offerings of copper and *Spondylus* shell, nearly half of all the post emplacements excavated at theses huacas contained sacrificial victims—some found blindfolded and physically bound to the remnant posts with rope, embracing the base of the column just below the floor level (Klaus and Shimada 2016).

Interestingly, the only comparable post emplacement structures contemporaneous to those at Huaca Colorada were found in the later occupation phases at Huaca Fortaleza in the Lambayeque Valley, where they were originally suggested to have served as storage containers before being independently interpreted as over-constructed post emplacements (Anders 1981; Day 1971, 1975; Haas 1985; Shimada 1994). With only two building phases, Huaca Fortaleza is not only one of the largest monumental structures attributed to the Moche culture but also by far the most quickly built, demanding an enormous and highly organized workforce (Shimada 1994, 179). Erected in an economic manner, the platforms were constructed using a "chamber-and-fill" method involving a honeycomb of rectangular walls filled with rubble, thereby reducing labor requirements and the overall amount of adobe needed for construction (Shimada 1994, 160). The platforms at this site were uniform in style and did not reveal the numerous construction phases that characterize most earlier Moche huacas of this monumental scale or even more modest sites such as Huaca Colorada, discussed above (Bawden 1996, 294). Huaca Fortaleza's rapid construction speaks to urgency in its creation and possibly other social pressures. It might also point to distinct ideologies of space and time. Indeed, Huaca Fortaleza was rapidly founded as a new node of social reproduction from which a territorialized community of a clearly different constitution developed. Archaeologically, we rely on these specific construction episodes of monumental centers to help us punctuate and interrelate the complexity of the shifting social conditions of ancient societies across the north coast of Peru. The initiating factors that brought about the establishment of such new communities are an inextricable product of both social and environmental conditions these ancient populations faced. However, it is in the way these specific, situated communities created and shared ideals and identities as members of a collective and intergenerational "house" that we can appreciate the power of place as fundamental to the establishment of cooperation and belonging.

CONCLUSION

To move beyond the continued categorization of Moche huacas as purely ceremonial locales designed to express and continually reiterate centralized political ideologies, the form of nuanced and long-term investigation that has been undertaken at Huaca Colorada is of vital importance. The close analysis of the specific object biography of this curated religious space allowed us to document the materialized

rhythms of social reproduction—as a moral ideal—of a particular ancient community. By appreciating that this form of collaborative intergenerational construction
project created and re-created the communities responsible for building them, we
gain a valuable glimpse into Moche *constructions* of both the cosmological and the
quotidian. Materially communicating ideals of domesticity centered on the house,
these specific architectural spaces appear to have symbolically bonded both partici-
pant and religious practitioner and "commoner" and "elite" in a ritual setting that
mimicked and celebrated domestic traditions. These structures were the central
focus of their communities, spaces where individuals became incorporated into the
social fabric of their society through a common understanding of place.

REFERENCES

Alva, Walter. 1999. *Sipán: Descubrimientos e investigaciones*. Lima: Edición del autor, version resumida de la edición de Backus y Johnson, S.A.A.

Alva, Walter. 2012. "El Cetro de Sipán." In *Microcosmos: Visión andina de los espacios pre
hispánicos*, edited by Adine Gavazzi, 114–117. Lima: Apus Graph Ediciones.

Alva, Walter, and Christopher B. Donnan. 1993. *Royal Tombs of Sipán*. Los Angeles: Fowler
Museum of Cultural History, University of California.

Anders, Martha B. 1981. "Investigation of State Storage Facilities in Pampa Grande, Peru."
Journal of Field Archaeology 8 (4): 391–404.

Bakhtin, Mikhail M. 1981. "Forms of Time and of the Chronotope in the Novel: Notes
toward a Historical Poetics." *The Dialogic Imagination: Four Essays*, edited by Michael
Holquist, 84–258. Translation by Caryl Emerson and Michael Holquist. Austin:
University of Texas Press.

Bastien, Joseph W. 1978. *Mountain of the Condor: Metaphor and Ritual in an Andean Ayllu*.
American Ethnological Society Monograph 64. St. Paul, MN: West Publishing.

Bawden, Garth. 1996. *The Moche*. Oxford: Blackwell.

Beck, Robin A., Jr. 2007. *The Durable House: House Society Models in Archaeology*.
Occasional Papers 35. Carbondale: Center for Archaeological Investigations, Southern
Illinois University.

Benson, Elizabeth P. 2012. *The Worlds of the Moche on the North Coast of Peru*. Austin:
University of Texas Press.

Billman, Brian R. 2002. "Irrigation and the Origins of the Southern Moche State on the
North Coast of Peru." *Latin American Antiquity* 13 (4): 371–400.

Bourget, Steve. 2001. "Rituals of Sacrifice: Its Practice at Huaca de la Luna and Its
Representation." In *Moche Iconography in Moche Art and Archaeology*, edited by Joanne
Pillsbury, 89–109. Washington, DC: National Gallery of Art.

Bourget, Steve. 2003. "Somos diferentes: Dinámica ocupacional del sitio Castillo de Huancaco, valle de Virú." In *Moche: Hacia el final del milenio: Actas del Segundo Colloquio sobre la Cultura Moche*, edited by Santiago Uceda Castillo and Eliaas Mujica, I: 245–267. Lima: Universidad Nacional de Trujillo and Pontifica Universidad Católica del Perú.

Bourget, Steve. 2006. *Sex, Death, and Sacrifice in Moche Religion and Visual Culture.* Austin: University of Texas Press.

Bourget, Steve. 2016. *Sacrifice, Violence, and Ideology among the Moche: The Rise of Social Complexity in Ancient Peru.* Austin: University of Texas Press.

Bradley, Richard. 2003. "A Life Less Ordinary: The Ritualization of the Domestic Sphere in Later Prehistoric Europe." *Cambridge Archaeological Journal* 13 (1): 5–23.

Bradley, Richard. 2005. *Ritual and Domestic Life in Prehistoric Europe.* New York: Routledge.

Castillo Butters, Luis Jaime. 2000a. *La Ceremonial del Sacrificio: Batallas y Muerte en el Arte Mochica.* Lima: Museo Arqueológico Larco Rafael Herrera.

Castillo Butters, Luis Jaime. 2000b. "La Presencia Wari en San José de Moro." In *Huari y Tiwanaku: Modelos vs. Evidencias*, edited by Peter Kaulicke and William H. Isbell, 143–179. Boletín de Arqueología PUCP 4. Lima: Pontificia Universidad Católica del Perú.

Castillo Butters, Luis Jaime. 2001. "The Last of the Mochicas." In *Moche Art and Archaeology in Ancient Peru*, edited by Joanne Pillsbury, 307–332. Washington, DC: National Gallery of Art.

Castillo Butters, Luis Jaime. 2003. "Los Ultimos Mochicas en Jequetepeque." In *Moche Hacia el Final Del Milenio, vol. 2*, edited by Santiago Uceda Castillo and Elías Mujica, 65–123. Lima and Trujillo: Fondo Editorial, Pontificia Universidad Católicadel Perú and Universdad Nacional de Trujillo.

Castillo Butters, Luis Jaime. 2007. *Programa Arqueológico San José de Moro, Temporada de 2007.* Lima: Pontificia Universidad Católica del Peru.

Castillo Butters, Luis Jaime, Solsiré Cusicanqui, and Ana Cecila Mauricio. 2011. "Las maquetas de San José de Moro: aproximaciones a su contexto y significado." In *Modelando el mundo: Imágenes de la arquitectura precolombina*, edited by José Canziani, Paulo Dam, and Luis Jaime Castillo Butters, 112–143. Lima: MALI (Museo de Arte de Lima).

Castillo Butters, Luis Jaime, and Christopher B. Donnan. 1994a. "La Occupación Moche de San José de Moro, Jequetepeque." In *Moche: Propuestas y Perspectivas*, edited by Santiago Uceda Castillo and Elias Mujica, 93–146. Lima: Travaux del'Institut Français d' etudes Andines.

Castillo Butters, Luis Jaime, and Christopher B. Donnan. 1994b. "Los Mochica del norte y los Mochica del sur." In *Vicús*, edited by Krzysztof Makowski and Christopher B. Donnan, 143–181. Lima: Colección Arte y Tesoros del Perú, Banco de Credito.

Castillo Butters, Luis Jaime, Andrew Nelson, and Chris Nelson. 1997. "Maquetas Mochicas de San José de Moro." *Arkinka* 22: 120–128.

Chapdelaine, Claude. 2006. "Looking for Moche Palaces in the Elite Residences of the Huacas of Moche Site." In *Palaces and Power in the Americas: From Peru to the Northwest Coast*, edited by Jessica Joyce Christie and Patricia Joan Sarro, 23–43. Austin: University of Texas Press.

Chapdelaine, Claude, Victor Pimentel, and Helene Bernier. 2003. "Informe del Proyecto Arqueológico PSUM (Proyecto Santa de la Universidad de Montreal) 2002—La presencia Moche en el valle del Santa, Costa Norte del Perú." Lima: Unpublished report submitted to the Instituto Nacional de la Cultura, Peru.

Day, Kent C. 1971. "Quarterly Report of the Royal Ontario Museum, Lambayeque Valley (Peru) Expedition." Toronto: Report Submitted to the Office of the Chief Archaeologist, Royal Ontario Museum.

Day, Kent C. 1975. "Mid-Season Report of the Royal Ontario Museum, Lambayeque Project." Toronto: Report Submitted to the Office of the Chief Archaeologist, Royal Ontario Museum.

Dillehay, Tom D., and Alan L. Kolata. 2004a. "Long-Term Human Response to Uncertain Environmental Conditions in the Andes." *Proceedings of the National Academy of Sciences* 101 (12): 4325–4330.

Dillehay, Tom D., and Alan L. Kolata. 2004b. "Pre-Industrial Human and Environment Interactions in Northern Peru during the Late Holocene." *The Holocene* 14 (2): 272–281.

Donnan, Christopher B. 1978. *Moche Art of Peru*. Los Angeles: Museum of Culture History, University of California.

Donnan, Christopher B. 1982. "Dance in Moche Art." *Ñawpa Pacha: Journal of Andean Archaeology* 20: 97–120. Institute of Andean Studies, Berkeley, CA.

Donnan, Christopher B. 2004. *Moche Portraits from Ancient Peru*. Austin: University of Texas Press.

Douglass, John G., and Nancy Gonlin. 2012. "The Household as Analytical Unit: Case Studies from the Americas." In *Ancient Households of the Americas: Conceptualizing What Household Do*, edited by John G. Douglass and Nancy Gonlin, 1–44. Boulder: University Press of Colorado.

Driessen, Jan. 2010. "Spirit of Place: Minoan Houses as Major Actors." In *Political Economies of the Aegean Bronze Age*, edited by Daniel J. Pullen, 35–65. Oxford: Oxbow Books.

Franco, Regulo, Cesar Gálvez, and Segundo Vásquez. 1994. "Arquetectura y decoración mochica el la Huaca Cao Viejo, Complejo El Brujo: Resultados preliminares." In *Moche: Propuestas y perspectivas*, edited by Santiago Uceda Castillo and Elias Mujica, 147–180. Actas del Primer Coloquio sobre la Cultura Moche. Lima: Travaux de l'Institut Français d'Études Andines.

Franco, Regulo, Cesar Gálvez, and Segundo Vásquez. 2003. "Modelos, function y cronología de la Huaca Cao Viejo, Complejo El Brujo." In *Moche: Hacia el final del milenio: Actas del Segundo Colloquio sobre la Cultura Moche*, edited by Santiago Uceda Castillo and Elias Mujica, 2:125–177. Lima: Universidad Nacional de Trujillo and Pontifica Universidad Católica del Perú.

Friedel, David. 1998. "Sacred Work: Dedication and Termination in Mesoamerica." In *The Sowing and the Dawning: Termination, Dedication, and Transformation in the Archaeological and Ethnographic Record of Mesoamerica*, edited by Shirley Boteler Mock, 189–193. Albuquerque: University of New Mexico Press.

Gillespie, Susan D. 2000a. "Beyond Kinship: An Introduction." In *Beyond Kinship: Social and Material Reproduction in House Societies*, edited by Rosemary A. Joyce and Susan D. Gillespie, 1–21. Philadelphia: University of Pennsylvania Press.

Gillespie, Susan D. 2000b. "Maya 'Nested Houses': The Ritual Construction of Place." In *Beyond Kinship: Social and Material Reproduction in House Societies*, edited by Rosemary A. Joyce and Susan D. Gillespie, 135–160. Philadelphia: University of Pennsylvania Press.

Gillespie, Susan D. 2007. "When Is a House?" In *The Durable House: House Society Models in Archaeology*, edited by Robin A. Beck Jr., 25–50. Center for Archaeological Investigations Occasional Paper 35. Carbondale: Southern Illinois University.

Golte, Jürgen. 2009. *Moche Cosmología y Sociedad: Una interpretación iconográfica*. Lima: Instituto de Estudios Peruanos.

González-Ruibal, Alfredo. 2006. "House Societies vs. Kinship-Based Societies: An Archaeological Case from Iron Age Europe." *Journal of Anthropological Archaeology* 25: 144–173.

Guengerich, Anna. 2014. "The Architect's Signature: The Social Production of a Residential Landscape at Monte Viudo, Chachapoyas, Peru." *Journal of Anthropological Archaeology* 34: 1–16.

Haas, Jonathan. 1985. "Excavations of Huaca Grande: An Initial View of the Elite of Pampa Grande." *Journal of Field Archaeology* 12: 391–409.

Halperin, Christina. 2017. "Vernacular and Monumental Maya Architecture: Translations and Lost in Translations during the Terminal Classic Period (ca. 800–950)." In *Vernacular Architecture in the Pre-Columbian Americas*, edited by Christina T. Halperin and Lauren E Schwartz, 113–137. Routledge: London.

Herva, Vesa-Pekka. 2010. "Buildings as Persons: Relationality and the Life of Buildings in a Northern Periphery of Early Modern Sweden." *Antiquity* 84: 440–452.

Hill, Erica. 1998. "Death as a Rite of Passage: The Iconography of the Moche Burial Theme." *Antiquity* 72 (277): 528–538.

Hobsbawm, Eric, and Terrence Ranger. 1983. *The Invention of Tradition*. Cambridge: Cambridge University Press.

Hocquenghem, Anne Marie. 1987. *Iconografía mochica*. Lima: Pontificia Universidad Católica del Perú.

Hocquenghem, Anne Marie. 2008. "Sacrifices and Ceremonial Calendars in Societies of the Central Andes: A Reconsideration." In *The Art and Archaeology of the Moche: An Ancient Andean Society of the Peruvian North Coast*, edited by Steve Bourget and Kimberly L. Jones, 23–42. Austin: University of Texas Press.

Inomata, Takeshi. 2006. "Plazas, Performers, and Spectators: Political Theaters of the Classic Maya." *Current Anthropology* 47: 805–842.

Jackson, Margaret. A. 2008. *Moche Art and Visual Culture in Ancient Peru*. Albuquerque: University of New Mexico Press.

Johnson, Ilana. 2011. "The Development of Semi-Autonomous Communities in the Late Moche Period (AD 600–900)." In *From State to Empire in the Prehistoric Jequetepeque Valley, Peru*, edited by Colleen M. Zori and Ilana Johnson, 51–64. BAR International Series 2310. Oxford: British Archaeological Reports.

Joyce, Rosemary A., and Susan D. Gillespie, eds. 2000. *Beyond Kinship: Social and Material Reproduction in House Societies*. Philadelphia: University of Pennsylvania Press.

Kirch, Patrick V. 2000. "Temples as 'Holy Houses': The Transformation of Ritual Architecture in Traditional Polynesian Societies." In *Beyond Kinship: Social and Material Reproduction in House Socieites*, edited by Rosemary A. Joyce and Susan D. Gillespie, 103–114. Philadelphia: University of Pennsylvania Press.

Klaus, Haagen D., and Izumi Shimada. 2016. "Bodies and Blood: Middle Sicán Human Sacrifice in the Lambayeque Valley Complex (AD 900–1100)." In *Ritual Violence in the Ancient Andes: Reconstructing Sacrifiuce on the North Coast of Peru*, edited by Haagen D. Klaus and J. Marla Toyne, 120–149. Austin: University of Texas Press.

Kolata, Alan L. 1993. *The Tiwanaku: Portrait of an Andean Civilization*. Cambridge: Cambridge University Press.

Kolata, Alan L, ed. 1996. *Tiwanaku and Its Hinterland: Archaeology and Paleoecology of an Andean Civilization*, vol. 1: *Agroecology*. Washington, DC: Smithsonian Institution Press.

Lévi-Strauss, Claude. 1982. *The Way of the Masks*. Translated by Sylvia Modelski. Seattle: University of Washington Press.

McClelland, Donald 2010. "Architectural Models in Late Moche Tombs." *Ñawpa Pacha: Journal of Andean Archaeology* 30 (2): 209–230.

Millaire, Jean-François. 2016. "Posts and Pots: Propitiatory Ritual at Huaca Santa Clara in the Virú Valley, Peru." In *Ritual Violence in the Ancient Andes: Reconstructing Sacrifiuce on the North Coast of Peru*, edited by Haagen D. Klaus and J. Marla Toyne, 342–358. Austin: University of Texas Press.

Mock, Shirley B. 1998. "Prelude." In *The Sowing and the Dawning: Termination, Dedication, and Transformation in the Archaeological and Ethnographic Record of Mesoamerica*, edited by Shirley B. Mock, 3–18. Albuquerque: University of New Mexico Press.

Moore, Jerry D. 1996a. "The Archaeology of Plazas and the Proxemics of Ritual: Three Andean Tradtions." *American Anthropologist* 98 (4): 789–802.

Moore, Jerry D. 1996b. *Architecture and Power in the Ancient Andes*. Cambridge: Cambridge University Press.

Moore, Jerry D. 2012. *The Prehistory of Home*. Berkeley: University of California Press.

Nash, Donna J. 2009. "Household Archaeology in the Andes." *Journal of Archaeological Research* 17: 205–261.

Ossa, Alanna, Michael E. Smith, and José Lobo. 2017. "The Size of Plazas in Mesoamerican Cities and Towns: A Quantitative Analysis." *Latin American Antiquity* 28 (4): 457–475.

Pauketat, Timothy R., and Susan M. Alt. 2005. "Agency in a Postmold? Physicality and the Archaeology of Culture-Making." *Journal of Archaeological Method and Theory* 12 (3): 213–236.

Prieto Burmester, Gabriel. 2008. "Rituales de enterramiento arquetectónico en el núcleo urbano Moche: Una aproximación desde una residencia de elite en el valle de Moche." In *Arqueología Mochica: Nuevos Enfoques*, edited by Luis Jaime Castillo Butters, Hélène Bernier, Gregory Lockard, and Julio Rucabado Yong, 307–323. Lima: Fondo Editorial Pontifica Universidad Católica del Perú.

Quilter, Jeffrey. 1997. "The Narrative Approach to Moche Iconography." *Latin American Antiquity* 8 (2): 113–133.

Quilter, Jeffrey. 2001. "Moche Mimesis: Continuity and Change in Public Art in Early Peru." In *Moche Art and Archaeology in Ancient Peru*, edited by Joanne Pillsbury, 21–45. Washington, DC / New Haven, CT: National Gallery of Art / Yale University Press.

Quilter, Jeffrey. 2002. "Moche Politics, Religion and Warfare." *Journal of World Prehistory* 16 (2): 145–195.

Quilter, Jeffrey, and Luis J. Castillo Butters. 2010. *New Perspectives on Moche Political Organization*. Washington, DC: Dumbarton Oaks Research Library and Collection.

Rucabado-Yong, Julio. 2006. "Elite Mortuary Practices at San José de Moro during the Transitional Period: The Case Study of Collective Burial M-U615." Master's thesis, University of North Carolina, Chapel Hill.

Shimada, Izumi. 1981. "The Batan Grande–La Leche Archaeological Project: The First Two Seasons." *Journal of Field Archaeology* 8: 405–446.

Shimada, Izumi. 1990. "Cultural Continuities and Discontinuities on the Northern North Coast of Peru, Middle-Late Horizons." In *The Northern Dynasties: Kingship and*

Statecraft in Chimor, edited by Michael Moseley and Alana Cordy-Collins, 297–392. Washington, DC: Dumbarton Oaks Research Library and Collection.

Shimada, Izumi. 1994. *Pampa Grande and the Mochica Culture*. Austin: University of Texas Press.

Shimada, Izumi, Crystal Barker Schaaf, Lonnie G. Thompson, and Ellen Mosley-Thompson. 1991. Cultural impacts of severe droughts in the prehistoric Andes: Application of a 1,500-year ice core precipitation record. *World Archaeology* 22 (3): 247–270.

Spence Morrow, Giles. 2018. "Scaling the Huaca: Synecdochal Temporalities and the Mimetic Materialization of Late Moche Timescapes." In *Constructions of Time and History in the Pre-Columbian Andes*, edited by Edward R. Swenson and Andrew Roddick, 207–238. Boulder: University Press of Colorado.

Spence Morrow, Giles, and Edward R. Swenson. 2019. "Moche Mereology: Synecdochal Intersections of Spatial and Corporeal Ontologies at the Late Moche Site of Huaca Colorada, Peru." In *Andean Ontologies: New Perspectives from Archaeology, Ethnohistory, and Bioarchaeology* edited by Henry Tantalean and Maria Cecilia Lozada, 150–182. Boulder: University Press of Colorado.

Swenson, Edward R. 2003. "Cities of Violence: Sacrifice, Power, and Urbanization in the Andes." *Journal of Social Archaeology* 3 (2): 256–296.

Swenson, Edward R. 2004. "Ritual and Power in the Urban Hinterland: Religious Pluralism and Political Decentralization in Late Moche Jequetepeque, Peru." PhD dissertation, University of Chicago, IL.

Swenson, Edward R. 2006. "Competitive Feasting, Religious Pluralism, and Decentralized Power in the Late Moche Period." In *Andean Archaeology III: North and South*, edited by William H. Isbell and Helaine Silverman, 112–142. New York: Springer/Plenum.

Swenson, Edward R. 2007. "Adaptive Strategies or Ideological Innovations? Interpreting Sociopolitical Developments in the Jequetepeque Valley of Peru during the Late Moche Period." *Journal of Anthropological Archaeology* 26 (2): 253–282.

Swenson, Edward R. 2008. "San Ildefonso and the 'Popularization' of Moche Ideology in the Jequetepeque Valley." In *Arqueología Mochica Nuevos Enfoques*, edited by Luis Jaime Castillo Butters, Hélène Bernier, Gregory Lockard, and Julio Rucabado Yong, 411–431. Lima: Fondo Editorial Pontifica Universidad Católica del Perú.

Swenson, Edward R. 2011. "Architectural Renovations as Ritual Process in Late Intermediate Period Jequetepeque." In *From State to Empire in the Prehistoric Jequetepeque Valley, Peru*, edited by Colleen M. Zori and Illana Johnson, 129–148. BAR International Series 2310. Oxford: British Archaeological Reports.

Swenson, Edward R. 2012. "Moche Ceremonial Architecture as Thirdspace: The Politics of Place-Making in the Ancient Andes." *Journal of Social Archaeology* 12 (1): 3–28.

Swenson, Edward R. 2013. "The Political Landscape of Early State Religions." In *A Companion to the Anthropology of Religion*, edited by Janice Boddy and Michael Lambek, 471–488. Chichester: Wiley.

Swenson, Edward R. 2015. "The Materialities of Place Making in the Ancient Andes: A Critical Appraisal of the Ontological Turn in Archaeological Interpretation." *Journal of Archaeological Method and Theory* 22 (3): 677–712.

Swenson, Edward R. 2018a. "Timing Is Everything: Religion and the Regulation of Temporalities in Pre-Columbian Peru." In *Religion and Politics in the Ancient Americas*, edited by Sarah B. Barber and Arthur A. Joyce, 210–233. Oxford: Routledge.

Swenson, Edward R. 2018b. "Topologies of Time and History in the Jequetepeque, Peru" In *Constructions of Time and History in the Pre-Columbian Andes*, edited by Edward R. Swenson and Andrew Roddick, 174–206. Boulder: University Press of Colorado.

Swenson, Edward R., Jorge Y. Chiguala, and John P. Warner. 2010. "Informe final de la temporada de investigacion 2009: University of Toronto, Pacasmayo, Peru." Lima: Unpublished report submitted to the Instituto Nacional de la Cultura, Perú.

Swenson, Edward R., Jorge Y. Chiguala, and John P. Warner. 2011. "Informe final de la temporada de investigacion 2010: University of Toronto, Pacasmayo, Peru." Lima: Unpublished report submitted to the Instituto Nacional de la Cultura, Perú.

Swenson, Edward R., Jorge Y. Chiguala, and John P. Warner. 2012. "Informe Final Proyecto Arqueologico Jatanca–Huaca Colorada, Valle Jequetepeque Temporada 2011: University of Toronto, Pacasmayo." Lima: Unpublished report submitted to the Instituto Nacional de la Cultura, Perú.

Swenson, Edward R., Jorge Y. Chiguala, and John P. Warner. 2013. "Informe Final Proyecto Arqueologico Jatanca–Huaca Colorada, Valle Jequetepeque Temporada 2012: University of Toronto, Pacasmayo." Lima: Unpublished report submitted to the Instituto Nacional de la Cultura, Perú.

Swenson, Edward R., Francisco Seoane, and John P. Warner. 2015. "Informe Final Proyecto Arqueologico Jatanca–Huaca Colorada, Valle Jequetepeque Temporada 2014: University of Toronto, Pacasmayo." Lima: Unpublished report submitted to the Instituto Nacional de la Cultura, Perú.

Swenson, Edward R., Francisco Seoane, and John P. Warner. 2017. "Informe Final Proyecto Arqueologico Jatanca–Huaca Colorada, Valle Jequetepeque Temporada 2016: University of Toronto, Pacasmayo." Lima: Unpublished report submitted to the Instituto Nacional de la Cultura, Perú.

Swenson, Edward R, and John P. Warner. 2016. "Landscapes of Mimesis and Convergence in the Southern Jequetepeque Valley, Peru." *Cambridge Archaeological Journal* 26 (1): 23–51.

Uceda Castillo, Santiago. 2001a. "Investigations at Huaca de la Luna, Moche Valley: An Example of Moche Religious Architecture." In *Moche Art and Archaeology in Ancient Peru*, edited by Joanne Pillsbury, 47–67. Washington, DC: National Gallery of Art.

Uceda Castillo, Santiago. 2001b. "El nivelalto dela Plataforma I de Huaca de la Luna: Un espacio multifuncional." *Arkinka* 67: 90–95.

Uceda Castillo, Santiago, and Elias Mujica. 1994. *Moche Propuestas y Perspectivas*. Lima: Travaux de l'Institut Français d'etudes Andines.

Uceda Castillo, Santiago, and Elias Mujica. 2003. *Moche Hacia el Final del Milenio*, vols. 1 and 2. Lima and Trujillo: Fondo Editorial, Pontificia Universidad Católica del Perú and Universidad Nacional de Trujillo.

van Gijseghem, Hendrick. 2001. "Household and Family at Moche, Peru: An Analysis of Building and Residence Patterns in a Prehispanic Urban Center." *Latin American Antiquity* 12 (3): 257–273.

Weismantel, Mary. 2014. "The Hau of the House." In *Religion at Work in a Neolithic Society: Vital Matters*, edited by Ian Hodder, 259–279. Cambridge: Cambridge University Press.

Wiersema, Juliet B. 2010. "The Architectural Vessels of the Moche of Peru (C.E. 200–850): Architecture for the Afterlife." PhD dissertation, University of Maryland, College Park.

Wiersema, Juliet B. 2012. "Vasijas arquetectónicas Moche: Pequeñas estructuras, grandes consecuencias." In *Microcosmos: Visión andina de los espacios pre hispánicos*, edited by Adine Gavazzi, 96–111. Lima: Apus Graph Ediciones.

Wiersema, Juliet B. 2015. *Architectural Vessels of the Moche: Ceramic Diagrams of Sacred Space in Ancient Peru*. Austin: University of Texas Press.

7

Households and Urban Inequality in Fourteenth-Century Peru

DAVID PACIFICO

Household archaeology never gets old because it was never new. Since at least the work of Johann Winckelmann at Pompeii in the eighteenth century (Ceram 1979, 13) and Louis Henry Morgan in the United States in the nineteenth century (Thomas 2000), anthropologists and social archaeologists have expressed a keen interest in houses and households. Change comes with respect to the nature of those interests: the kinds of questions anthropologists and archaeologists ask and the kinds of analyses they conduct on houses, domestic assemblages, and household residents. Changing approaches to houses and households reflect the ways anthropologists believe household archaeology can inform us about the broader anthropological topics the field is currently examining.

This chapter reports on research conducted in a fourteenth-century residential district, called Sector B South, of the city of El Purgatorio, capital of the Casma Polity, on the north-central coast of Peru. Research conducted in Sector B South examined how houses and households contributed to the nature of social diversity at El Purgatorio, especially with respect to hierarchy and inequality, among nonelites. A neighborhood archaeology approach here is based on household archaeology but provided considerably more comparative data than would have been collected in a more focused household archaeology strategy. Consequently, the commoner district at El Purgatorio contributes to our understanding of how houses, households, and the quotidian practices of commoners affect the social construction of cities and urban settlements (sensu Smith 2003). Specific to

DOI: 10.5876/9781646420919.c007

Andean archaeology, the character of commoner social diversity at El Purgatorio is a critical element in understanding the Casma State itself and, therefore, the history, politics, and culture of the north-central coast of Peru in the later Middle Horizon and Late Intermediate Periods. El Purgatorio is a key site for understanding the sociopolitical history of the North Coast and its relationship to the South Coast, Central Highlands, and areas further north because it was a complex settlement at the center of a polity with wide regional reach, it had a long urban history, and it resides within a spatial context of a deeper history of complex settlements in the Casma Valley stretching back to 1500 BC (Pozorski and Pozorski 2008).[1] An understanding of commoners at El Purgatorio also provides a unique opportunity to examine the interrelationship of urbanism, households, and everyday life in a longer-term perspective. Indeed, as the world is increasingly urban (Davis 2004) and industrialized countries like the United States are increasingly unequal in terms of material wealth (US Census Bureau 2014), the archaeology of urban households provides a much-needed long-term perspective on social changes experienced in our contemporary world.

From Sector B South we learn that fourteenth-century commoner households were diverse in terms of social status and household configuration. This finding complicates traditional approaches to household archaeology (e.g., Aldenderfer 1993; Stanish 1989; Wilk and Rathje 1982), which tend to view the household as the smallest repeating social unit as indicated by the smallest repeating domestic architectural unit. This traditional approach is important for identifying households but deemphasizes the diverse forms households may take within a single society or settlement. The discovery of diverse house and household forms among commoners at El Purgatorio supports more recent approaches to household archaeology in the Andes (e.g., Janusek 2004, 2009; Van Gijseghem 2001) and Mesoamerica (e.g., Robin 2004; Yaeger 2000), which assert the diversity of households and the complexity of everyday life in preindustrial societies.

Findings from El Purgatorio support the idea that there is a core set of repeating architectural units representative of houses and the households that occupied them; but these findings also demand that we recognize the multiple constellations in which these elements may form, constituting various household forms typical of a single society. In Sector B, storage, production, and living spaces were configured into several morphological constellations comprising the houses of low-, middle-, and high-status commoners. We should not be surprised, however, by these finds, given that ethnographic research (e.g., Horne 1982; Lobo 1992) has frequently demonstrated the diversity and dynamic nature of households that may exist within a single society. In El Purgatorio's commoner residential district, Sector B South, it appears that there were three different household configurations, each associated with a different commoner status. Low-status and high-status urban commoners lived in smaller residences (though built with different materials) occupied by small households. In contrast, middle-status commoners lived in sprawling patio compound households occupied by numerous small (perhaps nuclear) families. Together, these residents comprised a broad middle class in the Casma State social landscape. Elites lived in the monumental and semi-monumental districts of El Purgatorio, as evidenced by the size and material elaboration of their residences. The lowest-status Casma State residents likely resided in the seemingly countless smaller and less elaborate settlements stretching up- and downriver from El Purgatorio. Privileged proximity to the urban core—tempered by segregation to the monumental district's precipitous hillsides—suggests that the residents of Sector B South composed a differentiated middleclass of nonelites, or commoners.

The results of research in Sector B South are significant in a couple of broad ways. First, they suggest that preindustrial and prehistoric urbanism share fundamental and significant characteristics with modern urbanism and therefore can serve as legitimate case studies in broader considerations of contemporary issues. Specifically, the relationship between urbanism and material inequalities as experienced by households and families is a common theme in both ancient and contemporary cities. This theme deserves robust examination and comparison for positive application in the present. For example, preindustrial case studies may be compared to contemporary cases of urban "death" (e.g., Detroit), hypermigration (Lima and Trujillo, Peru), revitalization (Barcelona), and rapid urban establishment (e.g., Brasilia, Shenzen) in order to identify the results of these urban processes on household form, material wealth, access to space and other resources, and the experiences and quality of quotidian life. Research at El Purgatorio serves as a starting point by analyzing differential access to basic resources, including building materials, living space, staples, secondary necessities, luxury foodstuffs, and other portable material goods. The dynamics of household and family change, redistribution of wealth, and the tradeoffs of urbanism are highlighted by research in Sector B South. Future research in the valley will help bring those dynamics into clearer articulation with modern case studies. What is clear now, however, is that social hierarchy, material inequalities, economic productivity, and household diversity are interrelated at El Purgatorio. In a longer-term perspective, then, we might anticipate changes to household form and inequality during processes of urbanism, including urban growth, development, and decline (for example, Susser 1999; Venkatesh 2014). Consequently, city planners, architects, and policymakers may have access to longer-term perspectives on urbanism and its effects. These perspectives may then help develop more informed urban plans and policies.

At El Purgatorio, it appears that household form and material inequality were interrelated. They may also have been reconfigured during the rapid settlement of Sector B South. In-migration was likely motivated by the promise of secure access to foodstuffs and to sacred spaces—especially in the context of Chimú expansion to the north. Preliminary examination of periurban sites suggests that many are less densely populated than El Purgatorio. This preliminary comparison between El Purgatorio and hinterland sites raises the question of whether some households lost access to physical space when joining the dense urban landscape. Proximity to resources at El Purgatorio almost certainly meant proximity to the watchful eye of administrators and submission to labor taxes. Broader access to certain resources, gained by urban migration, may then also have led to the creation or exacerbation of other kinds of material and consequent social inequalities.

Inequality is one of the most pressing issues faced by both academics and the public. Anthropologists know that inequality has different configurations and consequences in different contexts. Consequently, archaeologists can engage in broadly meaningful discussions with the public by providing long-term and cross-cultural perspectives on inequality (e.g., Smith 2010a). Here I examine the configuration and consequences of material and social inequality among commoner households in an ancient urban neighborhood in Peru.

The research I report here was a component of the El Purgatorio Archaeological Project (PAEP) directed by Dr. Melissa Vogel (Clemson) between 2004 and 2011. I conducted excavations using a "neighborhood archaeology" (Pacifico 2014) strategy to examine the social organization of commoners and the significance of their everyday lives and domestic activities in the social production of El Purgatorio, capital of the Casma Polity or State. Neighborhood archaeology is a methodological and theoretical approach that builds upon the foundations of household archaeology and the archaeology of communities (e.g., Canuto and Yaeger 2000; Inomata and Coben 2006). Neighborhood archaeology examines multiple houses and households as well as their spatial setting as an interrelated complex of context and content (see Hutson 2016; Pacifico and Truex 2019; Smith and Novic 2012; Stone 1987 as extensive examples). Neighborhood areas, houses, and rooms are simultaneously the containers for and content of archaeological data. Neighborhood archaeology synthesizes spatial and artifact data to provide a more detailed understanding of ancient social life than is possible through household archaeology, though it tends to trade depth of detail at the household level for broader detail at the settlement level.

Here I argue that commoners at El Purgatorio were a complex, stratified population. In the context of fourteenth-century El Purgatorio, household configuration and social status were interrelated because different household configurations meant different levels of participation in citywide and neighborhood-focused redistributive and labor economies that focused on feasting (especially *chicha* [maize beer]). Larger households could provide more labor, were more productive, and therefore became "wealthier" in terms of domestic architecture and space. The wealthiest households were affiliated with El Purgatorio's elites, who lived in the city's monumental district. Smaller households provided less labor, were less productive, and therefore were "poorer" and of lower status with respect to these metrics. However, access to protein and agricultural goods was in some ways uniform among commoner Casmeños. Residential space, as well as the comfort and permanence it provided, were variables related to wealth, status, and household configuration. However, nutritional staples were widely available and equitably distributed among commoners at El Purgatorio (Pacifico 2014).

These conclusions raise additional hypotheses that will be addressed by future research in the Casma Valley and into the Casma State. First, because El Purgatorio's commoner residential districts were rapidly occupied in the fourteenth century, new residents may have already been related to one another by idioms of kinship and status that resonate with historical and ethnohistoric models of the *ayllu* (e.g., Allen 2002; Mayer 2002; Wernke 2013). If this is the case, then villages and hamlets in the Casma Valley hinterland were characterized by significant social and material hierarchies. If this were the case, then those hierarchies may have been reconfigured and concretized in the sociospatial construction of El Purgatorio's commoner neighborhoods. Potential material differences in terms of access to foodstuffs were equalized by the redistributive economy organized by El Purgatorio's elites and evidenced by artifacts found in Sector B South. Certainty about long-term change of Casma State society requires additional exploration of the hinterland (currently being conducted by the author). However, at present, research into El Purgatorio's commoners suggests that the nature of the Casma State was likely an economic apparatus for organizing the production and redistribution of foodstuffs bolstered by periodic rituals involving the massive consumption of *chicha* (and other things, like marine mollusks) in both residential and monumental districts.

CITIES, SOCIAL DIVERSITY, AND HOUSEHOLDS

Cities and social diversity have been conceptually linked at least since V. Gordon Childe's (1950) Marxian evolutionist approach, and so "diversity" often reads as "rigid social hierarchy." In a Childean schema, cities emerged when productive surplus allowed certain members of society to cease working and begin administering the works and products of others (see also Rousseau 1997[1755]). This separation of labor forms is associated with the development of cities in agrarian landscapes and the formation of permanent states with legible symbolic systems for representing and administering production (Childe 1950, 9). Alternative configurations for conceptualizing urban social diversity include structural-functional differentiation (Wheatley 1971); diversity in religion, social values, and ethnicity (Butzer 2008); positions in multilevel networks (Smith 2006); and role in long-distance trade (Hansen 2008), among other schema. These diverse schemas suggest that to understand urbanism and social diversity, an approach is needed that is flexible enough to be context-specific but sufficiently concrete to provide for cross-cultural comparison. Household identity and neighborhood role are one such approach in that together they show how social diversity was configured in the very domain in which most people spent much of their time (Keith 2003, 58).

Andean urbanism has largely been understood from the perspective of economic specialization, intensive settlement nucleation, and the concomitant social structures that emerge out of economic specialization in intensive settlements (Bawden 1982; Brennan 1982; Burger 1991, 293). This approach posits that Andean urban settlements emerged sometime between the late first millennium BC and early first millennium AD. Others (e.g., Pozorski and Pozorski 2008) argue that urban societies existed as early as the second millennium BC and indeed right in the Casma Valley, in the shadow of what would become El Purgatorio and Sector B South. The argument over the emergence of cities—and therefore urbanism's link to complexity—is founded on the belief that cities and social hierarchy are cogenetic: that they arise simultaneously. In this argument, cities are large, complex settlements with diverse functions within a wider social landscape.

Rather than disputing the genesis of social complexity and cities, an alternative approach to understanding inequality in a long-term perspective is to consider inequality to be a fundamental aspect of human society at all scales. In the context of cities, which I argue can be thought of as intensified human settlements (Pacifico 2014), we might rather ask *if* and *how* inequality was configured and how it changed during urban growth, development, and evaporation (not to mention collapse). At El Purgatorio, a capital city by many accounts, my research began this process by exploring *if* and *how* social diversity was configured among the commoner residents.

This question was particularly important because leading models of Prehispanic Andean cities (e.g., Kolata 1997, though see Kolata 2013 for an updated approach; Makowski 2008; Von Hagen and Morris 1998) suggest that they were political projects with few inhabitants compared to modern cities, limited social diversity, and no social factions. While the core of this political model holds up at El Purgatorio, its details require revision; El Purgatorio appears to have been a political project directed by strong central powers, but was also internally diverse. Internal economic and social diversity led to multiple loci of peripheral power in commoner households. To examine social diversity in its various forms (e.g., social hierarchy, material inequality, occupational specialization, ethnic diversity), architectural mapping, surface artifact collection, and systematic excavation were used to compare the material evidence for social diversity among numerous households inhabiting El Purgatorio's commoner residential district, Sector B South.

Results from Sector B South suggest a model of the household defined by people sharing a residence, productive pursuits, and a sense of commonality organized around a kinship idiom (see also Kenoyer 2008; Stone 2008 for allied approaches). This model was selected because it appears to correspond to significant social units as actually practiced in El Purgatorio's commoner residential district. Analysis of the standing architecture, described in more detail below, revealed a number of distinct structures with evidence of residential activity that linked the co-residing inhabitants in subsistence and social activities. As co-residents sharing subsistence and social activities, households in Sector B South support the composite definition of the household—one that encompasses demographic, spatial, practical, and conceptual elements for locating households, their residents, their significance, and their experiences in the processes of urbanism.

THE LATE INTERMEDIATE PERIOD, EL PURGATORIO, AND SECTOR B SOUTH

El Purgatorio is a very large archaeological site in the lower Casma Valley (figure 7.1), about 80 km due west of the highland center Huaraz and the nearby site of Chavín de Huantar. Located at the furthest reach of the foothills of the Cordillera Negra, the Casma Valley was an advantageous route from sea to sierra to *selva*. El Purgatorio is situated in the Casma Valley at the base and up the flanks of the mountain Cerro Mucho Malo, which rises over 700 masl (meters above sea level), so it is within sight and walking distance of the Early Intermediate Period ritual fortress Chankillo and the preceramic center of Pampa de las Llamas–Moxeke. El Purgatorio was identified in the 1930s by Julio Tello (1956), visited by Donald Collier (1962) and Donald E. Thompson (1964, 1974) in the 1950s, observed by Rosa Fung Pineda and Carlos Williams León (1977) in the 1970s, and surveyed by David Wilson (1995) in the 1990s. The PAEP began the first systematic investigations of the site in 2004 (Vogel and Vilcherrez 2004). Mapping, surface artifact collection, excavations, and a number of laboratory analyses have revealed that El Purgatorio was settled as early as the eighth century AD (Vogel and Pacifico 2011). Yet the massive commoner residential district was only occupied in the very late thirteenth through very early fifteenth centuries (Pacifico 2014; Vogel et al. 2012). These dating schemes mean that while the monumental and semimonumental

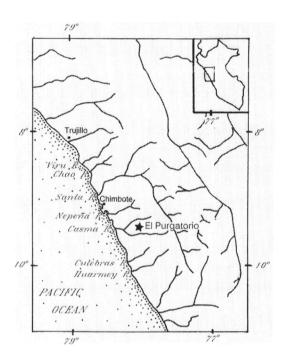

FIGURE 7.1. Location
of El Purgatorio on Peru's
North Coast

sectors had long lives spanning the eighth through the fourteenth centuries AD, the commoner residential district—which likely housed the majority of the city's inhabitants—was built, occupied, and abandoned all within about 120 years ranging from AD 1295 to 1405 (Pacifico 2014, 211). This rapid immigration, construction, and abandonment of Sector B South highlights the need to focus on urbanism as a process of social reconfiguration, a process that can be best understood at the household level and at the level of articulated households: the neighborhood.

El Purgatorio consists of four sectors defined by topographical separation and characterized by different forms of architecture and sector layouts (figure 7.2). Sectors A, B, and C were contemporaneously inhabited during the final century or so of El Purgatorio's occupation, as is demonstrated by numerous radiocarbon assays, consistent ceramic decorative motifs (Vogel 2011), and mimetic techniques utilized among the three sectors that were systematically investigated (Pacifico 2014).

Sector A is a monumental district characterized by large, rectangular, multi-function compounds constructed of adobe and stone (Vogel et al. 2010). The size, construction materials, and artifacts found within these compounds indicate that Sector A housed elites and hosted rituals with citywide importance (Vogel et al. 2010, 35). Sector A was also the site of administrative and productive activities

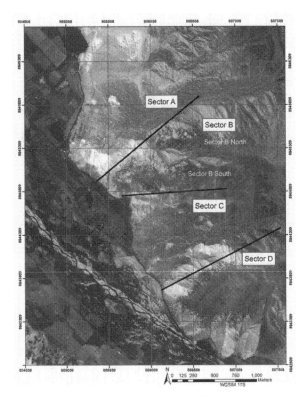

FIGURE 7.2. El Purgatorio overview showing Sectors A, B, C, and D

(Vogel et al. 2010, 35). Sector C is a less well-built portion of the city that also had multifunctional adobe and stone compounds. Sector C is characterized by rectangular compounds containing adobe and built largely of stone. However, it is not as well constructed as Sector A. Sector D contains rough building foundations and patches cleared of stone that may have been residences and animal pens, though its history and functions require further analysis.

Sector B was the commoner residential district of El Purgatorio. While Sectors A and C are located in the pampa at the western toe of Cerro Mucho Malo, Sector B climbs the two west-facing arms of Mucho Malo—a geography that divides the commoner residential district into northern and southern counterparts: Sector B North and Sector B South (figure 7.3). Sector B was identified as the commoner residential district because, unlike Sectors A and C, Sector B is characterized primarily by numerous repetitive structures made of piled, unworked field stones. Many of those structures are domestic terraces that climb Mucho Malo, much as *pueblos jóvenes* or *favelas* surround rapidly expanding cities in Latin America today. Sector

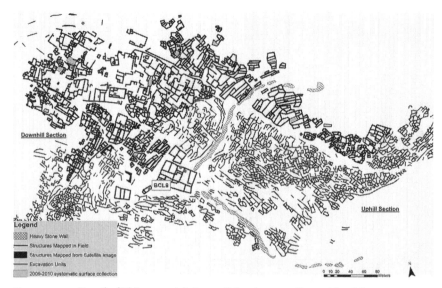

FIGURE 7.3. Detail of El Purgatorio's Sector B South, a nonelite residential area

B South is the focus of this chapter, and it is covered by the foundations of stone-based structures comparable to the SIAR at Chan Chan (Topic 1982) and is itself divided into upper and lower sections by a horizontal wall at about 268 masl.

RESEARCH METHODS AND RESULTS

Investigations in Sector B South used a methodology I call neighborhood archaeology. Neighborhood archaeology builds upon household archaeology and the more recent community archaeologies[2] of Marcello Canuto and Jason Yaeger (2000), Allison R. Davis (2011), Naoise Mac Sweeney (2011), and Steven A. Wernke (2006, 2007, 2013). Community archaeology improved upon household archaeology by recognizing that households are typically diverse, socially embedded, and politically salient units of societies (e.g., Keith 2003; Sampson 2012; Stone 1987). Neighborhood archaeology improves upon community archaeology by investigating the interrelation of demographic, spatial, and ideational components of communities to understand how large-scale social formations (e.g., cities, polities, states) were produced vis-à-vis their commoner residents' everyday activities.

Drawing on practice theory (e.g., Bourdieu 1972; de Certeau 1984; Giddens 1984), identity theory (e.g., Anderson 1983; Brubaker and Cooper 2000; Cohen 1985), and spatialized urban anthropology (e.g., Davis 1998, 2004; Holston 1999,

2008; Low 1996, 1999a, 1999b, 2011), neighborhood archaeology examines households in context with respect to their identities, everyday activities, spatial practices, and experiences to understand—in this case—how commoners contributed to social institutions at El Purgatorio and in the Casma Polity. Michael Smith and Juliana Novic (2012) defined neighborhoods as bottom-up social groups where individuals have face-to-face social relationships. Scott Hutson (2016) suggested that neighborhoods likely had fuzzy boundaries but could house no more than about 2,000 people. These guidelines are helpful in identifying and analyzing archaeological neighborhoods. However, it is most likely that neighborhoods were formed through the tensions of bottom-up *and* top-down forces (Pacifico 2019; Pacifico and Truex 2019). Moreover, it is unlikely that all neighborhood residents knew (or now know) one another face to face. Rather, neighborhoods are places where neighbors know one another *as if* they had face-to-face relationships (Pacifico 2019; Pacifico and Truex 2019). This experiential component of neighborhoods helps make potentially alienating and new urban environments tolerable, especially in periods of rapid urbanization—points elaborated by Hutson (2016), Monica L. Smith (2019), and David Pacifico and Lise Truex (2019; also Pacifico 2019). In this light, despite the internal wall, Sector B South should be considered a neighborhood in that it is spatially distinct from other parts of the city, its residents likely encountered one another virtually on a daily basis, and it includes areas where these neighbors came together periodically. These are the archaeological hallmarks of neighborhoods (Hutson 2016; Pacifico 2019; Smith and Novic 2012).

Two forms of analysis were used to analyze the structures in Sector B South: qualitative analysis and quantitative analysis.[3] Qualitative analysis focused on an examination of the morphology, materials, and construction techniques utilized in building the different residences in Sector B South as well as their location within the residential district. Melissa Vogel (2003, 58, 232) identifies a number of indicators of status in Casmeño settlements, including adobe, plaster, roofing, serving vessels in general, and stirrup-spout vessels in particular. Hendrik Van Gijseghem (2001, 264) identifies additional "indexical features" of prestige, including ramps and daises, which can be used to mark space as special and also formalize movement within spaces in accordance with spatialized strategies of authority (sensu Lefebvre 1991; Swenson 2006). Quantitative analysis focused on examining the consumption patterns of domestic space, ceramic assemblages, and organic remains found within the residences and other structures in Sector B South. Material richness can be measured in terms of the amount of material present (e.g., total volume of space consumed), the diversity of materials users accessed (e.g., diversity of species utilized), and the type and amount of skill and labor available for architectural projects.

To facilitate these analyses, a qualitative schema for sample selection was developed based on building morphology. I identified three different kinds of architecture in Sector B South: orthogonal, semiorthogonal, and irregular structures. Within these morphological categories, I identified three functional room types: processing rooms, storage rooms, and communal spaces. These room types were defined by their morphology and relationship to adjacent rooms. Processing rooms contained *batanes*; storage rooms were small, regular, and often clustered; communal spaces were defined by the largest room or rooms in a given structure, especially if they had multiple entrances. These categories provided a representative sample of architecture and artifact assemblages for interpreting the social dimensions of Sector B South. Indeed, excavations confirmed the residential functions of these structures but also revealed differences in supplemental functions, household configuration, and status hierarchy among commoners.

Unfortunately, there was no perfect calculus of household status differences. Rather, different lines of evidence provided insight on different aspects of social hierarchy and inequality in Sector B South. Architectural features provided the clearest and most unequivocal image of social diversity in Sector B South from both a qualitative and quantitative standpoint. Ceramic assemblages measured by volume, diversity, and density paint a mixed picture of inequality in the residential neighborhood.[4] Organic remains suggest a certain equality of access to staples. However, further examination is required to fully understand the organic remains from Sector B South at El Purgatorio.

Qualitative analyses showed that only orthogonal buildings (figure 7.4, figure 7.5) included labor-intensive construction materials such as adobe and mortar; extensive fill efforts to bring surfaces to level; "indexical features" of prestige, for example, ramps, daises, and platforms (Van Gijseghem 2001, 264); and orthogonal footprints indicative of a single, coordinated planning and building episode.

In contrast, semiorthogonal buildings (figure 7.6) consisted only of unmortared, unworked stone foundations topped with *quincha* walls, noted as commoner materials by Vogel (2003, 58). They conformed to the landscape with little or no leveling fill, and their footprints meandered. Their morphology suggests initial construction around a central orthogonal patio, with later, agglutinative expansions that drifted further and further away from the original orthogonal room.

Finally, irregular buildings (figure 7.7) also consisted exclusively of unmortared, unworked field stone with *quincha*-topped walls. Irregular footprints indicate that these buildings were built by their residents and crammed into whatever space was available after neighboring buildings had been constructed.

Quantitative analysis showed differential access to space and ceramic vessels but relatively uniform access to foodstuffs. Analysis of variance (ANOVA) (table 7.1,

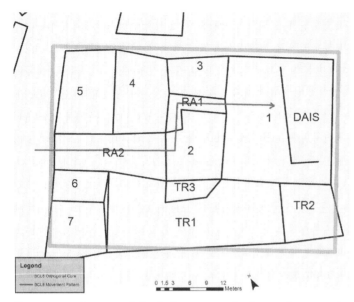

FIGURE 7.4. Layout and circulation pattern of orthogonal structure in Sector B South

FIGURE 7.5. Adobes and rock fill in Sector B South orthogonal structure

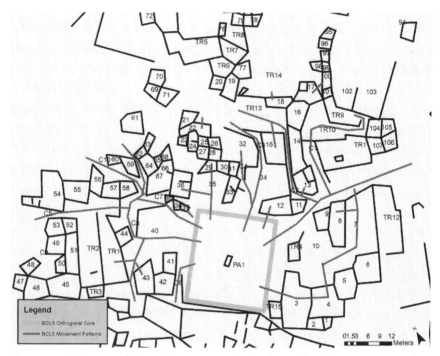

FIGURE 7.6. Layout and circulation pattern of semiorthogonal patio-group structure in Sector B South

table 7.2) reveals a statistically significant difference in space per room among these three different residence forms.[5] Orthogonal residences had the most room space, semi-orthogonal residences had a middling amount of room space, and irregular residences had the least room space per capita. Ceramic artifact assemblages complement these findings. Ceramic fragment density, overall abundance (within 2 m × 2m or 2 m × 3m sample units to sterile), and relative abundance (defined as the ratio between different functional vessel forms in the same unit)[6] indicate that orthogonal residences had access to more and higher-quality ceramic vessels.[7] In contrast, organic remains from foodstuffs, including marine mollusks, maize, and domesticated fruits, were relatively equivalent among these three residence forms.[8]

MATERIALIZING HOUSEHOLD FORM, FAMILY, AND SOCIAL INEQUALITY

Fourteen separate structures were mapped in Sector B South, and eight of them were excavated. The archaeological remains in Sector B South suggest that taphonomic

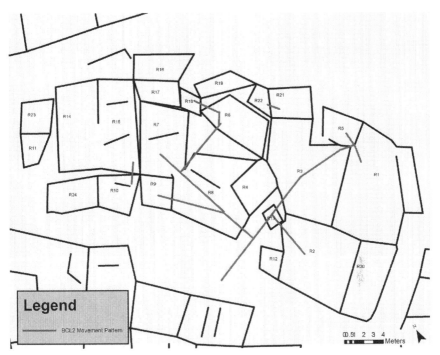

FIGURE 7.7. Layout and circulation pattern of irregular structure in Sector B South

processes left a relatively clear record of room functions. There were typically three strata to a depth of about 50 cm in rooms bounded by gabbro stone foundations rising above the current surface. The top layer was a mix of overburden and silt with artifacts that had washed into or been dropped onto their current location, which was probably not far from their last place of use. The next stratum was typically an informal—or sometimes prepared—use-floor supporting objects used or stored in the room and then left behind. Below this was a sandy, silty matrix with stone and rubble fill with some cultural material. Of seventeen radiocarbon assays, sixteen produced dates ranging from the late thirteenth to early fifteenth centuries, suggesting a very short lifespan for Sector B South.

Data were collected through mapping, surface artifact collection, and excavation, then processed through laboratory and spatial analyses—all of which were supervised by the author. Analyses indicate the presence of three different social statuses that composed the commoners at El Purgatorio. These three social statuses were part of a fairly broad middle class, as defined by their relationship to the means of production. In brief, it seems that whatever their status, as commoners

TABLE 7.1. Analysis of variance (ANOVA) of room area, by building morphology

	N	Mean	Std. Deviation	Std. Error	95% Confidence Interval for Mean		Minimum	Maximum
					Lower Bound	Upper Bound		
High-Status ORTHOGONAL	69	77.48640899	98.51145110	11.859385562	54	101	0.960589	422.053422
Middle-Status SEMI ORTHOG	706	40.03492079	61.10213902	2.299609145	36	45	2.193317	692.330310
Low-Status IRREGULAR	166	23.61220958	19.57337833	1.519188749	21	27	2.699715	138.273000

TABLE 7.2. Statistical significance of ANOVA

	Sum of Squares	df	Mean Square	F	Sig.
Between groups	149681.727	3	49893.909	13.989	0.000
Within groups	3363427.707	943	3566.731		
Total	3513109.435	946			

they did not own, grow, or broker the majority of the raw materials in the Casma economy. Rather, they provided the labor for manufacturing the raw materials into the staple goods on which El Purgatorio's economy was based. These diverse social statuses among the middle class correlate to different household configurations that typified Casma commoners. Household configuration, in turn, defined potential for participation in the redistributive economy that was central to the life of both the Sector B South neighborhood and the city at large. This economy likely centered on *chicha*, given the abundant evidence for its consumption and production: maize cobs, grinding stones, brewing, fermenting, and consumption vessels.

Several structures contained evidence of serving as focal nodes of production and consumption (sensu Hutson 2016). Those structures are BCL8 and BCL1, high-status urban commoner residences with additional public functions; BCL5, a middle-status urban commoner residence; and BCL2, a low-status urban commoner residence. Within the context of El Purgatorio and the wider hinterland in the Casma Valley, these divisions among the urban commoners suggest that El Purgatorio's commoners composed a broad and stratified middle class. The highest-status commoners may have been low-level administrators in charge of ensuring the neighborhood's overall productivity in the city's and state's economies. Middle-and low-status urban commoners would have been middle-class laborers and manufacturers (perhaps part-time specialists in food production and building construction). It is likely that a lower class of laborers lived outside the city. However, it is expected that these classes were not hermetically sealed. There were likely divisions within them, the potential for some mobility, and certainly porosity and fuzzy boundaries between them. Indeed, a classic Western class structure may not perfectly map onto ancient Casma society.

High-Status Urban Commoners: Nuclear Families and Nice Houses

Here I focus on four buildings that illustrate the archaeological and social differences among three distinct status groups and household forms among El Purgatorio's commoners in Sector B South: BCL8, BCL1, BCL5, and BCL2. The highest-status urban commoner households are represented by BCL8 and BCL1. Middle-status urban commoner households are represented by BCL5, and low-status urban commoners are represented by BCL2. BCL8 and BCL1 are two orthogonal buildings at different central points within the overall layout of Sector B South. They also represent two complementary functions within the neighborhood, both of which were carried out by the highest-status members of the urban commoners.

BCL8: HIGH-STATUS RESIDENCE AND OCCASIONAL
PRODUCTION AND CONSUMPTION CENTER

BCL8 is at the overall center of Sector B South (figure 7.3). The building is fairly large (tables 7.3 and 7.4), with an overall orthogonal footprint (figure 7.4) and orthogonal individual rooms that meet neatly at shared corners. BCL8 is located on a ridge line on the southern arm of Mucho Malo's western face. It is located up against the Heavy Stone Wall that traverses the 268 masl contour of Mucho Malo and also divides Sector B South into uphill and downhill sections (figure 7.3). Because of its location, BCL8 took on a number of important characteristics. First, it was built at a location that was both the nexus of, and the point of symbolic distinction between, residents of uphill and downhill Sector B South. The Heavy Stone Wall was neither defensive nor very effective for preventative functions. Rather, it likely provided a symbolic break between residents of different parts of a moiety-organized neighborhood. It also created a large terrace that may have served as a promenade. In that light, the imagined component of the neighborhood community in Sector B South likely drew on idioms of kinship, suggesting that households were likely reflexively conceived of as families of various configurations and sizes.

Residing at this key point in the neighborhood landscape, BCL8 had a commanding view of the lower Casma Valley and its extensive irrigated floor. Given that BCL8 also had the most extensive food-processing center in the neighborhood (Pacifico 2012, 2014), it is likely that BCL8 played an administrative role in the political ecology of the valley, at least insofar as that political ecology involved commoner households. Because of this centrality and its location on the spur, BCL8 was also meant to be seen. Beyond its material functions, BCL8 also played a symbolic function within the neighborhood community of Sector B South.

The symbolic function of BCL8 was tied to the status of the residents and chief users and was materialized in the construction materials used to build it. Those construction materials were unique in Sector B South and matched in the entirety of Sector B only by a single structure in Sector B North called BAS5, which is at the center of *its* arm of Mucho Malo. The construction materials that set BCL8 apart are the adobes used in its construction and the technique with which they were laid. BCL8 is the only structure in Sector B South to include adobes, and they were laid in a chamber-and-fill method using the *soga y cabeza* bricklaying pattern (figure 7.5). Adobes require choice sand, labor, and water—all of which are scarcer in the desert and require transportation to the construction site, in contrast to the unworked field stone that was used in virtually every other structure in Sector B South and Sector B North. Both adobes and water are heavy. They must have been hauled several dozens of meters uphill and over a kilometer away from the river bottom. The ability to marshal rare resources and skill is evidence that the residents of BCL8 were

TABLE 7.3. Ordinal comparison of overall building (cluster) area; clusters ranked by overall area (smallest to largest, in m²)

Arch. Type	Type 5	Type 5	Type 2	Type 2	Type 2	Type 6	Type 3	Type 3	Type 2	Type 3	Type 4	Type 4	Type 1	Type 1	Type 4
Cluster	BAS3	BAS2	BCL2	BCL9	BCL10	BAS4	BCL1	BAS5	BCL3	BCL8	BCL4	BCL5	BCL16	BCL15	BCL6
Total Area	71.68	321.16	542.84	598.6	864.74	964.6	1093.5	1257.74	1913.44	2030.72	2366.65	5141.39	5293.24	6539.23	8924.15

* mean = 2,528.25 m², median = 1,257.74 m²

TABLE 7.4. Ordinal comparison of mean room (enclosure) area; clusters ranked by mean enclosure size (smallest to largest, in m²)

Arch. Type	Type 2	Type 2	Type 2	Type 3	Type 3	Type 4	Type 4	Type 5	Type 4	Type 4	Type 4	Type 6	Type 5	Type 3	Type 3
Cluster	BCL10	BCL9	BCL2	BCL3	BCL1	BCL16	BCL4	BAS3	BCL15	BCL5	BCL6	BAS4	BAS2	BCL8	BAS5
Mean Enclosure Area (m²)	20.11	20.64	22.62	27.33	28.04	32.08	32.42	35.84	37.37	41.13	53.12	87.69	107.05	135.38	314.44

* mean = 66.35 m², median = 35.8 m²

among the highest-status residents in Sector B South. Their status was likely a function of their linkage to central authorities in other parts of El Purgatorio, especially Sector A. The use of adobes and the *soga y cabeza* (figure 7.5) bricklaying pattern are mimetic of the elite compounds of Sector A, many of which are *soga y cabeza* adobes atop stone foundations.

Architectural features of BCL8 also link its residents—and functions—to those of Sector A. "Indexical features" of prestige (Van Gijseghem 2001, 264) are architectural features that set apart buildings and their residents as distinct from others in Sector B South. BCL8's Room 1 is its largest room, and Room 1's back wall abuts the Heavy Stone Wall (figure 7.3). Indeed, to be in BCL8 Room 1 is to be at the conceptual and physical center of Sector B South. The main feature of that room is a dais (figure 7.4), an architectural marker of a special space, often used for audiences and other important events including feasts. Room 1 is approached by a zigzagging ramp that formalizes movement while traversing the rooms that front Room 1, rooms that likely supported the residential function of BCL8, as evidenced by ceramic and organic remains.

In addition to these indexical markers, which both formalized movement and the use of space in BCL8 while also symbolically marking it as special to those who saw it, BCL8 has one of the few overt instances of architectural decoration in Sector B South. BCL8 had significant roofed portions—noted by Vogel (2003) as indices of high-status spaces in Casma Polity settlements—as evidenced by the stumps of wooden posts once used to support the roof sections. Like adobe, wood is a resource-intensive material. One post found in BCL8 was particularly thick in diameter and, more important, was carved in a decorative "stacked saucer" form, much like an oversize wooden version of the bendable section of a plastic straw.

Complementing the architectural evidence from BCL8, the portable remains recovered there indicate high-status commoner residential features combined with public administrative and ritual functions (Nash [2009] noted that combined residential elite and public ritual functions are common in Prehispanic Andean settlements). Architectural elements emulated the elite architecture especially from the city's monumental and administrative core in Sector A.

BCL8's portable remains show that complementary and perhaps competing activities occurred in Sector B South. BCL8's Room 1 produced the most bowls (end-user serving vessels) recovered from any single data-collection unit (68 bowl fragments from surface collection [48.22% of all bowl fragments from surface collection]; the next closest unit produced 16 fragments in one excavation unit). In complement, a high number of jar fragments were also found in BCL8 Room 1 during surface collection (n=27, 29.67% of all jar fragments collected during surface collections). A high quantity of bowl fragments indicates that the room was a primary food and drink consumption area, while the jars—useful both in *chicha* brewing and decanting—suggest that the pouring and consumption of *chicha* happened with greatest intensity in BCL8's Room 1. It was also the location of the only stirrup-spout fragment found in all of Sector B South and produced the only sculptural vessel found in Sector B South, a duck-bellied vessel. Stirrup spouts were identified by Vogel (2003) as high-status vessels and are recognized as used for serving liquids. The organic remains from BCL8 Room 1 indicate that large quantities of marine mollusks, which provided the majority of the protein in Sector B South, were consumed in BCL8 Room 1.

In total, the architectural and portable remains from BCL8, especially Room 1, indicate that it served as a central structure in Sector B South that was the venue for intensive food-consumption episodes: feasts. The abundance of mollusk remains and the abundance of evidence for *chicha* production both in BCL8's Room 7 and elsewhere in Sector B South (Pacifico 2012) lead to the conclusion that BCL8 was a feasting venue in which mollusks and *chicha* were consumed in great quantity. Evidence for *chicha* production includes the ubiquitous maize cobs found throughout the neighborhood, brewing vessels (*tinajas*, jars), and grinding implements for rendering malted maize kernels into brewable mash.

Despite its ritual and production functions, BCL8 was also residential, and the household it sheltered was likely relatively small (likely conceived as a kin group, e.g., a family) compared to the middle-status urban commoners discussed below. The series of terraces and rooms that surround BCL8 show evidence of residential functions. Chief among these clues are a full suite of domestic vessels, including not only the bowls and jars used for serving and producing *chicha* and other foodstuffs, respectively, but also more mundane *ollas* used in cooking. There are also smaller food-production stations that indicate smaller-scale food-production episodes more suitable for a nuclear or small extended family than for feasting purposes. Specifically, grinding stones (*batanes*) found in small clusters in BCL8 Room 1 and a lone *batán* in BCL8 Room 3 indicate that small groups of people were producing relatively small amounts of food for relatively small groups of consumers. Small groups of *batanes* are the ideal setup for working, talking, and perhaps watching other people (e.g., children playing) while family foodstuffs are being processed. Taken altogether, the evidence from BCL8 suggests multiple scales of use within the residence of a high-status nuclear or small extended family.

These small groupings of *batanes* contrast with the line of eleven *batanes* in Room 7, which suggests that massive food-production episodes were conducted under the conditions of surveillance and with relatively little socializing. A single overseer would have been able to watch over all eleven processing stations in a single gaze. Because Room 7's line of eleven *batanes* faces a retention wall, only adjacent workers would have been able to converse. Moreover, the relatively small room and proximity of the retention wall mitigate the probability of multitasking while grinding food in Room 7. This arrangement of *batanes* suggests a contrasting context to smaller groups found elsewhere. Whereas smaller groups could have been used in daily, social production episodes, these eleven *batanes* are arranged for maximal production and minimal socialization.

Analysis of variance in spatial consumption (measured by average room size) indicates with statistical significance that this family had the privilege of lots of space per room, more than any other resident in Sector B South. They may also have had access to a second residence or been directly tied to a family living in BCL1, which also served as a public functional counterpart to BCL8.

BCL1: HIGH-STATUS RESIDENCE AND CENTRAL STORAGE

BCL1 is an orthogonal structure that occupies the center position in the *lower plain* of Sector B South (figure 7.3), surrounded by sprawling middle-status residences. It complements BCL8, and its storage complex is linked to BCL8's receiving room. BCL1 is smaller than BCL8 but is nevertheless orthogonal. Its overall footprint ends in clean orthogonal angles, and its internal rooms meet at neat corners. Unlike BCL8, BCL1 does not incorporate mortar; nor was there evidence of architectural decorations, like the post in BCL8. However, the morphology, location, and spatial consumption of BCL1 suggest that it complemented BCL8 demographically and functionally. It may have been an extension of the BCL8 household or family and appears to have had a centralized storage function in the neighborhood in complement to the consumption and processing functions of BCL8 in Room 1 and Room 7, respectively.

BCL1 is dominated by two features that suggest its dual high-status residential and public administrative function. The core of BCL1 is an open room or patio, perhaps with a large bench, that articulates in an open floor plan into a series of other rooms with multiple functions. Matching the small-family household configuration seen in BCL8, BCL1 has a single and a pair of grinding stones, suggestive of small processing episodes for small to moderate groups of consumers: nuclear or small extended families.

In parallel with this nuclear residential function, BCL1 also houses a formal complex of storage rooms unlike any others found in Sector B South. The northeast quadrant of BCL1 is a series of four, perhaps later expanded to seven, large and rectangular storage rooms. One such room was excavated and was larger than an analogous room excavated in the middle-status urban commoner residence BCL5. In addition to this orthogonal complex of storage rooms in BCL1 is a string of additional orthogonal storage rooms off its west edge. Fronting the main complex of

BCL1 storage rooms is a receiving room that is somewhat thin but fronts the length of the storage compartments. The receiving room has a rare, still-visible doorway that opens onto one of Sector B South's paths that extends up between a complex of low-status urban commoner residences located on the steep side of the spur atop which BCL8 resides. The path ends at BCL8 Room 8, a heavy-walled receiving room off the northwest corner of BCL8, a room that also contained a number of jar fragments.

Taken together, the central structures of BCL8 and BCL1 suggest that high-status urban commoner families occupied central spaces and central roles in the redistributive economy of Sector B South. They also linked the neighborhood and its ritual-economic institutions to the elites in Sector A, both symbolically and practically. BCL8 was visually symbolic—through architectural mimesis—of Sector A and the elite central authority that originated there. BCL1 supported the production and consumption activities that underwrote the extension of central authority into Sector B South by storing the goods to be consumed in BCL8 Room 1. Indeed, if this is the case, then high-status urban commoners in Sector B South, occupying BCL8 and BCL1, were likely a single nuclear family or a small core of an extended family in which the administration of elite-originating authority was vested.

MIDDLE-STATUS URBAN COMMONER RESIDENCES: EXTENDED FAMILIES
In contrast to these smaller but high-status commoner households in Sector B South, many of its residents lived in patio-group clusters of semiorthogonal form. These patio groups were inhabited by multiple nodes of extended families that occupied separate lobes around an orthogonal patio that served as their cluster's core. In terms of architectural materials, these patio groups had access only to limited construction materials and were probably built by their inhabitants and those with whom their inhabitants might be able to engage in labor exchanges (e.g., Mayer 2002; Smith 2007, 2011).

BCL5 is an excellent example of the patio group as a household and exemplifies the evidence that suggests that its residents were of middling status among the commoners in Sector B South. BCL5 (figure 7.6) is built entirely of stone foundations composed of unworked stones found right on the side of the mountain. Atop these stone foundations were *quincha* walls that are no longer present. In fact, no *quincha* itself was found, although the raw materials of *quincha* including *Gynerium saggitatum* and *Phragmites comunis* were recovered throughout Sector B South, including in BCL5.[9]

The morphology of BCL5 indicates the strategy of its construction. It was built around an orthogonal core of a rectangular patio. As families built and expanded their lobes off of the patio, their architecture strayed further and further from orthogonality. This semiorthogonal morphology suggests an expedient construction plan (Smith 2007). Expediently built structures begin with an ideal orthogonal core—in this case likely a central patio—but then extend outward, with less attention to the aesthetics of orthogonality and more attention to rapid construction of additional rooms built most likely by the residents of the structure. This vernacular architectural strategy requires less specialized labor and implies diminished visual impact from high-status urban commoner structures in Sector B South. However, it does not suggest a lack of a plan or skill. Rather, it is a separate planning scheme, skill set, and response to priorities from those employed in BCL8 and BCL1. Orthogonal structures were built with the same plan and perhaps the same planners and laborers as the monumental core in Sector A. Similarly, their functions were lightly residential and largely symbolic and public. In contrast, the semiorthogonal structures in Sector B South were largely residential in function and satisfied attendant priorities. Patios at the center of residential lobes provided places for communal work—evidenced by *batanes*—and for communal consumption—evidenced by the high number of bowl fragments excavated in BCL5 Patio 1 (n=14, 17.5% of the excavated bowl fragments).

In addition to these social priorities, residential comfort was also attended to in the design of middle-status commoner patio-group residences. Raised door jambs held in the cool air near the floor as the desert afternoon heated up, and patios interconnected by small apertures and passageways would have promoted airflow through these shared spaces.

In contrast, many of the rooms in the residential lobes are relatively small compared to their counterparts in high-status urban commoner dwellings (see table 7.1). They also contain individual *batanes* or act as smaller clusters of storage rooms than those of BCL1. These numerous but diminutive sets of resources fortify the conclusion that these patio groups were the residences of middle-status commoners at El Purgatorio. Indeed, ANOVA shows that the spatial consumption of these structures was of a middling magnitude: the average room size for these structures was categorically distinct from the sizes of the rooms of both high-status and low-status urban commoners. The rooms of these structures, on average, are medium in comparison to their neighbors of different statuses. They are not as roomy as high-status commoner dwellings but roomier than low-status commoner dwellings.

However, these structures have an *overall* large size. Why would middle-status households have such access to large spaces, though with limited per capita access to space as calculated by individual inhabitant or room? Clusters of multiple *batanes* suggest that these extended households were able to "earn" the right to such large overall spaces (though still less per capita than high-status urban commoners) by producing surpluses of food, likely for communal consumption outside the

TABLE 7.5. *Batán* configurations and distribution

Status	High	Middle	Low	Total
Batán config.				
Singles	3	189	29	222
Doubles	3	14	1	18
Triples	2	6	1	9
Quads	0	0	1	1
> 10	1	0	0	1

household. While most *batanes* were found as single processing tools in room corners, a number of clusters indicate that special intensive processing sessions were needed to supplement the production of single individuals (table 7.5). Why did they need neat rows of multiple *batanes* when single *batanes* would do in most cases?

Small clusters of *batanes* in these middle-status commoner residences mirror—in miniature—the intensive production center in BCL8 Room 7. Thus middle-status urban commoner households were able to marshal large amounts of labor and therefor claim large amounts of space overall for their families based on the argument that (1) the families were rather large and (2) large families could richly participate in the production of food for neighborhood feasts. Indeed, it appears that they had to make good on this promise, as there are numerous instances of multiple-*batán* installments in middle-status patio-group residences. Some of these are aligned, suggesting in-house surveillance of the production episodes and the administration of these in-house surplus production episodes. This production arrangement compares favorably with Payson Sheets's (2000) findings at Cerén, El Salvador. There, households produced surpluses for a vertical economy in which they exchanged household surplus goods for specialty goods acquired at regional marketplaces. At El Purgatorio, this household surplus was funneled into the vertical neighborhood economy for redistribution at neighborhood feasts or into the citywide economy as labor and goods tribute collected by elites in Sector A. Nevertheless, the limited resources for constructing these residences, the peripheral location in the neighborhood, and the per capita access to space indicate that these residents were of a middle status compared to the nuclear families living in adobe-lain structures of orthogonal morphology at central locations in Sector B South that made reference to the architecture of Sector A.

LOW-STATUS URBAN COMMONERS: CRAMPED QUARTERS

Low-status urban commoner households lived in irregular residences that appear to have been crammed into the space remaining after central, orthogonal, high-status

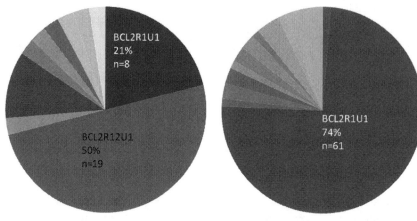

FIGURE 7.8. Chart visualizing ceramic jar fragments from excavations

FIGURE 7.9. Chart visualizing ceramic *tinaja* fragments from excavations

urban commoner households and peripheral, semiorthogonal patio residences had been built by middle-status urban commoners. BCL2 is an excellent example of a low-status urban commoner house. It is built only of unworked field stones and has a kidney bean–like overall footprint. Many of its rooms are irregular multilaterals, including its principle Rooms 1 and 2. Although they are the largest rooms in BCL2, neither is as large as the patios in middle-status urban commoner houses, and they do not form a central space in the residence of a large household. Rather, BCL2 was likely occupied by a nuclear family. The presence of just a single usable grinding stone, with a second recycled in a wall, suggests that the food preparation here was meant only for a small audience. Similarly, the overall small size of the structure suggests a small number of residents. Those residents also occupied the smallest rooms per capita in Sector B South.

However, the residents of BCL2 had access to an unusually large number of ceramics, measured by fragment density, and access to a large variety of vessel forms as well (n=7) (Pacifico 2014, 456). Among those fragments were a large number[10] of *tinaja* and jar fragments excavated, respectively, in Room 1, a large room with a *batán*, and Room 12, a storage room. These ceramic finds suggest that the residents of BCL2 may have been a small household specializing in brewing surplus *chicha* for communal consumption.[11] If that is the case, it is likely that the residents of BCL2 served as brewers in Sector B South. As brewers, they had access to lots of ceramic vessels but not to space, labor-intensive construction materials, or the architectural knowledge applied to orthogonal structures. They may also have been among the

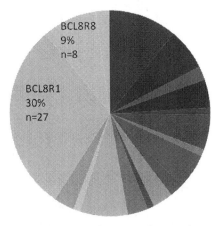

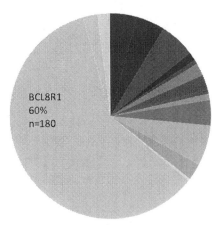

FIGURE 7.10. Jar fragments from surface collections

FIGURE 7.11. *Tinaja* fragments from surface collections

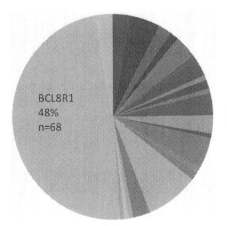

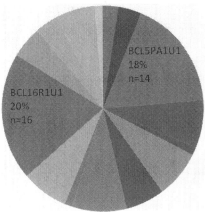

FIGURE 7.12. Ceramic bowl fragments from surface collections

FIGURE 7.13. Ceramic bowl fragments from excavations

last residents to move into Sector B South[12] and therefore were limited to occupying whatever space was left in the neighborhood, as was the case with the residents of other structures of irregular architecture. If that was the case, then it would suggest potential for social mobility in the Casma Valley during the final century and a half at El Purgatorio. Perhaps brewers, likely related to people already living in Sector B South, were brought into the neighborhood to further facilitate the neighborhood and city feasting economy. This move would likely have conferred upon the residents a higher status than that of those living outside the city, but still among the lowest status within the commoner residential neighborhood at El Purgatorio.

CONCLUSIONS, CAVEATS, AND FUTURE DIRECTIONS

A neighborhood archaeological approach at El Purgatorio's Sector B South revealed the extent and configuration of social diversity among commoners in a way focused household archaeology would not have done. Social diversity among commoners was configured around a three-tier status hierarchy that was likely related to family size, subsequent labor power, and perhaps additional qualities like relationship to people already residing in the city and date of migration into the city. Qualitative and quantitative analyses indicate three different status identities among the commoner households at El Purgatorio and the fact that these status differences had consequences in terms of material wealth. First, *high-status urban commoners* lived in orthogonal residences whose form and construction materials made architectural reference to the monumental compounds in Sector A.[13] High-status urban commoners were a social link to city elites, and they played a leading role in creating community in the commoner neighborhoods by hosting massive production and consumption episodes. Given the *overall* size of high-status urban commoner residences and the distribution of *batanes* within their residences, it is likely that high-status urban commoner households consisted of nuclear families or small extended families.

Second, *middle-status urban commoners* lived in sprawling compounds arranged around large central patios. These middle-status commoners lived in smaller rooms than high-status commoners, and they apportioned the greatest amount of their residential spaces for communal patios. These households were extended families composed of numerous nuclear groups, evidenced by the lobe-like sets of rooms and terraces that surround central patios containing redundant food-processing facilities. Due to the large number of people in these households and their numerous grinding stones, it is likely that middle-status households "earned" their right to have extensive overall spaces by providing large amounts of labor in brewing *chicha* for communal events in the neighborhood. These commoners also probably provided a large amount of *chicha* that was skimmed off by elites in Sector A as a tribute tax used in citywide rituals in the monumental district.

Low-status urban commoners lived in small, irregularly shaped residences with small rooms. They were likely nuclear families or small extended families. They did not enjoy the communal spaces of patios or typically have large numbers of grinding stones. Therefore, low-status urban commoner households could not participate robustly in the production of *chicha* for communal consumption, either in the neighborhood or in the citywide rituals held in the monumental district.

However, all the households had access to staple foodstuffs beyond their immediate ability to produce them personally. Although there was no evidence that residents of Sector B South were agriculturalists (as was also the case at Huacas Moche [Chapdelaine 2009]), all households had access to edible marine and terrestrial mollusks (especially *Perumytilus purpuratus* and *Semimytilus algosus*), maize, and domesticated fruits. Thus despite clear evidence of unequal access to architectural, spatial, and labor resources and notwithstanding a complex and unequal distribution of ceramic vessels, households in Sector B South all appeared to have had access to staple goods that they did not produce in raw form themselves: excavations turned up no agricultural implements; Sector B South is far away from and high above the fields and water; in contrast, its residents are very close to the ritual, administrative, and production facilities at El Purgatorio.

BROADER IMPLICATIONS: PRODUCTIVE AND RESTRICTIVE EMBEDDED INEQUALITIES

It is likely that these households and their hierarchies were existent in some form *before* the rapid development of Sector B South in the late thirteenth century AD. These families were probably drawn to the city for the easy and equitable access to foodstuffs arranged by elites in Sector A; in exchange, they provided labor for the production of *chicha* sent to the monumental district for distribution by city elites. However, once in the city, the context and configuration of social hierarchies was likely reconfigured. Preliminary research in El Purgatorio's hinterland (Pacifico 2019) suggests that immigration into El Purgatorio was not a simple translation of the village into the city. Certainly, moving into the city implies accepting many of the negative effects of social density in exchange for other benefits, and the production of neighborhoods can help mitigate the cons by creating a sense of structure, security, and belonging in the new setting (Hutson 2016; Pacifico 2019; Pacifico and Truex 2019; Smith 2019).

However, enduring the negative aspects of population density for access to goods and rituals may not be the only bargain new urbanites encountered. Some commoner households probably retained or attained high statuses through affiliation with elites. But that affiliation and status came with both the responsibilities and the benefits of organizing, hosting, and provisioning feasts. While hosting feasts can establish and concretize status among one's neighbors, hosting is a burdensome activity that requires secure access to and proper distribution of resources. It also comes with the risk of deposition in the case of failure (Dietler 2001; Durkheim 1995 [1912], 217–227; Foucault 1975, 63–69). Other households, those of middling statuses, worked for their access to ample space or were allotted ample space on the promise (viz. "credit" sensu Graeber 2012) of providing ample labor. They, too, gained access to secure marine and agricultural resources arranged by elites in Sector A, but middle-status households seem to have been required to produce relatively large amounts of *chicha* for intra- and extraneighborhood consumption. Finally, some households gained access to the city and the redistributive economy of foodstuffs but not to ample space, labor, or materials for building their houses. The draw of the city must then have been greater than the seemingly ample space of the countryside.

As a case study in preindustrial urbanism in an agricultural and marine resource area, El Purgatorio's Sector B South suggests that urbanism and urban hierarchies may have entailed a mixed bargain. Certain preexisting social hierarchies may have been reduced. For example, before moving to the city, many of El Purgatorio's resident households may have had less secure access to staples or perhaps access only to the foods they could produce or collect themselves. However, in the city they would have more secure and equitable access to marine and agricultural goods. In exchange, it is likely that before moving to the city, those households had more ample living space. They were also closer to the water and sand necessary for making the adobe that in the city was limited to the highest-status residences. Once in the city, space, labor, and building materials became premium goods with material consequences in terms of the physical comfort that is provided by ample space, breezy patios, and high doorjambs that trap cool air in the hot desert afternoons (Rapoport 1969).

More generally, research at El Purgatorio directs us to consider the historicity of inequality to understand its configurations and significances under different circumstances. Consequently, urbanism appears to be a sociospatial gamble. It provides opportunities to alleviate the consequences of certain forms of inequality but may create, exacerbate, and concretize new forms of inequality. These inequalities may have interrelated and unintended social, spatial, and material consequences that may lead to future social processes of settlement and neighborhood reconfiguration. Indeed, many of El Purgatorio's residents seem to have rapidly relocated to the new Chimú-Casma center at Manchán just after AD 1400.

NOTES

1. Including a mysterious hiatus of complex settlements as well (Collier 1962; Thompson 1964, 1974).

2. Not to be confused with the community archaeology of Marshall (2002), which aims to connect local, descendant communities to the excavation and interpretation of archaeological materials near their homes.

3. All of the data are available in tabular form in Pacifico (2014, appendix C), which is available for open access at the durable link https://pqdtopen.proquest.com/pubnum /3627869.html.

4. Ceramic assemblages came from both surface collection and excavation. I designed and conducted both phases of research and analyses, ensuring consistency in the integration of data.

5. 95% confidence interval for mean room area: orthogonal structures = 54–101m^2; semiorthogonal structures = 36–46m^2; irregular structures = 21–27 m^2; p = 0.000; n=947 (Pacifico 2014).

6. For example, the highest-status residence/ritual structure—BCL8—produced the most ceramic fragments during excavations, the second-widest variety of rim fragments, and the second-highest density of excavated fragments. It also had the highest density of fragments collected during systematic surface survey of vessel fragments (Pacifico 2014, 456).

7 Though select areas in some semiorthogonal structures had notably high numbers of fine bowls and one notable irregular structure also had a high number and wide range of ceramic vessel fragments.

8. All residents had access to between 21 and 29 species of the 46 identified in Sector B South, though mammalian remains (in the form of *cuy*/guinea pig, *Cavia porcellus*) were limited to high-status residences (Pacifico 2014).

9. Nash (2009) points out that commoner domestic structures are often built of ephemeral materials that do not survive at all.

10. Seventy-one percent (n=61) of excavated *tinaja* fragments came from Room 1; 50% of the excavated jar fragments came from nearby Room 12. Combined, 72% of excavated jar fragments came from these two proximal rooms in this small structure. Surface collections yielded the most jars (30%, n=27), bowls (48%, n=68), and *tinajas* (60%, n=180) in BCL8R1: the largest room in another building associated with food processing as well as feasting (figures 7.8–7.13).

11. But not grinding the maize in large quantities, it would seem.

12. Though with the narrow range of dates for Sector B South, it is hard to parse detailed structure histories using radiocarbon assays. BCL2's two carbon samples return ages of 660±33 and 629±34 years before present among a range of 714 to 629 years before present ±29 to 34 years before present (Pacifico 2014, 211).

13. Much like the "practices of affiliation" practiced by commoners at Xunantunich (Yaeger 2003).

REFERENCES

Aldenderfer, Mark, ed. 1993. *Domestic Architecture, Ethnicity, and Complementarity in the South-Central Andes*. Iowa City: University of Iowa Press.

Allen, Catherine J. 2002. *The Hold Life Has: Coca and Cultural Identity in an Andean Community*. 2nd ed. New York: Smithsonian.

Anderson, Benedict. 1983. *Imagined Communities: Reflections on the Origin and Spread of Nationalism*. London: Verso.

Bawden, Garth. 1982. "Community Organization Reflected by the Household: A Study of Pre-Columbian Social Dynamics." *Journal of Field Archaeology* 9:165–181.

Bourdieu, Pierre. 1972. *Outline of a Theory of Practice*. Translated by Richard Nice. Cambridge: Cambridge University Press.

Brennan, Curtis. 1982. "Cerro Arena: Origins of the Urban Tradition on the Peruvian North Coast." *Current Anthropology* 23: 247–254.

Brubaker, Rogers, and Frederick Cooper. 2000. "Beyond 'Identity.'" *Theory and Society* 29(1):1–47.

Burger, Richard. 1991. "The Second Season of Investigations at the Initial Period Center of Cardal, Peru." *Journal of Field Archaeology* 18:275–296.

Butzer, Karl. 2008. "Other Perspectives: Beyond the Disciplinary Boundaries." In *The Ancient City: New Perspectives on Urbanism in the Old and New Worlds*, edited by Joyce Marcus and Jeremy Sabloff, 77–92. Santa Fe, NM: School for Advanced Research.

Canuto, Marcello, and Jason Yaeger, eds. 2000. *The Archaeology of Communities: A New World Perspective*. New York: Routledge.

Ceram, C. W. 1979. *Gods, Graves, and Scholars: The Story of Archaeology*. 2nd revised ed. Translated by Edward Ballard Garside and Sophie Wilkins. New York: Vintage.

Chapdelaine, Claude. 2009. "Domestic Life in and around the Urban Sector of the Huacas of Moche Site, Northern Peru." In *Domestic Life in Prehispanic Capitals: A Study of Specialization, Hierarchy, and Ethnicity*, edited by Linda Manzanilla and Claude Chapdelaine, 181–196. Memoires of the Museum of Anthropology 46. Ann Arbor: University of Michigan Press.

Childe, V. Gordon. 1950. "The Urban Revolution." *Town Planning Review* 21: 3–17.

Cohen, Anthony P. 1985. *The Symbolic Construction of Community*. New York: Routledge.

Collier, Donald. 1962. "Archaeological Investigations in the Casma Valley, Peru." In *Akten des 34 Internationalen Amerikanistenkongresses, Wien, 1960*, 411–417. Horn-Wien, Austria: Verlag Ferdinand Berger.

Davis, Allison R. 2011. *Studies in Latin American Ethnohistory and Archaeology*, vol. 8: *Yuthu: Community and Ritual in an Early Andean Village*, general editor Joyce Marcus. Memoirs of the Museum of Anthropology 50. Ann Arbor: University of Michigan Press.

Davis, Michael. 1998. *City of Quartz: Excavating the Future in Los Angeles*. London: Pimlico.

Davis, Michael. 2004. "Planet of Slums: Urban Involution and the Informal Proletariat." *New Left Review* 26:5–34.

de Certeau, Michel. 1984. *Practice of Everyday Life*. Translated by Steven Rendall. Berkeley: University of California Press.

Dietler, Michael. 2001. "Theorizing the Feast: Rituals of Consumption, Commensal Politics, and Power in African Contexts." In *Feasts: Archaeological and Ethnographic Perspectives on Food, Politics, and Power*, edited by Michael Dietler and Brian Hayden, 65–114. Washington, DC: Smithsonian Institution Press.

Durkheim, Emile. 1995[1912]. *The Elementary Forms of Religious Life*. Translated by Karen Fields. New York: Free Press.

Foucault, Michel. 1975. *Discipline and Punish*. Translated by Alan Sheridan. New York: Vintage.

Fung Pineda, Rosa, and Carlos Williams León. 1977. "Exploraciones y Excavaciones en el Valle de Sechin, Casma." *Revista del Museo Nacional* 43:111–155. Lima.

Giddens, Anthony. 1984. *The Constitution of Society: Outline of the Theory of Structuration*. Berkeley: University of California Press.

Graeber, David. 2012. *Debt: The First 5000 Years*. New York: Melville House.

Hansen, Mogens Herman. 2008. "Analyzing Cities." In *The Ancient City: New Perspectives on Urbanism in the Old and New Worlds*, edited by Joyce Marcus and Jeremy Sabloff, 67–76. Santa Fe, NM: School for Advanced Research.

Holston, James. 1999. "The Modernist City and the Death of the Street." In *Theorizing the City: New Urban Anthropology Reader*, edited by Setha M. Low, 245–276. New Brunswick, NJ: Rutgers University Press.

Holston, James. 2008. *Insurgent Citizenship: Disjunctions of Democracy and Modernity in Brazil*. Princeton, NJ: Princeton University Press.

Horne, Lee. 1982. "The Household in Space: Dispersed Holdings in an Iranian Village." *American Behavioral Scientist* 25:677–685.

Hutson, Scott. 2016. *The Ancient Urban Maya: Neighborhoods, Inequality, and Built Form*. Gainesville: University Press of Florida.

Inomata, Takeshi and Lawrence Coben. 2006. "Overture: An Invitation to the Archaeological Theater." In *Archaeology of Performance: Theaters of Power, Community, and Politics*, edited by Takeshi Inomata and Lawrence Coben, 11–46. New York: Altamira.

Janusek, John. 2004. *Identity and Power in the Ancient Andes: Tiwanaku Cities through Time*. New York: Routledge.

Janusek, John. 2009. "Residence and Ritual in Tiwanaku: Hierarchy, Specialization, Ethnicity, and Ceremony." In *Domestic Life in Prehispanic Capitals: A Study of Specialization, Hierarchy, and Ethnicity*, edited by Linda Manzanilla and Claude Chapdelaine, 159–180. Memoirs of the Museum of Anthropology 46. Ann Arbor: University of Michigan Press.

Keith, Kathryn. 2003. "The Spatial Patterns of Everyday Life in Old Babylonian Neighborhoods." In *The Social Construction of Ancient Cities*, edited by Monica L. Smith, 56–80. Washington, DC: Smithsonian Institution Press.

Kenoyer, J. Mark. 2008. "Indus Urbanism: New Perspectives on Its Origin and Character." In *The Ancient City: New Perspectives on Urbanism in the Old and New Worlds*, edited by Joyce Marcus and Jeremy Sabloff, 183–208. Santa Fe, NM: School for Advanced Research.

Kolata, Alan. 1997. "Of Kings and Capitals: Principles of Authority and the Nature of Cities in the Native Andean State." In *The Archaeology of City States: Cross-Cultural Approaches*, edited by Deborah L. Nichols and Thomas H. Charlton, 245–254. Washington, DC: Smithsonian Institution Press.

Kolata, Alan L. 2013. *Ancient Inca*. Cambridge: Cambridge University Press.

Lefebvre, Henri. 1991. *The Production of Space*. Translated by Donald Nicholson-Smith. Malden, MA: Blackwell.

Lobo, Susan. 1992. *A House of My Own: Social Organization in the Squatter Settlements of Lima, Peru*. Tucson: University of Arizona Press.

Low, Setha M. 1996. "The Anthropology of Cities: Imagining and Theorizing the City." *Annual Review of Anthropology* 25:383–409.

Low, Setha M. 1999a. "Introduction: Theorizing the City." In *Theorizing the City: New Urban Anthropology Reader*, edited by Setha M. Low, 1–36. New Brunswick, NJ: Rutgers University Press.

Low, Setha M. 1999b. "Spatializing Culture: The Social Production and Social Construction of Public Space in Costa Rica." In *Theorizing the City: New Urban Anthropology Reader*, edited by Setha M. Low, 111–137. New Brunswick, NJ: Rutgers University Press.

Low, Setha M. 2011. "Spatializing Culture: Embodied Space in the City." In *The New Blackwell Companion to the City*, edited by Gary Bridge and Sophie Watson, 463–475. Malden, MA: Blackwell.

Mac Sweeney, Naoise. 2011. *Community Identity and Archaeology: Dynamic Communities at Aphrodisias and Beycesultan*. Ann Arbor: University of Michigan Press.

Makowski, Krystof. 2008. "Andean Urbanism." In *Handbook of South American Archaeology*, edited by Helaine Silverman and William H. Isbell, 633–657. New York: Springer.

Marshall, Yvonne. 2002. "What Is Community Archaeology?" *World Archaeology* 34(2):211–219.

Mayer, Enrique. 2002. *The Articulated Peasant: Household Economies in the Andes.* Boulder: Westview.

Nash, Donna. 2009. "Household Archaeology in the Andes." *Journal of Archaeological Research* 17:205–261.

Pacifico, David. 2012. "Chicha and Neighborhood Political Ecology in Ancient Peru." Paper presented at the 111th Annual Meeting of the American Anthropological Association, San Francisco, November 14–18.

Pacifico, David. 2014. "Neighborhood Politics: Diversity, Community, and Authority at El Purgatorio, Peru." PhD dissertation, University of Chicago, IL.

Pacifico, David. 2019. "Neighborhood as Nexus: A Trans-Historical Approach to Emplaced Communities." In *Excavating Neighborhoods: A Cross-Cultural Exploration*, edited by David Pacifico and Lise Truex, 114–132. Washington, DC: Archaeological Papers of the American Anthropological Association.

Pacifico, David, and Lise Truex. 2019. "Why Neighborhoods? The Neighborhood in Archaeological Theory and Practice." In *Excavating Neighborhoods: A Cross-Cultural Exploration*, edited by David Pacifico and Lise Truex, 5–19. Washington, DC: Archaeological Papers of the American Anthropological Association.

Pozorski, Shelia, and Thomas Pozorski. 2008. "Early Cultural Complexity on the Coast of Peru." In *Handbook of South American Archaeology*, edited by Helaine Silverman and William H. Isbell, 607–631. New York: Springer.

Rapoport, Amos. 1969. *House Form and Culture.* Englewood Cliffs, NJ: Prentice-Hall.

Robin, Cynthia. 2004. "Social Diversity and Everyday Life within Classic Maya Settlements." In *Mesoamerican Archaeology: Theory and Practice*, edited by Julia Hendon and Rosemary Joyce, 148–168. Malden, MA: Blackwell.

Rousseau, Jean-Jacques. 1997[1755]. "Discourse on the Origin and Foundations of Inequality among Men or Second Discourse." In *Rousseau: The Discourses and Other Early Political Writings*, edited and translated by Victor Gourevitch, 111–231. Cambridge: Cambridge University Press.

Sampson, Robert J. 2012. *The Great American City: Chicago and the Enduring Neighborhood Effect.* Chicago: University of Chicago Press.

Sheets, Payson. 2000. "Provisioning the Cerén Household: The Vertical Economy, Village Economy, and Household Economy in the Southeastern Maya Periphery." *Ancient Mesoamerica* 11: 217–230.

Smith, Michael E. 2007. "Form and Meaning in the Earliest Cities: A New Approach to Ancient Urban Planning." *Journal of Planning History* 6(1):3–47.

Smith, Michael E. 2010a. "Sprawl, Squatters, and Sustainable Cities: Can Archaeological Data Shed Light on Modern Urban Issues?" *Cambridge Archaeological Journal* 20(2):229–253.

Smith, Michael E. 2010b. "The Archaeological Study of Neighborhoods and Districts in Ancient Cities." *Journal of Anthropological Archaeology* 29:137–154.

Smith, Michael E. 2011. *Empirical Urban Theory for Archaeologists. Journal of Archaeological Method and Theory* 18(3):167–192.

Smith, Michael E., and Juliana Novic. 2012. "Neighborhoods and Districts in Ancient Mesoamerica." In *The Neighborhood as a Social and Spatial Unit in Mesoamerican Cities*, edited by Marie Charlotte Arnauld, Linda Manzanilla, and Michael E. Smith, 1–26. Tucson: University of Arizona Press.

Smith, Monica L. 2003. "Introduction: The Social Construction of Ancient Cities." In *The Social Construction of Ancient Cities*, edited by Monica L. Smith, 1–36. Washington, DC: Smithsonian Institution Press.

Smith, Monica L. 2006. "The Archaeology of South Asian Cities." *Journal of Archaeological Research* 14(2):97–142.

Smith, Monica L. 2019. "The Phenomenology of Neighborhoods in the Early Historic Period of the Indian Subcontinent (Third Century BC–Fourth Century AD)." In *Excavating Neighborhoods: A Cross-Cultural Exploration*, edited by David Pacifico and Lise Truex, 62–70. Washington, DC: Archaeological Papers of the American Anthropological Association.

Stanish, Charles. 1989. "Household Archaeology: Testing Models of Zonal Complementarity in the South Central Andes." *American Anthropologist* 91(1): 7–24.

Stone, Elizabeth. 1987. *Nippur Neighborhoods*. Studies in Ancient Oriental Civilization 44. Chicago: Oriental Institute of the University of Chicago.

Stone, Elizabeth. 2008. "A Tale of Two Cities: Lowland Mesopotamia and Highland Anatolia." In *The Ancient City: New Perspectives on Urbanism in the Old and New Worlds*, edited by Joyce Marcus and Jeremy Sabloff, 141–164. Santa Fe, NM: School for Advanced Research.

Susser, Ida. 1999. "Creating Family Forms: The Exclusion of Men and Teenage Boys from Families in the New York City Shelter System 1987–1991." In *Theorizing the City: New Urban Anthropology Reader*, edited by Setha M. Low, 67–82. New Brunswick, NJ: Rutgers University Press.

Swenson, Edward. 2006. "Competitive Feasting, Religious Pluralism, and Decentralized Power in the Late Moche Period." In *Andean Archaeology*, vol. 3: *North and South*, edited by Helaine Silverman and William H. Isbell, 112–142. New York: Springer.

Tello, Julio. 1956. *Arqueologia del Valle de Casma*. Lima: Editorial San Marcos.

Thomas, David Hurst. 2000. *Skull Wars: Kennewick Man, Archaeology, and the Battle for Native American Identity.* New York: Basic Books.

Thompson, Donald E. 1964. "Postclassic Innovations in Architecture and Settlement Patterns in the Casma Valley, Peru." *Southwestern Journal of Anthropology* 20(1): 91–105.

Thompson, Donald E. 1974. "Arquitectura y Patrones de Establecimiento en el Valle de Casma." *Revista del Museo Nacional* 40:9–29.

Topic, John. 1982. "Lower-Class Social and Economic Organization at Chan Chan." In *Chan Chan: Andean Desert City*, edited by Michael Moseley and Kent Day, 145–175. Albuquerque: University of New Mexico Press.

US Census Bureau. 2014. "Gap between Higher- and Lower-Wealth Households Widens, Census Bureau Reports: Release Number CB14–156." Originally published August 21, 2014. http://www.census.gov/newsroom/press-releases/2014/cb14–156.html.

Van Gijseghem, Hendrick. 2001. "Household and Family at Moche, Peru: An Analysis of Building and Residence Patterns in a Prehispanic Urban Center." *Latin American Antiquity* 12(3): 257–273.

Venkatesh, Sudhir. 2014. "The Hustler and the Hustled." In *The Urban Ethnography Reader*, edited by Mitchell Dunier, Phillip Kasinitz, and Alexandra Murphy, 831–848. Oxford: Oxford University Press.

Vogel, Melissa. 2003. "Life on the Frontier: Identity and Sociopolitical Change at the Site of Cerro la Cruz, Peru." PhD dissertation, University of Pennsylvania, Philadelphia.

Vogel, Melissa. 2011. "Style and Interregional Interaction: Ceramics from the Casma Capital of El Purgatorio." *Ñawpa Pacha: Journal of Andean Archaeology* 31(2):201–224.

Vogel, Melissa, Victor Falcon, and David Pacifico. 2010. "Informe Final (Temporada 2010): Proyecto Arqueologico El Purgatorio." Field report, Instituto Nacional de Cultura, Lima, Peru.

Vogel, Melissa, Victor Falcon, and David Pacifico. 2012. "Informe de los Fechados y del Analisis Isotopico, Proyecto Arqueológico El Purgatorio, Temporada 2010." Archaeological Field Report, Ministerio de Cultura, Lima, Peru.

Vogel, Melissa, and David Pacifico. 2011. "Arquitectura de El Purgatorio: Capital de la Cultura Casma." In *Andes 8: Boletín del Centro de Estudios Precolombinos de la Universidad de Varsovia, Arqueología de la Costa Ancash*, edited by Ivan Ghezzi and Milosz Gierz, 357–397. Warsaw: University of Warsaw Press.

Vogel, Melissa, and Percy Vilcherrez. 2004. "Informe Final (Temporada 2004): Proyecto Arqueologico El Purgatorio." Field report, Instituto Nacional de Cultura, Lima, Peru.

Von Hagen, Adriana, and Edward Craig Morris. 1998. *The Cities of the Ancient Andes.* New York: Thames and Hudson.

Wernke, Steven A. 2006. "The Politics of Community and Inka Statecraft in the Colca Valley, Peru." *Latin American Antiquity* 17(2):177–208.

Wernke, Steven A. 2007. "Negotiating Community and Landscape in the Peruvian Andes: A Transconquest View." *American Anthropologist* 109(1):130–152.

Wernke, Steven A. 2013. *Negotiated Settlements: Andean Communities and Landscapes under Inka and Spanish Colonialism*. Gainesville: University of Florida Press.

Wheatley, Paul. 1971. *The Pivot of the Four Corners: A Preliminary Inquiry into the Origins and Character of the Ancient Chinese City*. Chicago: Aldine.

Wilk, Richard R., and William Rathje. 1982. "Household Archaeology." *American Behavioral Scientist* 25(6): 617–639.

Wilson, David. 1995. "Prehispanic Settlement Patterns in the Casma Valley, North Coast of Peru: Preliminary Results to Date." *Journal of the Steward Anthropological Society* 23(1–2):189–227.

Yaeger, Jason. 2000. "The Social Construction of Communities in the Classic Maya Countryside: Strategies of Affiliation in Western Belize." In *The Archaeology of Communities: A New World Perspective*, edited by Jason Yaeger and Maurice Canuto, 123–142. New York: Routledge.

Yaeger, Jason. 2003. "Untangling the Ties That Bind: The City, the Countryside, and the Nature of Maya Urbanism at Xunantunich." In *The Social Construction of Ancient Cities*, edited by Monica L. Smith, 121–155. Washington, DC: Smithsonian Institution Press.

8

Continuity and Change in Late Intermediate Period Households on the North Coast of Peru

ROBYN E. CUTRIGHT

After the Moche collapse, household life went on in the coastal valleys of northern Peru, in many ways unchanged from previous centuries. In the subsequent Middle Horizon and Late Intermediate Periods (LIP), the household continued to be a focus for agricultural and craft production, social reproduction, and ritual. Household life was intensely local, based on the rhythms of irrigation agriculture, and households were linked in wider networks of kin and community.

However, households on the North Coast were confronted with new sociopolitical configurations at the valley and regional levels during the Late Intermediate Period. Coastal political strategies in the middle valley, and an end to the political fragmentation of the Late Moche Period, created new economic and political opportunities for households. The coalescence and expansion of the Chimú Empire reshaped the political landscape and imposed new economic demands on rural and urban households. Household strategies in conquered territories changed to meet these new demands while at the same time conserving key elements of household organization and daily life. In this chapter I examine the strategies of Late Intermediate Period households based on two examples from my own research in the Jequetepeque Valley. I argue that these households exhibited considerable resilience but that this resilience could manifest itself as adaptation and change or as continuity in household organization and practice.

DOI: 10.5876/9781646420919.c008

CONTINUITY AND CHANGE IN NORTH COAST HOUSEHOLDS
Theorizing Household Resilience

Households, especially lower-class rural households, have often been cast as essentially conservative and resistant to change. Marshall Sahlins (1972), for example, argues that peasant households resist intensifying production beyond subsistence levels. In this view, traditional households were oriented toward internal consumption and were essentially self-sufficient, inward-looking units. Pierre Bourdieu (1977) identifies the household as a site of enculturation through embodied practice, and Ian Hodder and Craig Cessford (2004) have employed practice theory to suggest that repetition of daily tasks in household spaces at Çatalhoyük helped to reinforce cultural norms and maintain long-term continuity. Patricia Crown (2000) has argued that cuisine, a central component of daily household life, is deeply conservative, as it draws on deeply held notions of identity, family, and memory.

However, households do change, and it is too simplistic to think of them as merely a tradition-bound, timeless substrate upon which more complex social configurations are constructed. Households adapt to larger political, cultural, and environmental contexts (Hirth 1993; Wilk 1991). This adaptation may maintain continuity, minimize risk, diversify patterns of production, or reshape family organization, participation in community institutions, cuisine, or other dimensions of household practice. As households respond to changing regional conditions, some aspects of domestic life may be more dynamic or more subject to change while others resist change (Bermann 1994, 1997; Falconer 1995; Wilk 1991). For instance, Marc P. Bermann (1994, 238) argues that as the community of Lukurmata experienced the expansion of the regional Tiwanaku polity, household architecture changed the most through time, signaling changes in the allocation of space to different activities. In contrast, artifact assemblages and, by extension, the set of tasks performed in households were relatively stable through time. Households pursue different strategies based on factors such as available resources, size and membership, status and class, and location, so all households should not be expected to respond to change in the same way.

In thinking about continuity and change in Late Intermediate Period households, I take what Richard R. Wilk (1991, 9) has referred to as a "historically sensitive cultural-ecological approach." In other words, I investigate how households adapted to local economic, political, and ecological conditions, constraints, and possibilities. In this chapter I consider two case studies of household continuity and change in the Jequetepeque Valley to explore some dimensions of household response to the sweeping regional changes of the Late Intermediate Period North Coast.

POST-MOCHE CONTINUITIES

During the Early Intermediate Period and into the Middle Horizon, the north coast of Peru was united by a broadly shared Moche culture. Reconstructions of Moche political organization vary: researchers have seen the Moche as a pristine state (e.g., Billman 2002; Moseley 1992), as three distinct politically opportunistic spheres (Castillo Butters 2010), or as a loose confederation bound by a shared religion or political ideology (Bawden 1995; Quilter and Koons 2012), among other models. Jeffrey Quilter's (Quilter and Castillo Butters 2010; Quilter and Koons 2012) syntheses of recent data in the context of models for Moche political organization emphasize political fragmentation and spatial and temporal diversity in the expression of Moche politics and religion and likely in what it meant to be Moche.

After the Moche collapse, the North Coast saw the rise and fall of several complex societies. To the north, the Middle Sicán polity coalesced at Batán Grande, then collapsed dramatically several centuries later; valley wide power was transferred to Túcume and other centers during the Late Sicán Period (Shimada 1981; Tschauner 2001). The Casma Polity emerged around the same time to the south, maintaining political control as far as the Chao Valley to the north (Vogel 2012). During this time, the Zaña, Jequetepeque, and perhaps Chicama Valleys were locally autonomous but participated in a shared Lambayeque tradition (Mackey 2011). To the south, the Chimú State emerged in the Moche Valley around AD 900 and then expanded beginning around AD 1300 to conquer the Lambayeque in the Jequetepeque, the Casma Polity to the south, and eventually the Late Sicán in the Lambayeque-La Leche Valleys to the far north.

Despite clear evidence of political and ideological changes at the regional level, many aspects of daily life remained stable throughout this period. Ilana Johnson (2010) argues that the basic worldview and organization of the Moche household did not change much through time. Domestic architecture consisted of multiroom complexes constructed of locally abundant materials that housed several families. Quotidian domestic activities such as eating, sleeping, child rearing, household rituals, and basic production tasks such as processing food and spinning and weaving cloth took place in kitchens and living rooms. Johnson (2010) also identifies a fundamental distinction between rural households and households in urban neighborhoods, which she argues gave up autonomy upon integration into socially and economically heterogeneous urban environments.

Post-Moche North Coast households could easily be described in these same broad terms, even while recognizing diversity at valley and community levels. At rural villages such as Pedregal in the Jequetepeque Valley and urban centers like Pacatnamú and Chan Chan, Late Intermediate Period households were characterized by rectangular, agglutinated domestic architecture and carried out a set of basic reproductive and productive activities similar to those described for Moche households (Cutright 2009, 2015; Gumerman 1991; Topic 1982). Urban domestic compounds, such as those documented by John R. Topic (1982) in the lower-class neighborhoods of Chan Chan, were generally larger; households there engaged in a wider variety of craft production activities but were less self-sufficient in terms of food than rural farming households.

Moche, Lambayeque, and Chimú societies coped with similar environmental risks within the framework of broadly analogous agricultural regimes and available resources. Rivers on the western slopes of the Andes run out of the foothills and across a narrow coastal plain before emptying into the Pacific. Lower valley residents relied on irrigation from the river to water the coastal desert and grew corn, beans, cotton, squash, and tree fruits. This system faced periodic risks of flooding during El Niño–Southern Oscillation (ENSO) events, which could be strong enough to wash out canals and seriously disrupt agricultural production. Farmers also faced risk from less predictable events such as multidecadal droughts, which occurred several times during the period in question (Shimada et al. 1991; Thompson et al. 1994). In addition to farming, coastal communities also relied on marine resources like fish and shellfish throughout these periods.

At other key moments of social transition in the Andes, such as the emergence of irrigation agriculture or the Spanish conquest, newly available products and technologies shifted the subsistence system, and local household economies saw clear changes (e.g., Kennedy and VanValkenburgh 2016). In contrast, the transition from Moche to Chimú may seem unlikely to have been accompanied by much change at the local level, and in fact the broad outlines do demonstrate a good deal of continuity. However, regional political processes such as the Moche collapse and Chimú imperial expansion did spur changes at the household level.

POST-MOCHE CHANGES

Between AD 650 and 900, the Jequetepeque Valley rural landscape was politically and religiously fragmented and agriculturally decentralized (Dillehay 2001; Dillehay and Kolata 2004; Duke, this volume; Swenson 2007a). The Late Moche Period settlement pattern consisted of a few large urban communities and scattered clusters of villages in the rural hinterlands. Sites like Huaca Colorada (Swenson and Warner 2016) were cyclically abandoned and then resettled and renewed. A profusion of Late Moche fortified hilltop settlements suggests a concern with defense, perhaps linked to increased factionalism or competition. Tom D. Dillehay (2001) and his team registered evidence of localized ENSO-related flooding across the Jequetepeque during the Late Moche Period; flood deposits were often followed by at least temporary site abandonment. Overall, this pattern indicates a preference for localized administration, political factionalism, and strategies for dealing with environmental risk that emphasized mobility and population dispersal (Dillehay 2001; Duke, this volume).

Elite burials at San José de Moro show that foreign influence intensified as the Moche collapsed (Castillo Butters 2010). Fineware ceramics from Cajamarca, Chachapoyas, and the Central Coast appear at Late Moche sites such as San José de Moro (Castillo Butters 2010) and Huaca Colorada (Swenson and Warner 2016). A highland enclave was constructed atop Cerro Chepén (Rosas Rintel 2007), and extralocal genes made a significant contribution to local populations (Zobler and Sutter 2016). All these lines of evidence suggest that the end of the Moche Period in the Jequetepeque was marked by social, political, and environmental turmoil that resulted in new political configurations and strategies. While in some communities, such as Talambo (Zobler, this volume; Zobler and Sutter 2016), post-Moche life may have continued relatively unaffected by collapse, the new political situation in the valley likely affected daily life in many local communities.

In contrast to Moche strategies, Late Intermediate Period Lambayeque and Chimú polities adopted a strategy of centralized investment in irrigation infrastructure (Dillehay and Kolata 2004), which created new potential for intensive agricultural production and new interest in monitoring and controlling key points of the irrigation network (Keatinge and Conrad 1983). This kind of strategy might be expected to decrease the autonomy of households and communities, which would now be more tightly integrated into broader networks. The population moved away from hilltop settlements and from locations most likely to be damaged by floods or dune encroachment. At the same time, rural hinterland political and ritual practice remained heterogeneous despite evidence for more political centralization (Swenson 2007b). This could indicate that local autonomy counterbalanced increasing political centralization or that Chimú elites were not concerned with controlling religious expression in the countryside as long as they could monitor agricultural production.

From a household perspective, some aspects of Late Intermediate Period domestic practice represented a clear break from Moche antecedents. Utilitarian ceramics changed notably from the Moche to Late Intermediate Periods in functional as well as stylistic terms. Several forms such as the high face-neck jars of the Moche disappeared, and other forms such as ceramic bowls and plates appeared and became common in household assemblages (Cutright 2009; Swenson 2004). Interestingly, a similarly clear break in household ceramics did not occur after Chimú conquest. In fact, new techniques like paddle-stamping that appeared during the Lambayeque Period continued through the Chimú, Inka, and Colonial Periods and even into contemporary ceramic production. If domestic ceramic assemblages reflect the culinary needs of households, then cuisine changed after the Moche collapse but remained fairly unchanged in Lambayeque, Chimú, and Inka households. This observation is consistent with a scenario in which Moche collapse was accompanied by a dramatic cultural upheaval, while Late Intermediate Period and even Late Horizon conquests were experienced as political and economic shifts but not necessarily cultural disruptions at the household level.

Another axis of household practice that shows a clear break between the Moche and Late Intermediate Periods is ritual, visible in the form of figurines generally representing female forms. These objects are often found in Moche households (Johnson, this volume; Ringberg 2008), suggesting that ritual linked to the home and to women's roles in the home was a common component of Moche life. While domestic rituals also pervaded Late Intermediate Period households (Cutright 2013a), they no longer regularly featured figurines. This change in the gendered content of domestic rituals along with the culinary change discussed above hint that the lived experience of household members changed in profound ways after Moche collapse, despite broad continuities in the basic worldview and organization of North Coast households.

To further elucidate how households, especially rural households and those located far from political centers, responded to the shifting political landscape of the Late Intermediate Period, I will examine two communities in the Jequetepeque Valley: Pedregal and Ventanillas. At Ventanillas, middle valley elites took advantage of broader Lambayeque coastal affiliation as well as local political opportunities, while at Pedregal rural farmers endured increased demands of Chimú administrators for agricultural production while maintaining considerable continuity in household practice.

CASE 1: LOCAL ELITE STRATEGIES IN THE
MIDDLE JEQUETEPEQUE VALLEY

The Jequetepeque River flows from the western edge of the Cajamarca Basin down to the Pacific, carving through the western slopes of the Andes until it passes the valley neck at Talambo, flows onto the wide coastal plain, and reaches the Pacific Ocean (figure 8.1). The lower valley had been intensively occupied since the inception of irrigation agriculture, by successive Formative, Moche, Lambayeque, and Chimú societies, and was eventually incorporated into the expanding Inka Empire around AD 1470 (Castillo Butters 2010; Dillehay et al. 2009; Hecker and Hecker 1990; Swenson 2004; Warner 2010). During the early part of the Late Intermediate Period (~AD 1000–1300), the Lambayeque polity occupied the lower Jequetepeque. Pacatnamú

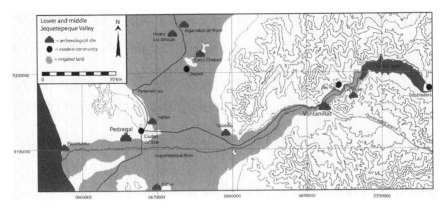

FIGURE 8.1. The Jequetepeque Valley

was the primary Lambayeque ceremonial and administrative center (Donnan and Cock 1997). It sat at the apex of a complex settlement system that included smaller centers such as Farfán (Mackey 2006, 2009) and Ventanillas (Cutright and Cervantes Quequezana 2012, 2014), elite residences at Cabur (Sapp 2011) and San José de Moro (Prieto Burmester 2010), and smaller rural villages (Cutright 2009, 2015).

Despite some broad similarities to Lambayeque/Sicán architecture to the north, such as large adobe platforms (huacas), ramps, and rectangular compounds, Lambayeque architectural and stylistic patterns at Jequetepeque sites such as Pacatnamú, Farfán, and Cabur followed a locally distinct template (Sapp 2011). Huaca quadrangles at Pacatnamú contained a large platform mound with a central ramp, accessed from a walled plaza with flanking platforms and corridors. A large rectangular enclosure that was divided into U-shaped rooms with niches, storerooms, patios, and winding, baffled corridors was located behind the huaca (Donnan 1986). Other characteristic Lambayeque architectural features include altars with ramps and low U-shaped benches known as *concilios* (Mackey 2011). Lambayeque burials at Farfán (Cutright 2011) were similar to contemporaneous burials at El Brujo, in the Chicama Valley to the south (Franco Jordán et al. 2007). This evidence suggests that the Jequetepeque was locally autonomous but participated in a broadly shared coastal cultural tradition during this period.

The extent to which coastal polities' influence extended past the valley neck into the middle valley is not yet well understood. Ongoing research (Cutright 2013b; Tsai 2012) indicates a Lambayeque presence in the middle Jequetepeque Valley beginning around AD 1000. Lambayeque occupation in the middle valley contrasts with a relative lack of prior Moche settlement in the region and suggests that the Lambayeque had a different set of strategic priorities or established new alliances

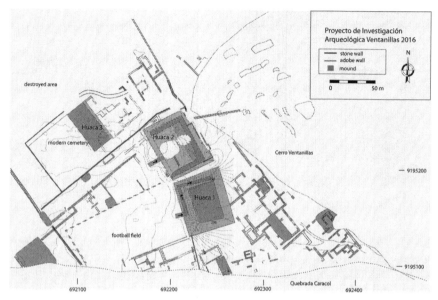

FIGURE 8.2. The site of Ventanillas

with middle valley populations. One of the most visible manifestations of this interest is the site of Ventanillas, which overlooks the intakes of canals running into the
lower valley and marks the confluence of two important routes from the coast to
the highlands (figure 8.1). Ventanillas was a large community. It included an extensive public sector, composed of a large rectangular compound containing three
adobe platform mounds, and two distinct residential sectors (figure 8.2). Stylistic
comparisons with regional architectural and ceramic chronologies and radiocarbon
dates from the Proyecto de Investigación Arqueológica Ventanillas (Cutright and
Cervantes Quequezana 2012, 2014; Cutright and Osores Mendives 2016; figure 8.3)
suggest it was occupied between about AD 1100 to 1400, the period leading up to
and spanning Chimú conquest of the Jequetepeque. While the dates (figure 8.3)
cluster in two groups, the first between cal AD 1200 and 1300 and the second
between cal AD 1300 and 1400, the stratigraphy shows no clear break in occupation, and the comparisons made here are synchronic across the site.

The monumental architecture at Ventanillas clearly references Lambayeque canons, featuring large adobe huacas with ramps, rectangular compounds, and narrow
corridors. The two better-preserved platform mounds, Huaca 1 and Huaca 2, were
constructed from adobes that fit general Lambayeque size and shape parameters
(McClelland 1986). Huaca 3 has been impacted by a modern cemetery, looting, and

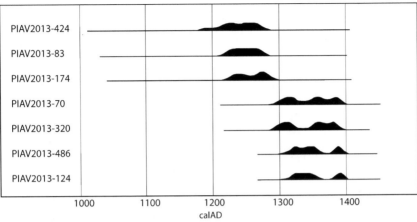

Project ID	Lab code	d13C value	Uncalibrated radiocarbon age	1-sigma error	2-sigma calibrated range (ShCal13)
2013-424	AA10359	-24.6	847	38	1177-1282 AD
2013-83	Beta- 445172	-27.8	830	30	1204-1284 AD
2013-174	Beta- 445173	-25.2	800	30	1220-1290 AD
2013-70	Beta- 445171	-24.7	680	30	1293-1393 AD
2013-320	AA106435	-24.5	690	25	1290-1330 AD (39.2%)
					1336-1392 AD (56.2%)
2013-486	D-AMS 007338	-22.8	658	21	1301-1365 AD (72%)
					1375-1399 AD (23%)
2013-124	D-AMS 007337	-24.3	651	23	1302-1365 AD (70%)
					1375-1402 AD (25%)

FIGURE 8.3. Radiocarbon dates from Sector D of Ventanillas

trash disposal and is harder to reconstruct but seems to face east upvalley rather than west toward to coast like the other platforms. Despite intensive looting, a honeycomb pattern suggestive of chamber-and-fill construction can still be observed at the summits of all three platform mounds. The top of Huaca 1 was accessed by a ramp that wrapped around the west and north sides. Huaca 2 had a more complex configuration—a short T-shaped ramp provided access from the middle of the western face onto a lower tier that was partially enclosed on the north and south sides. A higher tier ran across the eastern half of the platform and was faced with stone cobbles toward the slope of Cerro Ventanillas. Though a large open area now extends west from Huaca 1, this feature was created in the 1960s or 1970s when the area was bulldozed to create a soccer field. Both huacas are more similar to Late

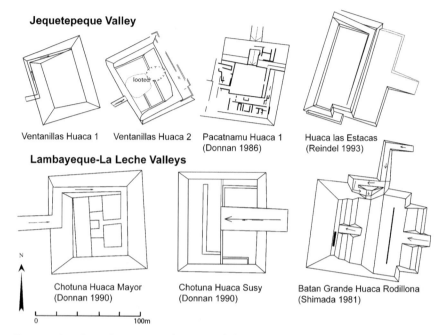

Jequetepeque Valley

Ventanillas Huaca 1   Ventanillas Huaca 2   Pacatnamu Huaca 1   Huaca las Estacas
                                              (Donnan 1986)   (Reindel 1993)

Lambayeque-La Leche Valleys

N

Chotuna Huaca Mayor   Chotuna Huaca Susy   Batan Grande Huaca Rodillona
(Donnan 1990)   (Donnan 1990)   (Shimada 1981)

0   100m

FIGURE 8.4. Some Late Intermediate Period platform mounds

Sicán platforms at Chotuna, in Lambayeque, than to contemporaneous architecture such as the huaca-quadrangle pattern in the Jequetepeque (figure 8.4).

Parallels with northern architecture raise the possibility that Ventanillas was an administrative outpost imposed by an expanding Lambayeque or Late Sicán State. Evidence from three seasons of fieldwork, however, is beginning to suggest a more complex picture in which local political dynamics were central to Ventanillas's development. Neighborhoods do not seem to have been organized by ethnic group, as might be expected if Ventanillas was an intrusive coastal administrative center, and higher status does not seem to be spatially associated with either coastal or highland styles as in a scenario of colonization and control. Instead, vessels associated with the middle valley, such as Coastal Cajamarca bowls, made up almost identical proportions of surface collections from domestic areas at the foot of the huacas (Sector D) and from the residential terraces on the north side of Cerro Ventanillas (Sector C) (Cutright and Cervantes Quequezana 2012). Carinated *ollas*, a utilitarian form associated with the coast, were likewise evenly distributed across both residential sectors. In other words, surface collections hint that Ventanillas residents across the site were drawing on coastal, middle valley, and possibly highland

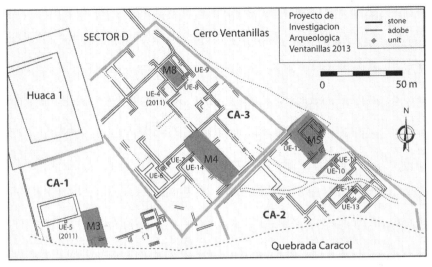

FIGURE 8.5. 2013 excavations in Sector D

traditions as they prepared and served daily meals. Given the lack of chronological control over surface collections, however, this evidence could also suggest that Ventanillas's cultural or political affiliation changed through time, from coastal to middle valley or vice versa.

To begin to test these distinct scenarios, in 2013 we placed ten 2 m × 2 m excavation units in Sector D, five in each of two compounds (CA-2 and CA-3, figure 8.5). Although they are located directly behind Huaca 1, these compounds lack characteristic features of the huaca quadrangles of Pacatnamú. Access is not restricted to a single entryway, no U-shaped rooms with niches or storage complexes seem to be present, and excavations revealed artifacts and features associated with domestic activities. The compounds were well constructed from plastered stone and adobe walls, and excavations encountered a higher concentration of metal fragments and objects such as tweezers, needles, and spindle whorls than in contemporaneous rural villages (Cutright 2009; Cutright and Osores Mendives 2018), lending an impression that wealthy or high-status families engaged in textile or copper production resided here. Each compound contained a maze of agglutinated rooms and open areas, and each featured a similar architectural configuration: an open patio next to a low adobe mound and a narrow flanking room (figure 8.5). This configuration recalls in a basic sense the platform-plaza pattern at Pacatnamú, described above, but lacks other characteristic features like niches and altars with ramps.

Over 1,300 diagnostic sherds were recovered from these excavations, reflecting a domestic assemblage concerned with wet cooking in *ollas*, serving and consuming food in bowls, and preparing, storing, and consuming liquids. High concentrations of grater bowls, jars, and large storage/*chicha*-preparation vessels recovered from two excavation units placed next to the patio in Compound 2 suggest that this area was a focus for food preparation and consumption during the Chimú Period and probably the earlier Lambayeque occupation as well. It may be the case that feasts or other celebrations were hosted in these patio-mound areas and that this activity took place in each of the compounds. Since these spaces were replicated in multiple household compounds, feasting and hosting could have been an arena for competition among extended family household groups.

Excavations revealed that coastal and middle valley/highland ceramic styles and food resources were not spatially or temporally separated either within household compounds or between the two compounds tested in 2013 and the Sector C terrace contexts excavated in 2016. Families across the site had access to coastal seafood as well as abundant middle valley resources such as land snails, tree fruits such as avocado and *guanábana*, and, of course, maize. Slight but significant differences existed between the two Sector D compounds in their use of coastal as opposed to middle valley resources, indicating perhaps that each family mobilized extended kinship ties differently to obtain exchange items. Table 8.1 compares the botanical and shellfish assemblages from the two compounds; CA-2 relied more heavily on local snails (*Scutalus proteus*) and the tree fruits that remain abundant in the middle valley today, while CA-3 apparently had greater access to marine species and maize.

Currently, I interpret the compounds in Sector D as local middle valley elite households drawing on coastal and highland ceramic, culinary, and architectural traditions to create a borderlands hybrid while taking advantage of a visible affiliation with powerful coastal polities. Ventanillas's huacas are visually arresting to a traveler approaching from the coast or the highlands and command a clear view toward the lower valley. The fact that Huacas 1 and 2 more closely replicate architecture from Chotuna rather than nearby Pacatnamú is intriguing if it represents a local effort to draw on wider traditions and hints at considerable diversity in stylistic influence or social affiliation during this period. Excavations in the public architecture at the foot of Huaca 2 in 2016 did not uncover any classic examples of Chimú administrative architecture or of southern Lambayeque features like altars with ramps or *concilios*. However, they revealed multiple episodes of remodeling and renewal of walls, small mounds, and internal spaces, suggesting a continual concern with reshaping public space throughout the Late Intermediate Period.

Members of the higher-status households at Ventanillas would have participated in larger political and religious events carried out in the public sector, perhaps

TABLE 8.1. Botanical and shellfish remains at Ventanillas

Botanical (percentage of total plant parts)

Category	Species	CA-2 %	CA-3 %	Overall %
Maize	*Zea mays*			
	maize	9.73	25.00	13.93
Tree/shrub fruits	*Annona sp.*			
	guanábana	76.55	56.74	71.10
	Persea americana			
	avocado	3.24	2.85	3.14
	Lucuma obovata			
	lucuma	0.79	0.39	0.68
	Inga feuillei			
	huaba	2.80	0.00	2.03
	Psidium guajava			
	guava	0.10	0.00	0.07
	Bunchiosa armenaica			
	ciruela del fraile	0.20	0.00	0.14
	Capparis ovalifolia			
	guayabito de gentil	0.05	0.39	0.14
	Capparis angulata			
	zapote	0.49	3.89	1.43
Other cultigens	*Ipomoea batatas*			
	sweet potato	0.00	0.26	0.07
	Lagenaria siceraria			
	gourd	1.23	2.46	1.57
	Cucurbita sp			
	squash	1.72	5.57	2.78
	Arachis hypogaea			
	peanuts	0.44	1.30	0.68
	Gossypium barbadense			
	cotton	0.20	0.13	0.18

continued on next page

TABLE 8.1—*continued*

Botanical (percentage of total plant parts)				
Category	Species	CA-2 %	CA-3 %	Overall %
Woody plants	*Prosopis pallida*			
	mesquite	1.72	0.39	1.35
	Acacia sp.	0.15	0.00	0.11
	cane	0.54	0.00	0.39
	wood	0.05	0.65	0.21
	unknown	1.03	1.42	1.14
	Total plant parts	2,034	772	2,806

Shellfish (percentage of total MNI)				
Habitat	Species	CA-2 %	CA-3 %	Overall %
Middle valley	*Scutalus proteus*	70.21	54.44	62.82
Pacific Coast	*Donax obesulus*	23.04	33.75	28.06
	Platyxanthus sp.	2.28	2.47	2.37
	Prisogaster niger	1.39	2.81	2.06
	Polinices uber	1.29	2.59	1.90
	Other/unknown species	1.79	3.94	2.80
	Total MNI	1,007	889	1,896

reaffirming their coastal affiliation or carrying out Lambayeque policy in the middle valley. At the same time, elites also facilitated local dynamics of celebration and competition by hosting feasts around family platforms. The emergence of a complex Lambayeque polity in lower Jequetepeque, its participation in wider exchanges of styles and ideas, and its interest in expanding beyond the valley neck may have offered new political possibilities for middle valley elites. Ventanillas residents responded by drawing on broad Lambayeque public architecture traditions, perhaps to emphasize a coastal political affiliation, but also by integrating coastal and highland products, styles, and technologies into a hybrid middle valley lifestyle that continued even after Chimú conquest of the lower valley.

CASE 2: RURAL STRATEGIES IN A LANDSCAPE OF CONTROL

Chimú conquest of the Jequetepeque around AD 1320 (Mackey 2011) imposed a new set of concerns on local households. Recent research summarized elsewhere (Cutright 2015) has called into question how much centralized control over local

TABLE 8.2. Change through time in key subsistence categories at Pedregal

	LIP Occupation	Total Plant Parts	Proportion	Chi-Square on Proportion
Maize	early	5,780	14.76	$X^2 = 142, p <0.0005$
	late	2,093	26.42	
Cotton	early	5,780	18.25	$X^2 = 85.17, p <0.0005$
	late	2,093	27.81	
Tree fruit	early	5,780	33.75	$X^2 = 147.88, p <0.0005$
	late	2,093	19.54	

populations the Chimú State really exerted. The Chimú made highly visible political statements in the valleys they conquered by altering settlement patterns and establishing provincial administrative centers. Aside from intensifying agricultural production, however, they exerted little economic control over lower-class populations.

Evidence from the rural agricultural village of Pedregal (see figure 8.1), where I conducted excavations in 2006, has revealed that focus on agricultural staples such as maize and cotton increased through time during the Chimú occupation (Cutright 2009, 2015). One of the inferred motivations for Chimú expansion to the north was the potential for agricultural production in these wide, well-irrigated valleys (Kolata 1990), so increased agricultural output at Pedregal could have been directed to state coffers or to fund state activities at the nearby provincial center of Farfán. As I have argued elsewhere (Cutright 2009, 2015; table 8.2), Pedregal households were incorporated into the extractive economy of the expansive Chimú Empire and responded by intensifying production of bulk staples.

At the same time that maize and cotton production and processing within households increased, emphasis on wild foods (nonagricultural plants, shellfish, and fish) decreased compared to domesticated resources (Cutright 2009, 2010). This could indicate a tradeoff in household labor or a shift in culinary preferences during the Chimú occupation. The overall range of foods consumed and activities carried out in Pedregal households did not constrict over time (Cutright 2009). While floor plans were changed and domestic spaces remodeled through time, there is no evidence that household size or makeup changed (Cutright 2009). Household and community ritual operated in similar ways throughout Pedregal's occupation (Cutright 2013a). Thus in this case, households did not lose self-sufficiency or autonomy even as they were incorporated into wider imperial systems. Intensification of production occurred without a radical reorganization at the household level.

This situation contrasts to what happened at Pedregal after Inka conquest around AD 1470. The Inka pursued conciliatory political strategies with local

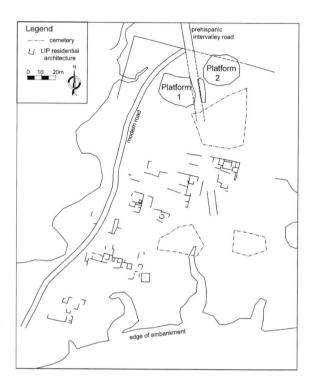

FIGURE 8.6. Inka road cross-cutting public and domestic architecture at Pedregal

Lambayeque lords at nearby Farfán (Mackey 2011) but placed an intervalley road through Pedregal (figure 8.6). The road cut through one of Pedregal's low platform mounds and bisected a residential compound. If the compound was still occupied, its use would have been dramatically reshaped by the construction of the road. Unfortunately, because of general continuities in household ceramics, it was not possible to identify the locus of Inka Period occupation, but Inka Period ceramics, including a fragment of a classic Chimú-Inka aryballoid vessel, were present in small quantities from later occupational strata across the site (Cutright 2009). Assuming that the site was still occupied, the impact of the road on this community must have been dramatic. Even as local lords enjoyed a resurgence of power under Inka rule at Farfán, as Carol J. Mackey (2011) has argued, at least some local communities were altered by Inka conquest, and previous strategies for preserving household traditions or community autonomy may have proved ineffective. The example of Pedregal, in context of the broader Chimú Period Jequetepeque, shows that local experiences of and responses to conquest were highly variable even during the same time period in the same valley and depended on location, resources, and status.

TIMELESS HOUSEHOLDS, SHIFTING TERRAIN?

In this chapter, I have presented two examples of Late Intermediate Period households dealing with the broader regional process of state expansion into new territories. One commonly held view when considering the relationship between households and the state is that households, especially those in rural hinterlands or political peripheries, were simply isolated from bigger political shifts. According to this view, conservative, inward-looking households would not necessarily alter economic or political strategies in a changing regional context unless such changes were forced on them.

However, my research at Ventanillas and Pedregal does not bear this view out. At Ventanillas, elite middle valley households strategically allied themselves and their community with a powerful coastal state and emphasized their new coastal affiliation with large-scale monumental architecture that is strikingly unique in the middle valley. They also invested in local dynamics such as textile production and kin-based competition, including feasting in household patio-mound areas. This kind of active alignment with new systems may have been more accessible to elites than to commoners, who may have been better situated to diversify economic or political strategies or who might have found themselves in the role of local intermediaries through which state control was articulated (Elson and Covey 2006; Hirth 1993). Additional work to identify the strategies of lower-class residents of Ventanillas may help confirm whether new opportunities were available only to relatively high-status or wealthy households.

Pedregal was so close to Farfán and the field systems stretching between Pacatnamú and Farfán that it would have been the first to be impacted by state policies to extract surplus and reorganize local communities. Yet at Pedregal, farming households adapted to new tribute demands while changing few other aspects of their organization. The example of Pedregal raises the possibility that the continuity we can observe from Moche to Late Intermediate Period households was in some cases the result of active or conscious strategies on the part of households and communities rather than representing a sort of "default setting" for North Coast households.

These two cases call into question a conservative, homogeneous view of Late Intermediate Period households. I argue that ancient households were not simply a passive substrate on which regional polities were constructed, a timeless "*lo doméstico*" that can be identified across the Andes throughout the past. Instead, households adapted in diverse, locally significant ways to the shifting political, economic, ideological, and ecological landscapes of particular historical moments. Their strategies varied along lines of socioeconomic status, location in the valley vis-à-vis state centers, and available political and economic opportunities in a given regional political context. These strategies, in turn, shape broader archaeological signatures of settlement, subsistence, and political economy. In other words, as Cynthia Robin (2013) points out, everyday life matters in our reconstruction of the past.

ACKNOWLEDGMENTS

Excavations at Pedregal, conducted in 2006, were directed by Lic. Jorge Terrones Zevallos and supported by grants from the Fulbright Commission, the Social Science Research Council, and the Wenner-Gren Foundation. Excavations at Ventanillas were conducted in 2011 and 2013 (co-directed by Lic. Gabriela Cervantes Quequezana) and 2016 (co-directed by Lic. Carlos Osores Mendives) and supported by Centre College, the Curtiss T. and Mary G. Brennan Foundation, and the Wenner-Gren Foundation. I would like to thank all those involved in collecting and analyzing data from these sites, as well as Ilana Johnson and David Pacifico for coordinating this volume and two anonymous reviewers for their helpful comments. All errors are my own.

REFERENCES

Bawden, Garth. 1995. "The Structural Paradox: Moche Culture as Political Ideology." *Latin American Antiquity* 6 (3): 255–273.

Bermann, Marc P. 1994. *Lukurmata: Household Archaeology in Prehispanic Bolivia.* Princeton, NJ: Princeton University Press.

Bermann, Marc P. 1997. "Domestic Life and Vertical Integration in the Tiwanaku Heartland." *Latin American Antiquity* 8 (2): 93–112.

Billman, Brian. 2002. "Irrigation and the Origins of the Southern Moche State on the North Coast of Peru." *Latin American Antiquity* 13: 371–400.

Bourdieu, Pierre. 1977. *Outline of a Theory of Practice.* New York: Cambridge University Press.

Castillo Butters, Luis Jaime. 2010. "Moche Politics in the Jequetepeque Valley: A Case for Political Opportunism." In *New Perspectives on the Political Organization of the Moche,* edited by Luis Jaime Castillo Butters and Jeffrey Quilter, 83–109. Washington, DC: Dumbarton Oaks.

Crown, Patricia. 2000. "Women's Role in Changing Cuisine." In *Women and Men in the Prehispanic Southwest,* edited by Patricia Crown, 221–266. Santa Fe, NM: School of American Research Press.

Cutright, Robyn E. 2009. *"Between the Kitchen and the State: Domestic Practice and Chimú Expansion in the Jequetepeque Valley, Peru."* PhD dissertation, University of Pittsburgh, PA.

Cutright, Robyn E. 2010. "Food, Family, and Empire: Relating Political and Domestic Change in the Jequetepeque Hinterland / Comida, familia, e imperio: Relacionando cambios políticos y domésticos en la periferia del Jequetepeque." In *Comparative Perspectives on the Archaeology of Coastal South America,* edited by Robyn E. Cutright, Enrique López-Hurtado, and Alexander Martin, 27–44. Pittsburgh: Center for Comparative Archaeology, University of Pittsburgh.

Cutright, Robyn E. 2011. "Food for the Dead, Cuisine of the Living: Mortuary Food Offerings from the Jequetepeque Valley, Perú." In *From State to Empire in the Prehistoric Jequetepeque Valley, Peru*, edited by Colleen Zori and Ilana Johnson, 83–92. British Archaeological Reports International Series 2310. Oxford: Archaeopress.

Cutright, Robyn E. 2013a. "Household *Ofrendas* and Community Feasts: Ritual at a Late Intermediate Period Village in the Jequetepeque Valley, Peru." *Ñawpa Pacha* 33 (1): 1–21.

Cutright, Robyn E. 2013b. "Lambayeque Politics in the Chaupiyunga: A View from Ventanillas." Paper presented at the Institute of Andean Studies meeting, January 11–12, 2013. Berkeley, CA.

Cutright, Robyn E. 2015. "Eating Empire in the Jequetepeque: A Local View of Chimú Expansion on the North Coast of Peru." *Latin American Antiquity* 26 (1): 64–86.

Cutright, Robyn E., and Gabriela Cervantes Quequezana. 2012. "Informe de Investigaciones Temporada 2011 Proyecto de Investigación Arqueológica Ventanillas." Report submitted to the Ministry of Culture, Lima, Peru.

Cutright, Robyn E., and Gabriela Cervantes Quequezana. 2014. "Informe de Investigaciones Temporada 2013 Proyecto de Investigación Arqueológica Ventanillas." Report submitted to the Ministry of Culture, Lima, Peru.

Cutright, Robyn E., and Carlos Osores Mendives. 2016. "Informe de Investigaciones Temporada 2016 Proyecto de Investigación Arqueológica Ventanillas." Report submitted to the Ministry of Culture, Lima, Peru.

Cutright, Robyn E., and Carlos Osores Mendives. 2018. "A Tale of Two Cities? Neighborhood Identity and Integration at Ventanillas." Paper presented at the Annual Meeting of the Society for American Archaeology, April 11–15, 2018, Washington, DC.

Dillehay, Tom D. 2001. "Town and Country in Late Moche Times: A View from Two Northern Valleys." In *Moche Art and Archaeology*, edited by Joanne Pillsbury, 259–284. New Haven, CT: Yale University Press.

Dillehay, Tom D., and Alan L. Kolata. 2004. "Long-Term Human Response to Uncertain Environmental Conditions in the Andes." *Proceedings of the National Academy of Sciences* 101 (12): 4325–4330.

Dillehay, Tom D., Alan L. Kolata, and Edward R. Swenson. 2009. *Paisajes Culturales en el Valle del Jequetepeque: Los Yacimientos Arqueológicos*. Trujillo, Peru: Ediciones SIAN.

Donnan, Christopher. 1986. "The Huaca I Complex." In *The Pacatnamú Papers*, vol. 1, edited by Christopher Donnan and Guillermo Cock, 63–84. Los Angeles: University of California.

Donnan, Christopher. 1990. "An Assessment of the Validity of the Naymlap Dynasty." In *The Northern Dynasties: Kingship and Statecraft in Chimor*, edited by Michael E. Moseley and Alana Cordy-Collins, 243–274. Washington, DC: Dumbarton Oaks.

Donnan, Christopher, and Guillermo Cock, eds. 1997. *The Pacatnamú Papers, vol. 2: The Moche Occupation.* Los Angeles: University of California.

Elson, Christina M., and R. Alan Covey, eds. 2006. *Intermediate Elites in Pre-Columbian States and Empires.* Tucson: University of Arizona Press.

Falconer, Steven E. 1995. "Rural Responses to Early Urbanism: Bronze Age Household and Village Economy at Tell el-Hayyat, Jordan." *Journal of Field Archaeology* 22: 399–419.

Franco Jordán, Régulo, César Galvez Mora, and Segundo Vasquez Sanchez. 2007. *El Brujo Prácticas Funerarias Post-Mochicas.* Trujillo, Peru: Fundación Augusto Wiese.

Gumerman, George, IV. 1991. "Subsistence and Complex Societies: Diet between Diverse Socio-economic Groups, Pacatnamú, Peru." PhD dissertation, University of California, Los Angeles.

Hecker, Wolfgang, and Giesela Hecker. 1990. *Ruinas, caminos y sistemas de irrigación prehispanicos en la provincia de Pacasmayo, Peru.* Patrimonio Arqueológico Zona Norte 3. Trujillo, Peru: Instituto Departamental de Cultura–La Libertad.

Hirth, Kenneth. 1993. "The Household as an Analytical Unit: Problems in Method and Theory." In *Household, Compound, and Residence: Studies of Prehispanic Domestic Units in Western Mesoamerica,* edited by Robert Santley and Kenneth Hirth, 21–36. Boca Raton: CRC Press.

Hodder, Ian, and Craig Cessford. 2004. "Daily Practice and Social Memory at Catalhoyuk." *American Antiquity* 69 (1): 17–40.

Johnson, Ilana. 2010. *"Households and Social Organization at the Late Moche Period Site of Pampa Grande, Peru."* PhD dissertation, University of California, Los Angeles.

Keatinge, Richard W., and Geoffrey W. Conrad. 1983. "Imperialist Expansion in Peruvian Prehistory: Chimú Administration of a Conquered Territory." *Journal of Field Archaeology* 10 (3): 255–283.

Kennedy, Sarah A., and Parker VanValkenburgh. 2016. "Zooarchaeology and Changing Food Practices at Carrizales, Peru Following the Spanish Invasion." *International Journal of Historical Archaeology* 20: 73.

Kolata, Alan. 1990. "The Urban Concept of Chan Chan." In *The Northern Dynasties: Kingship and Statecraft in Chimor,* edited by Michael Moseley and Alana Cordy-Collins, 107–144. Washington, DC: Dumbarton Oaks.

Mackey, Carol J. 2006. "Elite Residences at Farfán: A Comparison of the Chimú and Inka Occupations." In *Palaces of the Ancient New World,* edited by Susan Toby Evans and Joanne Pillsbury, 313–352. Washington, DC: Dumbarton Oaks.

Mackey, Carol J. 2009. "Chimú Statecraft in the Provinces." In *Andean Civilization: A Tribute to Michael E. Moseley,* edited by Joyce Marcus and P. Ryan Williams, 325–349. Los Angeles: Cotsen Institute of Archaeology, UCLA.

Mackey, Carol J. 2011. "The Persistence of Lambayeque Ethnic Identity: The Perspective from the Jequetepeque Valley, Peru." In *From State to Empire in the Prehistoric Jequetepeque Valley, Peru*, edited by Colleen Zori and Ilana Johnson, 149–168. British Archaeological Reports International Series 2310. Oxford: Archaeopress.

McClelland, Donald. 1986. "Brick Seriation at Pacatnamú." In *The Pacatnamú Papers*, vol. 1, edited by Christopher Donnan and Guillermo Cock, 37–46. Los Angeles: University of California Press.

Moseley, Michael E. 1992. *The Incas and Their Ancestors: The Archaeology of Peru*. New York: Thames and Hudson.

Prieto Burmester, O. Gabriel. 2010. "Aproximaciones a la Configuración Política Lambayeque: Una Perspectiva desde el Sitio de San José de Moro, Valle de Jequetepeque." In *Comparative Perspectives on the Archaeology of Coastal South America*, edited by Robyn E. Cutright, Enrique López-Hurtado, and Alexander Martin. Memoirs in Latin American Archaeology. Pittsburgh: University of Pittsburgh.

Quilter, Jeffrey, and Luis Jaime Castillo Butters. 2010. "Many Moche Models: An Overview of Past and Current Theories and Research on Moche Political Organization." In *New Perspectives on Moche Political Organization*, edited by Jeffrey Quilter and Luis Jaime Castillo Butters, 1–16. Washington, DC: Dumbarton Oaks.

Quilter, Jeffrey, and Michelle Koons. 2012. "The Fall of the Moche: A Critique of Claims for South America's First State." *Latin American Antiquity* 23 (2): 127–143.

Reindel, Markus. 1993 *Monumentale Lehmarchitektur an der Nordküste Perus: Eine Repräsentative Untersuchung Nach-Formativer Grossbauten vom Lambayeque-Gebietbis zum Virú-Tal*. Bonn: Holos.

Ringberg, Jennifer. 2008. "Figurines, Household Rituals, and the Use of Domestic Space in a Middle Moche Rural Community." In *Arqueología Mochica: Nuevos Enfoques*, edited by Luis Jaime Castiillo, Helene Bernier, Greg Lockhard, and Julio Rucabado, 341–357. Lima: Pontificia Universidad Católica del Perú.

Robin, Cynthia. 2013. *Everyday Life Matters: Maya Farmers at Chan*. Gainesville: University Press of Florida.

Rosas Rintel, Marco. 2007. "Nuevas perspectivas acerca del colapso Moche en el Bajo Jequetepeque." *Bulletin de l'Institut d'Etudes Andines* 36 (2): 221–240.

Sahlins, Marshall. 1972. *Stone Age Economics*. Chicago: Aldine-Atherton.

Sapp, William. 2011. "Lambayeque Norte and Lambayeque Sur: Evidence for the Development of an Indigenous Lambayeque Polity in the Jequetepeque Valley, Peru." In *From State to Empire in the Prehistoric Jequetepeque Valley, Peru*, edited by Colleen Zori and Ilana Johnson, 93–104. British Archaeological Reports International Series 2310. Oxford: Archaeopress.

Shimada, Izumi. 1981. "The Batán-Grande-La Leche Archaeological Project: The First Two Seasons." *Journal of Field Archaeology* 8 (4): 405–446.

Shimada, Izumi, Crystal Barker Schaaf, Lonnie G. Thompson, and Ellen Mosley-Thompson. 1991. "Cultural Impacts of Severe Droughts in the Prehistoric Andes: Application of a 1,500-Year Ice Core Precipitation Record." *World Archaeology* 22 (3): 247–270.

Swenson, Edward R. 2004. *"Ritual Power in the Urban Hinterland: Religious Pluralism and Political Decentralization in Late Moche Jequetepeque, Peru."* PhD dissertation, University of Chicago, IL.

Swenson, Edward R. 2007a. "Adaptive Strategies or Ideological Innovations? Interpreting Sociopolitical Developments in the Jequetepeque Valley of Peru during the Late Moche Period." *Journal of Anthropological Archaeology* 26: 253–282.

Swenson, Edward R. 2007b. "Local Ideological Strategies and the Politics of Ritual Space in the Chimú Empire." *Archaeological Dialogues* 14 (1): 61–90.

Swenson, Edward R., and John P. Warner. 2016. "Landscapes of Mimesis and Convergence in the Southern Jequetepeque Valley, Peru." *Cambridge Archaeological Journal* 26: 23–51.

Thompson, Lonnie G., Mary E. Davis, and Ellen Mosley-Thompson. 1994. "Glacial Records of Global Climate: A 1500-Year Tropical Ice Core Record of Climate." *Human Ecology* 22 (1): 83–95.

Topic, John R. 1982. "Lower-Class Social and Economic Organization at Chan Chan." In *Chan Chan: Andean Desert City*, edited by Michael Moseley and Kent Day, 145–176. Albuquerque: University of New Mexico Press.

Tsai, Howard I. 2012. *"An Archaeological Investigation of Ethnicity at Las Varas, Peru."* PhD dissertation, University of Michigan, Ann Arbor.

Tschauner, Hartmut. 2001. *"Socioeconomic and Political Organization in the Late Prehispanic Lambayeque Sphere, Northern North Coast of Peru."* PhD dissertation, Harvard University, Cambridge, MA.

Vogel, Melissa. 2012. *Frontier Life in Ancient Peru: The Archaeology of Cerro la Cruz.* Gainesville: University Press of Florida.

Warner, John P. 2010. *"Interpreting the Architectonics of Power and Memory at the Late Formative Center of Jatanca, Jequetepeque Valley, Peru."* PhD dissertation, University of Kentucky, Lexington.

Wilk, Richard R. 1991. *Household Ecology.* Tucson: University of Arizona Press.

Zobler, Kari A., and Richard C. Sutter. 2016. "A Tale of Two Cities: Continuity and Change Following the Moche Collapse in the Jequetepeque Valley, Peru." In *Beyond Collapse: Archaeological Perspectives on Resilience, Revitalization, and Transformation in Complex Societies*, edited by Ronald Faulseit, 486–503. Center for Archaeological Investigations Occasional Paper 42. Carbondale: Southern Illinois University.

9

Enduring Collapse

Households and Local Autonomy at Talambo, Jequetepeque, Peru

KARI A. ZOBLER

> You pile up associations the way you pile up bricks . . . Memory itself is a
> form of architecture.
>
> LOUISE BOURGEOIS (2000, 26)

Archaeologists have made significant advances in modeling societal change, particularly as it relates to political collapse and regeneration (Holling 1973; Holling and Gunderson 2002; Kolata 2006; Tainter 1988; Yoffee and Cowgill 1988). Cross-cultural analyses have revealed a range of interrelated internal tensions (e.g., corruption, economic overextension, and diminishing returns) and external challenges (e.g., environmental degradation, natural disaster, warfare, and disease) that catalyze societal destabilization (Railey and Reycraft 2008; Schwartz and Nichols 2006). A key component of many of these models is that sociopolitical change occurs across multiple intersecting scales—from regional to local and public to private.

Domestic contexts offer an analytically accessible scale at which regional societal variation may be examined (Deetz 1982). Moreover, the diachronic nature of the "house" as social unit, as well as its material ubiquity, makes it ideal for temporal and cross-cultural comparison. Yet despite the frequent application of household data to regional models of sociopolitical collapse, there has been comparatively little focus on long-term community endurance or how the challenges households face rarely disappear with the dismantling of elite power. From a household perspective, "collapse" is characterized less by epochal rupture than

DOI: 10.5876/9781646420919.c009

by prolonged precarity. Moreover, societal regeneration is not a product of unidirectional elite action but rather the endurance (or exhaustion) of locally created alternate social worlds.

On the North Coast of Peru, ancient households were constitutive social and economic units in community endurance and regional political change. Although the key role exchange networks played in Late Moche cultural continuity is well established in Moche archaeology (particularly for San José de Moro in the Jequetepeque Valley), community endurance strategies exhibited at economically insulated sites and the role water management played in Cajamarca territorial arrogation and local autonomy have not been fully explored.

This chapter presents evidence of household endurance in the Jequetepeque Valley of Peru in the Late Moche (AD 600–800) and Transitional/early Late Intermediate Periods (AD 800–1100) at the site of Talambo (figure 9.1). Talambo's location (near the intake for the Talambo Canal), water access, and socioeconomic independence enabled households to adopt alternative endurance strategies during a period of political and environmental destabilization surrounding the Moche collapse. Whereas elite centers (and those communities imbricated in their systems of exchange) perpetuated their own ceremonial ideology and the prestige of foreign connection, recent excavations of two contemporary domestic contexts demonstrate how Talambo maintained an alternate social world that operated at the margins of (or entirely outside) these prominent centers.

GIVE ME SHELTER: HOUSEHOLDS, "COLLAPSE," AND ALTERNATE SOCIAL WORLDS

The scale of the home defies easy classification—it is at once intimate and universal. For anthropologists, initial bounded conceptions of what constitutes a house have given way to a panoply of domesticities. The "house," as first conceptualized by Claude Lévi-Strauss (1982, 1987), is a social unit wherein co-residence underlies a network of social, political, religious, and economic ties (Wilk and Rathje 1982). As a constitutive social unit, the house embodies broader societal ideals and their selective application. It is the space where culturally defined social relationships are naturalized—at the intersection of community and individual.

In "Essay: The Love of Old Houses," poet Mark Doty highlights the intersection between household endurance and accumulated action. "A *building*," he reminds us, is "both noun and verb, / where we live and what we do" (Doty 2001, 54) Or, as artist Louise Bourgeois (2000, 26) would have it, "memory itself is a form of architecture." Although I am sensible that poetic engagements with the home quickly outpace the limitations of household archaeology, they nevertheless provide a useful avenue to

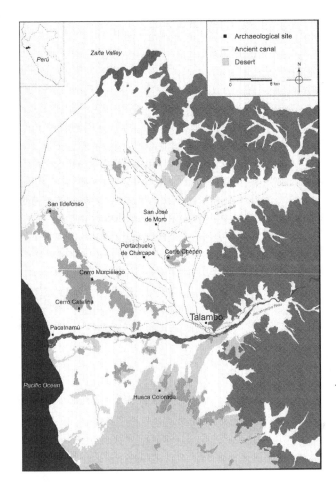

FIGURE 9.1.
Map of the lower
Jequetepeque Valley,
including important
Late Moche and
Transitional Period
sites, as well as the
northern irrigation
canals

critically assess the capacity of quotidian routine to insulate and sustain alternate social worlds. Doty's description of a two-centuries-old house, for example, shifts between past and present, as the structure's material continuity—a polished floor, a well-worn stair—elicits memories of previous habitation and an affective attachment to the house's former residents. It is central to Doty's narrative that a house encompasses much more than its architectural shell. Rather, the carapace of brick and mortar, wood and stone, is imbued with the past efforts of previous occupants, whose energies transcend even the most profound rupture.

By contrast, archaeological models of rupture, such as those that characterize sociopolitical change, are predominantly rooted in event-based perspectives of the past (Badiou 2005; Deleuze 2007). Borrowing from ecological models, these analyses have primarily focused on identifying the material correlates of emerging complexity, collapse, and (sometimes) regeneration (Faulseit 2016; Holling 1973; Holling and Gunderson 2002; Redman 2005; Schwartz and Nichols 2006). Such studies often rely on variations in elite material culture, which magnifies the visibility and importance of epochal change.

Domestic contexts provide an important counterpoint to elite-derived models of sociopolitical transformation. Households tend to function on a different temporal scale than prestige arenas. Unlike the moments of transformative rupture that often accompany macropolitical change, the opportunities and challenges faced by households in their daily maintenance are generally below the level of the catastrophic. Rather, societal collapse is more often a political disruption than a demographic loss (Dillehay 2001; Railey and Reycraft 2008). Moreover, the material culture of domesticity is more stylistically conservative than the prestige goods on which relative chronologies are usually based. Consequently, households often resist the cause-and-effect characterizations that are the hallmark of archaeological narratives of collapse and regeneration.

Given the extended temporality of domestic life, how do we reconcile the inherent stability of the household as a constitutive social unit with a macropolitical view of epochal change? Although most archaeological models of collapse and regeneration utilize the cyclical terminology of systemic resilience (Redman 2005), a growing body of anthropological research (within the context of Late Liberalism) problematizes the inevitability of these cycles by examining the processes by which state abandonment is repackaged as community failure (Berlant 2011; Nixon 2011; Povinelli 2011). Anthropologist Elizabeth A. Povinelli (2011, 2012) framed community potentiality in human terms—endurance or exhaustion, with exhaustion having mortal consequences. Moreover, Povinelli's (2011) "exhaustion" and Rob Nixon's (2011) "slow violence" underscore the oblique wounds that are endemic to prolonged precarity in communities.

By applying Povinelli's dichotomy between community endurance and its antonym to the household, I ascribe intentionality to even the most recursive domestic social production. "If we must *persist* in potentiality," Povinelli (2011, 128) wrote, "we must *endure* it as a space, a materiality, and a temporality. As we all know, materiality-as-potentiality is never itself outside given organizations of power." Seen thus, household continuity under strain is an act of endurance that carries material, mental, and emotional costs. If organizations of power endure, then community costs are amplified at a rate commensurate with their sociopolitical distance from the ideological center.

At the same time, by enduring the prolonged precarity of collapse, communities may develop alternate social worlds that diverge from the normative strategies of elite centers or, indeed, their own rural neighbors. These "otherwises," to borrow Povinelli's (2011, 2012, 2014) term, have the *potential* to be actualized and resonate more broadly, although this is never a certainty. It is at this regional scale that alternate social worlds most often gain archaeological recognition. Their origins, however, are always intensely local—living or dying by the energies of individuals and the resources to which they have access. Seen thus, moments of "transition" between collapse and regeneration are characterized less by unidirectional development than by uneven impasse. Transformative societal change occurs not in moments of elite conflagration but in the quiet potentiality of the domestic, where what was and what could be together hang fire.

LATE MOCHE AND TRANSITIONAL PERIODS IN THE JEQUETEPEQUE VALLEY

In the Late Moche Period, intermittent political and environmental instability on the north coast of Peru resulted in political decentralization along canal networks and a proliferation of inland settlement (Castillo Butters 2000a, 2003, 2007, 2009, 2010; Dillehay et al. 2004, 2009; Hecker and Hecker 1995; Swenson 2004, 2007). Elite centers that were strategically located at valley necks and canal nodes thrived as many of the prominent Middle Moche complexes in the lower valleys declined. In the southern Moche heartland, for example, elite settlement shifted from the Huacas de Moche[1] to the site of Galindo near the lower valley neck (Bawden 1977, 2001; Lockard 2005, 2008; Moseley 1978; Moseley and Deeds 1982). A similar move occurred in the northern Moche sphere, at Pampa Grande in the Lambayeque Valley (Johnson 2010; Shimada 1994). Meanwhile, hinterland communities proliferated—oscillating between autonomous and cooperative strategies that alternately paralleled or diverged from those of elite centers.

In the Jequetepeque Valley, Late Moche communities negotiated an amalgam of centralizing and divergent forces. First, expanded canal irrigation networks physically connected dispersed settlements while communities continued to manage their own subsistence economies. Second, prominent centers in the Jequetepeque Valley did not develop the same urbanism that characterized elite settlement in neighboring valleys. Rather, elite centers hosted ceremonies and cultivated ritual exchange networks that propagated elite symbols of power while hinterland "huaca communities" intermittently utilized or eschewed these icons. Finally, as the power of local elites waned and highland influence grew toward the end of the Late Moche Period, rural communities either mirrored the strategies of prominent centers or developed their own means of endurance.

CANAL IRRIGATION IN THE JEQUETEPEQUE VALLEY

The lower Jequetepeque Valley was irrigated in three phases, the last of which watered the northern sector between the Jequetepeque and Chamán Rivers. Although earlier efforts were more structurally unified, this final phase of canal construction was accomplished through building four separate canals (Chafán, Guadalupe, Chepén, and Talambo), each with an independent intake (figure 9.2). Thus each subsector of the northern valley could have been irrigated independently. The redundancy of this system has been linked to successive chronological episodes of construction, strategies of risk management, and increasing political factionalism (Castillo Butters 2010; Eling 1987).

The northern canal expansion dates to either the Middle Moche (AD 400–600) or Late Moche Period (AD 600–800). Luis Jaime Castillo Butters (2010) assigned construction to the Middle Moche Period, based on relative dating of the ceramic assemblage at San José de Moro and nearby settlements. Although the site of San José de Moro was not directly associated with a canal in the Moche era (the Moro subsidiary canal is a Late Intermediate Period expansion), Castillo argued against the likelihood of any significant settlement in the arid northern sector of the valley without canal irrigation.

Tom D. Dillehay (2001) and Edward R. Swenson (2004) have each argued for a Late Moche date of canal construction, based on radiocarbon dates and relative ceramic chronologies at hinterland sites. The association of sectional canal management with particular social groups is well established in the Andes (Netherly 1984) and is a common feature of many irrigation systems cross-culturally (Adams 1960; Fernea 1970). Given that the Late Moche Period was also characterized by increased fortification, they argue that these individual canals and their separate intakes were originally conceived as (or eventually became) the resources of politically autonomous communities.

Beyond chronological exactitude, the underlying question in this debate is whether irrigation of the northern Jequetepeque Valley emerged from political unity or fragmentation. In this chapter, I address this chronological question. My primary interest in Jequetepeque canal networks, however, has less to do with the original impetus for canal construction than with what role canal networks played in community endurance during and immediately after the Moche collapse.

LATE MOCHE RITUAL AND EXCHANGE

During the Late Moche Period, individuals intermittently gravitated toward the ritual mass of elite centers while remaining tethered to their increasingly autonomous source communities (Castillo Butters 2010; Dillehay 2001; Johnson 2011; Swenson

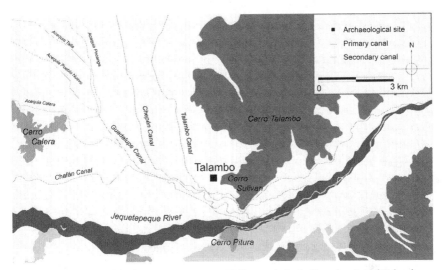

FIGURE 9.2. Map of the lower Jequetepeque Valley neck, including the site of Talambo and canal intakes for the northern valley

2004, 2006, 2007; Swenson and Warner 2012). A priestess cult flourished at the site of San José de Moro, which elevated this once marginal iconographic figure to the focus of funerary ritual and communal feasting (Castillo Butters 2001, 2006). Meanwhile, small "huaca communities" proliferated throughout the Jequetepeque Valley (Dillehay 2001; Duke, this volume), indicating that Late Moche ceremonial life was locally as well as regionally situated (Swenson 2006, 2008). Recurrent dedicatory and termination offerings at these complexes reinforced a materially vital and mutually sacrificial mode of being while elites simultaneously perpetuated the contradiction of an increasingly class-divided society (Morrow, this volume; Swenson 2015).

Newly established ritual exchange networks, emanating from San José de Moro, fostered greater cultural continuity among participating hinterland settlements (Castillo Butters 2010). Intricately painted fineline vessels associated with veneration of the Moro priestess have been found at sites throughout the valley (Johnson 2008, 2011; Swenson 2008, 2015; Swenson and Warner 2012). These wares are recovered most often in ceremonial or mortuary contexts, including within some huaca communities, along with mold-impressed face-neck jars that depict more generalized Moche religious imagery (Swenson 2006, 2008). Thus hinterland settlements engaged with regional symbols of power while simultaneously developing and reaffirming their own ancestral community narratives.

Castillo Butters (2010) has argued that the regional impact of San José de Moro's ceremonial ideology extended beyond cultural continuity to facilitate sociopolitical integration among settlement groups. These "opportunistic states," as he termed them, would have utilized the same ritual exchange networks that disseminated San José de Moro (SJM) fineline wares to manage regional defense and canal irrigation (Castillo Butters 2010, 106). Seen thus, ritual exchange at San José de Moro and the northern canal expansion were not only concurrent processes but also represented contingent parts of a semiunified political effort on the part of Moche elites.

If San José de Moro elites used existing ceremonial networks to organize irrigation management (during either the Middle Moche or the Late Moche Period), we might expect that all settlements located along these canal networks would have access to SJM fineline wares. Moreover, if elites occasionally mobilized communities under their influence to address shared opportunities and challenges (such as an influx of highland settlers or climatological instability), we might expect corresponding similarities between elite and hinterland material culture during periods of intensified interaction.

Before addressing these issues at the site of Talambo, it is helpful to briefly outline the shared opportunities and challenges faced by all Late Moche communities in the Jequetepeque Valley, as well as elite strategies of endurance.

SHARED CHALLENGES AND NEW NEIGHBORS: RITUAL NETWORKS TRANSFORMED

The El Niño–Southern Oscillation (ENSO) phenomenon, an ever-present variable on the North Coast, presented one such shared challenge to Late Moche (and contemporary highland) societies (Shimada et al. 1991; Swenson 2004; Thompson et al. 1985). El Niño disrupts the agricultural and maritime cycle and, in severe years, the warmer waters and shifting atmospheric currents can produce rains that flood canals and wash out agricultural fields. Given significant regional variation in the severity of El Niño effects (Billman and Huckleberry 2008; Dillehay 2001, 269; Sandweiss and Quilter 2012), some communities likely fared better than others. Thus in addition to their political significance, dispersed settlement patterns in the Jequetepeque Valley during the Late Moche Period may have reduced general subsistence risk.

Variable rains in the highlands (associated with ENSO) and the expansion of the highland Wari State brought new people, ideologies, and economies into the coastal sphere (Bawden 2001; Castillo Butters 2001; Castillo Butters et al. 2012). Highland and coastal populations coexisted in Jequetepeque in a variety of hierarchical and heterarchical arrangements. Biodistance results indicate that ethnically highland settlers from Cajamarca migrated into the middle and lower valleys (particularly Zaña and Jequetepeque) during the Late Moche Period (Zobler and Sutter 2016). Their interactions ranged from intrusive at Cerro Chepén (Cusicanqui and Caramanica 2011; Rosas 2007, 2010) to co-optive at San José de Moro (Castillo Butters 2001, 2010; Castillo Butters and Uceda Castillo 2008; Castillo Butters et al. 2012) to cohabitation at Las Varas (Tsai 2020).

In the lower Jequetepeque Valley, Cajamarquinos grafted on to the existing resources and ceremonial life of Late Moche communities. Cajamarca settlers established a new settlement at Cerro Chepén Alto, which surmounted the locally populated area of Cerro Chepén. Cerro Chepén Alto was an ideal location for a colony, as the Serrano Canal supplied ample water. Moreover, the ethnically Moche community of Cerro Chepén Bajo provided a ready source of agricultural labor (Rosas 2007, 2010).

In addition to Cerro Chepén Alto's favorable resources, the site's geographic proximity to San José de Moro facilitated highland participation in Late Moche ceremonial life. Cajamarca Floral Cursive wares[2] joined local SJM finelines in the elite mortuary assemblage of San José de Moro (Castillo Butters 2000b; 2001). Frequent co-occurrence of these wares evinces a level of (asymmetrical) cooperation between highland and local elites that likely benefited both groups throughout an era of environmental instability. These interactions facilitated and locally legitimized Cajamarca priorities related to subsistence and exchange while simultaneously transplanting the prestige of foreign authority to buttress local elite power in uncertain political times.

Some rural communities mirrored elite interactions by embracing highland wares. At the Late Moche site of Huaca Colorada, for example, Cajamarca vessels were found in elite ritual contexts alongside SJM fineline wares and face-neck jars (Swenson and Warner 2012). Meanwhile, at the more modest residential site of Portachuelo de Charcape, located approximately 50 km west of San José de Moro, SJM finelines were found together with Wari-related ceramic styles (Johnson 2008, 272). Despite evident differences in site size and location, both sites are located adjacent to irrigation canals (albeit different networks). Moreover, these settlements share a history of participation in San José de Moro ritual and exchange networks before highland influence entered the valley.

Although some hinterland settlements employed the same ceremonial assemblages as prominent centers, rural communities in the Jequetepeque Valley did not universally adopt the new highland wares. Recent surveys indicate that some hinterland settlements did not utilize Cajamarca wares (Cusicanqui and Barrazueta 2010; Dillehay et al. 2009; Ruiz 2004; Swenson 2004). Other sites, such as the remote settlement of San Ildefonso, continued to use SJM fineline wares but in an entirely different use pattern than elite centers (Swenson 2008). Moreover, San

Ildefonso's geographic remoteness (without easy access to irrigation) complicates the presumed relationship between SJM fineline wares and canal infrastructure.

Thus, despite facing shared challenges, some communities in the Jequetepeque Valley developed alternate strategies of endurance to negotiate the uncertainties of Moche collapse. While elite centers and some hinterland sites cultivated foreign connection, other settlements lacked access to (or chose to avoid) these relationships. What role did rural households play in creating and maintaining such alternate social worlds? Did these strategies ultimately contribute to the endurance or exhaustion of their respective communities?

TALAMBO HOUSEHOLDS DURING THE LATE MOCHE AND TRANSITIONAL PERIODS

The site of Talambo, located on the north bank of the Jequetepeque River at the neck of the lower valley, is well situated to address the role of canal irrigation, elite exchange networks, and foreign influence during the Late Moche and Transitional Periods. Although primarily known for its Late Intermediate Period (AD 1000–1476) role in the Chimú imperial scheme (Keatinge and Conrad 1983), Talambo began as a Moche era settlement. The site's initial function, by virtue of its location, appears to have been control and management of the nearby canal intakes and adjacent agricultural fields.

Results from my excavations revealed that Late Moche and Transitional households at Talambo engaged in small-scale subsistence and craft production activities, as well as local ceremonial practices, similar to other settlements in the valley. Unlike many of its contemporaries located along canal networks, however, Talambo was not imbricated in San José de Moro (and eventually highland) networks of ritual and exchange.

General Description of Site Features

The main sector of Talambo (also referred to as Talambo Oeste) consists of a large adobe enclosure, three huaca mounds, and numerous outbuildings (figure 9.3). The main compound was constructed of adobe bricks with a stone-and-daub foundation. It incorporated a huaca along the north perimeter wall, internal partitions and platforms, and an extensive adobe brick and field stone extension that abuts the entire eastern wall. The main compound is accessed through an entrance on the west side. Two additional huacas (including the site's largest) are located southwest of this complex. The ancient Talambo Canal flows a short distance south of these mounds. The modern canal, which was built as part of the Gallito Ciego Dam Project in the 1980s, bisects these huacas.

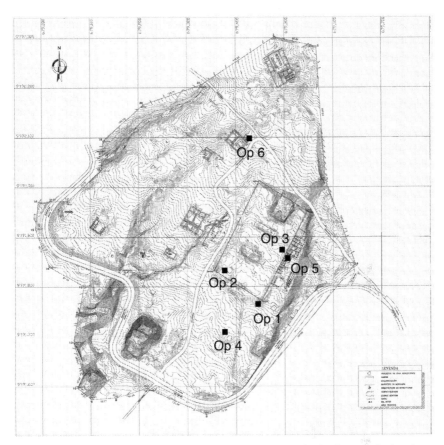

FIGURE 9.3. Topographic map of Talambo's core settlement (Talambo Oeste), showing the location of Proyecto Arqueológico de Talambo Oeste excavation units. Map also includes present-day features such as roads and the modern Talambo Canal.

A cemetery abuts the larger of these two mounds at its eastern base. Systematic surface collection (50% coverage) of ceramics in this mortuary sector indicates that it (and the adjacent huaca) was utilized during the Moche and Chimú Periods (Zobler n.d.). The ceremonial assemblage at the huaca summit and in the Moche sector of the cemetery (located closest to the huaca base) is typical of rural Moche settlements, consisting of face-neck jars[3] and quartz beads, along with a variety of food preparation and serving wares for feasting.

The main compound and huacas are surrounded by numerous smaller rectangular structures, particularly to the north and west of the core. The best preserved of these buildings was excavated by Richard W. Keatinge and Geoffrey W. Conrad (1983) in the late 1970s. They identified it as a Chimú administrative structure with architectural parallels (an *audiencia* and niched rooms) to contemporary sites such as Farfán and Chan Chan. Subsequent survey and modeling of the site have noted its place in the Chimú settlement hierarchy (Mackey 1987), to the near exclusion of other periods of occupation (with the exception of Eling 1987, 456; Shimada 1994, 121-122; Swenson 2004, 404). My excavation revealed that the majority of extant Late Intermediate Period and Late Horizon architecture in this core sector overlays an earlier history of continuous occupation beginning in the late Middle Moche Period, particularly in the southern portion of the settlement closest to the ancient Talambo Canal.

The Talambo Canal was the last major canal to be constructed in Jequetepeque and flows immediately south of the main sector of the site of Talambo. At its fullest extent, the 80 km-long canal irrigated over 30,000 hectares (Swenson 2004, 237) and linked the Jequetepeque River with the Chamán drainage. It included two main subsidiary canals (the Serrano Canal and Moro Canal) and eventually reached up to the Pampa de Colorado (Eling 1987). Given that there was no settlement on the Pampa de Colorado until the Late Intermediate Period, the Late Moche profile of the Talambo Canal would have been more modest in scope. Although the canal has not yet been directly dated, extensive survey and excavation of associated sites indicate that during the Late Moche Period, the Talambo Canal likely extended only as far as Cerro Chepén Bajo, where the Serrano Canal watered a Late Moche settlement (Rosas 2010). Talambo was thus in a privileged position of water access for itself and control for sites in the lower valley, including Cerro Chepén.[4]

The core of Talambo is flanked by numerous stone structures (including a small huaca complex) that are terraced into the nearby hillside of Cerro Sullivan (also referred to as Talambo Este). In this, Talambo is similar to other Moche sites such as Galindo (Bawden 1977; Lockard 2005, 2008) and Santa Rosa–Quirihuac (Billman et al. 1999; Gumerman and Briceño 2003), where settlement extended from the coastal pampa to the adjacent hillside. Systematic but not fully comprehensive survey of this hillside yielded a plethora of small and intermediate-sized field stone structures, including enclosures and platforms (Dillehay et al. 2009; Kremkau 2010; Zobler n.d.).

Grab-sampling at these sites revealed that with the exception of a few fine blackware fragments, surface sherds were generally *tinajas*, jars, and *ollas* made of coarse, low-fired, grit-tempered wares (sometimes with loosely applied bands of cream slip) used for storage and cooking activities. The variable presence of such diagnostic features as "King of Assyria" face-neck jars (Castillo Butters et al. 2008; Hecker and Hecker 1995, 46, 89-90; Swenson 2004, 407; Ubbelohde-Doering 1967, 24, 63), platform rims (Castillo Butters 2010; Donnan and Cock 1986), paleteada surface decoration (Cleland and Shimada 1998), and appliqué animal heads indicates that these sites conform to a date range spanning the Late Moche to Chimú-Inka Periods.

Excavation and mapping conducted by the Proyecto Arqueológico de Talambo Oeste (PATO) in the 2012 and 2013 field seasons were confined to the core sector of Talambo, where six individual operations were opened, ranging in size from 2 m^2 to 5 m^2 (figure 9.3). More than one vertical meter of continuous settlement was found, in which I recognize four occupational phases composed of perceived building levels or depositional events (Zobler n.d.). The four phases cover the Early Intermediate Period to the Late Horizon, with Phase I attributed to the late Middle Moche/Late Moche Period and Phase II to the Transitional/early Lambayeque era. Phase III represents the main period of occupation under the Chimú, and Phase IV marks an extensive Chimú-Inka occupation. Excavation in the southern sector of the site (Operations 2 and 4) revealed the earliest deposits (and Operation 2 included all four occupational phases). These operations are in relatively close proximity to the huaca complex and cemetery that were first associated with the Moche era. In addition, some domestic debris associated with Phase II was recovered to the northeast of Operation 2 (Operation 3), although no extant architecture and few artifacts remained. All other units were confined to the latter two phases. Phases I and II are discussed below.

PHASE I

Phase I, which corresponds to the late Middle Moche/Late Moche Period (AD 500–800), was characterized by domestic settlement throughout the southern sector of the site (closest to the Talambo Canal). The earliest deposits consisted of two partially cleared buildings constructed on sterile soil: a daub-and-cane (*quincha*) wall oriented east to west in Operation 4 (hereafter referred to as Building A) and a fragmentary *quincha* structure in Operation 2 (hereafter referred to as Building B). Although the paucity of architectural remains obviates any spatial reconstruction in either of these early contexts, the artifact assemblage is consistent with lower-status Moche households.

In Building A, an east-west wall constructed of *quincha* formed the sole architectural feature that was excavated (figure 9.4). Recovered ceramics were overwhelmingly utilitarian, including jar (*cántaro*), *olla*, and *tinaja* forms, associated with food preparation and storage. Scattered shell, animal bone, and macrobotanical remains were consistent with small-scale food preparation and consumption (although remains were sparse). The majority of shellfish consumed were *Donax obesulus* (80%), with *Scutalus proteus* (20%) forming the rest of the sample. A few camelid bone fragments formed the entirety of the terrestrial remains.

FIGURE 9.4. Photograph of Building A in Phase I showing the *quincha* wall (Operation 4)

To the northwest of Building A, excavations uncovered an occupational area (Building B) beneath the southwest corner of the primary Late Intermediate Period rectilinear complex at a depth of 1 m. Although no *quincha* walls were preserved *in situ*, cane and grass rope as well as a small hearth were found, indicating that *quincha* walls or a woven roof suspended by posts were constructed in this area. A single AMS radiocarbon date (1550 ± 30 BP, calibrated [2 sigma] in AD 520–635) recovered from a charred seed on the compacted, earthen floor of Building B places occupation within the late Middle Moche/early Late Moche Period.

At Building B, residents engaged in small-scale food preparation activities similar to Building A (figure 9.5). The vast majority of recovered ceramics were jar (52%) and *olla* (30%) fragments, as well as lesser quantities of graters (11%) and plates (3%). Remnants of a small hearth and cooking refuse evidence a diet that included shellfish, such as *Donax obesulus* (47%), *Polinices uber* (26%), and *Scutalus proteus* (19%), as well as smaller quantities of *Tegula atra* (5%), *Cantharus rehderi* (2%), and *Thais chocolata* (2%). Residents also subsisted on limited terrestrial (camelid, dog, and rat) and marine (fish and crab) species, as well as agricultural and foraged products (such as beans, maize, and *guanábana*). This modest diet is consistent with similar

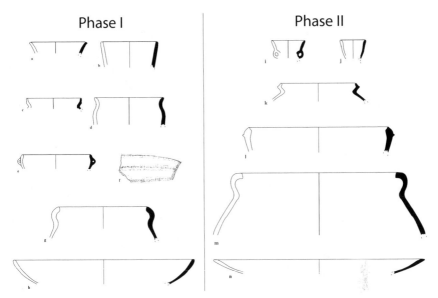

FIGURE 9.5. Common ceramic profiles from Phases I and II (Operations 2 and 4)

Moche settlements on the North Coast, such as Santa Rosa–Quirihuac, Santa Rita B, Ciudad de Dios, and Charcape (Johnson 2010).

Finer wares were also part of the ceramic assemblage at Building B, including a stirrup-spout bottle neck, face-neck jar, and figurine fragments (figure 9.6). These wares are of a similar style and quality as ceramics recovered in surface collection of the nearby huaca and cemetery complex and included red-on-white stirrup-spout bottles and jars with press-molded faces in the style of the "King of Assyria."

In addition, Building B's residents engaged in specialized craft production of stone beads (particularly quartz) that were identical to those found associated with the nearby huaca and cemetery. Both finished and unfinished beads were recovered, in addition to a copper needle and small bundles of cotton (the seeds of which were preserved), which were likely used for thread (figure 9.7). No spinning or weaving implements (such as spindle whorls or shuttles) were found in this phase, indicating that this cotton was likely part of the bead makers' toolkit rather than evidence of additional weaving activities.

Despite their otherwise typical Late Moche material assemblage, residents of Talambo avoided importing elite ceremonial wares. No SJM fineline wares were found in Buildings A or B. Moreover, no SJM fineline ceramics were recovered by

FIGURE 9.6. Figurine and face-neck jar fragments from Building B in Phase I (Operation 2)

survey from the nearby huaca and cemetery. Rather, Talambo's residents favored a ceremonial assemblage consisting of locally produced stone beads and face-neck jars that depicted more generalized Moche iconography. Thus geographic proximity to the Talambo Canal does not appear to have guaranteed community

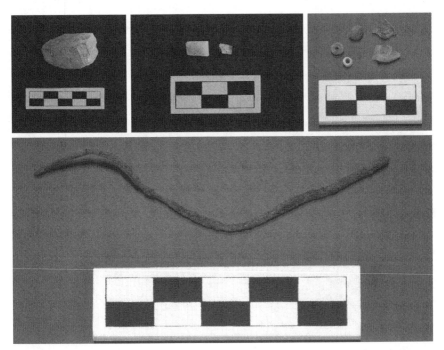

FIGURE 9.7. Bead makers' toolkit from Building B in Phase I (Operation 2). Includes cut quartz, quartz and shell beads, and a copper needle

access to (or interest in) the elite ritual and exchange networks emanating from San José de Moro.

PHASE II

Phase II occupation at Talambo corresponds to the Transitional Period/early Lambayeque Period (AD 800–1100). Settlement seems to have discontinued in Building A early in the Transitional Period. By contrast, the inhabitants of Building B thrived.

During Phase II, Building B was rebuilt along more permanent and extensive lines (figure 9.8). Four rooms of this complex were partially excavated. Its walls were built of adobe bricks that were set on a low stone footing. The tamped earthen floors associated with the Phase II rebuild were situated 15 cm above the loose ashy surface of Phase I. Excavation revealed no evidence related to the issue of access between rooms or entry/exit points in the area so far exposed. General parallels exist, however, between the Phase II occupation of Building B and other Moche

FIGURE 9.8. Photograph and plan of Building B in Phase II (Operation 2)

and Transitional era households. Although they exhibited variation in available resources, at their most essential, Moche households included a living space, a kitchen, and a storeroom (Johnson 2010, 176). More elaborate households added general-purpose rooms, spaces for specialized craft production, patios, and plazas.

Within their more materially permanent edifice, Building B's occupants continued to engage in small-scale food preparation and craft production activities, albeit with a broader range of goods. The majority of ceramic forms were jars (30%), *ollas* (29%), and *tinajas* (24%), as well as lesser quantities of plates (11%) and bottles (6%) (figure 9.5). Diagnostic wares included paddle-stamped decoration (*paleteada*) and two pendant figurines (figure 9.9). Phase II inhabitants consumed a diet similar to that of their Phase I predecessors, including shellfish (*Donax obesulus*, 65%), *Scutalus proteus* (12%), *Polinices uber* (7%), mollusk (7%), *Littorina aspera* (4%), *Tegula atra* (4%), *Cantharus rehderi* (2%); marine animals (fish and crab); and terrestrial mammals (camelid, dog, and guinea pig). Residents of this house also enjoyed the addition of consumables such as maté, which tend to be associated with more elite households.

Despite their evident increase in social status, residents of Building B remained unengaged with regional centers of power. Although they utilized ceremonial wares (face-neck jars and stirrup-spout bottles), regionally meaningful markers of elite connection—such as SJM fineline wares, Cajamarca ceramics, or Transitional Period hybridized wares—were once again wholly absent. Furthermore, only two Cajamarca sherds were found in the surface collection of the entire site of Talambo (figure 9.10).

Specialized craft production of stone beads continued in two of the rooms, indicating the likely continuity of Building B's inhabitants (possibly the same kin group) observed in Phase I. Finished stone beads were recovered, as well as bead blanks and raw quartz (figure 9.11). Needles of copper and bone were also found. In addition, many of the recovered shells were perforated, indicating that they may have been intended for personal adornment. Cotton and copper needles were found as part of the bead makers' toolkit.

FIGURE 9.9. Pendant figurines found in Building B, Phase II (Operation 2)

INTERPRETING ENDURANCE AT TALAMBO

In the Jequetepeque Valley, Late Moche and Transitional Period communities navigated political and environmental instability through a variety of convergent and divergent strategies. At Talambo, households played a significant role in enduring the Moche collapse. The community nurtured its own alternate social world—through careful water management and investment in craft production—that diverged from the more socially focused strategies of elite centers.

The earliest occupation at Talambo dates to the late Middle Moche/early Late Moche Period. Given the site's proximity to the Talambo Canal and its intake, this initial phase of occupation is most likely concurrent with canal construction. Thus canal expansion in the northern Jequetepeque Valley dates to the end of the Middle Moche Period. This date is consistent with the earliest occupation at San José de Moro (Castillo Butters 2010). As one of the settlements associated with canal construction, Talambo was likely occupied slightly earlier than many of the Late Moche rural hinterland settlements (Dillehay 2001; Swenson 2004) located further along the canal network or outside its catchment.

In addition to canal construction and maintenance, Talambo households engaged in small-scale craft production. Building B's residents fabricated quartz beads that were subsequently utilized in local ceremonial practices at the site's huaca and cemetery complex. Bead production in Building B continued (despite an architectural rebuild) throughout the Late Moche and Transitional Periods, indicating that household domestic economies at Talambo prospered throughout the Moche collapse. Moreover, the introduction of more permanent building materials, the addition of elite consumables, and a broader diet at Building B underscore increased wealth.

FIGURE 9.10. Cajamarca ceramic fragments found in surface collection of Talambo

FIGURE 9.11. Bead makers' toolkit from Building B in Phase II (Operation 2). Includes raw and cut quartz, quartz and shell beads, and a bone needle

Despite increasing status differentiation, the community of Talambo did not adopt the elite ceremonial assemblage of prominent centers. The elite ideology of San José de Moro spread to hinterland ceremonial spaces through well-established local patterns of exchange. Outside of these networks, Talambo and hinterland sites like it maintained their own alternate social worlds organized at the household level. Talambo's residents employed locally produced beads and the more generalized Moche iconography present on face-neck jars to illustrate their ritual narratives. Moreover, the absence of SJM fineline wares at Talambo indicates that the social processes responsible for their dissemination were organized independently from irrigation management. Thus, if Late Moche communities did intermittently unify to form "opportunistic states," it was likely more of a ceremonial union than an administrative one—evincing a path to elite legitimation and community integration not open to or desired by all.

As environmental instability on the North Coast contributed to community precarity, many households navigated the uncertainties of the Late Moche and

Transitional Periods through arrangements of convenience with Cajamarca. These new social connections functioned through established ritual and exchange networks centered at San José de Moro. Cajamarca settlers (from Cerro Chepén Alto) participated in ritual and mortuary practices at San José de Moro and co-opted local elite relationships with hinterland communities to disseminate highland wares. These highland efforts impacted communities that were already imbricated in San José de Moro networks of ritual and exchange and thus reproduced existing social relationships without expanding influence to new settlements.

Residents at Talambo chose an alternate strategy of endurance (enabled by their ample access to water and investment in local ceremony), which eschewed local elite and foreign connections. Despite the prevalence of Cajamarca wares at other sites, only two Cajamarca sherds were found at Talambo (none from an excavated context). Talambo's relative isolation from San José de Moro ceremony during the early Late Moche Period may have reduced household susceptibility to subsequent Cajamarca influence in later eras.

It is intriguing that Talambo was directly connected by canal to the epicenter of Cajamarca power in Jequetepeque at Cerro Chepén yet was not imbricated in Cajamarca's strategy of control.[5] Although Cajamarca settlers are hypothesized to have chosen Cerro Chepén as an ideal locus for colonization because of easy access to water (from the Serrano Canal) and labor (from Cerro Chepén Bajo), they appear to have taken little interest in securing the site at its headwaters. Perhaps they favored direct access to certain resources and elite relationships rather than valleywide control. Otherwise, Talambo would have been a priority for incorporation, as it was for the Chimú (Zobler n.d.).

Cajamarca settlement at Cerro Chepén Alto and highland influence proliferated in the Jequetepeque Valley throughout the Moche collapse and subsequent Transitional Period. During the Late Intermediate Period, San José de Moro continued to be a center of regional importance as the site of a Lambayeque palace long after highland influence had receded (Prieto 2010, 2014). Significantly, however, many of the hinterland sites (such as Huaca Colorada and Charcape) that utilized these same networks were abandoned before the LIP (Johnson 2008; Swenson and Warner 2012). Perhaps the increased interaction between coastal and highland communities that characterized the Late Moche and Transitional Periods afforded different social protections to elite centers than did hinterland settlements.

By contrast, the community of Talambo continued to thrive until the Late Horizon.[6] Talambo's detachment from San José de Moro elite networks and Cajamarca connections does not seem to have hindered community growth or hastened exhaustion. Rather, sustained local investment in an alternate social world, along with the resources to sustain it, fostered a rapid transformation toward more permanent settlement and the making of place.

CONCLUSION

In his topoanalysis of intimate domestic space, Gaston Bachelard (1958, 5) remarked that "an entire past comes to dwell at a new house." The Late Moche and Transitional Periods at Talambo illustrate that homes are more than microcosmic indicators of regional change, where the dictates of elite centers were writ small. They are a palimpsest of births and deaths, good harvests and El Niño rains, cook-fire gatherings and fortified retreats that together constitute a history of their own. Such "minor histories," to borrow anthropologist Ann Laura Stoler's (2009) term, intersect with the regional but constitute their own critical space. In periods of stress, these interconnections are magnified, strained, broken, and re-forged—revealing an intricate social tapestry that is all the more resilient for its patches. Distant politics, economies, and ideologies converge on and are transformed by the local. Seemingly small local events catalyze profound regional transformations. The "house" endures even as states rise and fall.

NOTES

1. Some reduced settlement continued at the site of Huacas de Moche through the Late Moche Period (Uceda Castillo et al. 2005).

2. Along with other ceramics accessed through the highlands, such as those from the central coast (such as Nievería) and southern highland Wari traditions (and to a lesser extent wares from Atarco, Pativilca, and Chachapoyas).

3. The style of face-neck jars in this area included Middle Moche motifs (such as owl faces) and Late Moche ("King of Assyria") designs.

4. Eling (1987, 253) notes the presence of two water reservoirs immediately west of Talambo. Depending on their date of construction, they may have played a part in the site's water management strategy and resultant autonomy during the Late Moche Period.

5. If there was a Cajamarca presence at Talambo, it is possible that it may have been located on the adjacent hillside (Talambo Este), similar to their occupational strategy at Cerro Chepén. If this was the case, however, one might expect a greater number of Cajamarca wares at Talambo Oeste. Future excavation will address this issue.

6. Although Talambo was no longer autonomous under Chimú and Inka rule (Zobler n.d.).

REFERENCES

Adams, Robert McCormick. 1960. "Factors Influencing the Rise of Civilization in the Alluvium: Illustrated by Mesopotamia." In *City Invincible*, edited by Carl Kraeling and Robert McC. Adams, 24–46. Oriental Institute Symposium. Chicago: University of Chicago Press.

Bachelard, Gaston. 1958. *The Poetics of Space*. Paris: Presses Universitaires de France.

Badiou, Alain. 2005. *Being and Event*. Translated by Oliver Feltham. New York: Continuum.

Bawden, Garth L. 1977. "Galindo and the Nature of the Middle Horizon in Northern Coastal Peru." PhD dissertation, Harvard University, Cambridge, MA.

Bawden, Garth L. 2001. "The Symbols of Late Moche Social Transformation." In *Moche Art and Archaeology in Ancient Peru*, edited by Joanne Pillsbury, 285–307. New Haven, CT: Yale University Press.

Berlant, Lauren. 2011. *Cruel Optimism*. Durham, NC: Duke University Press.

Billman, Brian, George Gumerman, and Jesus Briceño Rosario. 1999. "Dos Asentamientos Moche En La Parte Media Del Valle De Moche: Santa Rosa–Quirihuac Y Ciudad De Dios." *Revista Arqueológica SIAN* 7:3–8.

Billman, Brian R., and Gary Huckleberry. 2008. "Deciphering the Politics of Prehistoric El Niño Events on the North Coast of Peru." In *El Niño, Catastrophism, and Culture Change in Ancient America*, edited by Daniel H. Sandweiss and Jeffrey Quilter, 101–128. Washington, DC: Dumbarton Oaks Research Library and Collection, Harvard University Press.

Bourgeois, Louise. 2000. "Interview with Jerry Gorovoy, New York, 1999." In *Louise Bourgeois: Memoria y arquitectura*, edited by Mieke Bal, Lynne Cooke, and Beatriz Colomina, 1–30. Madrid: Museo Nacional Centro De Arte Reina Sofía.

Castillo Butters, Luis Jaime. 2000a. "La presencia de Wari en San Jose de Moro." *Boletín de Arqueología PUCP* 4: 143–179.

Castillo Butters, Luis Jaime. 2000b. "Los rituales Mochicas de la muerte." In *Los Dioses Del Antiguo Peru*, edited by Krzysztof Makowski, 103–135. Lima: Banco de Credito del Peru.

Castillo Butters, Luis Jaime. 2001. "The Last of the Mochicas: A View from the Jequetepeque Valley." In *Moche Art and Archaeology in Ancient Peru*, edited by Joanne Pillsbury, 307–329. New Haven, CT: Yale University Press.

Castillo Butters, Luis Jaime. 2003. "Los Últimos Mochicas En Jequetepeque." In *Moche: Hacia El Final Del Milenio*, edited by Santiago Uceda Castillo and Elias Mujica, 65–123. Lima: Universidad Nacional de Trujillo y Pontificia Universidad Católica del Peru.

Castillo Butters, Luis Jaime. 2006. "Five Sacred Priestesses from San Jose De Moro: Elite Women Funerary Ritual on Peru's Northern Coast." *Revista Electronica de Arqueologia Pontificia Universidad Catolica del Peru* 1 (3): 1–10.

Castillo Butters, Luis Jaime. 2007. *Tumbas De Elite En San José De Moro: 1000 Años De Prácticas Funerarias En El Valle De Jequetepeque.* Lima: Fondo Editorial de la PUCP.

Castillo Butters, Luis Jaime. 2009. "El Estilo Mochica Tardío De Línea Fina De San José De Moro." In *De Cupisnique a Los Incas: El Arte Del Valley De Jequetepeque,* edited by Luis Jaime Castillo and Cecilia Pardo, 208–243. Lima: Museo de Arte de Lima.

Castillo Butters, Luis Jaime. 2010. "Moche Politics in the Jequetepeque Valley: A Case for Political Opportunism." In *New Perspectives on Moche Political Organization,* edited by Jeffrey Quilter and Luis Jaime Castillo Butters, 83–109. Washington, DC: Dumbarton Oaks Research Library and Collection, Harvard University Press.

Castillo Butters, Luis Jaime, Francesca Fernandi, and Luis Moro. 2012. "The Multidimensional Relations between the Wari and the Moche States of Northern Peru." *Boletín de Arqueología PUCP* 16: 53–77.

Castillo Butters, Luis Jaime, Julio Rucabado, Martín Del Carpio, Katiusha Bernuy, Karim Ruiz, Carlos Rengifo, Gabriel Prieto, and Carole Fraresso. 2008. "Ideología y poder en la consolidación, colapso y reconstitución del estado Mochica del Jequetepeque: El Proyecto Arqueológico San José De Moro (1991–2006)." *Ñawpa Pacha* 29: 1–86.

Castillo Butters, Luis Jaime, and Santiago Uceda Castillo. 2008. "The Mochicas." In *Handbook of South American Archaeology,* edited by Helaine Silverman and William H. Isbell, 707–729. New York: Springer.

Cusicanqui, Solsiré, and Roxana Barrazueta. 2010. *Prospecciones en los sitios arqueológicos Cerro Chepén y San Idelfonso.* Lima: Pontificia Universidad Católica del Perú.

Cusicanqui, Solsiré, and Ari Caramanica. 2011. "Trabajos Arqueológicos En La Sector 5 (Zona Monumental) Del Sitio Arqueológico Cerro Chepén." In *Informe de excavación, temporada 2011: Programa Arqueológico San José de Moro,* 99–179. Lima: Pontificia Universidad Católica del Perú.

Deetz, James F. 1982. "Households: A Structural Key to Archaeological Explanation." *American Behavioral Scientist* 25 (6): 717–724.

Deleuze, Gilles. 2007. "On Spinoza." Lectures by Gilles Deleuze. http://deleuzelectures .blogspot.com.

Dillehay, Tom D. 2001. "Town and Country in Late Moche Times: A View from Two Northern Valleys." In *Moche Art and Archaeology in Ancient Peru,* edited by Joanne Pillsbury, 259–284. New Haven, CT: Yale University Press.

Dillehay, Tom D., Alan L. Kolata, and Michael E. Moseley. 2004. "Long-Term Human Response to Uncertain Environmental Conditions in the Andes." *Proceedings of the National Academy of Science USA* 101 (12): 4325–4330.

Dillehay, Tom D., Alan L. Kolata, and Edward R. Swenson. 2009. *Paisajes Culturales En El Valle Del Jequetepeque: Los Yacimientos Arqueológicos,* edited by Luis Valle Alvarez. Lima: Ediciones SIAN.

Donnan, Christopher B., and Guillermo A. Cock, eds. 1986. *The Pacatnamu Papers*, vol. 1. Los Angeles: Museum of Cultural History, University of California.

Doty, Mark. 2001. "Essay: The Love of Old Houses." In *Source*, 53–55. New York: HarperCollins.

Eling, Herbert, Jr. 1987. "The Role of Irrigation Networks in Emerging Societal Complexity during Late Prehispanic Times: Jequetepeque Valley, North Coast, Peru, vols. I and II." PhD dissertation, University of Texas, Austin.

Faulseit, Robert K., ed. 2016. *Beyond Collapse: Archeological Perspectives on Resilience, Revitalization, and Transformation in Complex Societies.* Carbondale: Southern Illinois University Press.

Fernea, Robert A. 1970. *Shaykh and Effendi: Changing Patterns of Authority among the El Shabana of Southern Iraq.* Cambridge, MA: Harvard University Press.

Gumerman, George, and Jesus Briceño. 2003. "Santa Rosa–Quirihuac y Ciudad De Dios: Asentamientos Rurales En La Parte Media Del Valle De Moche." In *Moche: Hacia El Final Del Milenio*, vol. 1, edited by Santiago Uceda Castillo and Elías Mujica, 217–244. Trujillo, Peru: Universidad Nacional de Trujillo.

Hecker, Giesela, and Wolfgang Hecker. 1995. *Die Grabungen Von Heinrich Ubbelohde-Doering in Pacatnamú, Nordperú: Untersuchungen an Den Huacas 31 Und 14 Sowie Bestattungen Und Fundobjekte.* Berlin: Dietrich Reimer Verlag.

Holling, Crawford S. 1973. "Resilience and Stability of Ecological Systems." *Annual Review of Ecology and Systematics* 4: 1–23.

Holling, Crawford S., and Lance H. Gunderson, eds. 2002. *Panarchy: Understanding Transformations in Human and Natural Systems.* Washington, DC: Island.

Johnson, Ilana. 2008. "Portachuelo de Charcape: Daily Life and Political Power in the Hinterland during the Late Moche Period." In *Arqueología Mochica: Nuevos Enfoques*, edited by Luis Jaime Castillo Butters, Hélène Bernier, Gregory Lockard, and Julio Rucabado Yong, 261–274. Lima: Fondo Editorial de la Pontificia Universidad Católica del Perú.

Johnson, Ilana. 2010. "Households and Social Organization at the Late Moche Period Site of Pampa Grande, Peru." PhD dissertation, University of California, Los Angeles.

Johnson, Ilana. 2011. "The Development of Semi-Autonomous Communities in the Late Moche Period (AD 600–900)." In *State to Empire in the Prehistoric Jequetepeque Valley, Peru*, edited by Colleen M. Zori and Ilana Johnson, 51–64. Oxford: British Archaeological Reports.

Keatinge, Richard W., and Geoffrey W. Conrad. 1983. "Imperialist Expansion in Peruvian Prehistory: Chimu Administration of a Conquered Territory." *Journal of Field Archaeology* 10 (3): 255–283.

Kolata, Alan L. 2006. "Before and After Collapse: Reflections on the Regeneration of Social Complexity." In *After Collapse*, edited by Glenn M. Schwartz and John J. Nichols, 208–221. Tucson: University of Arizona Press.

Kremkau, Scott. 2010. "Late Horizon Imperial Landscapes in the Jequetepeque Valley, Peru." PhD dissertation, Columbia University, New York, NY.

Lévi-Strauss, Claude. 1982. *The Way of the Masks*. Translated by Sylvia Modelski. Seattle: University of Washington Press.

Lévi-Strauss, Claude. 1987. *Anthropology and Myth: Lectures 1951–1982*. Translated by Roy Willis. Oxford: Blackwell.

Lockard, Gregory D. 2005. "Political Power and Economy at the Archaeological Site of Galindo, Moche Valley, Peru." PhD dissertation, University of New Mexico, Albuquerque.

Lockard, Gregory D. 2008. "A New View of Galindo: Results of the Galindo Archaeological Project." In *Arqueología Mochica: Nuevos Enfoques*, edited by Luis Jaime Castillo Butters, Hélène Bernier, Gregory Lockard, and Julio Rucabado Yong, 275–294. Lima: Fondo Editorial de la Pontificia Universidad Católica del Perú.

Mackey, Carol J. 1987. "Chimu Administration in the Provinces." In *The Origins and Development of the Andean State*, edited by Jonathan Haas, Shelia Pozorski, and Thomas Pozorski, 121–129. Cambridge: Cambridge University Press.

Moseley, Michael E. 1978. "An Empirical Approach to Prehistoric Agrarian Collapse: The Case of the Moche Valley, Peru." In *Social and Technological Management in Dry Lands: Past and Present, Indigenous and Imposed*, edited by Nancie L. Gonzales, 9–43. AAAS Selected Symposium Series 10, Boulder: Westview.

Moseley, Michael E., and Eric E. Deeds. 1982. "The Land in Front of Chan Chan: Agrarian Expansion, Reform, and Collapse in the Moche Valley." In *Chan Chan: Andean Desert City*, edited by Michael E. Moseley and Kent Day, 25–53. Albuquerque: University of New Mexico Press.

Netherly, Patricia J. 1984. "The Management of Late Andean Irrigation Systems on the North Coast of Peru." *American Antiquity* 49 (2): 227–254.

Nixon, Rob. 2011. *Slow Violence and the Environmentalism of the Poor*. Cambridge, MA: Harvard University Press.

Povinelli, Elizabeth A. 2011. *Economies of Abandonment: Social Belonging and Endurance in Late Liberalism*. Durham, NC: Duke University Press.

Povinelli, Elizabeth A. 2012. "The Will to Be Otherwise/the Effort of Endurance." *South Atlantic Quarterly* 111 (3): 453–475.

Povinelli, Elizabeth A. 2014. "Geontologies of the Otherwise." *Cultural Anthropology Online*. Published electronically, January 13. http://culanth.org/fieldsights/geontologies -of-the-otherwise.

Prieto, Gabriel. 2010. "Approximating Lambayeque Political Configurations: A Perspective from the Site of San José de Moro, Jequetepeque Valley." In *Comparative Perspectives* on the *Archaeology of Coastal South America*, edited by Robyn E. Cutright, Enrique López-Hurtado, and Alexander J. Martín, 231–246. Pittsburgh: Center for Comparative Archaeology.

Prieto, Gabriel. 2014. "El Fenómeno Lambayeque en San José de Moro, valle de Jequetepeque: Una perspectiva desde el valle vecino." In *Cultura Lambayeque: en el contexto de la costa norte del Perú*, edited by Julio Fernández Alvarado and Carlos Wester La Torre, 107–137. Chiclayo, Peru: Universidad Católica Santo Toribio de Mogrovejo.

Railey, Jim A., and Richard Martin Reycraft. 2008. "Introduction." In *Global Perspectives on the Collapse of Complex Systems*, edited by Jim A. Railey and Richard Martin Reycraft, 1–18. Anthropological Papers. Albuquerque: Maxwell Museum of Anthropology.

Redman, Charles L. 2005. "Resilience Theory in Archaeology." *American Anthropologist* 107 (1): 70–77.

Rosas, Marco. 2007. "Nuevas Perspectivas Acerca Del Colapso Moche En El Bajo Jequetepeque: Resultados Preliminares De La Segunda Campaña De Investigación Del Proyecto Arqueológico Cerro Chepén." *Bulletin de l'Institut Fraçais d'Éstudes Andines* 36 (2): 221–240.

Rosas, Marco. 2010. "Cerro Chepen and the Late Moche Collapse in the Jequetepeque Valley, North Coast of Perú." PhD dissertation, University of New Mexico, Albuquerque.

Ruiz, Karim. 2004. *Prospecciones en el valle de Jequetepeque: Evidencias de sitios Mochicas fortificados*. Lima: Pontificia Universidad Católica del Perú.

Sandweiss, Daniel H., and Jeffrey Quilter. 2012. "Collation, Correlation, and Causation in the Prehistory of Coastal Peru." In *Surviving Sudden Environmental Change: Answers from Archaeology*, edited by Jago Cooper and Payson Sheets, 117–141. Boulder: University Press of Colorado.

Schwartz, Glenn M., and John J. Nichols, eds. 2006. *After Collapse: The Regeneration of Complex Societies*. Tucson: University of Arizona Press.

Shimada, Izumi. 1994. *Pampa Grande and the Mochica Culture*. Austin: University of Texas Press.

Shimada, Izumi, Crystal Barker Schaaf, Lonnie G. Thompson, and Ellen Mosley-Thompson. 1991. "Cultural Impacts of Severe Droughts in the Prehistoric Andes: Application of a 1,500-Year Ice Core Precipitation Record." *World Archaeology* 22 (3): 247–270.

Stoler, Ann Laura. 2009. *Along the Archival Grain: Epistemic Anxieties and Colonial Common Sense*. Princeton, NJ: Princeton University Press.

Swenson, Edward R. 2004. "Ritual and Power in the Urban Hinterland: Religious Pluralism and Political Decentralization in Late Moche Jequetepeque, Peru." PhD dissertation, University of Chicago, IL.

Swenson, Edward R. 2006. "Competitive Feasting, Religious Pluralism, and Decentralized Power in the Late Moche Period." In *Andean Archaeology III: North and South*, edited by William H. Isbell and Helaine Silverman, 112–142. New York: Springer.

Swenson, Edward R. 2007. "Adaptive Strategies or Ideological Innovations? Interpreting Sociopolitical Developments in the Jequetepeque Valley of Peru during the Late Moche Period." *Journal of Anthropological Archaeology* 26: 253–282.

Swenson, Edward R. 2008. "San Ildefonso and the Popularization of Moche Ideology in the Jequetepeque Valley." In *Arqueología Mochica: Nuevos Enfoques*, edited by Luis Jaime Castillo Butters, Hélène Bernier, Gregory Lockard, and Julio Rucabado Yong, 411–432. Lima: Fondo Editorial de la Pontificia Universidad Católica del Perú.

Swenson, Edward R. 2015. "The Materialities of Place Making in the Ancient Andes: A Critical Appraisal of the Ontological Turn in Archaeological Interpretation." *Journal of Archaeological Method and Theory* 22: 677–712.

Swenson, Edward R., and John P. Warner. 2012. "Crucibles of Power: Forging Copper and Forging Subjects at the Moche Ceremonial Center of Huaca Colorada, Peru." *Journal of Anthropological Archaeology* 31: 314–333.

Tainter, Joseph A. 1988. *The Collapse of Complex Societies*. New Studies in Archaeology, series editors Colin Renfrew and Jeremy Sabloff. Cambridge: Cambridge University Press.

Thompson, Lonnie G., Ellen Moseley-Thompson, John F. Bolzan, and Bruce R. Koci. 1985. "A 1500-Year Record of Tropical Precipitation in Ice Cores from the Quelccaya Ice Cap, Peru." *Science* 234: 361–364.

Tsai, Howard. 2020. *Las Varas: Ritual and Ethnicity in the Ancient Andes*. Tuscaloosa: University of Alabama Press.

Ubbelohde-Doering, Heinrich. 1967. *On the Royal Highways of the Inca: Archaeological Treasures of Ancient Peru*. Translated by Margaret Brown. New York: Fredrick A. Praeger.

Uceda Castillo, Santiago, Elías Mujica, and Ricardo Morales, eds. 2005. "Proyecto arquelógico Huaca de la Luna: Informe técnico 2004." Unpublished final report submitted to the Instituto nacional de Cultura, La Libertdad.

Wilk, Richard R., and William L. Rathje. 1982. "Household Archaeology." *American Behavioral Scientist* 25 (6): 617–639.

Yoffee, Norman, and George L. Cowgill, eds. 1988. *The Collapse of Ancient States and Civilizations*. Tucson: University of Arizona Press.

Zobler, Kari A. n.d. "Empire Interrupted: Community Endurance and Serial Conquest at Talambo, Jequetepeque Valley, Perú." University of Illinois, Urbana-Champaign.

Zobler, Kari A., and Richard C. Sutter. 2016. "A Tale of Two Cities: Continuity and Change Following the Moche Collapse in the Jequetepeque Valley, Peru." In *Beyond Collapse: Archeological Perspectives on Resilience, Revitalization, and Transformation in Complex Societies*, edited by Robert K. Faulseit, 486–503. Carbondale: Southern Illinois University Press.

10

Diversity in North Coast Households

Rethinking the Politics of the Everyday

EDWARD SWENSON

The investigation of the material traces of past practices and routines sets archaeology apart from "history" as a discipline, though various schools of historiography are often brought to bear in interpreting these traces (e.g., whether, historical materialism, Annales). Household archaeology in particular excites the imagination in its potential to more holistically reconstruct past historical realities by focusing on how quotidian practices structured diverse social formations. Indeed, household archaeology is often championed as providing one of the few means of interpreting the lifeways of majority, lower-status communities and even the resistive practices of oppressed groups who were excluded from the production of "written" history (see Cutright, Johnson, Zobler, this volume). As Billman intimates in his review in this volume, household archaeology privileges bottom-up perspectives in explanations of social processes and historical change—a method opposed to event-based, teleological, or "big-man" interpretations of history (see also Zobler, this volume). In a sense, household archaeology encapsulates a quintessentially anthropological approach to the writing of history.

Although archaeologies of the everyday arrived late to the Andes and was even temporarily sidelined in the 1990s by the discovery of sensational tombs and temples (see Billman, this volume), the collective chapters in this volume showcase the significant advances that have been made in this subfield of archaeology on the north coast of Peru during the last twenty years. The authors demonstrate how a focus on routine practices, residential architecture, domestic modes of production, and

DOI: 10.5876/9781646420919.c010

materialized ideologies of place, family, and community is permitting historically sensitive understandings of the alternate political worlds created by Precolumbian Andean communities. In this concluding chapter, I focus on these political worlds by taking stock of an important revelation that emerged from the chapters—the remarkable diversity in the physical configuration and social organization of household units in the ancient north coast of Peru. In the first four sections of this review, I argue that this diversity forces us to critically assess models of historical change and to rethink coastal political, religious, and economic institutions. The rich empirical data presented by the authors reveal that we should also question taken-for-granted assumptions of house, home, identity, and social difference as well as their relationship to macropolitical forces, whether understood in terms of cities, states, or larger exchange networks. The authors of the volume make an important contribution by scrutinizing the relationship and often blurred boundaries between the quotidian sphere and seemingly higher-level political arenas.

Of course, the notable diversity in constructions of place framing quotidian lifeways often correlated with remarkable variability in social and economic organization. In this chapter, I offer interpretations of this variation and also consider some commonalities in everyday routines in different North Coast polities. As a complement to Billman's outline of good practices, my review concludes with a short discussion of method. The formulation of viable explanations for why North Coast households differed in spatial and social composition must rely on the creative playing off of different datasets. Ultimately, investigations of this kind will need to contextualize the material corpora of quotidian life as forming part of more encompassing political landscapes.

BEYOND DUALISMS OF HOME AND STATE: A CRITIQUE OF MATERIALIST AND STRUCTURALIST INTERPRETATIONS OF HOUSEHOLDS

Anthropologists have long recognized that the configuration of residential space is fundamental to understanding the ingrained cultural values and structures of practice that define a particular society. Pierre Bourdieu's (1973) famous ethnographic study of the Kabyle house demonstrated that the spatiotemporal framing of daily activities played a critical role in socialization and the reproduction of misrecognized power relations. In contrast, public ritual spectacle, political institutions, and specialized production have often been contrasted with the domestic setting by social scientists who espouse either materialist or structuralist viewpoints. Ritual celebrations in particular are equated with active ideological production, "discursive consciousness" (sensu Giddens 1984), and subject formation while the common household is identified with the taken-for-granted, "practical consciousness" (*habitus*), and the a-political (but see Hodder and Pels 2010; Marcus 2007; Swenson 2015; Swenson and Chiguala 2018). However, the contributors to this volume expose the simplicity of this dichotomy and challenge the assumption that the "household" refers to a universal spatial and social phenomenon (see also Hendon 1996; Robin 2002; Robin and Rothschild 2002).

Anthropologists have often implicitly approached the house as having conveyed little conscious meaning ("hyposignificant") or as having served instead as a totalizing symbol, that is, as "hypersignificant" (see Choay 1986). In the former, the house is interpreted first and foremost as the vehicle that fulfills basic subsistence and social needs and epitomizes routines of the everyday to the extent that it rarely constitutes the subject of religious and philosophical exegesis. The household imbued with hypersignificance likewise emphasizes the physical house and its constituents as crucial for social and economic reproduction but stresses in turn the symbolism and cosmological meanings of the residential space—for instance, as a microcosm *writ small* (Nash 2009, 206; Rapaport 1969). Surely, the physical "house" often serves as a powerful metaphor of ideal bodies, social orders, and cosmic forces (Banning 2011; Blier 1987; Boivin 2000; see Spence Morrow, this volume). Although such viewpoints recognize the ideological representation of the household as a reified thing ("social fact"), homologous correspondences of this kind would fail to account for the highly varied permutations of the house in different North Coast polities or among distinct status groups documented in this volume. Obviously, the two polarized interpretations are simplistic, and the somewhat artificial contrast drawn here serves to remind archaeologists that the specific *significance* of the domestic setting must be understood not according to universalist criteria, whether materialist or symbolic/structuralist, but within culturally particular frameworks of practice (see Swenson and Chiguala 2018).

Nevertheless, materialists tend to deemphasize the household nexus as critical to macroeconomic relations; production and exchange defining certain social formations are more commonly investigated in the context of the market, specialized workshops, or related public forums—the locus of the "political economy" as opposed to the "domestic economy" (which is commonly perceived as largely determined by the former) (Blanton 1994). However, as Chicoine and his coauthors note in their analysis of household organization in the Middle Horizon site of Caylán in the Nepeña Valley, specialized craft production and domestic living were inextricably intertwined in the elaborate compound structures of this center (see also D'Altroy and Hastorf 2001). They note: "It is indeed significant to nuance the traditional view that households typically engage in self-sufficient, low-intensity production while high-intensity production involved full-time specialists working from largely non-residential spaces." Similar conclusions have been reached by the investigators of Huacas de Moche (Chapdelaine 2001, 75; 2009; Uceda Castillo and Armas 1998). Intensified forms of food production were also noted by Cutright at the site of Pedregal during the Chimú occupation and by Pacifico at the Late Intermediate Period (LIP) center of El Purgatorio.

Comparable to materialist perspectives, structuralists often relegate the domestic setting to the conceptual realm of the private, female, and cyclical and downplay the political or public aspects of household social organization (Bowser and Patton 2004; Carsten and Hugh-Jones 1995; Guengerich 2014; Lyons 2007; Nash 2009). In fact, it is important for archaeologists to realize that a one-to-one correspondence does not always hold between the physical form of the dwelling and the social relations it mediated and materially represented. Fundamental social affiliations are not necessarily confined to the household space and may even have been deliberately misrepresented by the latter (see Chicoine et al., Duke, Pacifico, and Spence Morrow this volume). Spence Morrow, for instance, argues that the ideals of kinship, household, and territory found more explicit ideological expression in the rituals and ceremonial constructions of Moche elites than in the diverse dwelling architecture documented in urban and rural settings. Thus the aesthetics of residential constructions do not unambiguously reflect underlying social ideals, ideologies of private or public, or beliefs concerning home and identity. For instance, Bill Sillar (1996) has argued that cosmological principles of death, fertility, and regeneration symbolically linked the form and use of Inka open sepulchers (*chullpas*) with *colcas*, the famous storage constructions built of stone. The former served as repositories and drying houses for mummified ancestors, and the latter functioned as *depósitos* for potatoes, corn, and other materials. In this instance, an analogy between the "house of the living" and "house of the dead" (whether as homology or inversion) cannot be drawn—and the specific meanings of the *chullpas* would be lost if compared exclusively with classic household forms (i.e., wherein the house is uncritically accepted as a totalizing symbol, as documented in some other societies; see Blier 1987; Bradley 2005; Hodder 1984).

HOUSEHOLDS AS LYNCHPINS OF POLITICAL TRANSFORMATION IN THE ANCIENT NORTH COAST OF PERU

If places of residence and daily social interaction frame the cyclical routines of life, it would also stand to reason that the search for and interpretation of sociopolitical change must foreground household economies and social organization (see Billman, this volume; Costin and Earle 1989; D'Altroy and Hastorf 2001; Robin 2003, 2013). The *real* effects of imperial conquest, ecological perturbations, political revolution, social upheavals, religious revitalization movements, or technological innovations are best gauged through detected shifts in household size, layout, and composition as well as through notable changes to utilitarian artifacts, diet, private ritual, materials of construction, and the placement of residential units within settlement systems (see Billman, Pacifico, Zobler, this volume). Although this approach has yielded fruitful results, it tends to imply that politics and the forces of change are to be found outside the household (see critique in Cutright 2010, 2015). In other words, the domestic realm is rarely viewed as a fulcrum of such transformations beyond serving as instruments to naturalize political and economic norms deriving from outside the residence. As Brenda Bowser and John Q. Patton note (2004, 158), "It is necessary to ... avoid naturalizing the domestic context as a place of socialization while the real business of politics occurs outside of the home" (see also Billman, this volume; Guengerich 2014). It is often assumed that since the spaces of the everyday (e.g., dwellings, fields, privies, shared common areas) structure the routines and daily rhythms that make existence bearable—where society is unconsciously "reproduced"—these places must have been inevitably more static, conservative, and even amenable to universalizing theories of behavior. To be sure, all humans must eat, sleep, raise children, cooperate, seek leisure, and so forth to survive—and such routines can become either a refuge or a prison.

As implied by the last statement, however, routinized practices and social arrangements can be actively political (and, of course, structuring), and the contributions to this volume reveal that they were far from uniform or constant in different North Coast communities. Zobler's analysis of household strategies of endurance at the center of Talambo in Jequetepeque shows that the reach of Moche authorities was limited and that the presumed upheavals following the collapse of Moche polities failed to disrupt the lifeways and domestic economies of Talambo residents who refused to participate in Moche and Cajamarca exchange systems. In this regard, the continued production of beads in both the Moche and Transitional households at Talambo is as equally illuminating as the disappearance of Moche religious iconography in understanding sociopolitical developments in Middle Horizon Jequetepeque. Complementing Zobler's critique, Alfredo González-Ruibal (2014, 28–33) contends that the anthropological understanding of history as "transformation" betrays neoliberal biases, and he argues that the deep temporalities of quotidian routines and things (e.g., millennial traditions of grinding corn with *batanes*) illustrate the resiliency of fundamental structures of practice. The maintenance of these activities could often have been explicitly political, resisting sublimation to the realm of the doxic and unquestioned as Bourdieu (1977, 1990) would have it (perhaps even materializing a kind of communally guarded "cultural capital" as discussed by Billman in this volume) (see also Joyce 2009, 43–44, 50–51; Swenson 2017; Swenson and Roddick 2018). Therefore, in interpreting the household data from Talambo, Zobler compellingly argues that "households often resist the cause-and-effect characterizations that are the hallmark of archaeological narratives of collapse and regeneration." Cutright similarly notes that despite rather abrupt changes in elite architecture and fine ceramics, an array of cooking pots used to prepare feasting foods continued to be made in Jequetepeque well into the Chimú Period at sites such as Pedregal, pointing to important continuities in social and economic organization during the Late Intermediate Period.

DIVERSITY IN THE INTERRELATIONSHIP OF LOCAL TASKSCAPES AND NORTH COAST POLITICAL REGIMES

The chapters of the volume thus prove that the domestic realm exhibited formidable diversity on the North Coast in terms of its cultural construction, dependencies on suprahousehold structures of authority, and relationship to the social status and identity of its inhabitants. This diversity should not simply be interpreted as "microcosmic indicators of regional change where the dictates of elite centers were writ small" (Zobler, this volume) but as reflecting potentially contradictory political formations operating both within household units and beyond. Therefore, the chapters raise the important question of how macroreligious and political forces variably altered or were shaped in turn by *local* taskscapes and domestic economies—which, as mentioned, varied considerably throughout the North Coast during the Moche era and in subsequent periods (on taskscapes, see Ingold 2000; Swenson 2017). The value placed on mobility and the maintenance of temporary, seasonally occupied dwellings in Late Moche Jequetepeque (AD 600–850) (Duke, this volume) contrasts notably with the more sedentary settlement system documented by Christopher B. Donnan and his team at Dos Cabezas and Pacatnamú during the preceding Middle Moche Period (AD 400–600) (Donnan 1997, 12; 2007; McClelland 1997). I have argued that the establishment of the priestess cult at San José de Moro and transformations in gendered constructions of landscape and religious authority might explain the transition to more transhuman residential patterns and shifts in the political production of space (Swenson 2012). However, as argued by Duke, the settlement change may also reflect the newfound autonomy of local agriculturalists and fisherfolk to more flexibly renegotiate economic and political alliances during the Late Moche Period. Cutright (this volume) describes a similar scenario of political opportunism for the polity based at Ventanillas during the later Lambayeque Period. She argues that the elites of this mid-valley settlement promoted a hybrid identity of coast and highlands to maintain extensive interregional economic and kin relations. This interpretation speaks to a certain emphasis on shifting territoriality and the fluidity of emplaced identity distinct to this region of the North Coast. This particular scenario contrasted with conceptions of place and identity at Huacas de Moche, an urban settlement characterized by a multitude of permanent, multigenerational compounds that housed corporate groups of occupational specialists (Van Gijseghem 2001). Santiago Uceda Castillo (Uceda Castillo and Armas 1998), Claude Chapdelaine (2001, 2002, 2009), and others argue that Huacas de Moche was a synchoritic city[1] of middle-class residents, and the hypothesized absence of primary producers sets this premier Moche city apart from some of the sites discussed in the volume.

A consideration of the diversity in Moche household organization presented in this volume (see Duke, Johnson, Zobler, this volume) should even prove critical in resolving ongoing debates on the meaning of the Moche label and the degree to which Moche polities were centralized and territorially integrated. The fixed and orthogonally planned residential complexes of the urban centers of Huacas de Moche differ significantly from the more evanescent and seasonally occupied domestic constructions of Middle Horizon Jequetepeque explored by Duke. Evidently, the comparison demonstrates the absence of a generalizable grammar of domestic space that could be identified as unequivocally Moche. Of course, the stark differences in the household configurations of Galindo and Huacas de Moche have long been recognized, and the chapters in this volume lend further support to models that question the centralized and overreaching power of monolithic Moche states (Bawden 1996, 2001; Lockard 2009; Quilter and Koons 2012). Zobler argues that the opportunistic states of Jequetepeque during the Late Moche Period relied primarily on religious ideology rather than on political economic control, as reflected by Talambo's eschewal of Cajamarca tableware and Moro finelines despite its prominent location at the juncture of the valley's massive irrigation system. The somewhat more permanent and continually occupied constructions of Talambo contrast with the ephemeral *temporales* that proliferated throughout Jequetepeque and speak to the coexistence of distinct lifeways or "alternate social worlds" in the same river valley (see Zobler, this volume). This juxtaposition of permanent and temporary architecture has also been recorded at the large Late Moche center of Cerro Chepén in the Jequetepeque region. Possibly intrusive highlanders lived in much more elaborate and permanent stone structures in the high monumental district of the site, while the more than 700 domestic terraces documented in the lower zone (sector Bajo) appear to have been occupied by pilgrims or lower-class dependents, who perhaps resided here seasonally as indicated by the shallow stratigraphy encountered in excavations (see Cusicanqui 2010, 48, 54; Johnson 2012, 57; Rosas 2010, 547, 590).

Evidently, the adoption of Moche ideologies in different regions of the North Coast did not necessarily translate to the alteration of ingrained, embodied routines or everyday perceptions of reality (as seems to have been the case at Talambo). Johnson's examination of Moche female figurines also shows that the ritual practices and spiritual preoccupations of lower-status household dwellers often diverged from elite religious programs. Still, she recognizes that certain dimensions of Moche ideology must have been drawn from everyday concerns of fertility, health, and parturition (and perhaps "home" and "territory," as argued by Spence Morrow in this volume) (for a similar argument in Maya archaeology, see Lucero 2003). The shared aesthetic conventions of Moche elite and commoner ritual paraphernalia would further suggest that the intimate rituals conducted by the inhabitants of the Southern Piedmont at Pampa Grande cannot be simply understood as a "hidden transcript" of resistance (sensu Scott 1992).

At the same time, it cannot be discounted that the propagation of certain Moche cults, perhaps even sectarian in nature, could have resulted in the transformation of long-standing dispositions, leading to new material realities and naturalizing novel experiences of time and place. The emergence of transient or "peripatetic" populations in Jequetepeque (see Duke, Spence Morrow, this volume; Swenson 2012) during the Late Moche Period was likely related to the allure of elite organized feasts and Moche-inspired ceremonies sponsored by different centers such as San José de Moro and Huaca Colorada. The constant movement of peoples among fields, cemeteries, hamlets, and ceremonial centers—resulting in makeshift and temporary residential constructions—was dictated in part by the adoption of Moche religious liturgies, calendars, and gender ideologies (see also Swenson 2012; Swenson and Warner 2012).

Cutright further notes that radical shifts in everyday life coincided with the fall of the Moche religious complex in Jequetepeque and elsewhere. These changes appear to have been much more profound than the transformations wrought by the Chimú and Inka conquests of the North Coast, given significant alterations in food production and utilitarian ceramic assemblages toward the close of the Middle Horizon Period. In other words, this abrupt transformation in daily material culture differs notably from the remarkable continuity in ceramic repertoires spanning the Late Intermediate and Late Horizon Periods. However, the demise of the Moche did not lead to the abandonment of corporate households at Talambo, as Zobler's research would indicate. Therefore, both the penetrating reach of Moche value systems and the eventual disruptions caused by the Moche collapse were clearly uneven in different regions of the North Coast.

To be sure, many of the authors of the volume argue that the impact of supralocal institutions on the domestic sphere and rural life was often minimal. As discussed above, Zobler refers to the resilience of households at Talambo, emphasizing the considerable continuities in domestic activities between the Late Moche and Transitional Periods. She even posits that this strategically important site rejected (or at least ignored) the ritualized exchange network centered on San José de Moro and Cerro Chepén. On the basis of her analysis, it appears that domestic constructions at Talambo became more fixed and permanent in the Transitional Period. However, it is also worth considering whether the earlier Moche occupants of the site may have maintained more temporary dwellings, burial grounds, and kin shrines at other sites in the valley, including San José de Moro, Pacatnamú, or Huaca Colorada. In other words, could Talambo have been the site of specialized administrative functions, perhaps explaining the absence of diacritical artifacts related to ritual feasts and celebrations? Were the Moche inhabitants of Talambo as mobile as the residents of JE-64 discussed by Duke (but possibly living at Talambo—as a kind of home-base community—for longer periods of time)? Certainly, the continuities in bead production within the same dwelling structure point to the long-term maintenance of a shared corporate identity.

Cutright's analysis of continuity and change in Late Intermediate Period households in Jequetepeque similarly affirms that the spaces and rhythms of quotidian tasks, including farming, child rearing, food preparation, and so forth, were intensely local and resilient. Thus Chimú imperialism never led to the colonization of everyday routines and dispositions at sites such as Pedregal. Still, Cutright rightly claims that households cannot be viewed as "a tradition-bound, timeless substrate upon which more complex social configurations were constructed." Her research at Ventanillas and Pedregal reveals that residential contexts serve as sensitive barometers of sociopolitical transformation. Household configurations may have changed little over the course of the Late Intermediate Period, but the extractive political economy of the Chimú resulted in significant shifts in diet, as indicated by the intensified consumption of domesticates (especially maize) at Pedregal after AD 1300. Zobler and Cutright similarly contend that continuities in household constructions between the Moche and later periods represent conscious strategies by local communities. Hence, continuities in domestic practices cannot simply be interpreted as reflecting cultural conservativism or the inertia of unconscious habitual practices and technologies (see above and González-Ruibal 2014).

INTERPRETING SOCIAL DIFFERENCE, IDENTITY, AND ALTERNATE POLITICAL FORMATIONS FROM ANCIENT NORTH COAST HOUSEHOLDS

Questions of identity and inequality constituted another overarching theme of the volume. Analyses of domestic contexts can provide the interpretive means to move beyond simplistic analyses of power as predicated on a reductive, bimodal playing field of elites versus nonelites or urban versus rural communities (see Pacifico,

Spence Morrow, this volume). The diversity of household social organization also challenges common understanding of the home as well as conventional typologies of larger political formations, including cities and states.

In her study of gendered spaces and domestic practices among the Moche, Johnson notes that the material assemblages of residences did not simply reflect social relations and political dependencies but actively created them. In fact, conceptions of "domesticity" among the Moche were likely far removed from idealized Western understandings of the house or home (Guengerich 2014; Spence Morrow, this volume). Therefore, the case studies point to alternative modes of being, dwelling, and habitation that challenge storied theories on how attachments to place are predictably implicated in the creation of subject positions. As Duke notes, variations in Moche household constructions and residential mobility in Jequetepeque call into question some of our basic assumptions of complex, sedentary societies. Indeed, identity and status were far from fixed but changed in accordance to the different places experienced by mobile social groups (see also Spence Morrow, this volume; Swenson 2012, 186–187).

Unsurprisingly then, the chapters demonstrate that different domestic spaces often configured historically particular fields of social distinction and political action. Pacifico's research on residential architecture at the LIP site of El Purgatorio in Casma reveals a political world far more complex than simplistic models of elite domination and nonelite resistance or compliance. Although status differences are expressed in the three distinct types of domestic structures at this center, inhabitants of Sector B South ate comparable diets, leading Pacifico to conclude that inequalities actually decreased when rural communities rapidly relocated to the capital—a possible consequence of an instituted redistributional economy put in place by the settlement's leaders. It would be interesting to consider whether the three different structural types might also reflect a developmental cycle of household social units. Perhaps members of affiliated houses moved from one structural form to another as people married, had children, aged, or died. Such household development cycles have been documented in the Andes and elsewhere and point to the mutable and contingent nature of status differences rarely considered by archaeologists (Goodman 1999; see also Billman, this volume; Goody 1971; Prossor et al. 2012).

Pacifico's study is worth comparing with Cutright's argument that rural communities, defined by more informal domestic structures, exercised greater political and economic autonomy than households residing in nucleated urban centers—the implication being that people were freer in the countryside. This perspective is reminiscent of Peter J. Wilson's (1991) controversial argument that the adoption of more formal and regimented residential architecture imposed severe constraints on people's dispositions, activities, and perceptions of the world. However, Pacifico's and Chicoine and coauthors' research reveals that urbanization does not predictably result in increased inequality or powerlessness. Despite the planning and formal construction of the more than forty compounds documented at the Early Horizon center of Caylán, the repetition of semipublic patios and the privacy the *cercaduras* afforded point to the considerable autonomy of multifamily corporations comprising the larger settlement.

Turning to Spence Morrow's chapter, even though house types differed considerably across the Jequetepeque landscape, he raises the fascinating question of whether an "ideal house" may have underwritten Moche ideologies of place and political affiliation. Spence Morrow's chapter was refreshing, for it considered Moche conceptions of house and home. Following Henri Lefebvre (1991), archaeologists have much to gain in examining how everyday practices structuring residential spaces complemented or contradicted ideal representations of both public and intimate places. Comparisons of this kind would allow for more probing analyses of how political identities were fashioned through the production of real or imagined attachments to place. The summit of Huaca Colorada appears to have served in part as a residence for religious specialists and political leaders. Still, I remain uncertain whether the *société à maison* sociological model can effectively explain the great variability in Moche settlement and residential constructions, and Johnson's and Zobler's chapters indicate the coexistence of a number of competing discourses on place among the Moche.

The house society heuristic may hold some potential for interpreting the multiple compounds at Huacas de Moche but perhaps less so for Sipán, San José de Moro, and other sites defined by lordly mausoleums. Nevertheless, Spence Morrow's theory is certainly worthy of consideration, and his thought-provoking study demonstrates that there is much to be gained by examining ideologies of home and territory and testing models derived from ethnography to our archaeological datasets, including theories on house societies. The dispersed *temporales* could be interpreted as expressing the general lack of rootedness among the peripatetic populations of Late Moche Jequetepeque (see Duke, this volume). However, as Spence Morrow argues, mobile communities possibly forged a strong sense of place and community belonging by affiliating with a lordly temple dwelling that was visited during religious festivals. These celebrations might have involved the exchange of marital partners, sacrifices for group renewal, consultations with oracles, joint worship of revered huaca ancestors, and the reestablishment of social and political alliances. Feasts sponsored by possibly semidivine lords would have economically and ideologically united disparate communities, including the fisherfolk and agriculturalists discussed by Duke—perhaps as members of one extended and imagined "household." As Spence Morrow argues, "The *huaca* . . . served as a sign embodying the

connection between the wider community and a deified elite through incorporative acts of construction, sacrifice, and dedicatory termination rites." In fact, social
identity in the Andes has traditionally been negotiated in terms of pulsating cycles
of dissolution and confederation among different peoples, places, *wak'as*, and things
(as expressed, for instance, in the notion of *tinkuy*) (Allen 1988, 205–206; Harris
1994, 47; Sallnow 1987, 136; Skar 1994; Swenson and Jennings 2018). In the south-
central Andes, Peter Gose (1991) similarly describes the practice of dual residence
and the seasonal disbandment and reconstitution of domestic groups—an analogy
that might have relevance to understanding the particulars of the Jequetepeque
settlement data. As Spence Morrow intimates, the archetypical house may have
constituted an all-important master symbol for Jequetepeque communities, for the
ideal house was so rarely built, seen, or experienced.

Finally, the notable variations in household social organization and their varied
articulations with institutions of authority expose the limitations of our standard
political typologies. The case studies presented in this volume demonstrate that
searching for the material correlates of cities, chiefdoms, or states would tell us very
little about the multifaceted political, social, and economic practices of North Coast
households, ranging from the multifamily compounds at Caylán and El Purgatorio
to the smaller but prosperous residences at Ventanillas. To take just one example,
the domestic practices of Late Moche Jequetepeque, as explored in the chapters
by Duke, Spence Morrow, and Zobler, were equally as complex as the Moche and
Lambayeque Valleys, dominated by their massive urban centers. Jequetepeque was
characterized by high populations, sophisticated religious and agricultural infra-
structures, a cosmopolitan international style, and flexible corporate structures that
negotiated local and global political networks comparable to urban households
and neighborhoods documented at Huacas de Moche. The unique social geography of the region was the product of specific religious and political ideologies that
were materially fashioned at various (and often overlapping) scales of sociospatial
interaction, including ephemeral households, more permanent residences, neighborhoods, elite temples, and cemeteries. In sum, North Coast households were
more than passive receptacles or reflections of higher-level political institutions but
were integral to their realization.

CONCLUDING NOTE: CONTEXT MATTERS

The chapters in this volume prove that domestic practices cannot be divorced from
the cultural constructions of broader landscapes in which they formed a part. In
this sense, the archaeological interpretation of the alternate political (even ontological) worlds materialized in quotidian life can only proceed through systematic

contextual analyses of interrelated datasets. Thus residential layouts and occupation histories must be systematically compared with changing artefactual distributions and other dimensions of the built and natural environments. As illustrated in the case studies presented in this book and briefly summarized above, whether temporary hamlets built in the vicinity of agricultural fields in the Jequetepeque Valley or the planned precincts of Caylán, patterned variation in the form, quality, and configuration of dwelling architecture does not necessarily correlate with generic, vertical differences in social status but points instead to the distinct political regimes that structured the social formation in question and the ideologies of religion and identity that underwrote these regimes.

I concur with Billman that the interpretation of households must rely on multidisciplinary research based on the systematic screening of fill and occupation layers and the comparative analysis of multiple databases. Perhaps self-evident, but good contextual archaeology is grounded in identifying the conjunctions, disjunctions, and unexpected lack of fit between different suites of data. Examples of this approach are illustrated throughout the edited volume, methods that shed valuable light on the distinct socioeconomic and political foundations of quotidian life on the north coast of Peru. For instance, Chicoine and colleagues interpret the skewed ratio of surface *batanes* and *chungos* as evidence that food production was managed at the suprafamily *cercadura* level of social cooperation. In addition, Pacifico's comparison of the distribution of organic remains with differences in the quality of residential constructions at El Purgatorio shows that social inequalities were surprisingly muted in the realm of food consumption. The data support his theory that a redistributive economy was in play at El Purgatorio and that the rapid migration to the center from rural zones was likely voluntary and motivated by the desire to secure access to dependable food supplies. Cutright also plays off culinary data with artefactual and spatial indices to show that the expansion of the Chimú Empire resulted in shifts to subsistence strategies and diet despite surprising continuities in house layouts and artefactual assemblages. She develops a strong case that the Chimú were concerned with overseeing the economy of the region and were little interested in the ritual observances and identities of local people.

In a similar manner, Spence Morrow compares iconographic depictions of architecture with excavated building plans to develop his thesis that Moche conceptions of home, territory, and community departed significantly from Western conceptions. Johnson's analysis of female figurines and their changing distributions through time further indicates that the Moche label designates more than an elite political theology; various Moche-inspired folk religions were clearly in play throughout the North Coast, and, as Johnson notes, these traditions were not always aligned with state-instituted religious doctrine. It is intriguing that identical figurine and whistle types cross-cut very different kinds of domestic contexts; for instance, the Labretted Lady has been recovered in residential debris at both Pampa Grande and Huaca Colorada. Therefore, despite notable differences in household organization and the degree of sedentism between separate river valleys, the religious observances of different communities may have been largely equivalent (dealing with parturition, female procreation, and similar concerns). In this regard, different taskscapes (rhythms of daily practice) do not always correspond to distinctive traditions of gender, constructions of personhood, or community organization. Once again, our reading of domestic remains must always be sensitive to the larger context in which they are embedded.

To provide one final example, a contextual approach of this kind can also help make sense of the role of ancient North Coast households in larger ritual economies. For instance, feasting played an important role in creating and *emplacing* both real and imagined communities in very different North Coast settlements (see chapters by Chicoine et al., Cutright, Duke, Pacifico). However, the scale of production/consumption and the degree to which feasting was centralized seem to have determined the size and physical contiguity of co-residential units as well as the value placed on privacy, enclosure, public gatherings, and so forth. Thus it is intriguing that mass public spectacles of feasting and sacrifice documented in Jequetepeque (Huaca Colorada, San José de Moro) coincided with a regional settlement pattern characterized by ephemeral and makeshift domestic constructions at a number of different sites (Castillo Butters 2010; Swenson 2012; Swenson and Warner 2012). In contrast, feasting appears to have been the prerogative of competing multifamily groupings in Caylán. This particular social arrangement could explain the multiplication of elaborate frieze-adorned compounds at this important Early Horizon center. In fact, the remarkable standardization of the *cercaduras* at this site was unlikely the result of centralized planning by a paramount authority; instead, it appears to have expressed the autonomy and fiercely protected identities of parochial *cercadura* alliances—perhaps comparable to the parish churches of the *contrade* of Siena or the multiple towers of feuding families in medieval Tuscan hill towns. In contrast and as argued by Spence Morrow, the little effort and few resources expended in many of the residential structures of Jequetepeque seem to have been offset by great spectacles of communion and collective effervescence at sites such as Huaca Colorada.

In the end, the case studies of this volume serve as a reminder that analogical inference can do much more than simply identify continuities in quotidian practices through time. As Alison Wylie (1982, 392–393) argued in her assessment of the Gould-Watson debate, analogy is not just about the search for equivalence between source and archaeological case study. Our mobilization of the analogue of "house," "home," or "community" is meant to uncover and make sense of both commonalities and variation in past residential structures and everyday lifeways. The chapters in this volume do an excellent job of interpreting this variation, and the authors have significantly improved our understanding of the ancient civilizations of the north coast of Peru.

NOTE

1. Synchoritic urban formation refers to a city lacking resident farmers (Rowe 1963).

REFERENCES

Allen, Catherine. 1988. *The Hold Life Has: Coca and Cultural Identity in an Andean Community*. Washington, DC: Smithsonian Institution Press.

Banning, Edward B. 2011. "So Fair a House: Göbekli Tepe and the Identification of Temples in the Pre-Pottery Neolithic of the Near East." *Current Anthropology* 52 (5): 619–660.

Bawden, Garth. 1996. *The Moche*. Malden, MA: Blackwell.

Bawden, Garth. 2001. "The Symbols of Late Moche Social Transformation." In *Moche Art and Archaeology in Ancient Peru*, edited by Joanne Pillsbury, 285–306. New Haven, CT: Yale University Press.

Blanton, Richard. 1994. *Houses and Households: A Comparative Study*. New York: Plenum.

Blier, Suzanne P. 1987. *The Anatomy of Architecture: Ontology and Metaphor in a Batammaliba Architectural Expression*. Chicago: University of Chicago Press.

Boivin, Nicole. 2000. "Life Rhythms and Floor Sequences: Excavating Time in Rural Rajasthan and Neolithic Çatalhöyük." *World Archaeology* 31 (3): 367–388.

Bourdieu, Pierre. 1973. "The Berber House." In *Rules and Meanings*, edited by Mary Douglas, 98–110. New York: Hammondsworth.

Bourdieu, Pierre. 1977. *Outline of a Theory of Practice*. Cambridge: Cambridge University Press.

Bourdieu, Pierre. 1990. *The Logic of Practice*. Stanford, CA: Stanford University Press.

Bowser, Brenda P., and John Q. Patton. 2004. "Domestic Spaces as Public Places: An Ethnoarchaeological Case Study of Houses, Gender, and Politics in the Ecuadorian Amazon." *Journal of Archaeological Method and Theory* 11 (2): 157–181.

Bradley, Richard. 2005. *Ritual and Domestic Life in Prehistoric Europe*. New York: Routledge.

Carsten, Janet, and Stephen Hugh-Jones, eds. 1995. *About the House: Lévi-Strauss and Beyond*. Cambridge: Cambridge University Press.

Castillo Butters, Luis Jaime. 2010. "Moche Politics in the Jequetepeque Valley: A Case for Political Opportunism." In *New Perspectives in Moche Political Organization*, edited by Luis Jaime Castillo Butters and Jeffrey Quilter, 1–24. Washington, DC: Dumbarton Oaks.

Chapdelaine, Claude. 2001. "The Growing Power of a Moche Urban Class." In *Moche Art and Archaeology in Ancient Peru*, edited by Joanne Pillsbury, 69–87. New Haven, CT: Yale University Press.

Chapdelaine, Claude. 2002. "Out in the Streets of Moche: Urbanism and Sociopolitical Organization at a Moche IV Urban Center." In *Andean Archaeology*, vol. 1: *Variations in Sociopolitical Organization*, edited by William H. Isbell and Helaine Silverman, 53–88. New York: Plenum.

Chapdelaine, Claude. 2009. "Domestic Life in and around the Urban Sector of the Huacas of Moche Site, Northern Peru." In *Domestic Life in Prehispanic Capitals: A Study of Specialization, Hierarchy, and Ethnicity*, edited by Linda Manzanilla and Claude Chapdelaine, 181–196. Ann Arbor: University of Michigan Press.

Choay, Françoise. 1986. "Urbanism and Semiology." In *The City and the Sign, an Introduction to Urban Semiotics*, edited by Mark Gottdiener and Alexandros Lagopoulos, 160–175. New York: Columbia University Press.

Costin, Cathy Lynne, and Timothy K. Earle. 1989. "Status Distinctions and the Legitimation of Power as Reflected in Changing Patterns of Consumption in Late Prehispanic Peru." *American Antiquity* 54 (4): 691–714.

Cusicanqui, Solisiré. 2010. "Investigaciones en el Sitio Arqueológico Cerro Chepén: Levantamiento Topográfico en la Zona Monumental y Excavaciones Arqueológicas en el Sector Habitacional de Bajo Rango." In *Programa Arqueológico San José de Moro: Informe de Excavación Temporada 2010*, edited by Luis Jaime Castillo Butters, 47–59. Lima: Pontificia Universidad Católica del Perú.

Cutright, Robyn E. 2010. "Food, Family, and Empire: Relating Political and Domestic Change in the Jequetepeque Hinterland." In *Comparative Perspectives on the Archaeology of Coastal South America*, edited by Robyn E. Cutright, Enrique López-Hurtado, and Alexander Martin, 27–44. Pittsburgh: Center for Comparative Archaeology, University of Pittsburgh.

Cutright, Robyn E. 2015. "Eating Empire in the Jequetepeque: A Local View of Chimú Expansion on the North Coast of Peru." *Latin American Antiquity* 26: 64–86.

D'Altroy, Terence N., and Christine A. Hastorf, eds. 2001. *Empire and Domestic Economy*. New York: Kluwer Academic/Plenum.

Donnan, Christopher B. 1997. "Introduction." In *The Pacatnamú Papers*, volume 2, edited by Christopher B. Donnan and Guillermo Cock, 9–16. Los Angeles: Fowler Museum of Cultural History, University of California Press.

Donnan, Christopher B. 2007. *Moche Tombs at Dos Cabezas*. Los Angeles: Costin Institute of Archaeology, University of California Press.

Giddens, Anthony. 1984. *The Constitution of Society: Outline of a Theory of Structuration*. Cambridge: Polity.

González-Ruibal, Alfredo. 2014. *An Archaeology of Resistance: Materiality and Time in an African Borderland*. New York: Rowman and Littlefield.

Goodman, Melissa. 1999. "Temporalities of Prehistoric Life: Household Development and Community Continuity." In *Making Place in the Prehistoric World*, edited by Johanna Brück and Melissa Goodman, 145–159. London: UCL Press.

Goody, Jack. 1971. *The Household Developmental Cycle*. Cambridge: Cambridge University Press.

Gose, Peter. 1991. "House Rethatching in an Andean Annual Cycle: Practice, Meaning, and Contradiction." *American Ethnologist* 18: 39–66.

Guengerich, Anna. 2014. "Monte Viudo: Residential Architecture and the Everyday Production of Space in a Chachapoyas Community." PhD dissertation, University of Chicago, IL.

Harris, Olivia. 1994. "Condor and the Bull: The Ambiguities of Masculinity in Northern Potosí." In *Sex and Violence: Issues in Representation and Experience*, edited by Penelope Harvey and Peter Gow, 40–65. New York: Routledge.

Hendon, Julia. 1996. "Archaeological Approaches to the Organization of Domestic Labor: Household Practice and Domestic Relations." *Annual Review of Anthropology* 25: 45–61.

Hodder, Ian. 1984. "Burials, Women, and Men in the European Neolithic." In *Ideology, Power, and Prehistory*, edited by Daniel Miller and Christopher Tilley, 51–68. Cambridge: University of Cambridge Press.

Hodder, Ian, and Peter Pels. 2010. "History Houses: A New Interpretation of Architectural Elaboration at Çatalhöyük." In *Religion in the Emergence of Civilization: Çatalhöyük as a Case Study*, edited by Ian Hodder, 163–186. Cambridge: Cambridge University Press.

Ingold, Timothy. 2000. *The Perception of the Environment: Essays in Livelihood, Dwelling, and Skill*. New York: Routledge.

Johnson, Ilana. 2012. "Investigaciones Arqueológicas en el Asentamiento Moche Medio, Sector 1 del Sitio Arqueológico Cerro Chepén." In *Programa Arqueológico San José de Moro: Informe de Excavación Temporada 2010*, edited by Luis Jaime Castillo Butters, 50–81. Lima: Pontificia Universidad Católica del Perú.

Joyce, Arthur. 2009. "The Main Plaza of Monte Albán: The Life History of Place." In *The Archaeology of Meaningful Places*, edited by Brenda J. Bowser and Maria Nieves Zedeño, 33–52. Salt Lake City: University of Utah Press.

Lefebvre, Henri. 1991. *The Production of Space*. Malden, MA: Blackwell.

Lockard, Greg. 2009. "The Occupational History of Galindo, Moche Valley, Peru." *Latin American Antiquity* 20 (2): 279–302.

Lucero, Lisa J. 2003. "The Power of Ritual: The Emergence of Maya Classic Rulers." *Cultural Anthropology* 44 (4): 523–558.

Lyons, Diane E. 2007. "Building Power in Rural Hinterlands: An Ethnoarchaeological Study of Vernacular Architecture in Tigray, Ethiopia." *Journal of Archaeological Method and Theory* 14 (2): 179–207.

Marcus, Joyce. 2007. "Rethinking Ritual." In *The Archaeology of Ritual*, edited by Evangelos Kyriakidis, 43–76. Los Angeles: Costen Institute of Archaeology Press.

McClelland, Donna. 1997. "Moche Fineline Ceramics at Pacatnamú." In *The Pacatnamú Papers*, vol. 2, edited by Christopher B. Donnan and Guillermo Cock, 265–282. Los Angeles: Fowler Museum of Cultural History, University of California Press.

Nash, Donna. 2009. "Household Archaeology in the Andes." *Journal of Archaeological Research* 17: 205–261.

Prossor, Lauren, Susan Lawrence, Alasdair Brooks, and Jane Lennon. 2012. "Household Archaeology, Lifecycles, and Status in a Nineteenth-Century Australian Coastal Community." *International Journal of Historical Archaeology* 16 (4): 809–827.

Quilter, Jeffrey, and Michelle Koons. 2012. "The Fall of the Moche: The Critique of Claims for South America's First State." *Latin American Antiquity* 23 (2): 127–143.

Rapoport, Amos. 1969. *House Form and Culture.* Englewood Cliffs, NJ: Prentice-Hall.

Robin, Cynthia. 2002. "Outside of Houses: The Practices of Everyday life at Chan Nòohol, Belize." *Journal of Social Archaeology* 2 (2): 245–268.

Robin, Cynthia. 2003. "New Directions in Classic Maya Household Archaeology." *Journal of Archaeological Research* 11: 307–356.

Robin, Cynthia. 2013. *Everyday Life Matters: Maya Farmers at Chan.* Gainesville: University of Florida Press.

Robin, Cynthia, and N. A. Rothschild. 2002. "Archaeological Ethnographies: Social Dynamics of Outdoor Space." *Journal of Social Archaeology* 2 (2): 159–172.

Rosas, Marco. 2010. "Cerro Chepén and the Late Moche Collapse in the Jequetepeque Valley, North Coast of Perú." PhD dissertation, University of New Mexico, Albuquerque.

Rowe, John H. 1963. "Urban Settlements in Ancient Peru." *Ñawpa Pacha* 1: 1–27.

Sallnow, Michael J. 1987. *Pilgrims in the Andes: Regional Cults in Cuzco.* Smithsonian Series in Ethnographic Inquiry. Washington, DC: Smithsonian Institution Press.

Scott, James. 1992. *Domination and the Forms of Resistance: Hidden Transcripts.* Hartford, CT: Yale University Press.

Sillar, Bill. 1996. "The Dead and the Dying: Techniques for Transforming Peoples and Things in the Andes." *Journal of Material Culture* 1: 259–289.

Skar, Sarah Lund. 1994. *Worlds Together, Lives Apart: Quechua Colonization in Jungle and City*. Oslo: Scandinavian University Press.

Swenson, Edward. 2012. "Warfare, Gender, and Sacrifice in Jequetepeque Peru." *Latin American Antiquity* 23 (2): 167–193.

Swenson, Edward. 2015. "The Archaeology of Ritual." *Annual Reviews of Anthropology* 44: 329–345.

Swenson, Edward. 2017. "Timing Is Everything: Religion and the Regulation of Temporalities in the Ancient Andes." In *Religion and Politics in the Ancient Americas*, edited by Arthur Joyce and Sarah Barber, 210–233. New York: Routledge.

Swenson, Edward, and Jorge Chiguala. 2018. "Relaciones entre Espacio Ritual y Doméstico en el Valle Jequetepeque, Perú." *Publicaciones IFEA* 47 (2): 195–216.

Swenson, Edward, and Justin Jennings. 2018. "Introduction: Place, Landscape, and Power in the Ancient Andes and Andean Archaeology." In *Powerful Places in the Ancient Andes*, edited by Justin Jennings and Edward Swenson, 1–54. Albuquerque: University of New Mexico Press.

Swenson, Edward, and Andy Roddick. 2018. "Rethinking Temporality and Historicity from the Perspective of Andean Archaeology." In *Constructions of Time and History in the Ancient Andes*, edited by Edward Swenson and Andy Roddick, 3–44. Boulder: University Press of Colorado.

Swenson, Edward, and John Warner. 2012. "Crucibles of Power: Forging Copper and Forging Subjects at the Moche Ceremonial Center of Huaca Colorada, Peru." *Journal of Anthropological Archaeology* 31 (3): 314–333.

Uceda Castillo, Santiago, and José Armas. 1998. "An Urban Pottery Workshop at the Site of Moche, North Coast of Peru." In *Andean Ceramics: Technology, Organization, and Approaches*, edited by Izumi Shimada, 91–110. MASCA Research Papers in Science and Technology. Philadelphia: Museum Applied Science Center for Archaeology, University of Pennsylvania, Museum of Archaeology and Anthropology.

Van Gijseghem, Hendrick. 2001. "Household and Family at Moche Peru: An Analysis of Residence and Building Patterns in a Prehispanic Center." *Latin American Antiquity* 12 (3): 257–273.

Wilson, Peter J. 1991. *The Domestication of the Human Species*. Hartford, CT: Yale University Press.

Wylie, Alison. 1982. "An Analogy by Any Other Name Is Just as Analogical: A Commentary on the Gould-Watson Dialogue." *Journal of Anthropological Anthropology* 1 (4): 382–401.

Contributors

BRIAN R. BILLMAN, University of North Carolina–Chapel Hill

DAVID CHICOINE, Louisiana State University

ROBYN E. CUTRIGHT, Centre College

GUY S. DUKE, The University of Texas Rio Grande Valley

HUGO IKEHARA, Pontifical Catholic University of Chile

ILANA JOHNSON, Sacramento City College

JESSICA ORTIZ, Ministry of Culture of Peru

DAVID PACIFICO, University of Wisconsin–Milwaukee

GILES SPENCE MORROW, Vanderbilt University

EDWARD SWENSON, University of Toronto

KARI A. ZOBLER, University of Illinois at Urbana-Champaign

Index

Page numbers in italics indicate illustrations.